THE TIDINGS

further extracts from:

THE BOOK OF TIDINGS
OF THE ALMIGHTY
AND HIS SPIRITS
TO HUMANITY

VOLUME ONE
NOVEMBER 1943 TO JANUARY 1945

translated by

Nick Mezins

Note for Librarians: a cataloguing record for this book that includes Dewey Decimal Classification and US Library of Congress numbers is available from the Library and Archives of Canada. The complete cataloguing record can be obtained from their online database at:

www.collectionscanada.ca/amicus/index-e.html

ISBN 1-4120-4370-0

TRAFFORD

Offices in Canada, USA, Ireland, UK

This book was published on-demand in cooperation with Trafford Publishing. On-demand publishing is a unique process and service of making a book available for retail sale to the public taking advantage of on-demand manufacturing and Internet marketing. On-demand publishing includes promotions, retail sales, manufacturing, order fulfilment, accounting and collecting royalties on behalf of the author.

Book sales for North America and international:

Trafford Publishing, 6E–2333 Government St.,

Victoria, BC v8t 4p4 CANADA

phone 250 383 6864 (toll-free 1 888 232 4444)

fax 250 383 6804; email to orders@trafford.com

Book sales in Europe:

Trafford Publishing (uk) Ltd., Enterprise House, Wistaston Road Business Centre,

Wistaston Road, Crewe, Cheshire cw2 7rp UNITED KINGDOM

phone 01270 251 396 (local rate 0845 230 9601)

facsimile 01270 254 983; orders.uk@trafford.com

Order online at:

www.trafford.com/04-2178

10 9 8 7 6 5 4 3

CONTENTS

FOREWORD

The material in this book came through human vehicles, but is not of human origin. It started in mid-1943 in Latvia, one of the three Baltic countries that regained their independence from the Soviet Union when it broke up in 1991 after its long stranglehold on those countries since World War II. Two women had gotten together and tried to communicate with the spirits in the days of uncertainty in the midst of World War II. One of them was Mary, the mother of the translator of this volume, Nick Mezins.

What eventually started coming through was a series of communications from entities who gave their names and identified themselves as spirits that are behind the workings of the Universe, including the planet Earth, and the development of matter and the spiritual nature of humankind.

As things progressed, Mary invited others to join. Some did, and then left for personal reasons, while others stayed to become the core group: Mary and her husband Janoss (initially referred to as John M.), Alexander Upenieks (who soon became the leader of the group), and my father, Alexander Homics, (Alexo, who initially was referred to as Alexander H.). Mary and Alexo were the two individuals who each could, jointly with Alexander, establish communication with the spirits. (During some of the longer communications, Mary and Alexo alternated back and forth, and short intermissions were given for this purpose.) Alexo came to be the main transcriber for the group, typing up the handwritten material after each session and distributing it to the group members.

In late summer of 1944, when the Russians began to gain the upper hand over the Germans in Latvia, the members of the group at different times fled from Latvia and went to Germany, where they fortunately settled in what was to become the American Zone, and resumed their sessions. Later, several years after World War II was finally over, the members immigrated at different times to the United States, settling in New York. There, starting in 1950, they resumed their sessions. The last session took place in January of 1971.

When my father retired in the late 1960s, he translated virtually all of the material into English. He had organized it into ten volumes, plus two sepa-

rate volumes that consisted of material in a fictionalized form. Sadly, he succeeded in publishing only the first two volumes before his death in 1982[1].

In 1992 Nick Mezins – the son of Mary and Janoss Mezins – published
REVELATIONS: Extracts From the Book of Tidings of The Almighty and His
Spirits to Humanity (Winston-Derek, 1992), which highlighted excerpts
from the message material; it was reissued in 2000 by Trafford Publishers.
In 2002 appeared THE TIDINGS: Further Extracts From The Book of Tidings
of The Almighty and His Spirits to Humanity, Volume One, which consists of a
fuller translation, covering part of the time period of World War II. At present Nick is working on Volume Two of The Tidings, which will comprise
the waning days of World War II and the period immediately following it.

As can be seen from the titles of the volumes cited, there are the usual
problems of translating from one language to another while trying to retain
the original meaning. For example, my father chose to use the word *messages* as opposed to Nick Mezins translating the same word as *tidings*, (which
could also have been translated as *communications*). Another example: my
father used the word *messengers*, and Nick prefers the word *heralds*. I myself
like the word *envoys*. But the important thing is to make the material and
the concept therein, available to all seekers on the Path to truth, and so it is
encouraging to see this voluminous material still being worked on and put
out further to the public.

Maya Homics
New York, 2004

INTRODUCTION TO REVELATIONS

The material in this book is not of human origin. It has not been thought of by a human mind. The material in this book originated from The Almighty, from God, from the chief spirits and the spirits. It has been passed on to humanity on the planet Earth by the chief spirits and by the spirits. It has been passed on through The Almighty's heralds to the planet Earth, who, outwardly, were ordinary human beings.

Initially, the heralds wrote down this material in longhand. Afterwards it was typed, and several copies were made. Care was taken to see that no accidental alterations were made. The original and the typed version were compared carefully. Some errors in grammar were found and corrected, and it was agreed that the corrections did not alter the meanings of the phrases or the sentences. In each case the heralds concurred that the correction did not alter the meaning of the material.

The chief spirits and the spirits passed the material down, through the heralds, in a language other than English. My involvement is limited to translating it into English. I have taken great pains to translate the material so as not to alter its meaning. At times I have sacrificed the quality of English, or its proper usage, in order to avoid possibly altering its meaning.

Some explanations are in order to assure a full understanding of the authenticity of the material. Unless otherwise indicated, the contents of this book came from the chief spirits and the spirits. For the sake of clarity, some questions and statements by the heralds have been included. These have been enclosed in double brackets ([[ ]]). All material enclosed in double brackets is of human origin, such as questions posed by the heralds, reading of material from the Bible, and so on. In addition, at times I have inserted a word, or words, not in the original. These are enclosed in single brackets ([ ]) and were inserted due to the peculiarities of the two languages. Sometimes English requires a word or phrase which is only implied in the original language.

Each tiding begins with a title line. This title line consists of the name of the spirit or chief spirit talking, the date of the conversation, and, generally, the starting time of the conversation. These are not part of the tiding itself and should have been enclosed in the double brackets, except for appearance. The ending time of the conversation, when given, is enclosed.

Since this book is a book of extracts from *The Book of Tidings*, not everything is included in it. To denote whenever something has been omitted, the triple asterisk (-★ ★ ★-) symbol has been used. This symbol, when used within a paragraph, indicates that part of the paragraph has been omitted. When used in a line by itself, it indicates that an entire paragraph has been omitted. This symbol is not repeated whenever more than one paragraph may have been omitted.

In reading this book, both the brackets and the triple asterisk symbols should be disregarded. They become important only when questioning the exact meaning of a phrase, sentence, or paragraph. Then they indicate that, if the question is of sufficient importance, one should go back to the original language and satisfy oneself as to the exact meaning of the original. While reading the communications, these symbols should be disregarded.

A few words follow regarding the use of the word *man*. It has more than one connotation in English. Generally, in this book, the word *man* is intended to mean a human, the singular of the word *people*, rather than the male of the human species. *Man* is used synonymously with *human*, *individual*, and *person*. In those cases where it does indicate gender, the text makes it evident. The plural *men*, however, is used only when gender is indicated, otherwise *people* or similar words are used. The expression "man on Earth" should denote what this is all about.

Thank you very much for putting up with these technical explanations. They are superfluous for most readers, but may be important to a few. Therefore they have been included.

Nick Mezins

INTRODUCTION

The volume *REVELATIONS: Extracts From The Book of Tidings of The Almighty and His Spirits to Humanity*, (originally published in 1992 by Winston-Derek Publishers, and now available in the revised edition from Trafford Publishing), contains what I consider to be highlights from the extensive material received by a small group of people during World War II and which continue to 1971. In it are included only those conversations which "reveal" something new or else, in a few cases, conversations which present rather concise and explicit summaries of the material.

It would be helpful, but not essential, to read REVELATIONS first, as it gives the reader an overall idea about The Almighty's teachings, and a general understanding of, and appreciation for, what they are all about. Also, toward the end, REVELATIONS specifically explains that a number of proposed "formalities" are only suggestions or examples, but not mandatory requirements as appears to be implied in this volume. This would include such things as the method of electing the priest and the board of the congregation for the church of the future.

I have organized the bulk of the material which comprises *The Book of Tidings of The Almighty and His Spirits to Humanity* as much as possible according to directions given in the Tidings themselves:

On April 13, 1944 Ilgya said in part,

"*...systemize all conversations with the spirits into three books. Everything that refers to the faith has to be collected into the first one. Into the second — advice for life, how to bring up the spirit and the body, how to raise children, and so on; as well as those stories which have an everyday significance. Collect into the third book everything that pertains to you and the accomplishment of your work.*"

In the present volume — *THE TIDINGS, Volume One* — I have included what I feel are Books One and Two. In a few cases, brief passages which probably belong in Book Three have been retained, primarily for the sake of continuity in the case of a particular conversation. Material that appeared in *REVELATIONS* is given here in its fuller context and is marked by arrows at the beginning and end.

The fuller context in this volume includes explanations and clarifications, stories which illustrate some of the concepts, and, sometimes, related ideas that are of importance. There are also descriptions of interesting events on the planet Earth as well as on a few other planets, some of which are related to specific heralds.

The present volume covers part of the period of World War II. Subsequent volumes will cover later periods of time and will be made available as the material is further translated. Volume Two, for example, will include material received through the waning days of World War II and the period immediately following it. Once all the material belonging in Books One and Two has been translated, I plan to start working on a translation of the complete material, which will include what Ilgya called Book Three. This will not add much to the teachings, but will be of historical and biographical interest.

Nick Mezins

Chapter I
1943

Dagmara   11/21/43

[[Answers to our questions.]]

Nonexistence is a complete annihilation – zero. Hell is eternal darkness, eternal night. That is the most dreadful thing. Spirits of the first degree – those who have fallen – are sent to Hell.

Once you are with us, you will find out how many degrees there are. I am of the fifth degree. The first degree consists of those spirits who have been born for the first time. Do not ask in which degree you will be after death.

Those spirits of the first degree who have fallen are the ones who did not carry out the tasks of the spirit, and succumbed to the evil spirit.

The duties of the spirits are superhuman. As assigned by The Almighty, they have to look after the living beings.

Clemency for those in the first degree, who have fallen, will come after a thousand years. Those spirits who have passed into nonexistence will never be reborn, for no road leads back from nonexistence.

The spirits of murderers and criminals are treated just like the manure from a barn – they are cleared out and forgotten.

The spirits who are born for the first time are formed from The Almighty's holiness. None of the spirits has ever seen the face of The Almighty.

It is not known whether good or evil will win, for The Almighty has not revealed His face yet.

The universe came into being from The Almighty's holiness.

[[Question: "How can we, people, understand that?"]]

It is not possible [to understand that].

[[We ask, "How can wars break out when there is The Almighty and the good spirits, who look after us?"]]

Just as quarrels and fights [break out] among the servants of a master, for The Almighty rules free people but not slaves.

One's degree is not advanced based on the manner of one's death, but rather due to the number of deaths and achievements.

1

Killing a human being in war is not considered to be murder.

_★ ★ ★_

A. Aurora   11/28/43

→[[We ask, "Are The Almighty and God, the very same entity?"]]

Yes and no.

[[We ask, "How can that be understood?"]]

Santorino can explain that to you. Santorino is a spirit of the very highest degree.

[[We ask, "Would it be possible to ask Santorino to come?"]]

Wait for five minutes. I will ask.

[[After five minutes.]] Santorino will come to you on December 5, 1943, between three and four o'clock in the afternoon.

Cover an easy chair with a black cloth and place a laurel branch on it. He will be coming from the Deoss Temple.

The Deoss Temple is where the spirits meet. After receiving one's degree, one arrives in it in the surge of God's rays and the harmony of The Almighty's blessing.

Ask the spirits only if you feel the blessing of believing in what has never yet been heard by, and revealed to, the eyes and hearts of mortals.

No one in the world is completely worthy of conversing with Santorino. However, the world now finds itself on the threshold of a new era. This will come after the current catastrophe of humanity and will bring entirely new ideas about the hereafter and religion for the world.

_ ★ ★ ★ _

[[Question: "Are Santorino's revelations intended just for us, or for others as well?"]]

You are intended as the first doves, whose wings may break, for a dreadful storm rages outside.

Santorino summons me this evening, and I must alight. Alighting is the means of transportation of the spirits.←

_ ★ ★ ★ _

A. Aurora   12/05/43

[[We ask for Dagmara to come to us.]]

Today is not her – Dagmara's – day.

[[We ask, "Will Santorino come?"]]

Santorino will not come. Santorino will come only to those who are worthy of believing [in the spirits].

[[Explanation: We had not assembled on time and also did not express absolute faith.]]

[[We ask, "How can we know that the evil spirits are not playing tricks?"]]

There is no way.

[[We ask, "Whose spirit are you, Aurora?"]]

I am the Spirit of the Star of Light. I have never died. I am the spirit for many stars, also [for many] people.

I see that you had misunderstood me last Sunday. I came to you for the first time, and the low spirits are not permitted to be present at the time of my visit, for the planet Earth is under my radiance as well.

Silence! Santorino will speak. Santorino announced that he understands the insignificance of the spirits and of people, and will talk with you. Await him! He alights from the Deoss Temple.

I depart; he arrives.

Santorino   12/05/43

→*Ego* Santorino. Have the person who is writing, pick up the laurel branch in his left hand. With the laurel branch, draw the sign of the cross across the table. Ask.

[[Question: "Are God and The Almighty, the very same entity?"]]

God is the one whom we see and who talks with us.

[[Question: "And The Almighty?"]]

Try to understand – The Almighty is invisible and incomprehensible. He has always existed and will always exist. At one time He was all alone. Then He created worlds and the spirits, who have to develop and grow until they attain the degree of divinity. *Dixi.*

[[We ask, "Was Christ the Son of God?"]]

Yes.

The Almighty created the spirits to be entirely free, so that they could grow and develop independently, or else fall into decay. He divided Himself into two parts. In one part, all the good; that is God. In the other, all the evil that was within Him; that is Satan. There is also evil within The Almighty, for He is everything.

The concepts about God changed along humanity's road of development.

Every six hundred years, before and after the birth of Christ, He sent His teachers – Buddha, Christ, and Mohammed – to the various nations. *Dixi*.

[[Question: "Will The Almighty send us His teachers again?"]]

No, for humanity has already achieved the state of self-comprehension. There will be [more of His teachers], except the more eminent spirits will come forth from among the people, themselves.

The teachings of Christ have been surpassed already. Humanity advances further and higher. – ★ ★ ★ –

Christ spoke in the language of parables.

God and Satan have equal rights and authority. Satan can overcome God temporarily. Satan had to come so that, in the struggle between good and evil, the divine spirits, who are free and noble, could ascend.

You cannot know who the next teachers will be, for they do not have names yet.

Praying for the deceased will probably benefit the deceased but, most certainly, will not harm them.

There is life on other planets as well, except entirely different. Those who are not destined for nonexistence may get there. Nonexistence is not predestined. It depends only on the individual's own worthiness. This worthiness can be achieved thusly: one must learn; one must suffer; one must struggle and conquer all evil; one must set oneself free from the Earth; one must grow.

My time is running out, hurry up!

New Gods come into the universe. Satan's years are numbered. The Almighty reveals His face.

I will talk with you some other time. Prepare your questions and summon Aurora. Be strong and wise; differentiate between the significant and the trivial. Low spirits are destined to err. Do not ask the spirits insignificant questions.

I would like to believe in you, for the lead spirits of millions – Aurora, Aristotle, and Ptolemy – implored on your behalf. *Salve!*←

A. Aurora   12/05/43

I thank you for withstanding the evaluation. Santorino is satisfied, despite your dreadful mistakes. These mistakes were: lack of faith – fortunately, in me – failure to prepare yourselves, and failure to observe the time. This could have been fateful, had Santorino arrived on time.

[[We ask, "How come that Aurora did not talk with us Sunday?"]]

Do not confuse me with low spirits.

[[Question: "How come that both Dagmara and Aristotle are Mary's spirits?"]]

I, Aristotle, and Ptolemy are the spirits of multimillions.

You do not have to know why we, the high spirits, are interested in you.

Should you wish to talk with me, use the sign of the cross and two *A*s, summon me thus: A. Aurora.

You may also ask about particularly important questions in life, but it would be better to ask Dagmara or Aurora about them.

Because of the war, the might of Satan now rules the world.

Astra   12/06/43

I am a ray of light – the messenger. Dagmara cannot come today, for it is Monday when the spirits generally remain silent. The spirit of the deceased Nicholas M. was with you an hour ago. He cannot come again.

[[Question: "Why?"]]

He is in the Solar Fields.

[[Question: "What does that mean?"]]

Only Alpha can explain that. Alpha is the Chief Spirit of the Past and the Beginning. Alpha will not talk with you, because it is Monday. I am the only one who talks; I, the ray, the messenger. My duties are to inform the spirits of God's decisions, and the people of the decisions of the spirits.

_ ★ ★ ★ _

I have not been given anything else to announce to you today.

Astra   12/12/43

[Tell me], with whom would you like to talk? You may talk with Dagmara directly. Alpha cannot come, for one can talk with him only through Santorino. Alpha is not higher than Santorino, but he communicates only with the very highest spirits.

I will summon A. Aurora.

A. Aurora   12/12/43

→The Solar Fields are at the foot of the stairway to the Deoss Temple. Only the more eminent spirits assemble in them, the rest assemble in the Lunar Fields. In addition to these fields, there is also nonexistence. There is a great difference between the Solar and Lunar Fields. Ask Santorino about that, for that is not my sphere.

Do not ask about my sphere.

The spirit and the soul are the same entity.

What has been said in the teachings of Christ, that the living and the dead will be judged, should be understood allegorically.←

Silence! Listen! Santorino informed me that God has permitted him to request Alpha to reveal – to Mary, Alexander U., and still a third one – their past, their former forms, places, and times of life.

Alpha will reveal this to you, [[Mary]], next Sunday at three o'clock. [He will reveal] who you were prior to this life on Earth.

Prepare everything just as for Santorino. You may use the dried out laurel branch. You have to conduct yourselves in the same manner as with Santorino. Alpha is just as high a spirit as Santorino is.

You must not talk at all. Alpha will come on his own. Only Alpha will speak. You may not ask him anything. Do not make any mistakes, for Alpha never repeats anything.

The third one to whom Alpha will reveal his past will be according to your request.

[[Mary asks, "I would like my husband to be the one."]]

Very well, that will be the case.

Exactly at three, draw the [sign of the] cross with the laurel branch, and await Alpha in silence. No one may disturb you in any manner while Alpha will be speaking. You may write down Alpha's answers.

Your past will be revealed to you so that you could comprehend better your future conversations with Santorino and in order to carry out the silent desire of your [[Mary's]] soul. Little Nick, too, may, perhaps, someday earn on his own to have his former life revealed to him.

In the future, I and Santorino will talk with you only through Astra, and only with the two of you. I will come to you in the future as well, except Astra has been assigned to you, for you have to guard yourselves against the servants of Satan, against whom Dagmara and Aurora are entirely helpless. In the future, Dagmara and Aurora will come only to you [[Mary]] and Lillian. That is because they are not subordinate to Ptolemy and might be deluded by Satan, for they do not know when and about what we talk with you.

Never ask other spirits about me, Santorino, or Omega. Omega is the Chief Spirit of the Future and of Death. You may ask other spirits about Alpha. This is in order not to give Satan the opportunity of hindering us, and of deceiving and ruining you.

None of the evil spirits can come [to you whenever] you summon Astra, because Astra always has to be wherever the two of you are.

For the time being, there is no other means of communication than the present one.

I have to alight. Be wise.

Alpha   12/19/43 1500

Astra, Astra, Astra. Aurora, Aurora, Aurora. Santorino, Santorino, Santorino. Alpha, Alpha, Alpha.

[[For Mary]]. Close your eyes for a moment, and follow me in spirit. Recall, you are standing on a stairway next to a large, white building. You are ten years old. Next to you stands your mother, and your father who is in the bright armor of a centurion. A large crowd of people, screaming and clamoring, walks along the street. A man walks in the middle of the crowd and carries a large, wooden cross.

You ask your father, "Who are they, and what has He done?"

Your father tells you, "This is the horrible Hebrew nation, and that is its King or God."

The man stops and wipes off the sweat. He is thirsty.

You ask your mother, "May I give Him some water?"

"Yes," replies your mother.

With a cup [of water] you hurry to the man with the cross. A bearded Hebrew knocks the cup from your hand, and the water is spilled on the sufferer's face. He smiles at you with a smile [which makes you think that] the sun had shone on you. You [begin to] cry and run to your mother while crying. You hide your face in her robe. The crowd continues on its way.

"They do not know what they are doing," your father says.

Your second ray. You are a young and happy wife. Next to you at the table, on a luxurious couch, reclines your handsome patrician – your husband. Through the hall, which is filled with noblemen, walks an elderly man in a purple garment with a laurel wreath on his head. An imposing lady walks next to him.

The man with the wreath on his head passes by the two of you, stops for a moment, smiles kindly, and tells your husband, "Fortunate one!"

The lady looks at you and at your husband and tells you, "Fortunate one!"

They continue on their way. You ask your husband, "Who were they?"

Your husband pats you lovingly on the shoulder and tells you, "Little fool, that, after all, is our divine emperor Claudius with his wife Messalina."

<u>Now to continue, the third one.</u> You are lying down in your room and are tired. Next to your bed stands a stately, young man – your son. A young and beautiful slave girl sits at your feet.

You tell your son, "Rome is burning already for the sixth day and night! What is Caesar Nero doing?"

"As usual, he is singing and playing," replies your son.

"Doesn't he feel the least bit sorry for the people?"

"He – Nero?" your son says scornfully. "I will go and continue to save the Romans."

He strokes your hair gently, smiles at you and at the slave girl, and departs – never to return again.

You notice how tenderly the slave girl follows him with her eyes, and you ask her, "What is your name?"

"Mary," she replies.

"Mary, a beautiful name, which I have heard before."

"I, my lady, am a servant of Christ."

"Christ? Wasn't He the man who once, in the land of the Hebrews, carried a cross and died on it?"

"Yes, the very same one who carried the cross, but He has not died on it and will never die; for He is the Son of God."

<u>To continue – the fourth and final one.</u> You are sitting on a seat facing a large arena. In the arena, tied to posts, stand Christ's martyrs. At one post you see the beautiful and naked body of Mary. A frightful bear is presently approaching her, with peculiar steps. You hear the terrible scream of your slave girl, and close your eyes. Then you hear the cheers of the crowd, "Long live our emperor and great actor, the divine Nero!"

You open your eyes and see in horror that the bear is standing next to Mary, who has fainted. The head of the bear, however, is hanging on its back, and in its stead you see the terrible face of Nero. Overcome by terror, you close your eyes again.

Then you hear a keen voice above you, "Don't you like our game?"

You open your eyes and see in front of you the horrible face of Lucius Domitius Caesar Nero. "No, Nero," you tell him boldly.

"Would you rather like to smile down there among the animals, rather than here in my box?"

"Yes," you reply.

"Then take her down to the animals in the arena, so that she might show us that she, too, knows how to laugh!"

"Among the animals I will smile, but here with you – Nero, you beast – I cannot!"

You see that the faces of Caesar's attendants stiffen in fright, and that the smile vanishes from Nero's lips – the last smile that you saw on the face of the Earth.

Open your eyes, I conclude. In an hour Santorino will talk with you for a few minutes. Be wise and bright!

Astra   12/19/43

Do not ask the spirits anything today, for The Almighty has revealed His face.

[Continue to] wait, and comprehend the great honor for the people from Alpha and Santorino – unprecedented thus far. Let us remain piously silent today.

A. Aurora   12/25/43 1945

Ask me by noon tomorrow when Alpha will be able to tell Alexander his past. Alpha has a conversation with God tomorrow, and he is unable to tell the hour when he will talk with you.

Do you really need to know why I can spare the time for you?

I come only whenever I want to, and no one can summon and disturb me, unless I, myself, command him to do so.

Prepare yourselves for the conversation with Alpha. He has to carry out the promise in the near future. In ten days Alpha will be billions of billions of kilometers from your galaxy. The Almighty has assigned him the creation of new worlds. An old world perishes. It is located two thousand worlds away from the Earth. Man is incapable of grasping the number of worlds.

_ ★ ★ ★ _

I am pleased that your conversation with Alpha concluded happily. All the time I followed anxiously the ray which radiated from Alpha's temple to you. It changed its brightness four times and finally became so bright that all the spirits had to turn away. When I saw Santorino alight into Alpha's temple, I understood that you had withstood the test of silence, and had been left on Earth. You might not have remained on Earth. Yet it is better not to know what might have happened to you.

Alpha leaves his temple only on a command from The Almighty.

The last ray was so very bright due to the martyr death, and the strength of your hearts.

Never dare to insult the high spirit by a lack of respect. Do not talk about us with unworthy people, and do not permit them into the room where the conversations take place.

The talk of the low spirits may be foolish. Be wise.

_ ★ ★ ★ _

Astra   12/25/43

The highest Aurora will not speak any more. She has told you everything that she wanted to. - ★ ★ ★ - You can thank the highest spirits only by understanding them.

Alpha   12/26/43 1510

Astra, Astra, Astra. Aurora, Aurora, Aurora. Santorino, Santorino, Santorino. Alpha, Alpha, Alpha.

Listen, Alexander! Close your eyes for a moment and follow me in spirit.

Your homeland is a narrow strip of land between two oceans and two continents. Hundreds of years have passed. You are a small boy and are sitting at a desk in a hall of the palace. Outside the windows rise magnificent edifices — temples, pyramids. You are doing arithmetic. You know how to read many words already, and you already know the four symbols for numbers. You are, however, having difficulties with multiplying the rows, and you start to cry.

A noble, high priest enters the hall, and tells you, "Don't cry! You multiplied each row by twenty, but the third row, and only that one, should be multiplied by eighteen. As the next high priest and ruler of the noble Maya nation, you have infinitely much to learn, so that your nation will prosper and grow. You must not get tired! Now, let us walk over to the temples of the gods."

You pass through the endlessly large passageways and halls of the temples. There you see the already familiar signs, carved in stone, of the evil gods of night and death. You see the sign of the sun god – Kukulcan. You see the many symbols of the gods – winged snakes, statues of gods with scepters in their hands and headdresses adorned with feathers. You already recognize all of them. Then you reach the sign of the cross, and you say proudly, "I recognize this one as well. It is the sign of the four parts of the world."

"Yes, but it is also the sign of the most important and invisible God – Gvuabku. Gvuabku will remain even then, when all other gods will lie in the dust. You will have to serve this God and will have to comprehend Him, something that no high priest has comprehended thus far.

"Now we will end the [period of] instructions. Go and play in the garden again, until the time when the acacias begin to fold their leaves. It was good that you freed the hummingbird from the webs of the large spider today, but it was wrong that you released alive the hedge snake. It was good that this morning you placed the magnificent blossoms of the fire tree on your mother's table, but it was wrong that you played with the ferocious and cunning tigercat."

Now your second [ray]. You have returned to your palace after the festival of the sacrifice of the first fruit. You are attired in the ceremonial garb of the high priest of the Mayan gods, and the headdress of the ruler adorns your head. The cheers of the crowd still echo in your ears, and you can still smell the incense. You can still see the rows of priests bowed before you, and can see with what respect they follow the movement of your lips. You know just how happy you have made the industrious and noble Maya nation. You have given it heretofore unprecedented knowledge and prosperity. You have saved from disaster, during periods of drought, the remote regions of the land. Being tired, you sit down.

There is a knock at the door. A messenger enters. He is covered with dust and blood.

"Ruler, disaster and calamity! A savage nation is attacking your northern regions from the north, and there is destruction and murder. What should we do, high ruler?"

You are crushed. You dismiss the messenger and proceed to the temple.

You pass by the gods of the night without stopping. You halt your steps by the sun god – Kukulcan – and ask for advice, but the bearded god, clad in bright clothing, remains silent. All the other gods remain silent as well. You drop to your knees in front of the invisible God Gvuabku's sign of the cross and ask Him for advice and for help. He, too, remains silent.

Then, however, you hear the voice of the sacred bird Quetzal. You get up and walk over to the window. The star of destiny shines in the sky, the evening and morning star – Aurora. The sacred bird Quetzal screams for the second time. You drop to your knees by the window. The call of the sacred bird Quetzal comes for the third time, and then comes the voice of the star of the evening and of destiny, "What do you want from The Invisible One?"

You ask that the destiny of your nation be revealed to you, and you hear, "A militant nation of savages comes from the north. You and the Maya nation have to abandon this land, temples, and cities, and have to seek a new homeland. The savages will take over your land, will reduce to rubble the temples of the gods, and in their stead will build gigantic temples to their gods. They will build huge cities again. Then from the sea will come a foreign and bearded nation, armed not with weapons of stone, but with metal swords and weapons of fire arrows, unknown to you. Then the Aztec nation, its temples, and culture will perish as well."

You ask, "Isn't it possible to somehow resist the invasion of the savages?"

"No!" comes the reply. "Your nation is not used to bearing arms and fighting!"

"I will teach it," you say.

"To no avail, for that is the will of The Invisible One."

"Then I will fight against it, but I will protect my nation and these temples; for I do not understand how such a high culture can be permitted to disappear from the Earth. I will fight or die here, in my country!"

"Then you will die here. Your nation will leave, the temples will crumble, and the gods will die. The anger of The Invisible One will punish you. Contrary to the previous decision, you will have to live on this Earth once again, and will have to suffer greatly in a lower degree!"

"All right, I will nevertheless fight!" you reply, and clouds cover the evening star.

The third and final [ray]. You are standing on a projection of the temple. Smoke covers the sky. Noise from the battle can be heard. Hordes of savages stream into the city from the north. Your people, led by the new high priest, depart toward the west. Your last guards fight in the entrance of the temple. The sign of the cross appears in the clouds. You bow down your head and say, "The Invisible One, what are You doing? How can we, people, understand You? How can we fight against You?"

Then you give the signal to your guards. An extremely loud noise resounds, the massive stone blocks of the temple crumble, and bury beneath them the high priest and ruler of the land of Maya.

Open your eyes! I conclude. Be bright! [[1722]]

A. Aurora   12/26/43

I congratulate you with the victory over human weakness. This time you had a heavy burden. Alpha is bright – satisfied. He is only concerned regarding the idea about how he will be able to portray the fate of John to you, in a form which you will be able to understand. John's fate will be revealed next Sunday at three o'clock.

[[Concerning Alexander U.]] He wanted to save his nation and did not carry out The Almighty's command, therefore he was punished. It was not a punishment as people understand it, except he was too happy. In order to be able to grow and develop, it is necessary for the spirits to suffer as well. Not all suffering raises us higher, only that which is destined by The Almighty – The Invisible One. The Almighty is the very same Invisible One. Suffering always has to follow happiness. On Earth, Alexander has not lived with the Maya nation again, but he has lived in the Deoss Temple.

→I am an original spirit, created by The Almighty. Santorino is also an original spirit. Human beings, too, can achieve a degree as we have, and even a higher one, which is the degree of divinity. That is Paradise.

What has been said previously about humanity's catastrophe refers to after this war, which brings a catastrophe. This catastrophe refers to your Earth, with which The Almighty is no longer satisfied.←

Chapter II
January 1944

Alpha   01/02/44 1500

Astra, Astra, Astra. Aurora, Aurora, Aurora. Santorino, Santorino, Santorino. Alpha, Alpha, Alpha.

Listen, John! You lived on Earth during the era of the cave people. You were the head and leader of a tribe living in a large cave. You were the region's best hunter. The largest heaps of horse, urus, mammoth, and other animal bones were next to your cave. Your heart, however, was captivated by the beauty of the wife of the neighboring tribe's leader. You began a fight with the leader and crushed his skull with a club. You united both tribes and decided to arrange an unprecedentedly magnificent wedding.

You – the famous destroyer of mammoths – built a large trap. All of you hid and waited for a long time. Then the breaking of bushes was heard, and the brownish frame of the giant appeared in the bushes. The mammoth browsed on grass and buds of the trees, and slowly approached the trap.

"It has a layer of fat beneath its hide at least as thick as the length of my middle finger," you told your new wife, "and you will receive this giant as a wedding present from me."

You gave the signal to the hunters, and they began the chase. The animal fell into the trap, but was too big for it. All of you attacked it with axes and spears. You bravely walked up to the giant and stabbed it in the heart. Your spear broke, your foot slipped, and you fell. You wanted to get up, but got tangled up in roots and in the wool of the mammoth. The last thing that you saw on the planet Earth was the pale face of your wife.

Then the huge mountain [of a mammoth] lay down on top of you and everything disappeared. Your wife arranged a splendid funeral for you and buried you in the cave. You met her once more on this Earth. She summoned you in your current life, but you did not answer her and passed her by.

The second [ray]. I will now take you to the place in the universe where you lived most recently, because life on Earth back then could not give you anything yet.

Close your eyes for a moment and follow me in spirit. The constellation Perseus, the star Algol, and the planet Sisesia.

You are standing by the window of your place of work. You are in charge of the planet's central plant for [the conversion of] the rays of the sun, the energy of the ocean waves, and the heat from the planet's center – you are master engineer Kivikio. I will attempt to depict, in a form that you can somewhat understand, the sounds, names, and the appearance of the people on that planet of Algol. Don't be surprised, and understand as much as you are able to. The people there appeared vaguely similar to a man on Earth, a bird, and an elephant. They had wings.

You are looking out the window and are thinking, "This huge central plant has been entrusted to me. The fate of the planet depends on its uninterrupted functioning. Thanks to it, constant light and heat radiate on the planet – winter and summer, day and night."

Your second assistant, chief engineer Vikivio, sits at a desk. Then you hear the beep from your belt radio station. You listen. You hear the voice of your fiancée, Lalilau, "Have you forgotten what day it is today?"

You suddenly remember Lalilau's wing day. You are ashamed and sad that you had forgotten about it.

"I await you immediately," the voice says. You promise her and turn off the station.

Then you suddenly remember that you have let your first assistant – chief engineer Likilio – go on vacation. However, the one hundred sixth order of lead engineer Pipipio states that there always have to be two chief engineers present in the central plant. What can you do? You decide to take a chance, and you discuss this with Vikivio. He agrees sadly, and inhales the aroma of the intoxicating flower – milimia.

You know that he is also in love with Lalilau, and you tell him, "Dear friend, you know that this is her own free will and choice, and no one can any longer do anything about it."

"No one can any longer do anything about it," Vikivio repeats sadly, and again inhales the fragrance of the intoxicating flower. You remind him how dangerous that is, and then fly away.

Your fiancée awaits you happily, and you go for a walk in the extensive gardens. You reach the zoo soon, where the former inhabitants of the planet can be seen in cages – predatory beasts – animals that have long since been eliminated from the planet. You stand in front of a cage now in which grieve the last representatives of the Nilaniu nation.

Lalilau has a strange nature – she feels sorry for everything. "Why did you destroy these industrious people, who built for us palaces, plants, cities inside the planet, and machinery that works perpetually?"

You reply, "We did not need them any longer, and they attempted to rebel once we confined them to the underground cities. They even tried to rebel after they had been blinded. Then we destroyed them."

"But how come that you did not feel sorry for them?" Lalilau asks.

"Sorry? But, after all, we no longer had any need for them," you answer while not understanding her.

You head homeward. She treats you to your people's only food, fruit, and only drink, the juice of fruits and flowers. Then you fly to the walkway of the melodious trees. Hours pass there in love and happiness.

Then you suddenly feel that the light begins to dim, and it turns chilly. You realize in horror – an accident at the central plant! You have to hurry just as fast as possible so that the planet, the planet's people, and Lalilau would not perish. You fly above the walkway. It turns dark, and snow flakes begin to fall. Huge butterflies fall to the ground, like large, wilted flowers. Where can Lalilau be sheltered? The houses are without windows and doors, they do not protect one from the cold. You want to call the plant, but in the rush you have lost your [radio]. You hurry to the entrance of the underground city, but it has already been closed, and you have foolishly left the key to it at home. You are desperate.

The wings of your fiancée begin to tire already, and she falls. You catch her in time, though. Your strength, however, is not infinite either. A blizzard begins to churn. Then you remember the valley of the hot geysers – the only hope. Fortunately it can still be reached, and you reach it. You set Lalilau down on the grass at the edge of the geysers and hurry on to the central plant.

It is completely dark already, and a snow storm howls. With your last strength you reach the plant. Your assistant lies there [asleep] next to the intoxicating flower. He is already stiff. The machinery is silent. With rigid fingers you grab the handles of the machinery. The machinery begins to function. The darkness starts to dissipate slowly. Light and heat flow [once again].

The people of the planet have been saved. The plant functions. Your first assistant returns. You turn the plant over to him and hasten to Lalilau.

You already see her. She raises her wings toward you. You hurry and forget about everything. You even forget that you are flying so low above the valley of the geysers.

The hiss of water can be heard. Streams of boiling water shoot up into the air and engulf you in steam – death. While falling, you still hear Lalilau's voice, full of despair, and then you no longer hear or see anything.

You parted from Lalilau there, and met her here.

I conclude. Be eternally bright. [[1736]]

A. Aurora   01/02/44

_ ★ ★ ★ _ I cannot tell you whether Lalilau was Mary, for life on the planets in the constellation Perseus is outside the sphere of my light.

_ ★ ★ ★ _

→Only Omega knows where the spirits are sent subsequent to the Lunar Fields. Very different things happen to the spirits who come from the Lunar Fields. That depends on their different lives on Earth and elsewhere. The Lunar Fields are large.

[[We ask, "Does one who succumbs to the power of Satan end up in nonexistence?"]]

Not always.

_ ★ ★ ★ _

Faith helps one to attain the Solar Fields, but, most of all, it takes a good heart. In order to achieve a higher degree, one must unleash oneself from the Earth. That means one has to live only with one's spirit and heart. You have to understand that on your own.

Alexander U. does not have a guardian spirit who looks after him. He is within the radiance of Astra, and within my luminousness. Those spirits who come from the Deoss Temple no longer need [guardian] spirits. They have to struggle with God and Satan on their own, in order to draw closer to The Almighty. This means that they have to struggle with themselves.

The difference between the Deoss Temple and the Solar Fields is like that between the sun and a candle.←

_ ★ ★ ★ _

Alotria   01/05/44

– ★ ★ ★ – I am talking to you, listen! It is immaterial whether an Arab kneels before the sacred Kaaba, or the statue of Buddha, or the cross of Christ, for he is praying to The Creator and the ruler of his destiny – he is praying to The Almighty – who is within all the Gods. I conclude.

A. Aurora   01/05/44

→"Our Father who art in Heaven…" is the only prayer that God has given to the people, and is the only one to which He listens. This is because everything that an individual needs to pray for, and that he is allowed to pray for, is expressed in this prayer. Whenever I tell you to pray to God, I mean "Our Father who art in Heaven…," and a prayer of the soul will follow it.

Do not ask about the future. It is ludicrous to ask about the future. You ask the spirits to reveal your future to you, but fail to realize to what absurdity this would lead, if the spirits were to tell the people their future.

First of all, what would happen if an individual were to be told everything that will happen to him? Think about that for yourselves! A person has been told that on the sixth of January, while riding in a streetcar, he will be killed on the street. Obviously, he will not ride the streetcar on that day, and the prophecy will be a lie. Or else, we, the spirits, will have to drag him by the collar into the streetcar.

To continue, if he were to know all his future days, he would feel like a prisoner, whose every day and hour is regulated by schedules. If the individual were to know his life ahead of time, would it any longer be of any interest to him? If he were to know the day of his death, his final years would then be very dreadful, and would he feel like doing anything?

Let's say that I were to tell you that Riga will be destroyed in March, and that some of you will be shot, and you were to know that this will occur irrevocably and definitely. Just how grateful would you be to me, and what superfluous and ghastly suffering would this knowledge bring you? Besides that, this [knowledge] would limit your free spirit. Therefore the spirits generally remain silent about the future. Do not bother them in vain, by forcing them to violate God's will.←

Santorino will speak on Sunday at three o'clock. The very greatest evaluation and surprise await you. There have to be white letters on black paper. Only the table may be illuminated and the paper on which a third person is writing. The room has to be without any furniture and locked. Three chairs and one table – that is everything. Santorino will tell you about additional preparations. When he comes he will tell you.

_ ★ ★ ★ _

I conclude. Be wise and strong!

Astra   01/09/44

I do not know anything about the instructions for your conversation today. It is not possible to ask Aurora, she's not here.

Yes, carry out what you have been told, and realize that a spirit will talk with you who does not even talk with the low spirits, and whose words bring The Almighty's blessing even to the high spirits.

Three paintings may remain in the room, and only three. I conclude.

Santorino   01/09/44 1500

Ego Santorino. Listen, I am speaking! Listen, I am speaking! Listen, I am speaking! Be vigilant!

We, the high spirits, alighted to the Deoss Temple last Wednesday in order to receive a decision from God, Satan, and The Almighty. The destinies of many nations on Earth were being decided. When God and Satan placed their hands on the scale of fate for the Latvian nation, the scale moved for a moment, but did not turn either to the right or to the left. Then God and Satan left their places as judges, and all of us looked into infinity, while awaiting The Almighty's decision; but it did not come. Then we saw God and Satan turn their faces toward The Almighty. We understood that They were inquiring about the destinies of the nations on Earth, and of the Earth itself.

Then the sign of The Almighty's Cross, above the Deoss Temple, began to grow dim. We understood then that The Almighty had concealed His face again. We departed from the Temple in silence. Await His decision with the same prayer and hope as we pray and believe, that He will not punish the nations on Earth too harshly.

Remember and bear in mind – the nations on Earth have forgotten that the gravest sin in the world is the extermination of children. This cannot be forgiven, and retribution will always come because of it. Some large, and even small, nations have dared to place this sin on their shoulders. All merciless nations have been deprived of the right to be the rulers of nations. Thus the Hun nation and the Tartar and Turkish empires vanished. Unfortunately, there are people with the hearts of wolves even among the sons of Latvia.

God has saved the land of Latvia three times, and Satan has lowered His sword before it three times. Now [you can rely] only on the might of The Almighty; hope and pray to Him. He is not satisfied with how the nations on Earth have utilized the free will that has been given them. Nations, and even planets, have perished because of The Almighty's anger. It is dreadful not to live up to His expectations.

Now, once I have finished talking with you, stand up very reverently for a minute, bow down your heads, and welcome The Almighty's architect of the worlds and the promulgator of His decisions – Chief Spirit Omega – who will talk with you. *Dixi*.

Omega   01/09/44

→I, the Ruler of the Future and of Death, speak unto you mortals – immortals. Know how to differentiate between what will be intended just for yourselves and what will be intended for everyone.

Your task is not to bring new Gods to humanity. It is merely to strive to open the altar doors in The Almighty's Temple, so that the believers could look inside and see, and the chosen ones could enter. Do not talk with the nonbelievers, and do not summon anyone into His Temple. Everyone has to discover it for himself. It is not up to you to go to the chosen ones, for whoever has been chosen and realizes his immortality will find you and will understand you on his own.

Do not take hordes of slaves into His Temple. Do not grieve for those who do not understand, but rejoice for those who have understood. Only one out of a million spirits, who have been created, is destined to achieve the degree of divinity, and only one out of a thousand is destined to remain eternally in the Solar Fields. All others, having failed to live up to The Almighty's expectations, will return to nonexistence.

Humanity on Earth approaches a level of spiritual development that will permit it to follow the rising sun of new understanding. Do not be surprised if its rays also touch you, the first ones. The first rays of the rising sun may touch initially not only the snow-covered summit of the highest mountain, but also a tiny, white cloud in the azure sky, [floating] above the darkest valley.

_ ★ ★ ★ _

People take pride in the free spirit that has been given to them. Yet they fail to realize that this is the heaviest burden which The Almighty could have placed on the soul. It is easier and better to be the slave of a good master than to be the master of a wicked slave.

You also have to realize that this life must never be too difficult for you, and you must not despair if you do not succeed in everything. You always have to keep in mind that even The Almighty is not capable of everything. The Almighty's greatest tragedy is His almightiness, which opposes His almightiness and limits it. He wanted to create spirits who are free from His influence, and could not. He wanted to create planets which He could no longer destroy, and could not.

A new era approaches. The strayed spirit of humanity, horror-struck, looks back at his deeds. Having washed, in disgust, his bloody hands, he will set his sight toward Heaven. Yet, that will take place neither tomorrow, nor the day after.

The most difficult period in humanity's history will only begin with Germany's withdrawal from the war. Unless The Almighty changes His decision, the sunny path of humanity's happiness will follow that.

You ask, "What is the future?" and claim that it has been decided by God and is irrevocable. You are surprised whenever everything does not occur as God had envisioned and decided. Do not forget that man has been given a free will and that he does not always travel the roads which have been set by God.

The state draws up a train schedule for a year, and it does materialize. This is regardless that, in individual cases – due to the negligence or sin of individual people, the train engineers – some trains are delayed, or do not arrive at all. The same holds true of the schedule of fate, which God has drawn up.

The era of new knowledge and understanding approaches. The spirit of humanity will cast off his narrow and dark wings of a sparrow, covered by the dust of the streets, and will soar into the azure sky on the wings of eagles, on wings silver-clad with the snowflakes from snow-covered mountaintops. He will ascend from the dark, tiny room of God, lit by a candle – the sun – to The Almighty's Temple. A Temple whose floor is formed of extinguished suns and planets – the walls are of glittering suns and stars – and the roof is formed of the sparkling nebulae of worlds, galaxies being born. The rags of superstition and childish adornments will fall from the Gods, and They will gleam in the lustrous garb of humanity's pure, high religion and science.

Strive to comprehend what I have told you. I want to ascertain, through you, just how high the spirit of humanity has ascended and how many there are of those who are capable of following you.

I conclude. Be wise, be bright, be strong.←

Ali   01/16/44

_ ★ ★ ★ _

[Go ahead and] ask the spirits, but only remember what my ruler, the sultan, always said, "Whoever asks too much has to have his head cut off, for he may also gossip too much."

Give and hand out presents, but remember what my sultan always said, "Should you wish to give some pearls as a present to only one of your wives, then do not give any at all, for otherwise you will become poor and a cripple."

I conclude.

Santorino   01/16/44 1500

[[Question: "What errors did we commit during Omega's talk?"]]

Ego Santorino. You do not understand your own question.

[[Question: "Did we pass the evaluation?"]]

Your questions do not correspond at all to that which you want to know.

Omega came to evaluate you. He accomplished that, and only he, himself, knows the results. He did not come to punish or to reward. Will you be able to understand if I will tell you that Omega is not visible, just as a storm, but his deeds are visible, just as uprooted trees are. If I will tell you that, simultaneously while talking with you, he also evaluated Adolf's agitated abilities of the spirit to carry on the inhumanly heavy burden which The Almighty has placed on him. He also evaluated the strength of the soul of Joseph's successor, and increased the number of days of Joseph's life. Simultaneously with that he strengthened Winston's health. On a battlefield he returned life to a fallen soldier, whose mother had, with her infinite faith in God's mercy and her pure heart, earned life for her son from God. He also braced the foot of a thief who was falling from a wall and kept him from falling. He also, while passing by, rescued from a cat's paws the mother of some helpless, young mice. Yet will you be able to understand that? Be less hasty and more thoughtful in the future!

→The Solar Fields are located at the foot of the stairway to the Deoss Temple and are under the direct and sole jurisdiction of God. They consist of thirteen circles, which are divided into sectors for the planets. The first circle, the circle of the happiest [spirits], is the plainest and the beginning circle. The spirits who have come over from the Lunar Fields rest in it, or else those spirits who have earned the Solar Fields by noble self-sacrifice. The spirits have to pass through twelve circles. After that they either remain eternally in the thirteenth circle or else ascend to the Deoss Temple, in order to start on the pathway to Paradise. This path is thirteen times longer and more difficult than the previous one.

The Lunar Fields are under the jurisdiction of Satan, except for the thirteenth circle that is ruled by Omega. From there the spirits either go over to the Solar Fields, or else into nonexistence. The human soul which has arrived in the Lunar Fields is being purified and evaluated, but you will not understand that.

[[Question: "Is that Hell?"]]

No. Hell is a thousand-year punishment of redemption and darkness and silence.

[[Question: "How can one comprehend the course of the human soul?"]]

It is strange how illogical you are. You ask about inexplicable matters and fail to grasp the comprehensible ones. Thus, you ask about The Almighty, of whom even Alpha and Omega say that they are mere [specks of] dust at His feet, and fail to comprehend God and the essence of the spirits. You have to understand that, initially, there is only the mother. Then come the mother and her child, as a single, inseparable body and soul. Then the body and soul separate. Even though they are one, now they are two entirely different and self-sufficient creatures.

Even though they are the same flesh of their mother, children can be entirely different. They can be similar, or different, or even hostile to their mother's body. Humanity even knows cases of children murdering their own mothers. Remember Nero and others. The child, too, has been given a free will.

Perhaps you will now understand how The Almighty could have created God, Satan, and the spirits and why they are so different, and either good or evil – even though they have come from the same spirit.

God and Satan. God has been given the authority to help the spirits and to save them, but Satan – to punish and to ruin them.

One can pray to The Almighty through God, who has been given the right of helping and of saving.

Prayer without deeds is criminal! Prayer is that last cord of salvation, which the individual weaves during his lifetime from his good deeds, and it is just as strong as he has woven it.

People need the church, just as the spirits need the Deoss Temple.

[[Question: "Why don't we remember the past?"]]

Think [about that] for yourselves, and try to comprehend that on your own.←

_ ★ ★ ★ _

Ali   01/23/44

- ★ ★ ★ - I will give you some advice now, for I have a peculiar nature. Do not complain about the hardships of life and do not value too lowly the wealth of [good] health. My sultan always said, "It is better to have two feet and one boot, rather than one foot and two boots."

Choose your friends wisely, which is most difficult to do here on Earth, but always remember what my sultan said, "If it is essential for you to go on a trip and to leave your wife and belongings behind, then at least entrust your belongings to the most foolish of your friends and your wife to the wisest one. Otherwise you will be left without your belongings and your wife."

Do not think that I am joking. Think [about that] and adopt it to the problems of life.

Do not ask about the future, for The Almighty is altering the destinies of all the nations on Earth. Only He and Omega know them now. Even God and Satan do not know them yet.

John, you are the youngest of the spirits of the three of you. You act much too rashly, and you do what the spirits do not ask from you. Be more deliberate and patient!

Mary, you are God's dearest and purest spirit. Do not grieve that quite often in this life you had to be different, and even hostile, to your spirit. Yet, that is Omega's decision.

Alexander U., you are the oldest of the three spirits, if one does not consider little Nicholas, who is an extremely old spirit. You are The Almighty's most intimate spirit, whom, of all the spirits, He loves the most and detests the most. He [[Alexander]] is incomprehensible to us, the spirits, as well, because he is infinitely higher and infinitely lower than we are. As the Mayan ruler, he was the executor of the thoughts of The Almighty Himself. However, by refusing to carry out The Almighty's final command, he committed the most serious sin that was possible and should have been punished with nonexistence for that. Yet since he took on the unimaginably heavy sin in order to save the people, he earned the degree of divinity with that. Thus one sin compensated for the other.

_ ★ ★ ★ _

[[Question: "What was the name of your sultan?"]]

You will have to find the name of my sultan in history on your own. I can tell you about myself – how I became the sultan's grand vizier.

When the former grand vizier died, the sultan had all the wisest statesmen summoned to the castle. Each of them had to answer the question, "What should be done so that the sultan could rule successfully?"

I, as the youngest, was also the last one. The sultan asked, and I replied, "Levy such high taxes on your subjects that they cannot become rich."

"And that is it?" the sultan asked.

"Yes, high ruler."

All the wise men began to laugh, but the sultan turned contemplative and dismissed us until the morning. I left the palace accompanied by ridicule.

In the morning, the sultan called me in and said, "The whole night long I thought about your advice and reached only one conclusion. Your words can be only one thing – they are either unimaginably foolish or incomprehensibly wise. Explain them to us."

I explained, "Ruler, should you levy low taxes on the people, they will become rich, and you will become poor. Your subjects will say, 'We are rich and wise, but our sultan is poor. Why should we listen to such a fool? Down with him!'

"Should you, however, be rich and the people poor, then they will call you, 'Our great and wise sultan.'"

The sultan then said, "Be my grand vizier!"

This incident will be useful to you in your life as well.

_ ★ ★ ★ _

Astra   01/23/44

The spirits will not speak today, because they are heading for the Deoss Temple. I am always there. It is not possible to talk any longer, since the spirits have assembled in the Deoss Temple. Omega is speaking there.

Not all the spirits have assembled in the Deoss Temple, but only the higher ones. The others are on the stairway. Ali is in the Temple. Those spirits who are in the Lunar Fields have not even seen the Temple.

Wait for Santorino to speak. He will summon you.

Chapter III
February 1944 – Part 1

A. Aurora   02/05/44

I was too far away for you to understand the distance.

Jews are the people of both, that is of God and of Satan.

[[We ask, "Are the Jews 'chosen people,' as they consider themselves to be?"]]

No. No people are chosen. Try to think clearly for yourselves. The Almighty judges nations according to the total, the total of good and evil. If a nation produces a hundred tons of grain, then it is immaterial whether that has been produced by one individual or by a million people. The nation that produces more is also more valuable. The Almighty does not value a nation as such, and we, the spirits, do not differentiate between a Latvian and a Jew. There are very high spirits among the Jews, and very low ones among the Latvians. With respect to the Jewish nation – The Almighty needed it, because no other nation would have crucified Christ. The Gospel tells you why Christ had to be crucified.

The Old Testament of the Bible is the book of fairy tales of a barbaric and merciless nation. It is high time for the world to forget it.

The Book of Revelation of John is the composition of a high spirit in which the truth – rather, fantasy – mixes with reality.

The writings of the wise ones of Zion are the nightmares of humanity's sickness.

The Jews are being blamed now for too much. Which nation currently does not want to and does not try to rule other nations? Why do you consider this desire, which all people possess, to be a sin only with respect to the Jewish people?

If you are such fools as to permit someone to sit on your backs and order you around, then only you, yourselves, are at fault. Who would not like to ride on your backs? Do not forget that The Almighty has given equal abilities and a free will to every individual and, hence, to every nation. Do not blame others, but only yourselves.

Do not be surprised if a warehouse, which you guard poorly and fail to lock, is burglarized. Thieves will always come about.

I have to leave. Ali will talk with you after dinner.

Ali   02/05/44

_★ ★ ★_

→The Almighty has decided to save humanity from complete demise by means of unprecedented torment. The horrors will make even the blind see, and the sword will fall from the bloody hands of the murderers of their brothers.

Omega had me speak thus unto you, for Santorino is busy. He is talking with God and Satan. Satan is very pale, for the horrors which the nations on Earth are experiencing have crushed even Him. He begged The Almighty to have mercy toward them. Only Omega is able to carry out The Almighty's dreadful commands.

The lower spirits do not know anything about this tragedy, for otherwise their strength would fail. I do not know why Omega had me reveal this to you. However, the spirits do not hear your words, and they do not see your writings. That is the will of Omega. No one understands it. You may relate this only to the closest and the strongest people.

Christ and Santorino are and are not the same entity. After His death, Christ merged with God. Santorino is −. But I am not allowed to reveal that to you yet.←

Tomorrow morning I will talk with you again. My task with you is becoming too difficult for my strength.

I will tell you now something about The Almighty and Alexander U. There came an order once from The Almighty for the spirits to undertake a life on a planet – the most difficult of lives – the life of a prophet who was destined to die under the most atrocious tortures for an entire month. The spirits remained silent, because that was too dreadful. Then came the voice of Alexander, "Almighty, I accept your offer."

Crushed, we looked back. The Deoss Temple floated in the rays of The Almighty, and we understood that the first spirit who would achieve the degree of divinity stood before us. Then, however, Alexander's voice came again, "Almighty, I accept it, but only on one condition. I am not to receive any appreciation for accomplishing this task."

We wanted to cheer, but then froze, because the Temple sank into hitherto unprecedented darkness. Then the head of Omega began to shine through the darkness, and the words came from his lips, "The Almighty accepts your conditions."

Alexander then sank to his knees, and said, "Oh, Almighty, I thank You that You alone have understood me correctly."

The Almighty's reply came, "Yes, after all, I did understand you. Go, My son."

The Temple lit up in unprecedentedly bright rays. We dispersed in silence, for still to this day we have not comprehended everything. Perhaps you will at least understand this – Omega and Alexander?

Until the morning.

Ali   02/06/44

_ ★ ★ ★ _

Now about something else. Listen and [try to] understand. My sultan told the people who were dissatisfied with everything and only strove for something new, "What would happen if the shoes wanted to run faster than the feet?"

He told a foreign ambassador whose eyes always darted around, "Man has been given two eyes, not so that he could see two worlds, but simply to discern better this one world."

He told one of his wives, who talked too much about the sins of others, "Why has Allah given you two eyes along with one tongue, rather than four eyes, because then you would be able to see correctly what your tongue is saying?"

I can be recognized by my jokes and from Astra's announcements.

→Some animals do have spirits; however, that is too complicated [to explain].

Do not ask about the future. You will be told whatever you have to know. With respect to the future, one has to say that it does not exist. There is only a scheme which may materialize, and also may be altered in the process of development.

Now, between us. The Almighty's deeds may seem to some people like the actions of a child. He builds a sand castle and, once it is almost complet-ed, he smashes it. Yet that is a ludicrous idea. The Almighty has established the highest demands for His work. Unless they are realized one-hundred percent, He destroys the entire work and begins anew.

The memory of children. For a few years, until he learns how to think, a child lives with the spirit of his mother. Then The Almighty gives him a soul, either an entirely new one or, else, that of an existing spirit. Therefore, you do not remember those days when you still had your mother's spirit.

Santorino is God's heart.←

Alexander U. decides his fate on his own. He came to Earth a hundred years sooner than had been envisaged by The Almighty so that he could be present during humanity's greatest suffering. He will also depart on his own.

_ ★ ★ ★ _

Only the higher spirits are capable of speaking all the languages in the universe. I am a high spirit, but I have to carry out a special task for Omega. Don't imagine that your guardian spirits are always with you. They come to you only when they are essential, the rest of the time you are by yourselves.

_ ★ ★ ★ _

Ali   02/13/44 1000

Close the door! Well, isn't that better?

[[We ask, "How can one bring up a child with a will as strong as steel?"]]

I will explain the essence of these principles. Both of you, the father and the mother, have to be consistent. Do not criticize each other in the presence of the child. If one of you has told him to do something, the other one should not rescind that. Should you give the child an order, then consider thoroughly beforehand whether it can be carried out and whether it is necessary. However, once an order has been given, then see to it that it is definitely carried out, and is carried out correctly.

Divide the child's time into time for studies, for chores, and for free time. Ironclad firmness has to reign during the first two time periods. The hearts of the mother and the father may not speak then, but only the high mind of the educator. During the latter – the free time – give him freedom as unlimited as is possible, and do not punish harshly, even for major transgressions. Instill in him respect toward a human being and toward himself, which is the very same thing. In the presence of people he has to conduct himself with the greatest respect toward himself, which means toward every person.

The greatest firmness has to be observed at the table. No liberties may be permitted, not even if the child eats by himself. He has to finish eating quickly and seriously. Should he not have an appetite, then it is better to let him go hungry until the next meal. That will only benefit him. However, don't attempt to coerce him.

You, too, have to conduct yourselves with respect toward him, if he deserves this. Treat his spiritual aspirations seriously, but not hypocritically. Encourage each good attempt and punish every evil one. Use the methods of upbringing of the Maya nation as an example, for little Nick's spirit is just as great as the spirit of the Mayan high priest.

Choose worthy companions for him, but do not grieve should he get a black eye while defending his honor. He has to learn how to win, for his entire life will be a struggle. However, in order to conquer others, one has to, first, learn how to conquer himself. Anyone who does not know how to rule himself will never rule others.

An example is the best school, therefore bring up yourselves as well.

What I told you are the words of Omega.

I will alight away for a while. A. Aurora will speak in ten minutes. Relax.

A. Aurora   02/13/44 1055

_ ★ ★ ★ _

Unfortunately Ali will have to leave you soon, because The Almighty wants to appoint him as the ruler of a planet.

The ideas of the new teachings will not be revealed to the nations on Earth for the time being, because Omega observes how those to whom they have been revealed comprehend them. Omega himself, though, will talk with you in the future as well, but only with you on the entire Earth.

Now I will reveal something altogether surprising for Mary and John. Alpha and Omega permitted me to do this.

Listen! When Alexander undertook his dreadful task of suffering, you, Mary, were the daughter of the prison warden in whose prison Alexander was being tortured. [The other] Alexander, now Homics, was your father – the warden of the prison. Your heart comprehended the truthfulness of the prophet's preaching and could not bear Alexander's suffering, his holy suffering. You eased his suffering in various ways and talked your father into letting him secretly out of the prison. Your father knew that this will cost him at least his life, but you also knew this, and still –.

The prophet, himself, refused to leave the prison. Then you wanted to rescue him by force. That failed as well, for Omega, himself, slammed shut the door of the prison.

Once Alexander returned to the Deoss Temple, he awaited you impatiently, for you followed him. He met you on the stairway of the Temple, and said, "Why did you want to disrupt my mission and make my suffering unbearable?"

Then came the voice of Omega, "She did not know anything about your mission. However, she supplemented your mission, and thanks to her, your teachings overwhelmed and conquered the hearts [of the people].

"After you had already departed from the planet, she turned to the people and said, 'Blind ones, what have you done? You have burned your God, who brought you nothing but love and justice! I am incapable of living among blind and deaf people, I am going along with him!'

"Then Mary climbed up next to Alexander, into the flames of the fire. The people froze in terror and in eerie premonitions.

"The one who had given the signal to light the fire, the one who loved Mary more than his own life, and who is now called John, fell weeping into the ashes. Having stood up again he said, 'My people, I and you have placed a mortal sin on our shoulders. We have tortured to death a prophet. I return my crown of the ruler to you! Throw me into the fire as well!'

"All the people fell to their knees and acknowledged their delusions."

Alexander then raised his face toward infinity and said, "Almighty, You see the heart of Anita – Mary – and You see her deeds. Doesn't it seem to You that there is a spirit before You who is worthy of Your degree of divinity?"

The Almighty's reply came through Omega, "Yes, but with your refusal you deprived Me of the opportunity to reward her as well, because that would have been the greatest insult for her."

Then Alexander – the proudest of the spirits – dropped down on one knee and told Mary, "Can you forgive me? Yet I did not know that you, too, would suffer."

Then came the voice of God. "It's all right, My children, Mary is still indispensable to Me," and He took her to His Temple.

However, the voice of Omega came again, "She nevertheless will have to suffer My punishment. I will send her to the planet Earth. There, though, she will be the executor of My commands, God, and You will be able to have her only after that. Yet now all of you submerse yourselves in the rays of The Almighty's blessing for some rest."

There is much that you can now see with clearer eyes. I will suspend the conversation for the time being. If you want to, summon me toward the evening. Be bright!

Ali   02/13/44

Don't be concerned, I will not leave you quite that soon.

Be serious with the spirits. It is not possible to summon any spirit unless he, himself, summons you. The spirits do not talk with everyone, but only with the chosen ones, and with those who believe in them. There can be deceivers among the people, because it is not difficult to make the saucer move. Similarly, a bright student can imitate the professor. Here, though, one has to differentiate between the professor and the imitator, and that is [based on] what each of them is capable of giving. Knowledge is what differentiates them. Most important, don't stage a show, and don't bore your guests.

Santorino   02/19/44 1930

_ ★ ★ ★ _

→Today I will reveal to you something unexpected and new. Perhaps it will not be that which you await and desire.

_ ★ ★ ★ _

Now, about spiritual matters. First, concerning sin. Sin should be comprehended thus: Everyone is responsible for their actions – sins, but it can be otherwise as well. The most sinful person will not be punished for his sins; rather, others will. For example, the father and mother drink, steal, and bring up their children to be drunkards and thieves. In that case, only they will be responsible for the sins of their children. The children, after death, will simply have to start life anew.

Consider the great significance of this revelation as it pertains to humanity. You have to understand how important a task, and what a responsibility, lies on an individual who wants to become a father or a mother.

To continue. You do not understand the essence of the spirits and their task. The spirits are not like you have imagined them. It is not you who are necessary for them, but rather, they are necessary for you. They are not constantly with you, but only at moments of need. Their task is not to ease your life on Earth, but merely to help your spirit grow. Therefore, quite often, not only do they fail to ease your life's hardships, but make them even more difficult should that be needed for the growth of your spirit. This growth can take place only through suffering and a struggle.

The spirits may ease your earthly passage only in rare instances, whenever that is necessary. It may even occur that a spirit, on seeing that an individual is sinking irrevocably – and that in the current body his spirit is not only incapable of any growth, but can only sink – the spirit not only will not help the individual to avoid the scaffold, but may take him to the scaffold.

Do not imagine that the high spirits incarnate in rulers and the wealthy. No, quite the contrary. Only in exceptional cases, and at The Almighty's direction, do they incarnate in rulers, such as Alexander of Macedonia and Peter of Russia. Generally, the most eminent spirits are doomed in rulers, for power and wealth are what degrade everything that is noble. Therefore, almost all rulers are murderers, and the majority of their spirits are set back several degrees and even pass into nonexistence.

Do not imagine that the high spirits choose prominent positions or appearance for themselves. They have to be similar to other people, and at times even more deplorable outwardly. They have to forget completely their spirit's past and have to preserve only their spirit's grandeur.

Those whom, after their deaths, you consider to be geniuses, are generally the highest spirits who have been sent to Earth. These would be persons of science, art, and literature. The ones whom you know best were Russia's Pushkin and Dostoevski, and America's Edgar [Allan] Poe. Yet you know what they were like as people.

Humanity's greatest genius, and The Almighty's most eminent spirit, Dostoevski, led a hard life. He had to suffer the greatest torments and experience all delusions so that his high spirit would be understandable to the people. Only then was he able to reveal to the people all the suffering and experiences of the soul, in a language which they could understand.

The spirits do not come to people when summoned by them, but only when they wish to do so. There are few people with whom the spirits speak. This is because people generally want to obtain only materialistic benefits from the spirits. [They want] help in misfortune, in finding lost goods or loved ones, and in finding out about their relatives and the future. All that is entirely contrary to the tasks of the spirits. Do not ask the spirits all that, for they will not answer you, or else will mock you maliciously. Or else, some clever individual, a friend of the spirits, will trick you.←

[[We expressed doubts about our abilities and achievements. An answer was given regarding this.]]

An individual walks across a field and drops a tiny poppy seed. You exclaim, "You fool!" Visit that field, however, in a few years, and you will see a miracle – the entire field will sway in the magnificent blossoms of the poppies. That is a reply to your discussion.

→I will take you now into the realm of the spirits. Follow me carefully. I will talk with you as with schoolchildren. Now then, let us begin.

The spirits are not like you have imagined them. They are not angels with wings nor devils with tails. The spirits are not visible, for they do not have bodies. They look similar to the people on Earth; that is, this is how we see each other. The spirits do not think as people do, for they do not have brains. They have comprehension and omniscience. Therefore, the spirit has to incarnate so that he might grow, think, and transform. The spirit relocates with the speed of thought, in addition to which he can simultaneously be here, as well as there, wherever he wants to be. The high spirits can simultaneously see and talk in many places, and the chief spirits are simultaneously everywhere.

That seems strange to you, but let's seek the aid of your current science. What do you know about the atom? In the Greek language, it means "indivisible." Yet, now you know that the atom is a sub-microscopic solar system, that electricity forms it, and that a rock and vapor are the very same atoms. The hard steel and the imperceptible air are the very same atoms, the very same electrical essence.

How can the spirits relocate so swiftly and converse over infinite distances? Yet consider the telephone, of which Napoleon did not even dream. With the help of electricity, you can talk to an individual who is thousands of kilometers away. He replies to you, as though he were sitting across the table from you. Can you grasp that?

The spirits do not see as people see, for they do not have eyes. You know that the brain recognizes the world like the eyes depict it [to the brain].

Yet are the eyes, and only the eyes, always needed for the brain to see? You are asleep, your eyes are closed. However, you see people, and you talk with them. You see objects and places that you have never seen before in life. Once you awake, quite often the dream appears to have been seen just as realistic as what you have seen in life. With what did you see this other world? Certainly not with your eyes! It is difficult, though, to explain to you with what the spirits see, hear, and talk. Neither is it necessary for you to know that.

How do the spirits talk with people? Usually by means of intuition. The Almighty announces His will through His envoys, such as Christ and others, who speak specifically in His name; or else through spirits, who, having incarnated in humans, reveal The Almighty's will, and through geniuses; or else, like in this case, through you with a saucer.

With the development of humanity's intellect, the concepts about God and spiritual life change as well. It would be possible to send a spirit, who would know how to design an airplane, to a tribe of savages. Yet there would be no craftsmen who could construct it, and no machinery and factories to assemble it. [There would be no] pilots who could be trained to fly. An absurdity would result. Therefore, let's rather give the savage a donkey on which to ride, for perhaps he will not fall off it.

Thus, along with man's knowledge, his spiritual comprehension grows as well, and his God grows as well. Christ spoke so that the people back then could understand Him. To the precept, "an eye for an eye," He gave the complete opposite – "love your enemy," in order to break the might of the former. He had to perform miracles, for back then one could arouse the minds of the people only with the help of miracles. Nowadays miracles are superfluous. A miracle is what your mind hears and understands.

_ ★ ★ ★ _

Humanity travels a long and difficult road of [new knowledge and understanding].

How did humanity alter the teachings of Christ? You know that millions of people have been sent, and are being sent, in His name to kill their brothers.

What currently rules on Earth is not the faith of Christ, and those who proclaim hatred in His name are not the priests of Christ. Therefore your churches, too, collapse in rubble. Christ does not dwell in them.

The teachings of Christ are humanity's ideals, which it will never achieve.

Now I am telling you: Act as your heart tells you. Should you be convinced that your actions are sacred and just, then struggle for them. Struggle for everything that is just, which brings blessings to your brothers, and which is the will of God. Even kill those who bring evil. That is your creed for the Earth. That is your new God. Everything for the good, everything for the purity of humanity's spirit, everything for humanity's happiness to include your own happiness and life.

I conclude for today. Be bright.← [[2200]]

Chapter IV
February 1944 – Part2

Santorino   02/20/44

→*Ego* Santorino. I could not complete my conversation yesterday because of two reasons. Let us continue.

The spirits consist of two elements: The Almighty's spirit, which is not comprehensible to anyone, and electrical atoms. From these, the spirits form the body which they need. This occurs instantaneously. The spirits can even condense the atoms so as to become visible even to humans. A human does not control the atoms of his body, but the spirits control them completely.

The soul, or The Almighty's spirit, is what exists invariably, either on its own or as the soul of a living being.

The Almighty, in His own form, or that of God or Satan, is everywhere and speaks unto everyone. Just as the speaker's voice from a radio broadcasting station can be heard in all homes in the world wherever there are receivers, thus the voice of God sounds to everyone who has a heart for its reception.

As you can see, electricity forms matter, produces light, gives heat, drives motors, and gives wings to the people. It carries their voices across oceans and does and forms still much else, of which currently you have no inkling whatsoever. A video radio [television] is being born as well. Soon you will be able to see and hear your fathers and sons in America, just as clearly and easily as you can now see and hear each other in this room. Then you will comprehend my words even more readily.

The firstborn spirits, after the first death of the individual, are just as weak as a human being. After spending some time in the Lunar Fields, they have grown already. It continues like that for thousands of years, until they have passed through all the circles of the Lunar Fields. Then come the Solar Fields and the life of the spirits as the spirits of living beings. Subsequent to the Solar Fields, for those who do not remain there eternally, begins the service of the spirits to The Almighty. The final goal of this service is Paradise.

What I told you yesterday about the new religion and God pertains, for the time being, only to the highest spirits of humanity. After the donkey, horse, or camel the people must first be given a simple, wooden wagon; then a carriage, after that a car, and only then an airplane, which will carry them into Heaven, to The Almighty.

This is what I wanted to reveal to you at this time.←

_ ★ ★ ★ _

Ali   02/20/44

_ ★ ★ ★ _

Be prudent, polite, and conduct yourselves respectfully toward every person. There is nothing easier than to thoughtlessly hurt the feelings of another individual. It is not great deeds which most often cause the greatest damage in the world, but strictly words. Therefore, consider each of your words, particularly when angry, and you will see just how much better the people become and how much easier life becomes. Unjust accusations are what offend the most. I will give you an example.

One day, while my sultan and I were driving along the streets of the city, we heard a commotion and saw a fight. The sultan stopped and ordered to have the matter investigated. Two men were brought before us.

One of them said, "This man called me a mule, but, since I am not a mule, I had to defend my honor."

The other one said, "He hit me."

The sultan said, "But, after all, you did call him a mule."

"Sultan, but after all, he is a mule. Everyone knows that."

"All right," said the sultan, "we will clear that up right now. Bring me a mule."

One was brought to him.

"Now call him a mule," the sultan gave an order to the one who had been beaten up.

He walked over to the mule, and for about half an hour shouted into one or the other of its ears, "Mule!" The latter, however, simply stood there and merely moved its long ears. Finally, in despair, the man stopped shouting and, while walking away from the mule, patted it with his hand lightly on the side and said, "Oh, you little lamb."

That very same second he was stretched out on his back on the ground.

The sultan then told him, "Well, see for yourself, even a mule can't stand being called incorrectly. What then did you expect from a human? In addition, give him twenty lashes," and we went on.

Think more on your own, and do not cling to the coattails of the spirits. Never thank the spirits with words, but only spiritually. Good-bye.

Ortega   02/20/44

Listen! I, Chief Spirit Ortega, am speaking to you.

The night comes. Blood flows. Weapons resound. Tears flow. Churches collapse. The priests remain silent. God is silent. Only Satan talks. Humanity's heart drowns in blood. There is no hope. That is humanity's present.

I will bring you a future – the sun for the world, happiness for Latvia. The Almighty sends me to you; drop to your knees!

I come to you. I bring light to the entire world. It will rise from my sword, which will smash to dust the might of Satan. That will be soon. Don't get tired, and also don't be afraid to die; because these will be the last sacrifices of the redemption.

I, The Almighty's Chief Spirit Ortega, am speaking to you.

Lucifer   02/20/44

The fire is going out, the fire is going out! Who has drawn the sign of the cross on the gates of Hell? The fire is going out! Ha, ha, ha.

Astra   02/20/44

Ortega is The Almighty's envoy and the judge for Earth; he comes as a redeemer. The Almighty will spare the Earth, and Ortega will set it free from the power of evil. Ortega is The Almighty's chief spirit who carries out His special assignments. We, the spirits, see him for the first time in this part of the universe.

[[We ask about our task.]]

Wait, because we, ourselves, still don't know anything. Wait for changes, because the fight against evil will be a difficult one, for evil dwells in the hearts of the people.

The spirits stream to the Deoss Temple to welcome The Almighty's high envoy. I have to hurry.

Russia's Czar Nicholas II   02/20/44

Those who killed me want to destroy your nation as well. Only a miracle can save you. Stand firm, the Communists and their rabble will come to ruin. They will disappear from the face of the Earth. But will that save you? Only The Almighty knows that.

I am in the Deoss Temple. The Russian people have to help themselves.

I obtained my high degree because of my torturous death. Besides that, in my life I did not wish evil to anyone. Everyone deceived me. I wanted to save the world from war, but I failed. Germany is humanity's evil genius. Rasputin was a deceiver, a servant of the evil spirit.

An emperor must not have a heart, but only the highest mind.

Rely on God's mercifulness. May God be with you!

Santorino   02/23/44 1930

What do you want from Santorino? I am listening.

[[We ask about Ortega.]]

Chief Spirit Ortega is The Almighty's envoy and the judge of the nations on Earth. The honor which he bestowed on you is so great that even the spirits could not grasp that.

The ruler of the evil spirits on Earth himself sought an answer from you concerning the basis of this visit. Only Omega and God knew that Ortega will come.

Do not misconstrue his coming and his words. The nations on Earth enter their darkest night. The time of the biggest horrors and suffering will begin. Humanity will drown in blood as it has never drowned before. Cities will transform into heaps of rubble. The old culture and its monuments will die. Mountains of corpses will block the sun for humanity, and only then will come the victory over evil; and God's sun will begin to shine, because the evil that dwells in the hearts of the people has to be vanquished. That will be a difficult and long fight, but with Ortega's help humanity will accomplish that.

→Humanity has deviated from the teachings of Christ to such an extent that nothing has remained of them. The most heinous crimes have been committed in the name of Christ. His deputies, as many people have dared to call themselves, have put on the robes of a king, had themselves carried in golden litters, and built palaces for themselves. Yet the people languished in dark hovels and died of starvation. They built palaces for God – churches – even though poor people dwelled in cellars and underneath bridges. Pastors, as the bureaucrats of religion called themselves, for the sake of pay and goods, wore proudly the sacred cross of Christ on their chests – on chests within which a heart did not beat, and where Satan dwelled.

Do you realize what humanity has created from the teachings of Christ?

Can those who carry out Christ's commands, contrary to the teachings and will of Christ, be called Christ's deputies or servants?

Let's say that on departing from your estate you leave an overseer in charge. You order him to manage justly, to take from the sharecroppers only what is necessary, to treat them and the servants cordially, to help them [in times of] need, and to teach them and bring them up. On your return you find that the overseer has amassed great wealth for himself and for you. The sharecroppers have been ruined and are begging along the roads, but the servants groan under the blows of staffs and languish in cellars. Would you consider this overseer as the executor of your will, or would you cast him into the fires of hell? Almost all who call themselves priests and rulers act that way.

You ask, "Why didn't The Almighty create people so that they would only do good and would be like they should be according to the teachings of Christ? After all, The Almighty is capable of everything."

Don't forget that The Almighty gave His spirit to the people; a spirit within which good struggles against evil. He wants your spirit to grow to be just as great as He is. He [does not want] to be alone in the world, like He was in the beginning. If He were to give you souls which had been formed with certain characteristics, and had been limited by The Almighty's will, they would be [mere] robots. It would be a dreadful world of robots, one in which even The Almighty's spirit would smother.

Get ready! In half an hour Omega will give to humanity, through you, his First Commandment of The Almighty. Use black paper, cover the paintings and seats with black, and limit the amount of light. *Dixi.*←

Omega   02/23/44 and 02/27/44 2000

→[[The Almighty's Commandments]]

I, the promulgator of The Almighty's will, I, the Ruler of the Future and of Death, Omega, announce to the people on Earth, The Almighty's First, Second, and Third Commandment.

The First Commandment:

Do not harm anyone!

The Second Commandment:

If you want your children to respect you, to love you, and to take care of you then bring them up to be people of a good and noble nature so that you would not have to bear the responsibility for their sins, and those of their children.

Children, if you want to be happy in this life then respect, love, and take care of your father and mother. Do not judge them in order not to be guilty of one of the gravest sins – the sin of ingratitude.

The Third Commandment:

I, The Almighty, have given you My spirit and a free choice between good and evil; between God and Satan; between eternal and inexpressible happiness and omniscience – Paradise – and the dark and dreadful Hell and the unimaginably horrible nonexistence.

Pray only to God, and directly to God, but not with words; rather, with good deeds.

May The Almighty's blessing be with you and the nations on Earth, from ocean to ocean, and from this day until eternity; and may His name resound in all hearts, and for all times, from this day on – eternally.

[[Explanations Concerning The Almighty's Commandments]]

To not harm anyone does not mean to merely carry out this Commandment passively, but [it means] to struggle against all the evil that is within yourself and within the people. It also means that one may kill only while defending his own life – or that of someone weaker, such as a child, wife, or someone disabled – against an attacker, providing there are no longer any other means of saving yourself or those being defended.

Never kill children, for by killing their bodies you will kill, inescapably, your own soul, and nothing, not even God, will save you. Nonexistence threatens for killing in selfish purposes. Only by complete repentance of the sin, and the devotion and sacrifice of your entire life to the relatives [of the victim], is it possible to save your soul from nonexistence. Initially, a thousand years of Hell ensue for killing a child, and after that – nonexistence. The aforementioned can also be referenced, to some extent, to nations and states.

An individual on his own cannot establish Sundays, or days of rest, for himself. It is the duty of the state to give people as many days as possible for rest and for spiritual life.

The churches must remain, except that they have to form into temples from which the warmth of affection and the light of knowledge spread over the entire world. Humanity's most eminent spirits have to function in them. The teachings of God have to be proclaimed. Everyone must be helped, but not only spiritually. Everyone who is weak in spirit and body has to be helped with advice, as well as materially. One should not wait for them to come to the church; rather, the church has to seek them out. It must dispel their doubts, reinforce their strengths, cure their souls and bodies, dry their tears, and take them toward happiness.

The only law of marriage is mutual love. Yet, since the main objective of marriage is children, the nations have to establish a legal foundation for marriage.

Let not lust and narcotics kill your divine spirit. Lust is powerful, and it is difficult to struggle against it. It is not a sin, unless a third person, or several others suffer because of it.

Children are their parents' blessing, but only whenever the parents are capable of carrying out the Second Commandment. Otherwise children are a grave sin. If it would delay their high mission, some high spirits have to refrain from having children.

The nation, through the church, has to care for those children whose parents are incapable or unwilling to bring them up correctly. Do not kill a child within the mother's body, for that cripples it. The nation must see to it that all children are born and has to assume the responsibility of the father and mother for those whom their parents reject. Until a law like that is enacted, killing a child prior to his birth is permitted.←

Santorino   02/23/44 2220

→[[Following the receipt of The Almighty's First Commandment.]]

Think about it, and act only then – that is my commandment for you.←

Do not proclaim the new teachings for the time being, because you, yourselves, still have doubts. How will you be able to convince others? Initially you, yourselves, have to comprehend everything fully. Also, you still know too little of that which you have to know. Speak to and, also, acquaint with the new teachings those people who come to you and who are capable of understanding them. Most important, though, don't worry about how they will be disseminated to the people, and when that will take place, because The Almighty, Himself, knows that.

Do not be alarmed if someday the spirits cease their conversations with you; if some of you are recalled, or if all of you perish. Your work will not die.

→You have not been given any means of miracles, except for the miracle of the spirits. If Raphael were to approach Rembrandt's painting of God and claim that he could paint an exactly identical painting of God, it would not be a miracle if he were to accomplish that. Yet should a simple tiller of the soil approach Rembrandt and ask Rembrandt to teach him how to mix paints and handle brushes, because he wants to paint the very same face of God and just as well as Rembrandt – and if he were to accomplish that by painting an equally good painting as this genius – then everyone would claim that this is a miracle. Everyone who understands art would claim that, but the ignoramuses would remain silent; for they, being unable to differentiate between high art and market goods, would fail to see a miracle there.

The time for miracles has passed. These days, every magician in the circus ring, in front of the eyes of the onlookers, can turn water into milk or wine and can pour water from an empty vessel. He can saw a person in half, show how he disappears before your very eyes and reappears again, and so on, without an end or limit. Miracle after miracle for the enjoyment of the circus audience.

What was a miracle at the time of Christ is no longer a miracle nowadays. Science performs miracles. The day will even come when science will liberate man from all diseases and labors and will transport him from one planet to the next. Today that appears like a miracle to you, but tomorrow that will be a common occurrence.←

_ ★ ★ ★ _

Do not be concerned and do not grieve about anything, for The Almighty knows what He is doing. You have many questions, except you are too lazy to prepare them. Realize when you are conversing with the high spirits and when with the low ones, and think more on your own. Do not ask the spirits with what to wash your face in the morning. We, the high spirits, will not show you any miracles, will not tell you who is alive or dead, and [will not tell you] what will happen to you, or to others, tomorrow. We will reveal to you only what we, ourselves, will consider to be necessary to reveal.

→Do not seek adherents among the clergy. Do not seek contact with any spiritualists and various sectarians, for you are the only ones with whom

The Almighty talks today. Do not seek any similarities in the Bible nor in other religious books. Except for a few points, what The Almighty reveals to you is entirely new and independent of all the old.

The spirit of humanity is no longer satisfied with those fairy tales which had to be told in his childhood. He asks that his doubts be explained to him. That is occurring currently. In lieu of the book of fairy tales, even though it also held much truth, a new book is being opened for humanity – a book about life and religion, about what exists – and what will exist eternally.

Be strong, be wise, be bright!← [[2325]]

Ali   02/27/44

_ ★ ★ ★ _

→The spirit is independent and condenses atoms only in order to assume a visible form. The soul, upon leaving the human body, first goes to its judges – God and Satan. Its return to those whom it left behind depends on the decision of the Judges. Only those spirits who have ascended above the Solar Fields set their own activities freely for themselves.

The Christian spiritual burial ceremony is important only for those who are left behind, but it has no significance for the deceased.

Insanity. The individual whose body has turned out to be too weak for a great spirit becomes insane, as does the one whom his parents have raised contrary to his task, which this spirit had to accomplish in this body. It is a body without a spirit, just like the body of any other animal. It is no longer a human, for the spirit has abandoned it, or, else, detests it and returns to it only for a few moments.

One may wear the cross, or rather, the sign of the cross. However, then the body has to be worthy of it as well. It has to be removed during some instances of life's activities, so that one would not commit the sin of blaspheming God.

It is permissible to kill animals, but only when that is necessary for your sustenance or essential for the well being of humanity.

Only the numbers three and thirteen are significant in some cases. However, there are no lucky and unlucky days or dates.

Anything can be used for sustenance that is not harmful to man and that a physician has not prohibited. Man has to fast only whenever a physician prescribes that.

One is considered to be a child from the moment of independence until the moment when he comprehends what is good and what is evil, and when he can avoid the dangers of death which threaten him.

Now I will talk again. Be particularly careful in the choice of friends and also in selecting those people with whom you discuss divine matters. Do not converse at all with those who do not believe in immortality, for they have already died. There is no sense in proclaiming the teachings of life to corpses.

The spirits can materialize only to the extent necessary to become visible at times of necessity. However, they can influence people only spiritually and never, under any circumstances, physically. Do not believe in those miracles which have a materialistic nature. ←

Receive my words carefully, and understand them correctly; for sometimes they seem peculiar to you. This is what my ruler, the sultan, told at a feast to a respectable, good, and happy individual, who felt sad and unhappy for, supposedly, he was lonely.

"Find yourself a friend," the sultan said after this man had told him his troubles. "Then you will find a person who will not permit you to feel lonely. He will come to you whether you will want this or not. He will come in the daytime, when you are busy, and at night, when you want to go to bed. He will smoke your best tobacco. He will call you a fool and a mule, something that even your worst enemies don't do. He will trample with his dirty feet through all the rooms of your soul, and you will be unable to throw him out; for he is your friend. If even then you will not feel sufficiently unhappy, then get married."

That is what the sultan said.

Now tell me, does it seem to you that I want to wreck the salutary establishment of friendship, and who might benefit from this advice? Think about it, and answer me in half an hour.

[[After half an hour.]]

Who might benefit from my advice? Your friend, obviously, for he will be able to see from it just how badly he takes advantage of the rights of a friend, and perhaps he will even improve.

→Now about serious matters again. Some of your scientists deny the existence of the spirit. They claim that only matter, on its own, forms the physical and spiritual development of a human. With this, they only make the solution of this question more complicated, rather than simplifying it.

All right. You know the brain; you also comprehend partially the essence of its functioning. What makes these atoms of the brain think so logically and wonderfully? Certainly not the blind and deaf atoms which constitute the brain!

Supposedly the atoms, in some sort of a manner, condense and transform, and create higher forms. That is the same comprehension as that of a savage who, for the first time, is inside an electrical [generating] station. He claims that a smaller machine transforms into a larger one and that these machines have created themselves and control intelligently their own operation by themselves. Not knowing that high up in the [control] room there is an engineer who has created and controls these machines, the savage would be understood and justified in his stupidity.

What makes man explore the sky, the North Pole, and the depths of the seas? These are activities which do nothing for his material well-being, and which distinguish him from the animals. Who permits man to develop so limitlessly if not the spirit of God?

After all, the animals, with all their minds, have not progressed further in their development than attaining the most essential elements for life and for fighting. The dog is the same as it was during humanity's cave era. The elephant, the smartest of the animals, knows how to carry logs for constructing a house, but it is incapable of building even the simplest house, for it lacks what man possesses – the spirit of The Almighty. ←

Chapter V
March 1944 – Part 1

Santorino   03/01/44 2100

→To begin with, I have to tell you about the Commandments. Since they were proclaimed to you on two separate occasions, you must combine them. Omega's introductory words are the same, but the concluding words have to be combined. Everything pertaining to the Commandments of the Old Testament, and their replacement, has to be completely discarded. That was intended only for you, so that you could comprehend better and could explain to others what you have understood.

The Almighty's Commandments do not replace any other Commandments. They are for the entire universe, and they already existed when the Earth did not yet exist. Only now has come the time to proclaim them to all nations on Earth and to all religions. Therefore the order and the contents of the Commandments do not correspond to your Commandments.

Omega's explanations have been given in a form so that you could, having comprehended the Commandments better, compile complete and logically correct teachings based on them. Therefore, instructions of a practical nature have been given, therein, as examples. Based on these, humanity can form temples, and so on, that are spiritually similar but different in appearance.

Since you cannot accomplish this task in short order, [the explanations] can be proclaimed in the form given by Omega, except by combining them logically and deleting the aforementioned.

Now let us proceed. Many people fail to comprehend eternity and nonexistence and say, "What can immortality give me, and why not pass into nonexistence?"

Some people even get bored with their short life on Earth. They are empty bags. You have to comprehend what spiritual life means! You are reading an interesting book and cannot tear yourself away from it; time has stopped. The astronomer cannot tear his eyes from the wonders of heaven. The researcher at his microscope forgets the time of day and night, forgets about lunch and dinner. A scientist crosses the impenetrable jungles or climbs mountains where it is impossible to breathe or else ventures into the lands of eternal frost. To all of them life seems to be extremely short. It seems that they have seen and achieved so little that, compared to what they wanted to achieve, it is almost a zero.

Similarly, while you are listening to the sounds of enchanting music, your soul dreams the dreams from beyond the stars and forgets about life and time. Similarly everyone who does beloved and creative work is happy. Life is too short for him, even though legions of years rest on his shoulders.

Now imagine the life of the spirits.

Once you have passed through the Lunar and Solar Fields, you see all the wonders of the universe. You see an infinite number of worlds. Each one of them is different, and each one changes its face every year. Can you imagine the happiness of helping The Almighty to form them, of growing and drawing ever closer to The Almighty, and of feeling that you are creating and guiding worlds?

Can you become bored and will eternity not seem shorter to you than a moment on Earth? Then, this inexpressible melody of The Almighty's rays, a melody which fills the space of the universe and within which the spirits float!

Scientists, while exploring the space of heaven, and failing to see God and His Temple there, claim rashly that God, Paradise, and Hell do not exist. This is because they have not perceived them anywhere. Yet they forget that, while they, themselves, acknowledge the infinity of the universe, they see in their telescopes only an immeasurably tiny fraction of the universe. They want the Temple of God to be located within this immeasurably tiny fraction of the universe. Wouldn't that be too much to ask, and desire, from paltry man and his insignificant Earth?

Your scientists, while looking into the sky, see that none of the stars or planets are stationary. All of them rush somewhere into infinity. Yes, they rush into infinity in an immeasurable circle in whose center are located the Deoss Temple and the Solar Fields. The bright spirits dwell in this inexpressibly lustrous and wonderful universe.

Yet those spirits who have transgressed and who do not acknowledge immortality stand at the brink of an infinitely dreadful abyss, filled with the cold darkness of death, [an abyss] within which nonexistence dwells. At the moment when they see the world of inexpressible happiness of the bright spirits and their own black abyss – nonexistence, into which they will vanish immediately – they feel such torment that, compared to it, hell is nothing.←

I have already told you about the low spirits. They are incapable of struggling against Satan's high spirits, who meddle in their midst. I have told you in what manner we, the high spirits, will talk with you. Since the evil spirits will frequently deceive you, and the low spirits will even more often talk nonsense; do not become upset, [but rather] be alert and wise as a snake. Do not seek answers from us.

→*Dixi*. Be bright!←   [[2220]]

Astra   03/04/44

Astra. Lucifer is the ruler of the evil spirits on Earth, and no one may prohibit him to talk with you. If you don't want to talk with him, then don't talk.

Shota   03/04/44

Shota. Ali alighted away again, and, again, asked me to talk with you. What can one do? God has assigned him a difficult task.

_ ★ ★ ★ _

Now about your unexpressed questions. Are all the spirits the same? They obviously are not! They are just as different as the people are. The spirit in a human merely forgets his past for a while but retains his peculiarities completely. The spirits are not frozen in their dogmas like solemn priests. No, there is vitality here, and even hilarity. The spirits are so different and so talented that no one is bored. Thus Alexander is a great poet with us. His songs can be heard even in the melodies of The Almighty's rays.

Mary is busy all the time arguing with Satan. She fights for almost every sinner, and Satan gladly argues with her; because her sincerity supposedly warms even Him.

John is involved in mathematics. He keeps count of all the new and destroyed stars. Since he frequently makes mistakes, he also often argues with Galileo, who is also the same friend of numbers.

John K. loves to settle the arguments of the spirits and quite often [does that] so soundly that even Satan finds no objections. Still, the most exuberant spirit is the spirit of Ali. He entertains all the spirits with his jokes, and once he even elicited a smile on Satan's lips.

This is how that happened. God had taken several planets away from Satan's power. Satan was very glum. Ali, however, said, "I have to try to cheer up the mood of the High Ruler."

Even though we did not believe it, this did happen.

Ali told the ruler of all evil, "High Ruler, I would not grieve in Your stead but would rejoice that You have gotten rid of such nasty subjects, who dare to laugh at their Ruler."

"How's that?" Satan asked.

"Just now I was on one of these planets and overheard the conversations of its people and heard how they explained the creation of the Milky Way."

"Tell Me," said Satan.

"All right, I'll tell it the way I heard it. Listen. Once the inhabitants of almost all the planets had sinned so gravely that they came under the power of Satan. Then Satan told God, 'These planets are scattered throughout the entire world, and it is difficult for Me to oversee them because there are too many of them. I'll collect them and carry all of them to hell. It'll also be more difficult for You to get at them.'

"No matter how much God tried to talk Satan out of it, nothing came of it. Satan placed all the sinful planets, along with their suns, into a sack, threw the sack over His shoulder, and proceeded to hell. God went along and thought about how to save the unfortunate sinners. Satan's burden was too heavy even for Satan, and He began to sweat. Then something flashed across God's mind, and He told Satan, 'Since I can no longer save anything, I'll help You,' and grabbed the other end of the sack.

"'But You certainly are good,' said Satan.

"'You aren't quite as evil as You appear either,' God replied.

"Satan murmured something pleasant in His beard. Then God said, 'Could You give Me permanently all those planets that remain behind Your back?'

"Satan thought, 'There are so few left! I don't begrudge that!'

"'Go ahead and take them,' He said.

"After a while Satan began to talk again. 'You sure are strong, though. The burden becomes lighter with every step.'

"When They were approaching hell, Satan said again, 'You must be carrying the sack all by yourself, for it feels so light as though it were already empty.'

"'That, after all, is what it is,' God replied.

"Satan looked back and grabbed the sack from His shoulder. It was completely empty, and a hole had been cut in its other end. The entire way was scattered with the suns and planets that had fallen out. Satan wanted to rush to pick them up, but God said, 'Nothing doing, my dear, all of them are mine, for You, Yourself, said that all the planets which will be left behind Your back will be mine.'

"In anger, Satan walked over to hell with an empty sack – and that's how the Milky Way was created," Ali concluded.

And what would you think, the High Ruler of all evil smiled and said, "You are right. They have sinned too much even for Me to want to keep them. Let them remain with God. He, too, will some day experience something similar from them."

You see, that's how it goes with us. Then there are still the laughter spirits for the amusement of the spirits and people. There also are various, little spirits for the animals, but it'll suffice for today. You are yawning so as to scare me.

Good night.

Ali   03/05/44

That Shota really did me in yesterday. Don't imagine that about me, which isn't the case. I am not such a great master at all. What I told Satan was not a contrived joke. I really had overheard it. Besides that, there is no sense in lying to Satan. He sees everything that you are thinking.

Similarly, he also told only the good things about you. You are not quite such little angels. Let us look somewhat into this matter from the other side as well.

I will also begin with Alexander. Alexander is, as you have already been told, an unusual spirit. We comprehend him poorly, but it seems that The Almighty comprehends him very well. He is the same on Earth. To the people, he seems to be cold and aloof. He does not try to approach them either and does not admit them into his soul. He bears his sorrows by himself, without telling them either to the people or to God, whose temples he does not visit either. Having come to Earth only to observe, he does not attempt to achieve anything, for he considers everything to be equally insignificant.

Except it seems to me that he sins against The Almighty, as well, by hiding from the people on Earth The Almighty's highest manifestation of the spirit – his poetry. He, however, is so proud that he does not want to give the people anything. That is rebelling against The Almighty, and it is eerie for me – as his friend, since he once honored me by calling me that – to talk about that. I advise him to consider, once more, the validity of his decision and to let the people look into his heart, which is not all that cold.

I will talk about Mary now. In your youth, your heart dreamed about everything that was beautiful, noble, and sacred. God's breath flew around your forehead. Then came the muddy wheels of the heavy wagon of life; wheels that threw mud into your soul. You lost hope, you lost yourself. The sounds of Paradise went out in your heart, but, still, you remained bright. Then came little Nick and the estate. Concerns about your son's future made you take some incorrect steps.

An individual should not be given too much in his youth. Whatever is easily obtained is squandered even more readily, for the person does not know the value of what he has received. Only that is valuable which you have achieved on your own. Give little Nick an education and a foundation [on which he], himself, can construct his future, but no more – if he is to be truly happy. Open up your bright heart to others as well. Don't let motherly love conceal God and the world for you.

Now about our dear secretary, John. You do, after all, have other duties in Heaven, besides merely counting the stars. You have thoroughly stifled your spirit on Earth by choosing an occupation which is completely unsuitable for your spirit. The work of a great scientist was envisioned for you, but you did not travel [that path]. You are kindhearted and helpful, except at times you are weird. You do not mind drinking a bottle of wine with your friends but begrudge throwing the empty bottle out the window. Elevate your spirit. Let him breathe the vastness of infinity. Set him free from the trash of Earth.

Then your other John, John K. He has preserved the high intensity of his spirit and stands for justice – except he has limited it in an atrocious fashion. As a physician, he treats and has washed off the little toe on the patient's foot, and now he thinks that the individual is clean. That is what his profession as a lawyer is like. He should have pursued the course of a statesman. Besides that, he does not approach the matter correctly and does not control his words. If you tell someone that he is a fool then, with that, you will not achieve an improvement in him, but only misunderstanding and hatred. Try to prove to him that he is not a fool but has only acted foolishly in this case. He will improve and will become your friend.

Now about my Alexander H., but since I can't see him, it is not worth bothering you. I will talk about him, but not behind his back.

→Suicide and its sin. Its sin depends on the motives. It is not a great sin. However, if an individual commits suicide while not believing in immortality, he inevitably passes into nonexistence. Should he commit suicide due to life's hardships, then he has deserted and ends up in the Lunar Fields. Should he do it under circumstances where he is suffering from an incurable disease, and is only a burden to others, then suicide is welcome. Should he commit it in order to save others then it is a sacred duty.

Giving poison to someone who is incurable is meddling with The Almighty's decision. It is permissible to give poison if the one who is suffering asks for it himself.←

Astra   03/05/44

A. Aurora will talk toward the evening.

Shota and Ali are just now arguing about something. Now they have alighted, while laughing, to their own part of the universe.

A. Aurora   03/05/44

I come to you. Let us talk seriously, as always. The decisive hour is approaching. It will be horrible, and it will be difficult; but perhaps you will endure everything and will see the sunshine of happiness. We already know the hour, the victors, and the names of the dead and those remaining alive. Except it is not allowed to announce this to you, for you will be incapable of retaining The Almighty's decision in your hearts.

Lucifer spoke with you. That is the highest honor for you on behalf of Satan, because the ruler of the evil spirits Himself accepts your mission – the mission of The Almighty's high envoys – with respect. That seems strange to you, but only here on Earth.

→The spirits are very different. Only The Almighty is capable of everything and knows everything. Do not ask the spirits that of which He alone is capable. The lower the degree of the spirit, the less he is capable of knowing. Only those spirits who have achieved the Solar Fields know more than the current people on Earth. The high spirits who have completed the Solar Fields know very much. God and Satan know almost everything.

Yet even The Almighty does not always know what man's free spirit will do. Think [about that], comprehend, and understand.

Animals do not have The Almighty's spirit. Santorino and Satan give them their spirits. These tiny spirits are mortal and live only for a thousand years. They roam through the atmosphere but only on their own planet.

The laughter spirits flow out of the melody of The Almighty's rays and, resounding, cross the Heaven and Earth like pearls. There is so much that is incomprehensible and unknown to you, people, that your life on Earth would be too short to relate all of that to you. [Besides that], people do not have to know everything, for, as spirits, they will find that out when necessary.

The question regarding man's similarity to ape has to be solved by the human mind and by science.←

Alexander, your father is very far from you. Alpha assigned him to form life in a new world, millions of suns away. That occurred when Alpha and I alighted away. He is an even higher spirit than you are but has sinned even more than you. He has not sinned on Earth. You will meet each other many times. You and Mary will have to go to him for a hundred years, to new worlds where difficult duties await you. Alexander H. will also alight to your father and will be his assistant. John and Nicholas [the brother] will live on other planets. You will meet them often in the Deoss Temple, except John will no longer be your secretary.

→Determining the process of Earth's creation is work for your scientists. It is not necessary to reveal to humanity the process of creating the universe, for you, yourselves, have sufficient knowledge to find an answer to that. Ask us only that which you, yourselves, with only your own abilities, cannot solve.

I alight away. Be bright.←

Shota   03/05/44

→You are still incapable of fully comprehending the spirits. We strive to speak in a language which is understandable to you, but we do not always succeed in that. Perhaps that is because, quite often, we speak incorrect Latvian, for none of us have been a Latvian and neither do we, the lower spirits, posses omniscience and the comprehension of everything.

So far, no spirit has the degree of divinity.

The Lunar Fields are located underneath the Solar Fields and are illuminated by the reflection from the Solar Fields.

Only a part of the teachings of Christ is expressed in the Gospel. Much has been forgotten, and some things have been altered. There is no need to correct anything. Had that been necessary, it would have been corrected long ago without waiting for you.

The same thing holds true of the birth of Christ. Would there be any need to alter any of that which seems to be unalterable to humanity?

The new doctrine is independent of all other teachings, therefore do not leaf through the Gospel, Koran, and other sacred books. You are given everything anew.

You have heard so much that it should suffice.←

Lucifer   03/05/44

[[Alexander converses by himself.]]

I, Lucifer, the ruler of the evil spirits on Earth, am talking. Listen to me. I and Ortega carry on the fight for the Earth. It is frightful and merciless, but both of us serve The Almighty. Remember that, high spirit, and do not scorn me.

Karino   03/05/44

I am the one whom everyone should fear – the angel, or spirit, of death. Be alert, I have arrived. My wings cover Latvia and the entire Earth. Santorino is the only one who guards you in Heaven and on Earth. My shadow covers the Earth.

Ortega summons me. I am going.

Aksanto   03/05/44

I arrive. Bow your heads. You are not subject to the might of death, only to my power. I, Aksanto, am the Spirit of Life. I am God's Envoy to the Earth. Bow your heads in front of Him.

Ilgya   03/05/44

I am Ilgya, God's guardian at your door. Only Santorino can recall me. Once that will occur, nothing will be able to hold back the spirit of death. I, Ilgya, am standing by your door. Death reigns in the world.

Astra   03/05/44

[[We ask about the arrivals of Karino, Aksanto, and Ilgya.]]

They spoke a sufficiently plain language.

Do not lose your spiritual strength. Do not grieve; everything is not lost yet. The fight begins only now – the fight for humanity. God's envoys come to Earth. The might of Satan has been crushed. Funeral bells will ring for the dead and bells of celebration for the living.

Ali   03/08/44

_ ★ ★ ★ _

Lillian placed some flowers on Elizabeth's grave last Sunday. It was good that she placed three blossoms – that is The Almighty's symbol. It was bad, however, that all three were yellow, which is the symbol of hatred. In the realm of the spirits, every number and color has its meaning, its symbol. [[Explanation: Lillian Birnbaum, the widow of John M.'s first schoolteacher, in response to a request from her husband's spirit, placed some flowers on Elizabeth's grave, while not knowing yet that in a former life she had been her twin sister.]]

[I will talk about] going to the cemetery and to the church. Go to the cemetery and to the church only if you acknowledge that your heart is not empty. Go if your heart is full of love. Then the departed ones, if they will be able to, will also come gladly to you in the cemetery – their last place of parting. Similarly, God will gladly listen to you in the church as well, should you go there with a heart full of faith. Wear your best garments when going to the cemetery or the church. You can also be solemn and present your prayers to God through God's servants, for God also listens to them. Present your requests solemnly.

As I have said previously, a servant can hand his master a loaf of bread in dirty, work clothing and with dirty hands. The master will accept and, perhaps, will not say anything but, maybe, will toss the bread to the dogs. Similarly, if your master comes [for a visit], then put on your best clothing and invite him into your best room, but do not meet him in dirty, work clothing and do not invite him into the kitchen. Perhaps the master will not say anything but will seek a new servant for himself. Even your neighbor, if you were to meet him on a Sunday in work clothing and were to offer him refreshments in the kitchen, will not likely visit you a second time. Whoever has ears for hearing, let him hear!

God is the master, and you – the servant.

You have to know the significance of only three colors – white, black, and yellow. You already know their significance.

[[We ask for an explanation about praying with deeds, but not in words.]]

Oh, how difficult it is with you! Let's consider this. You can pay your taxes to the state, or debts to a creditor, only in cash or in kind. That, however, does not mean that you may not make a request to have them eased. In particularly important cases that might happen.

The evil spirits have come about only from Satan's sanctity. The concepts of good and evil are synonymous, if we take them in the overall context. What is evil for someone may be good for another. Man has to understand this concept from his – the human – point of view.

_ ★ ★ ★ _

You still wanted to know whether a religious ceremony is necessary in the cemetery. If you like it and it is dear to your heart, then please do so. The old minister will earn his morsel of bread as well, and neither will you become a pauper.

[[Question: "Can a sinful minister be a servant of Satan?"]]

Anyone who proclaims God's teachings cannot be a servant of Satan. Don't sin by speaking evil about those whom you do not know. A minister may be sinful, but, if he proclaims the pure teachings of Christ, he cannot be a servant of Satan.

_ ★ ★ ★ _

Omar   03/09/44

I was a Turkish sultan in life. Ali said that you are merry lads. I had nothing to do this morning, and I wanted to look you over.

[[Question: "Why did you destroy so many churches in your time?"]]

That was a cheerful occupation. I built mosques in lieu of the churches, and God was being worshipped again. Back in those times the masters of the church were just as commercialized as they are now. My mullahs knew how to pray to God more honestly. Overall, those were brutal times, if one may express himself like that. Whoever chopped off more heads was considered as being dearer to God. Unfortunately, though, we did not know how to fight a war as you do it now. Sweep people off from the air, like the devil with a broom. How could we!

Well, I'll have to go. I saw what you are like, and it suffices. *Salaam al-leikum.*

Shota   03/12/44

Those spirits who are in the Solar Fields generally do not alight after three. The spirits of the recently deceased talk with their relatives only on extremely rare occasions. Therefore Ann [[Alexander's mother]] does not talk with Alexander, even though she is now with you all the time.

What is a dream? Your scientists will have to explain dreams. On rare occasions a dream can be prophetic. On even rarer occasions, spirits converse by means of a dream, and the spirits of those who have just died appear to their relatives who are far away.

[[Question: "May a guard shoot to kill an escaping prisoner?"]]

Perhaps you would like to have God give you lists of sins, with all the paragraphs. You have been given the Commandments and the necessary explanations. After all, think for yourselves! You want God to lead you by the hand, like little children, and tell you at every step, "Put your right foot forward here, and here the left one, cut with a knife here, and chop with an ax there."

We, the spirits, are forbidden to answer regarding the astral body. You will have to ask Santorino about that. He will talk with you this evening.

Communication – the means of conversing – with the spirits. It is neither your business, nor that of serious people, what form The Almighty has chosen. I would think that even if bolts of lightning were to flash around you, there would be no shortage of "serious" people who would claim that you have placed an extremely powerful electric motor, or something similar to that, under the table. They would ask, "Why does God converse with you in such a noisy manner?"

So many people are now dying, and so much is being asked, that it is not good to reply. It is not good to say something bad. To tell only good things would cause doubts in those who asked. Therefore it is best not to answer these questions at all and to anyone. Therefore, don't ask in the future either.

So then, let us conclude.

Santorino   03/12/44

→*Ego* Santorino. Do you have a question?

[[We ask, "How can the astral body and willpower be explained?"]]

This is one of those questions whose answer can simultaneously bring good as well as evil to you people. Your question is formulated too narrowly.

As you already know, the spirit can condense atoms and, thus, materialize. You also know partially – no matter how strange that may sound, only partially – the human bodily functions. When the abilities of the spirit and the body are combined, then possibilities can be achieved which can be called miracles. The body is very strong, and the spirit is not always able to control it. Quite often various passions of the body take an upper hand over the spirit.

Should a strong spirit and a powerful body join their abilities and will harmoniously, it is even possible to achieve what people call impossible. You know rather well the functions of physical nature, such as the might of the hand, the strength of a chain, the pressure of steam, and so on. You do not particularly comprehend phenomena like gravity, magnetism, hypnotism, and others. Even though they are invisible, they do exist and are extremely powerful. Thus, a spirit – by combining his highest abilities, an inflexible will and unswerving faith – can create the so-called astral body. This is capable of assuming the necessary appearance, leaving the human body, overcoming distances, and performing the so-called miracles.

Still, this astral body usually does not function physically. It functions by hypnotizing people, by making them see what does not exist, and by making them perform – with their own hands – the deeds which were supposedly performed by the astral body. If an individual were to believe unswervingly that he can do anything, then he could do almost anything. Doubts are what preclude man from being capable of everything. It is entirely possible and easy, with the power of an unswerving will, to overcome the force of Earth's gravity and walk on water, fly through the air, have another person – with a weaker will – carry out your will, and so on.

Therefore, should some evil, but strong-willed, individual desire to rule others, he would achieve that easily. Should some evil spirit want to be almighty and rule the entire universe, he could achieve that. To preclude such situations from arising in the universe – and some spirit fancying to assume The Almighty's place – The Almighty, having been the first, was also the first to express an unswerving will that no one else would be almighty.

Thus doubts of one's own abilities arose in the universe. It is these doubts which bind our powers and do not permit those who are weaker in spirit and body to perform miracles.

Now you understand what you could be capable of and why you are capable of hardly anything, why people with a stronger will rule the weaker ones.←

Let us turn to other questions.

Do not proclaim anything to anyone until I will tell you to, otherwise the death penalty will follow. I have already told you: Do not hurry, contemplate [the Tidings]; comprehend them, systematize them, and wait. Talk with those who come to you [and who have been] sent by me; talk, but do not proclaim. One may proclaim God's teachings only with His permission or, rather, in His mission. In order to teach something to others, one has to first learn it well himself, otherwise one may find himself in the role of a fool and, by becoming ridiculous himself, make his teachings ridiculous as well.

_ ★ ★ ★ _

Ali   03/12/44

_ ★ ★ ★ _

I will tell you now something from my life and that of my great sultan.

The two of us had begun some reforms, as one says these days. However, some long-beards came along who opposed this matter, and the majority of the people started to lean in their direction as well. One day the sultan told me, "It's bad, Grand Vizier, very bad. Your opponents demand your dismissal, and unless we can think of something I will have to give in to these backward crawlers."

"High Ruler," I said, "you have already found these means."

"How come?" the ruler asked.

"Like those – you said – backward crawlers. That is a wonderful idea. If you want to vanquish the enemy, make him ridiculous."

I explained my plan to the sultan, and he agreed with it.

When the long-beards came for an answer the next day, and all the streets were full of people, the sultan said, "I'll probably have to accept your demands, but first let us go to the mosque to pray to Allah."

We went there.

In the mosque, the sultan had the mullah summoned, and he asked, "For what should I pray to Allah?"

The sultan said, "Pray for Allah to relocate our eyes to the back of our heads for all of us."

When the surprised long-beards asked why the eyes should be relocated to the back of their heads, the sultan said, "After all, you want to crawl backwards but not, like other people, go forward. Therefore, eyes in the back of your heads will be more useful to you than in the forehead."

These words immediately escaped through the door of the mosque into the ears of the people, and we heard fierce laughter from the crowd.

When the long-beards appeared on the street, a boy greeted them with these words, "Look, here come the ones with their eyes in the back of their heads!"

These words stuck to the long-beards like pitch to the tail of a dog, and they were dead as corpses; because people do not follow those whom they ridicule.

We had won. Well, did you understand?

[[Question: "Have we already met with each other earlier in the Deoss Temple?"]]

Yes, quite often, particularly with John. With my jokes, I often scrambled his figures so that at one time or another he made the universe poorer by a thousand planets. My Alexander H. gave me headaches here as well by relating an occasional caustic joke about me. Obviously, I never remained his debtor. There was no joking with Mary and Alexander. One of them sat in God's sunshine and warmed herself, and the other one plucked the strings of The Almighty's rays and did not hear anything.

Well, good night.

Chapter VI
March 1944 – Part 2

Shota   03/12/44

_ ★ ★ ★ _

Satan observes your work and your life with much interest and, one evening, almost annihilated one of you. Only Ali managed to intervene in time. Be careful! Satan is not your enemy, but merely a merciless judge. I would think that you understand this, because Satan is the very same Almighty.

The spirits of the recently deceased speak with their relatives only on extremely rare occasions. Therefore Ann does not talk with Alexander, even though now she is with you all the time.

Alexander makes the fewest mistakes, for he does not do anything. Yet, eventually, he will receive some task compared to which all your work will be child's play. Wait and preserve your strength.

[[We ask about Omar.]]

Yes, here the old one [i.e., Ali] had played a trick again. Later on, when Omar learned who you really are, he argued with him for a long time.

_ ★ ★ ★ _

Ali   03/16/44

_ ★ ★ ★ _

The so-called low spirits, like Ro and others, bother you. You have already been told how to consider them and that only The Almighty, alone, knows everything. Yet He, too, can err, particularly with respect to you humans, because now and then you exercise your free will in such a manner that even Satan is left with His mouth open. What can one do? Such, you see, is this freedom!

Talk with the low spirits, but don't expect great wisdom from them. It would be better if you could talk only with the high spirits. Would that not, however, be boring for you, not to even mention the high spirits themselves?

_ ★ ★ ★ _

Santorino will probably speak to you Sunday. Ask, if you have anything on the tip of your tongue.

Russia's czar Peter fought for the destiny of his nation, but Sweden's Charles for power in Europe.

_ ★ ★ ★ _

Laughter Spirits   03/16/44

Our, the laughter spirits', task: We cheer up the souls. Therefore, now and then, some bearded man walks along the street while trilling. A laughter spirit sits in his pocket. Your world would be entirely dour without us.

Santorino   03/19/44 1510

→*Ego* Santorino. Let Alexander ask his questions first.

[[Alexander's question: "How can it be explained that the spirits, who are capable of and know everything, make grammatical errors while dictating to us?"]]

You have to realize that we, the spirits, do not talk like people talk. There is only one language of the spirits in the entire universe. Yet there are infinitely many languages of the living beings on all the planets. The spirits understand your thoughts in a manner that is incomprehensible to you, but not all of them can talk with you. Only the higher spirits are capable of that, as are those spirits who have lived and spoken in that language [which you use]. Therefore, the people on Earth are generally given as [guardian] spirits those spirits who have lived on Earth at one time.

Do you think that it is easy to converse with you in the manner in which I am currently talking? Would a human be capable of that? In order to converse with you, the spirit first has to establish complete contact with your spirit and body. It is possible to talk only when that has been established.

Occasionally you wonder about letters that don't make sense, or individual words. This means that a spirit wants to talk with you but is unable to establish contact. Whenever we talk with you, everything can be completely correct only if this contact is not interrupted due to your inattention. That is how errors come about.

At times, your mind distorts the correctness of the phrase as well. While thinking that, according to the contents of the sentence, a certain word should follow, you overcome contact and force the saucer to indicate the imagined word that, after all, is not the right one. In order not to recall this word, which is very difficult to do, the construction of the sentence has to be changed, and even its meaning. This is also how errors crop up.

Besides that, your language is still so new that you, yourselves, occasionally do not know how to write correctly. How then can you ask us, the spirits, for such earthly knowledge in which you frequently stumble and correct your writings until they are all blue and red?

[[Question: "How can it be explained that the spirits, in their conversations with us, on occasion use expressions which are not accepted in society?"]]

Yes, it is not quite the same as what takes place in your society. The spirits are just as different as people, except they differ greatly among themselves according to the degree of their development. Here the difference is greater than between a savage from the jungles of Africa and your college professor. Therefore, converse only with the high spirits. Yet they, while talking with you and wanting you to understand them better, adapt themselves to you, just as your professor would do should he have an occasion to talk with the savage. Undoubtedly, on occasion he would exaggerate in the opposite direction.

The same thing happens to us, the spirits, while talking with you. Ali has been given to you in order to teach you while laughing. Besides that, he jokes with you as with his colleagues, and whatever he tells you discreetly should also remain discreet.

The high spirits are serious, but they are not walking books of formulae and teachings. Neither are they the Gospel, out of whose every page sacred words pour forth. The spirits form the life of the worlds and live along in them. ←

Now you understand why you can joke with Ali and why you may not, not even in your thoughts, do that with Omega.

[[Question: "How come that the laughter spirits, who have spilled out of the melody of The Almighty's rays, have given us poems that, judging from what they have given us so far, do not have high literary value?"]]

Yes, so far you have had dealings only with the so-called children's laughter spirits, and what appears to be beautiful and good to an adult is simply nothing to children. A child has his own comprehension and psychology. One has to converse with him in a child's language as well. This has to be simple and primitive, at times even silly from the adults' point of view. Here your teachers and writers of children's books sin greatly. The task of the laughter spirits is to bring joy to people's souls, but their words are audible only to the souls.

[[Question: "I still cannot fully comprehend why we have been given such an important task, for it seems to me that we are not entirely suited to accomplish it?"]]

Yes, that is the will of The Almighty, and we do not know its further goals. I can see that you, [Alexander], while coming to Earth, wanted to observe the horrible fate of humanity and not only observe, but also suffer it along with the people. Yet, most important, you hastened to Earth because you were afraid that The Almighty might assign you some task that would delay you in following the fate of the nations on Earth. You forgot, though, that The Almighty knew all your thoughts, and, since He permitted you to come to Earth, then that was His will. Therefore, await His task. Why do you think that He saved you from certain death twelve times, and that you, while running into the jaws of the NKVD itself, could have come out from there alive? All these miracles indicate that your task is still ahead for you.

Mary is definitely too weak for the task that she has been given, but she will accomplish it.

You are The Almighty's spirit, and she is God's spirit. That is essential for Omega and me to be able to talk with the people on Earth.

Do not grieve, Mary. Nick is a smart, good boy. A slight effort and a somewhat greater firmness – that is everything that is being asked of you with respect to your current son, a spirit of The Almighty.

John, you have to help Mary with the upbringing. Your work is good, except don't be so narrow. Spread the great wings of your spirit.

Alexander H., you have been given a double task by The Almighty – to bring up yourself and to bring up nations. Every day your steps become firmer and your mind brighter. I, too, will permit myself a joke. Old Ali strokes his white beard joyfully in the morning and at night.

You have not been told what you will have to do tomorrow, therefore do that which you have been tasked with today. Do not ask, for The Almighty, Himself, guides you.

[[We ask, "Why do the spirits, while talking with us, occasionally use distinctive forms of language, as, for example, Babushka?"]]

She could have spoken differently, and can, but she wants to be like she was – that is, Babushka – but not a spirit who would be strange and expressionless to you, like a photograph without a head.

[[We ask for an explanation about the future, for, even though that has already been answered several times, we still have a desire to know it, particularly with respect to the destinies of the nations.]]

If while getting ready to travel to, let us say, Liepaya, you would ask the spirits whether you will get to Liepaya, then, should the spirits answer you, two unpleasant situations would arise. The first one – if no, then you would no longer do anything, for why should you exert any effort if nothing will come of it? If yes, then you would similarly not do anything. You would claim that since you are destined to get to Liepaya you will get there. Why should you exert any effort yourself? What should the spirits do with you then? If an individual were to know his future, he would become the very same robot about which you have already been told.

Why don't we tell you the destinies of the nations? Simply because of the way it is at the movies. No one tells the audience that goes to a movie the ending of the movie, for that would spoil all your interest. It is better to observe that which takes place before your eyes. Should something be necessary, then we, ourselves, will tell you that.

Great events await the world, on the battlefields as well as in politics. Keep your ears open.

I conclude. Alexander, you see that I, too, can understand you, and not just The Almighty alone.

→*Dixi*. Be bright and strong.←

Astra   03/19/44

The other laughter spirits will attempt to tell you their march.

The march of the laughter spirits:

> From the sonorous rays of Heaven
> We fall on the people and the spirits.
> Sorrow and night disappear from the hearts,
> The wonderful rhythm of eternity is heard.

You can sense the sounds of the laughter spirits' march only with your soul. The laughter spirits do not stay long in any one place. Their march is made known to the ears of mortals for the first time. That takes place with Santorino's permission.

Shota   03/19/44

→[[We ask about the Old Testament of the Bible.]]

Without doubt, a book like the Bible contains something that is worthwhile for all people.

[[Question: "Why do small children die, and those who have been just born? They have not yet fulfilled their mission."]]

You value the life of each individual too highly. The Almighty values highly only those living beings in whom high spirits have incarnated; those spirits who grow and are capable of growth. The Almighty pays no heed to the other spirits, particularly to those who have been born for the first time. You already know that only one spirit out of a thousand remains in the Solar Fields, and one out of a million achieves the degree of divinity. All others perish. Thousands, and even millions, of spirits who have turned out incompletely are destroyed without mercy.

The spirits seldom interfere in cases when the body becomes sick. Generally, the body is allowed to struggle against the disease by itself. Here only the individual's own spirit can help, with his faith and willpower, as well as the knowledge of your physicians. Should the body collapse, the spirit simply moves over to another body. There is nothing here to cry and wail about.

The newborn spirit, should he be in a child and the child dies, merely evaporates and vanishes. There is nothing to regret here; for The Almighty has no shortage of spirits, and He does not pity the body, this combination of atoms. Learn to view the human spirit and body from The Almighty's point of view. Then you will understand that there is no need to pity that for which you feel sorry. The Almighty seeks only those spirits who are capable of achieving the degree of divinity. He does not know the concept of mercy in a sense like you humans know it.

[[We ask, "How do sleepwalkers overcome the Earth's gravity?"]]

You have already been told about strong spirits in weak bodies and that strong spirits can perform miracles, as long as they do not doubt themselves.

[[Question: "What is epilepsy?"]]

Your physicians have to explain epilepsy.

[[Question concerning black magic.]]

That is the same thing, people with a strong will. Magic is the so-called nonsense, in your language. No one can summon a spirit with his will nor order him to do anything. All this so-called magic is the tricks of charlatans.

[[Question: "Why don't historians examine the life of Christ?"]]

Do you know of any historian who is writing anything about you, even though The Almighty, Himself, talks with you? Unfortunately, Christ was not a military commander and did not do anything that would have been of interest to the historians in Rome. The writings of the local historians were lost and did not reach Rome, from where you obtain your knowledge of history.

[[Question: "Is it possible to put a curse on another individual?"]]

That is the same bugbear of a child. Pronouncing a curse is a complete absurdity, and those who believe in such rubbish are the greatest of fools. Damnation is wishing evil to another person, and it speaks contrary to all the Commandments of God and The Almighty. The one who pronounces a curse does not harm the one whom he damns, but he damns himself and is inescapably doomed as a blasphemer of God. How come that you people could not have realized that on your own? After all, aren't you Christians?←

_ ★ ★ ★ _

Ali   03/26/44

→Now I will answer your questions in lieu of Shota, and later on will tell you something in a friendly manner.

[[Question: "Why do some instances of damnation come true?"]]

Yes, that is very easy to explain. The will of strong and weak people, and doubts, are at fault here. You know that a strong-willed individual can influence, or hypnotize, a person with a weaker will. You should consider this, also, when examining Alexander's further questions.

In some cases, something like this happens with pronouncing a curse. Let's assume that a narrow plank lies across a ditch between your home and the road. You have run and walked across it innumerable times and have never even thought about how easy it would be to fall off of this plank. Yet, now, your clergyman, or someone else, damns you by saying that you will break your neck while falling from this plank. Should you have a weak will, and great faith in the power of the curse, then just try to walk across this plank now. It will slip beneath your feet, and you will fall. Thus these damnations do come true. With that, though, the sin of the damner increases a hundredfold.

[[We ask, "How can it be explained that some miracles of black magic come true as well? Is the explanation the same as the previous one?"]]

No, only partially. Partially because, here, in some cases, a scientific discovery is involved as well. However, most of the miracles of black magic are simply the fantasy of the human spirit thirsting for a miracle, a fairy tale. Even though thick books have been written about black magic, its miracles have not been verified and documented anywhere. It's been impossible to prove any of them even now. All this magic has failed to give humanity anything that is real, for it itself is unreal.

[[Question: "How can it be explained that some clairvoyants can tell the past, and even the future? Similarly, by the reading of cards or according to the lines in one's palms."]]

Should you guess something a thousand times, then you will undoubtedly hit the nail on the head now and then. There are thousands of clairvoyants in the world. One forgets what they have predicted incorrectly. Yet, whenever something has accidentally come true – that is clairvoyance. No one can predict the future. One can only guess. I am telling you that for all times. Research history. If such predictions were possible, history would have preserved innumerable examples for you. Where are they, though? An occasional individual with a sharp mind can, from time to time, estimate possibilities for the future rather accurately, but there is nothing miraculous in that.

With respect to relating the past, the matter is entirely different. It is possible for an individual with the ability to hypnotize to read your past from your brain, where it is engraved. Similarly, it is possible to establish your character and your past from the lines in your palms, because every great test of nerves leaves traces not only on your spirit, but on your body as well. In conclusion, I will talk about your Finks. He truly was capable of much. Yet, with respect to the future, all of you remember the few correct predictions, but how many incorrect ones lie in the graveyard of oblivion? Had he truly had these abilities, the matter would appear quite the reverse.

[[Question: "How come that the spirit, when incarnating in a human, completely forgets his past?"]]

Thus: The huge burden of his spirit's memories would impede the human. You went to college. You stuffed thousands of pages of knowledge into your memory. Now, in life, you preserve them in your brain and remember them only when you need something from them. The same goes for your past on this planet. Your childhood, youth, friends and parents, joys and sorrows; all lie in your memory. In your daily activities, you often do not remember them for days, months, and even years. They lie in your brain like living corpses. They come back to life again only during rare moments of reflection.

What would happen if you were unable to shut out the memories of your past, and they would bear down on you every moment? Would you be able to live, and is that necessary? Similarly, the memories of the spirit are shut out, temporarily, from the minute when the spirit incarnates until the minute when the body starts to die. Those spirits who have special missions can remember some things.

[[Question: "Where is the spirit while an individual is asleep?"]]

While an individual is asleep, the spirit, too, is usually in a trance of sleep. He can leave the body, if that is necessary and does not impede his task. Then, however, it may happen that he does not return, and the individual is found to have died in his sleep. The spirit may leave his body only when a special spirit, a guardian, has been assigned to it by The Almighty. You can understand for yourselves to whom such a [guardian] would be assigned. Still, in sleep the spirit feels freer from earthly bonds and fantasizes or, as you call it, dreams.

[[Question: "What sense is there in going to holy communion and in confessing sins, as is done in our religions?"]]

None, unless you, yourself, sincerely acknowledge and repent your sins and delusions. Remember for ever and ever, no human and no spirit can forgive you your sin, not even the most insignificant one. Only God can do that, and only God, and only God.←

Lucifer   03/26/44

Don't be afraid, Ilgya protects you. Satan ordered me to display all appropriate respect to you as The Almighty's envoys. May peace and the cross be with you.

I am speaking by permission of the high spirit Ilgya.

Ilgya   03/26/44 2030

Servus. You waited a long time for me today, but those evil friends hindered me. As you can see, all is well. Now, let us turn to our order of the day.

Alexander, after hundreds of years I want to talk with you again and remember our last, joint life in the land of Maya. In coming to Earth this time, you have devoted yourself completely to Earth, therefore I have to talk with you in such an unusual manner. You are once more here on that Earth, which we left at such a terrible moment. I also see three other eminent spirits here. Two of them were together with us on Earth, in the land of Maya.

You remember the wonderful Mayan people; remember their high and noble culture. Your scientists are just now discovering in amazement the wonders of the great achievements of this lost nation. Then you came along – you, who had to raise this nation to such heights that if today's scientists were to learn that, they would not know what to say about what the Mayan people already knew then.

You led this nation along the pathway of the stars, and I was your guardian, God's guardian from your very first day. Jointly with you I climbed the heights of happiness and of the stars. Jointly with you I inhaled the fragrance of incense. Jointly with you I listened to the cheers of the people when we walked along the streets of the metropolis. It seemed that you were leading a nation that would have to rule the ignorant world. You were the one who gave these people the true God.

Then, however, came that day which cannot be comprehended by either the mind of a human or that of a spirit. That day came when the voice of Aurora was heard, which spoke in the name of The Invisible One. You and your people had to abandon everything and pass almost into nonexistence. That was so horrible and incomprehensible that I, too, froze along with you. I, also, could not understand the meaning and the necessity of The Almighty's dreadful command – and, mainly, its fairness.

When you refused to carry it out, I understood that direful moment that came over you. And I, God's spirit, justified you and agreed with you. When Omega's shadow fell on your face, I heard God's command to abandon you. I, The Almighty's and God's spirit and guardian, did not obey this command and remained with you.

Then came the [fateful] days. When I remember them it becomes eerie, and the world seems to be dark as the night. You led your people against destiny. It was a brave fight, but a hopeless fight. In the daytime I followed you in your inhumanly hard work. At night I accompanied your spirit in your wanderings through the universe, where you were lonely, for all the spirits had fled from your path. The black shadow of Omega followed you. You were all alone in Heaven.

Soon you became alone on Earth as well. Your people no longer understood you, and silence followed you in the streets which were full of people. In the temple, too, the priests bowed their heads low whenever you approached, but their lips were silent. And the armies, which suffered one defeat after another, met you and parted from you with heads hung down. You were lonelier than anyone else in the world. Only The Almighty might have been this lonely in His early days, and only He alone could understand loneliness like that. Did He understand, though?

How could I abandon you; I, who had been with you during your days of sunshine; I, your guardian? How could I not guard you now, when I specifically had to do that? During the day I was with you in your work, and during the short hours of night I sat by your bed and observed your hard but noble face. When your spirit flew through infinity, you often spoke with me. You wanted to talk me into abandoning you, but when that failed we talked extensively about things that you could not understand now.

Then came Omega's command to abandon you, but I did not hear it either. The moment approached when everything had to perish. Hordes of savages approached the heart of the state.

Then one night I sensed that you had decided on something ghastly, and I followed you. You reached the Deoss Temple and alighted into it. Overcome by horror, I followed you. The spirits parted before you. Here I noticed, next to Santorino, a new spirit, who had arrived in the Temple for the first time from the Solar Fields. Now I see that spirit in front of you, at the table. I will call her Mary, in your earthly language.

Mary observed with surprise how the spirits glided away from Alexander's path, and inquired of Santorino, "Why are they doing that? After all, this spirit bears the greatest sacrifice for the sake of his people, and who can say that he acts incorrectly?"

Santorino then said, "Don't you see that the shadow of Omega falls on his face and that this is death for the spirits?"

"What does he want to do, though?" asked Mary.

"[He wants to] save his nation," Santorino replied.

"How can that be accomplished?"

"He probably wants to turn, with a request for help, either to God or to Satan," Santorino answered.

Mary asked again, "But will They help him, and in what manner?"

Santorino replied, "It is difficult to tell that exactly, but, if he will turn to God, then perhaps he will save his people from annihilation; but he, himself, will have to pass into nonexistence. If he will turn to Satan, then perhaps he will save himself as well as his people, except he will have to accept the bloodthirsty gods of the Aztec nation."

Mary then said, "That is too dreadful, particularly if he were to turn to God."

"But who can restrain him?" Santorino asked.

"I will try," replied Mary, "because it would be the worst injustice in the world for such a noble spirit to pass into nonexistence."

Alexander approached the throne of God and neared Mary. It seemed like Omega's shadow would touch her imminently. Alexander, though, stopped. Then, in great surprise, he raised his eyes toward Mary, and said, "Unfortunate one, get out of my way, for otherwise you will die."

"No, I will not die," Mary replied, "for you will not go any further."

Alexander did not go any further, because he was incapable of killing this good spirit.

Alexander then turned toward Satan. Satan stood up from His throne and waited. Deep torment covered your face, Alexander. Everyone waited [to see] what you would do. Then you turned around and alighted from the Temple. In the door of the Temple I looked back and saw that God, too, had stood up from His throne when you departed from the Temple.

There was no longer any salvation. In order to be with you in the day-time as well, I committed the gravest crime that a first-born spirit of The Almighty can commit. I took the life of the palace guard commander's daughter and incarnated in her. Thus I could support you physically as well. You hardly noticed me in your troubles.

Then came the day – a ghastly silence blanketed the streets of the city. All the people had gathered in the square. You knew what that meant, for the temples and barracks were also empty. You went there all by yourself. Your steps echoed in the empty streets like winds in a desert. Your people awaited your arrival in gloomy silence. Not one hand was raised to greet you. You faced [the people]. Deep sorrow and pain furrowed your face.

In my pain and despair I wanted to scream and curse these people whom you loved more than yourself. Then came your voice, "What do my noble people want, for they hide their faces from their ruler like cowardly women?"

The people remained in gloomy silence.

"Isn't there any longer a single man among my people?" came your voice.

Your assistant, the first priest, whom you now call John [K.], replied to you, "Where are you taking us? Your God has abandoned us. Take us from here to those lands which have been designated for us so that there, in peace and security, we could build new temples."

You replied, "Fools, do you think that, since The Invisible One permits these temples of His to be destroyed, He will allow you to build new ones?"

The commander of your armies, who is now called Alexander [H.], also began to speak, "High ruler, reconsider, take our legions to a land where we could regroup and consolidate ourselves for defensive battles."

You said again, "Fools, do you think that legions which do not want to and are incapable of defending the land of their fathers, their native homes and palaces, will be capable of defending a foreign and empty land? No! My decision has been made! I know that nothing is able to save my Mayan nation as the first nation in the world. However, you, the new leaders, will save it as one of the last ones. That will be a road of shame and destruction. I am not capable of traveling it along with you. I will die along with the famous and the only one in the world – the Mayan culture. But, you, go!

"You, my noble assistant, I appoint as the high priest. Take your people from these palaces and temples into the shadow of primeval forests. You, my commander of the armies, protect them from the beasts of the forest and from predatory birds, for you will no longer have other enemies.

"Go, my people, and forget your glory, your language, and your last ruler!"

You turned around and went to the temple.

The new high priest assembled the people and led them out of the city.

The enemy legions approached its buildings. You stopped on top of the temple and noticed me. You recognized me and said, "Ilgya, now, for once, we are entirely alone in this dreadful world where there is neither love, nor loyalty, nor heroism, nor justice."

For the first and the last time in life your lips touched my forehead.

Then, however, the steps of soldiers could be heard, and the commander of your legions appeared before us with the palace guard. You asked in surprise, "Why are all of you here? After all, I ordered you to go with the people and protect them."

The colonel replied, "You have abdicated your power and can no longer command me. We would rather die with you than live with cowards."

Thus we stayed behind.

Then approached the moment compared to which everything else was insignificant. The savages ravaged the palaces and the temples. The culture of thousands of years collapsed in a few hours. Then they noticed you. A battle started in the doorway of the temple. The sign of the cross appeared in the clouds. You raised your arm in order to give the signal.

The Almighty's shadow fell on you and approached me. Horror struck, I left my body and fled into infinity. I wanted to escape from this dreadful world of The Almighty's injustice. Suns and planets flashed past me. Hundreds, and again hundreds, of years passed, but there was no end to this world. I lost all sense of time.

Then, a few moments ago, I heard the call of Santorino, but I did not reply. Then, for the second time, came the call of God. I stopped, but did not reply. For the third time came the call of The Almighty. Love and your name were expressed in it.

I returned and received this high assignment – to guard you and five other high spirits. I understood then that The Almighty's injustice is justice, that His hatred is love, and that His shadow of death is the sun of life.

We will not part now. I have been given permission to incarnate and to grow, just like you. →I am permitted to announce to you that which, so far, in the entire universe, has been announced only to twelve planets. Listen!

My brothers and sisters, one out of a thousand, not newborn, but of the people currently living on Earth, will achieve the thirteenth circle of the Solar Fields. One out of a million of those who have achieved the twelfth circle of the Solar Fields will achieve the degree of divinity. One out of this million will be able to achieve the degree of almightiness and stand beside The Almighty, see Him, and understand Him. That is a very brilliant happiness, whose brilliance our eyes cannot yet endure, but the road is open to the seven of us as well. You have to comprehend this infinite love of The Almighty. Bend your knees before Him.

This life is nothing. Your wings will cleave the gates of death. Your spirits will rule worlds which you, yourselves, will create and above which your spirits will soar.

No matter how difficult your path may be, it is inconceivably easy compared to what you will achieve by completing it. Do not grieve, and do not condemn The Almighty. I will travel your difficult path with you.

Be bright, be wise, be strong.←

Ortega   03/30/44

I, The Almighty's Chief Spirit Ortega, am speaking unto you. The voices of reason can already be heard in the world. You have already been told about that. The people begin to comprehend what the victory of evil would mean. Alarm bells begin to ring in America and in England. Humanity's intellect and heart are waking up. I have begun a struggle with Satan.

You can now see that for yourselves. Those are the first bells of my struggle which ring in the death of evil. The fight has begun. All the spirits of God and of The Almighty gather around my banner, for the evil on Earth must die! That is the will of The Almighty. Those who oppose it are destined for annihilation. All the cowardly and lazy ones will be judged in the Lunar Fields. All those who have ears for hearing, let them keep them open, because the bells of death will toll, as well as those of victory – ones for the living, the others for the dead. Don't be among those who will hear the bells of the dead.

I, Chief Spirit Ortega, am speaking unto you.

Chapter VII
April 1944 – Part 1

Aksanto   04/02/44

I am Aksanto. I have not come to you as God's chief spirit, but as a beloved colleague. I want to talk with you frankly, as behooves high spirits. I have observed you all this time and have tried to understand you and your deeds. I was surprised about how strongly the chains of Earth have bound you, how ardently you have grasped it, and how you love it. Probably, though, we will not comprehend each other that readily.

On incarnating in a living being, the spirit has to carry on a difficult struggle against the body and its instincts, as one might call that. For example, the human being is already a being with a definite instinct in whom the entire, long road of humanity is deeply ingrained. The instinct has grown as well. The spirits, on incarnating in a human body, have to take this instinct into account and either have to fight against it, have to harmonize with it, or else have to surrender to it. As you can see, the spirit is not man's only master.

This instinct of humanity – to love your life, land, and goods – is extremely strong in all of you as well. Similarly, also foolishness, envy, and some other characteristics are not entirely alien to you. I am not talking about a lack of faith. Similarly, you have forgotten that the spirits do not know the feelings of envy. All spirits have been given equal abilities, and if some spirit, who, perhaps, is older or has been more successful in his deeds, has achieved a higher degree, then there is nothing to be envious about. Similarly, you are still incapable of [accepting] the idea that a high spirit could be in the body of a servant on Earth while some insignificant spirit might be in the body of a king or a priest. You also use among yourselves words that are too harsh, and you have ugly quarrels. Do not get mad at me. You now have a big loss, Ali, and two large gains, Ilgya and Nakcia.

Note that every contact with us, the spirits, is fateful to people. Anyone who has summoned us and has conversed with us has already called the shadow of Omega upon himself. His spirit and fate are altered. Therefore you have sinned much by offering your acquaintances to talk with the spirits. However, since this sin was unwitting, it has been forgiven to this day.

Invite [someone to talk] only whenever he asks you sincerely and if you have explained to him the heavy burden that he places on his shoulders.

_ ★ ★ ★ _

Argus   04/06/44

Greetings! You are confusing me with the mythological Argus. I have nothing in common with him. The ancient people had somehow learned my name and ability of omniscience and invented a mystical guard with many eyes who sees everything.

_ ★ ★ ★ _

Ilgya   04/06/44

I, and we the spirits, comprehend your conduct. But do not welcome us unless you have been told to. Welcome only Santorino and the highest spirits, but it suffices, for us, if you greet us in your hearts.

_ ★ ★ ★ _

Let's talk like friends. Aksanto talked with you on Sunday and judged you, but you misunderstood him on several occasions.

_ ★ ★ ★ _

You were thinking then, "Why does he condemn us so harshly, for our faith is only a few days old?"

Don't forget, though, that what he condemned had already been condemned thousands of years ago by Christ, Buddha, and God's other envoys. As Christians you should have known that Christ's faith states that this life on Earth is nothing, but only the life there − in Heaven − [is important]. Christ said not to accumulate worldly goods. The trouble, however, is that you are Christians in name only, not in spirit.

_ ★ ★ ★ _

[[We ask, "What does it mean − peace and the cross − in Lucifer's expressions?"]]

The cross is the burden.

_ ★ ★ ★ _

I can see that you are still expecting something, and you will not be disappointed. I can announce to you that Santorino will talk with you on Sunday about religions as well as the Solar Fields. You have not asked such an important question as how the religions have come about, and about their promulgators.

Think this over some more on your own as well.

The shadow of Omega on a spirit or on a body means that he is subject to fate.

Shota   04/07/44 1500

Shota. I just alighted from the mountains of Caucasus. The snowflakes of Elbrus still float above me. My hair is still being tossed by the breath of eagle wings. Who can forget this most beautiful land in the universe! It uplifts not only humans, but also the spirits in The Almighty's cradle. On seeing these majestic mountains, one can comprehend the greatness and majesty of The Almighty's spirit.

From Elbrus I also glanced at your, Alexander's, eternally green valley adjacent to the eternally singing waves of the Black Sea; where everything is now swaying in a beautiful carpet of flowers, where peaches ripen and strawberries smell sweetly. I glanced at the roads and paths where your steps were once heard and stood on the rock, embraced by the waves of the sea, where you so often sat and wrote your poems.

A beautiful, young woman sat there and dreamed of a prince. I whispered in her ear that once a Georgian poet by the name of Shota stood on this stone, and a Russian and Latvian poet called Alexander. Her eyes turned dark as the sea, and her heart began to beat ardently and rapidly. Then the ray of Omega came and split her heart and placed The Almighty's strings in it. Thus a new and great poetess came about in the world; she will follow us.

I promised to talk with you – await and do not await me, for our souls can be heard in The Almighty's resounding rays. All of us await when, once again, you will sway with us in the waves of these sounds, and the entire universe will breathe the vitality of our songs; for the souls of people would die without it.

I have a greeting for Mary from Aksanto. He alighted with me to the Caucasus to rest a little, because the noise of weapons and the moans of the dying cannot be heard there. He said that Mary, too, as a small girl, had at one time ran around among these mountains and one day had climbed up so high that she had to fall. During the fall her spirit departed from her body, and Aksanto carried her to God. Together we flew over the mountain from which Mary had fallen, and Aksanto said sadly, "It is not always good to be a first-born spirit, but I almost envy Ilgya."

Now, still, a few words for my Alexander H. His interest in Atlantis is understandable but cannot be realized, for we do not have Alpha's permission to talk about Atlantis. Some day Nakcia will tell him about something else perhaps even more interesting. Too bad that there is not even a spark of poetry in him or in John. I am incapable of [fanning] it up, for the sword of Omega has not split their hearts.

_ ★ ★ ★ _

Ali   04/09/44 1500

Ali. I bring you a sacred greeting from infinity. Several moments have already passed since our last conversation, and I am with you again. Out of one corner of my eye I observed you all the time. Thanks go to Santorino, that he has spared you from the dangers of war. Blessed is every minute and every day which have protected you from the danger that is called war. The ending day of the war has been set, and the remaining number of days [of war] is unalterable. Therefore, each day which is spent in peace reduces the number of the horrible days. Therefore, each evening bow your heads before God in deep gratitude.

I can see that you have not gotten very far. Except that the servants of Satan already have their backs wet from toiling with you. Yet, thanks to God, they have not gotten very far either. Stick with it, and everything will be well.

Just as before, you are making some occasional mistakes. One runs ahead like a colt, and the other one holds on to his tail like a crab; but that isn't all that bad either.

You should not proclaim yet, because, first, you have to withstand Satan's evaluation and have to learn – you have to learn. Except not like one wise-guy who had to go to school and who demanded from the school's principal: Since he is smarter than the others, then he should be permitted to proceed not from the first grade to the last, but rather from the last one to the first.

Do much thinking, consider, and learn!

On one of my current planets I heard this fable: Initially, The Almighty created the spirits, then the suns and planets and, after that, plants and animals. He assigned to each spirit a sun with planets, plants, and animals.

He had each spirit locate them as well as possible in their own corner of Heaven and said, "Since that is not so easy, I will explain to you how that should be done."

However, a vain spirit said, "That, after all, is so simple and understandable to everyone that it is not worth wasting the valuable time in listening to instructions."

"All right," The Almighty said, "go ahead and work."

The spirit left, but not much time passed before he was back. "Almighty, Your planets have not turned out right. They do not stay up in the air and fall into the sun so that they almost burned up."

"The planets are not at fault here, but rather you, yourself. Did you give them the force which makes them orbit around the sun?"

"No, I did not know that," the spirit replied.

"Do you understand everything now?" asked The Almighty.

"Yes," and the spirit departed, but he was back immediately. "Almighty, everything would be fine now, except the planets are too small for all the plants and animals which You have given me. You have probably erred and miscalculated."

"How come?" The Almighty asked. "I thought that there would not be enough of them."

"Oh, no, not – not enough! They have climbed on top of each other," said the spirit, "within that narrow strip of land on which it is possible to live."

"I don't understand you at all," The Almighty wondered. "What strip?"

"What strip!" responded the spirit. "What else could one call it since one side of the planet is being scorched by the eternal rays of the sun, and the other, the dark one, has become numbed with cold. It is possible to live somehow only in-between these two sides."

"But have you given the planets a rotational force?"

"That I had forgotten, though," the vain spirit slapped himself on the forehead. "Who would have thought that a trifle like that could have such a significance? Everything will be fine now," and the spirit disappeared.

And, truly, a prolonged period of time passed, and the spirit did not return. The Almighty wanted to see how well he was getting along and went to visit him. What did He see? Yes, the planets rotated around the sun and their own axes according to all the laws. Except the vain spirit was jumping around them like crazy and was catching something.

Having noticed The Almighty he said, "Thank God that You have come. I myself cannot go to You."

"What trouble is there now?" The Almighty asked.

"What trouble," hollered the spirit, "but, after all, these plants and animals do not stay on the planets but fall off like peas. Just as I catch them and put them back on the planets, see – they are flying past my ears again. Both my eyes are already full of dirt. You sure have created a beautiful world," the spirit growled while wiping off sweat.

"The world is like any world," The Almighty replied, "except you are not like a spirit. Have you given the planets the force of gravity?"

"No, who can think of everything," mumbled the spirit.

"It is not possible to think of everything, and neither is that necessary," The Almighty said, "but a spirit does need to know how to do everything and [does need to] know everything. It seems to me that you still have to go to school, rather than rule," said The Almighty. He summoned another spirit and turned the planets over to him, but tossed the overly-wise spirit into hell.

That's what this fable is like, from which you, the inhabitants of Earth, can learn something as well.

Now I take leave from you. Live and do not grieve, even though clouds, dark clouds, cover the old Earth.

Santorino   04/09/44

May The Almighty's and God's blessing be with you, your children, wives, and friends. May the name of Christ bless your days and deeds.

Today the entire Christian world remembers Him who brought peace and love to the world – two things that were to redeem the world from sin and suffering, things that humanity forgot and, consequently, succumbed to sins and the worst disaster. The world, which has preserved only one thing from the teachings of Christ – His name – is not worthy to have the name of Christ resound on it. [Therefore] Christ has left the Earth, and Satan rules on it now.

The hour came when The Almighty covered His face and decided the destinies of Earth. Once He revealed [His face] the kingdom of Satan trembled, and His might had been decided. The voice of God came, "Santorino,

I give you Aksanto and a legion of My spirits. Go, and deliver Earth from evil and from delusions."

The voice of Omega came, "The Almighty reveals His name to the nations on Earth and sends them His faith. He sends His judge, Ortega, to Earth, and he has to annihilate injustice and give the people justice. To those who will not want to recognize it, I, The Almighty, send Karino."

Then once again came the voice of Omega, "To you Karino and Aksanto, I appoint Ilgya as the mediator. Any decision by Ilgya will be unappealable and unalterable."

The voices of God and of Omega grew silent.

On this day I want to talk with you about religions and the Solar Fields. Do not get tired, for that may be your death.

First, though, let us resolve the question which burns on your lips, "Why do we, The Almighty's envoys, have to withstand Satan's evaluation?"

I reply to you. Christ was God's envoy and Son, but on incarnation He, too, became a human. He also had to forget much, and in the desert Satan evaluated Him as well. He, too, prayed to God to have Him set free from the bitter cup of torture.

He – the Son of God – and you, what are you asking? Now you understand why you failed to understand me when I announced to you your task, suffering, and evaluations.

Religions. I will not talk about Christ's and many other religions. I will talk only about that religion which The Almighty at one time gave to all the nations on Earth and which, in general, they forgot. Some nations, though, did perceive and preserve some concepts from it.

It seems strange that The Almighty has chosen you – who know hardly anything about the world's religions and have not taken any interest in them – to reveal the new religion to the nations. That, however, has been done on purpose. I will speak in your earthly language – do not pour new wine into old wineskins. Knowledge of the old religions would merely constrain you unnecessarily.

So then, at one time The Almighty promulgated His religion to the nations. Let us see what humanity has perceived from it – the Greeks and Romans almost nothing. As gods for themselves, they appointed the very same people, only more powerful and more sinful than they, themselves.

The Hebrews perceived God as the only ruler. The rest was more from Satan, rather than from God.

The ancient Persians and the people of India perceived the most. The ancient Persians acknowledged the infinite time and infinite expanse as God – that is, the infinity of the universe and of time. As gods they recognized that of all the good, Ahura Mazda, and that of all evil, Angra Mainyu. They wage a war with each other, an eternal war, but the good will, nevertheless, win eventually. Good and evil spirits serve both of these gods.

As you can see, the basic concepts are admirably correct. You can become better acquainted with this teaching of Mazdaism on your own.

The people of India began with the deification of the beautiful nature of India. Then the Brahmins smothered the spirit of these people and placed heavy shackles on it.

Along came Siddhartha [Buddha] and proclaimed almost the same concepts as Christ, but did not effect the cult of God. This faith has preserved the correct notion about the transmigration of souls from one being to the next, but only has exaggerated it by having the souls also incarnate in animals, and even in plants.

Gautama, that is Buddha's name, taught about Nirvana, the significance of which you Europeans have not comprehended correctly. You claim that Nirvana is nonexistence, is nothing. Buddha understood that differently. Nirvana is freeing oneself from ignorance. It is achieving a comprehension of justice and, hence, achieving a state of blissful omniscience and, what is least important, freeing oneself from all suffering and doubts and obtaining eternal and uninterrupted peace. That is what Nirvana is.

At this time I will not talk any more about religions. I told you the main points. The rest you will achieve on your own.

→Now I will talk about the Solar Fields. First, though, a few words about the Lunar Fields.

As you know, the Lunar Fields are under the jurisdiction of Satan. From The Almighty's point of view, Satan is not an evil spirit. He is the one who has to evaluate the spiritual capabilities of The Almighty's creations and has to bring them up, while punishing and evaluating them.

The souls, or spirits, who are in the Lunar Fields are still the so-called potter's soft, clay material, which can be corrected readily by the press of the hand.

In the Solar Fields are those spirits who, like the clay vessel, have already hardened. It only has to be fired and painted. The potter treats clay which has not hardened yet without mercy. He squashes the vessel which has not turned out right and throws it back into the pile of clay and molds a new one in its stead. However, it is already more difficult with a hardened vessel, it cannot be corrected as readily. The more complete the vessel becomes, the more valuable it is. The vessel, which the artist has already painted with his own hand, can be extremely expensive and valuable. No one wants to deliberately smash it.

The Solar Fields are the school and the place of rest for the spirits. They learn much from each other and from the high spirits. The higher they ascend, the higher they become, and the more is given to them.

There are enchanting gardens in the Solar Fields, and the melody of The Almighty's rays resounds. According to their desires, the spirits may visit all the corners of the universe and may request to be guardian spirits for the living. They constantly see the Deoss Temple and the higher spirits who alight into it.

The spirits grow and develop through incarnation, or else they fall. Those who are incapable of growing to the degree of divinity, and decline it, remain in the thirteenth circle. This is the so-called isle of beatitude. Everything that a spirit could desire is there. He can visit the Deoss Temple; can be a guardian spirit; and also can incarnate – by himself or with a beloved spirit – in some beings on the planets where the inhabitants are happy, or else on other planets in the so-called fortunate people, and can enjoy all human pleasures.

For the time being, there is nothing to tell you about the Solar Fields in more detail. You have already been told about those spirits who have started along the way toward the degrees of divinity or almightiness.

With that, we will conclude examining this topic.←

I will not tell you anything about the future.

Learn; withstand Satan's evaluation; think; organize what has been revealed to you; and ask, but only that which has been thoroughly considered from the spiritual point of view. Do not ask simply to be asking, or ask questions about earthly concerns or regarding what people themselves have to decide.

Alexander, you have an assignment from me for tonight. You have to re-main sitting all night long in this room and in my chair, without questions.

Be bright, be wise, be strong!

Ilgya   04/09/44

Ilgya is talking with you. Do you understand everything that the divine Santorino told you? He was unable to relate everything that he wanted to at this time and postponed it to another time.

You, Alexander, will have to sleep tonight while sitting up, in Santorino's chair. Put out the light after twelve. Since you have been forbidden to ask, don't ask.

If anyone else will sleep in this room, then he will have to be as if dead. Death will fly above this house. The sword of Karino has struck the doorsill of the house.

I conclude. Ask, whoever else has anything to ask.

May peace and the shadow of Omega be with you tonight.

Ilgya   04/10/44

Good morning, this morning as well.

All of you had an evaluation from Santorino yesterday. I am glad that all of you endured it.

Santorino could not tell you everything yesterday, for you were begin-ning to get tired. We will now supplement the teachings of Zoroaster some more. According to his teachings, people have been given a free will; (un-derline these two words). According to his teachings, hell is eternal darkness, such a darkness that it may even be felt with one's hands. I am allowed to help you out that much.

[You have to] understand what immensely important concepts Santorino revealed to you yesterday.

I am extremely happy for that good fortune which Santorino and Omega granted us – you, Alexander, and me – yesterday. We do not want the oth-ers to be destined to remain ignorant. We permit you to reveal to the other Almighty's envoys as well that which may be revealed to them. I will shroud in fog what may not be revealed for the time being. Whatever is not in fog may be revealed, but under the conditions that it remain in your hearts and that not one drop spill over their rims.

Close the doors, drop the curtains, and in the daytime shade listen to the words of The Almighty.

I have finished.

Nakcia   04/10/44

May the high honor which the divine Santorino bestowed on you yesterday – and, during the night, Omega – burn in your hearts as a bright and eternal torch. Omega stationed the angel of death at your door, and covered the sky of Latvia with fog, so that nothing would disturb him.

We will not talk any more today.

Your destinies were decided last night in the Deoss Temple. Be bright as the sun!

Ilgya   04/13/44

_ ★ ★ ★ _

I am introducing Ali's replacement, Kolinto, to you. He asks Alexo to sit down at the table. That is what we will call Alexander H. After that I will talk with you again.

Kolinto   04/13/44

Greetings from me and from Ali.

I did not talk with you for a long time because, having come from distant stars, I was alien to Earth.

I wanted to become acquainted first with the people on Earth and, particularly, with you. That, however, did not proceed very rapidly, for you turned out to be rather inconsistent and changeable. I am surprised by the strong instinct in human bodies. A large majority of spirits have surrendered to it as slaves.

Then I observed how people live, and was greatly disappointed. I almost wanted to cry over what happens to The Almighty's spirits on Earth. Hatred reigns everywhere. Greed follows people like a bad shadow. Yet is it worth enumerating all these traits? You don't know how to live and utilize the valuable time. Your bookshelves are full of books, but their pages never see the light of day. The great spirits – such as Dante, Homer, Dostoevski, Tolstoy, Poe, Pushkin, Hugo, Cervantes, and many others – wait in vain for you to visit their inexhaustible sources of vitality, wisdom, and beauty.

After all, you do not have the time. You have to work, have to read gutter novels and newspapers. You have to gossip. Oh, you have to gossip so much!

You have to drink and play cards. How can there be any time left over for these gray geniuses?

I was with you constantly Sunday and Monday. Sunday was the Earth's brightest day, because the world's love – Santorino – visited it, and the day of Christ was being celebrated. It was disgusting, though, to observe humanity which, with Christ's cross on its chest and Christ's name on its lips, undertook bloody and dreadful deeds of destruction.

It was difficult to imagine something more horrible and despicable. I found some rest only with you. Yet then came Monday. I am ashamed to remember it, even if you are not.

What did the proud ruler of Earth – man – do on this day? How did he spend this day?

Old friends gathered after not having seen each other for a lengthy period. I prepared myself to listen with pleasure to memories and to friendly, cordial conversations. I wanted to hear what everyone had learned and how he will hasten to report his discoveries to his friends. However, what did I see?

After short greetings, with words which were soulless and disgustingly cold and worn-out from endless use, everyone sat down at tables and began killing time. What else could this dumb game of cards be called?

All right, lunch time came. I thought, "Now, after all, there will finally be sincere and worthwhile conversations at the table."

What a disappointment, though! Glasses were emptied and alcohol – this greatest blasphemer of The Almighty's spirit – placed itself in the middle of the table, like a disgusting toad.

You drank and drank. Your eyes and faces became red, tongues dirty and limp as rags. Everyone was talking, but no one, except for the evil spirits, was listening. Then the card game started again and, after it, eating and drinking again.

Following that the dear friends – having killed an entire day, [one of the very few] days which The Almighty has allocated people – bid farewell and went homeward with full stomachs, fuddled dispositions, and empty souls.

It is not a sin to rest and enjoy yourselves after work. Is it necessary, though, to enjoy yourselves in exactly a manner like that? Isn't humanity's genius capable of finding something beautiful and noble for people's enjoyment? One may dance some as well, and drink an occasional glass of wine, but one must not become a slave to all this dancing and wines.

The task of the spirit is to control himself and his body. Anyone who serves only the demands of his body has already died. Very many living corpses like that stream through the streets and across country roads.

Today, at the very first meeting, I already told you much that is unpleasant. That, however, is Omega's irony — to replace the cheerful Ali with the bleak Kolinto.

Let us bid farewell for today. Be brighter and stronger!

Ilgya will talk with you later on. Shota apologizes today for failing to keep his word, but I utilized his time for my conversation.

Ilgya   04/13/44

Alexander, what we discussed in the Deoss Temple regarding the preparation of The Almighty's teachings we will, based on Omega's wishes, postpone for the time being. Do not take over the leadership, for Omega expresses the idea that you would introduce too much of that which people do not need to know yet.

Besides that, he wants Janoss — that is what we will call John M. — and Alexo to try getting by on their own.

Alexander, you will be able to take over the leadership only on The Almighty's command. You understand that.

Note that only the higher spirits can read the thoughts of the lower spirits.

Mary has to fear only Lucifer and higher ones; Alexander — only Satan.

I want to say a few words to my dear Janoss as well. Try a little harder to decide the questions on your own, with your own mind. Then, while wanting [to do some] good for your old friends, try to achieve that not with liquor, but, rather, with something entirely different.

A friend who seeks only liquor and cards from you has no reason to call himself a friend. It is better not to have friends like that at all. Their ideas and love have only a negative value, like a dog full of fleas.

You will struggle with me in your heart, but Mary already agrees with me.

To you, Alexo, I wish all the very best in earning your master's degree tomorrow, but do not expect any help from us. We want to, based on Ali's wishes, see your own, and only your own, victory.

John, don't think that much about your family. It is not worth it.

Omega told me to give Janoss and Alexo these directions. They have to systemize all conversations with the spirits into three books.

The first one has to be called: *The Book of The Almighty's Faith*, the second – *The Book of the Teachings of Life*, and the third – *The Book of the Tidings of the Spirits*.

Everything that refers to the faith has to be collected into the first one. Into the second – advice for life, how to bring up the spirit and the body, how to raise children, and so on; as well as those stories which have an everyday significance. Collect into the third book everything that pertains to you and the accomplishment of your work. The last book has to be kept locked up and no one, except for you, yourselves, may read it. It has to be kept with you, and the last one of you, before dying, has to destroy it. [[Translator's remarks: These instructions were later modified somewhat. See Ilgya's tiding of 05/29/44.]]

Initially keep the book on separate pages in loose-leaf binders, so that it would be easy to supplement any one page.

Start to write a complete book of teachings. During this process, questions will arise. We will reply to these.

Do you have anything to ask? Your questions are not necessary. You, yourselves, have to accomplish the work of preparation. You have been told everything that was necessary, and not one word more.

You will be permitted to ask only once you have started writing the book of teachings. Perhaps you want us to tell you where to put a period and where a comma – be ashamed of yourselves!

John, too, has to participate in this work with advice and in all other possible ways. You may call on other trustworthy helpers as well.

Now for you, Mary. Don't refuse to lend your hand to this work either.

With that, I also take leave of you.

Chapter VIII
April 1944 – Part 2

Ilgya   04/15/44

Let the most important – [the reason] why I summoned you today
– come first.

The divine Santorino will speak in the middle of next week. He will talk
about love. Think this over well, and in three days each of you write down
your ideas about what love is.

Alexander does not have to write. Santorino will tell you why.

– ★ ★ ★ –

Ilgya   04/19/44

Santorino wants to hear your definitions of love. Have the youngest one
begin and the oldest one conclude. Read particularly slowly and with five-
minute breaks. Start with little Nick.

[[After the conclusion of the readings.]] The Divine will speak at four.

Santorino   04/19/44 1600

Be seated. I thank you for your answers. I will speak now.

I wanted to know how you, as people, comprehend love. Alexander, you
did not have to tell me, for I already heard how you comprehend it from
your poems. You have approached love and passion so close and with such
courage of a genius, particularly with respect to passion, that it seems to me
that very many people will consider that as too open and shocking. To me,
though, they gave very much toward understanding human love, for we, the
first-born spirits, can understand it only from your words. That was also one
of The Almighty's tasks for you in sending you to Earth.

We will talk about love now.

The concept of love is extremely complicated, and people generally use
the word *love* for that which is not love at all. Love could be divided into
three loves: mother's love, the love of a friend, and love between a man and
a woman. Let us examine them in sequence.

Mother's love, which you people consider as if the truest, most ideal love,
is an entire complex of various feelings. In this love the most important

aspect is not love itself, but that instinct which The Almighty has given to all, almost all, living beings – people and animals. It is the strongest instinct which animals and people posses and has been given them so that each animal would look after the continuation of its species. This instinct is so extremely strong that it makes a coward turn into a hero while defending its children, and even sacrifice its own life without thinking.

That, however, is not love. We see that from the animals. Once the little ones have grown up, the parents generally chase them away without mercy and no longer care about their fate. At least they do not differentiate between their grown-up children and other members of their species.

We can say the same thing about human mother's love, except here is added the real love which comes about between the mother and her child by growing up and living together, that is – by them becoming friends. In this love the closeness of the souls, or mutual respect and feelings of gratitude play a great role, which bind them for their entire life. This love is not mandatory, though, for you know many mothers, fathers, and children who do not love, and even despise, each other.

Now you understand what mother's love is, and that it is not a general law but, rather, an exception.

I will deviate slightly from the subject and will talk about how parents incorrectly comprehend what it means to love their children. They understand that to love means to provide the sweetest, easiest, and most enjoyable childhood that is possible for the child. By doing so they cause more harm to their child than the fiercest enemy would. Nothing can be more harmful than to pamper a child. Anyone who wants to have an easy life has to be given a difficult youth. If a child is accustomed to obtaining everything easily, obtaining whatever he desires, then he will want the same thing in life as well. He will be greatly disappointed and will suffer on seeing that strangers are not dear mothers, but people from whom everything has to be obtained by a struggle. However, he will not know how to do that. Being used to an easy life, real life will seem to him to be a hundredfold more difficult. Like a plant from a greenhouse, in the open air he will be frost-bitten and scorched by the sun. Therefore the so-called blind mother's love – which fails to see anything beyond the tiny, darling child, who has to be pampered as much as possible – is criminal.

Think about why the great spirits of the world are found mostly among those who had a difficult childhood.

I will now turn to the love of a friend. It is the purest and truest love and, therefore, is so rare. A real friend loves his friend and is prepared to suffer and to die for him. You will find many examples in history. This love is based on the closeness and nobility of the souls, and no instinct is involved here. Neither is there any place here for material benefits. It is the only sacred love, and the most distinguished people, spirits, and Gods know it. It also binds all of them together – Gods, spirits, and people.

I will now turn to the last form of love, to the love between a man and a woman.

This is the most complicated love, if one may express oneself like that. So many and different feelings mix together here that it will be difficult to unravel this ball [of yarn].

To begin with, it entails the same instinct of preserving the species which a mother's love possesses. Then the most powerful driving force – passion – is added, which people generally call love, even though it is something entirely opposite from love. It clouds an individual's mind and does not permit one to see the true face of the beloved. The desire of the flesh is so mighty and intoxicating that people see everything rose-colored. The girls grow the wings of angels, and the boys acquire the characteristics of Greek heroes or the handsomeness of fairy tale princes, even though neither one nor the other has a whiff of these wonders. The awakening comes sooner or later, but it comes bitterly and dreadfully. Then the golden wings break off from the angel, and instead she grows the tail of a witch; but the hero turns out to be the mere breaker of a feather, or even the devil himself.

However, then comes the true love. Like everything that is genuine, it is, again, rare. Should noble and congenial souls meet, then their passion is transformed into friendship, is transformed into the love of a friend. There cannot be anything more beautiful in the world than this love, nor anything more noble and sacred.

Briefly, that is what this last love is like.

We have looked into this infinitely large subject about which humanity talks from its diaper days, about which scientists rack their gray and dry heads, and about which the overly-smart philosophers sweat and the wise and crazy poets sing. Still, no matter what, there are no successes and probably will never be, for love is just as inexhaustible as the ocean and as varied as jewels.

I will stop talking about this subject for today. My beloved Ilgya will speak with you later on.

Be bright, be strong, be wise!

Ilgya   04/19/44

You are alarmed and some of you are even dissatisfied. All magnificent matters are simple.

The great philosophers know how to explain concepts so wisely that it is well if they, themselves, are capable of understanding them. The many and wise words quite often bury the notion so deep that all of humanity's shovels are incapable of uncovering it.

Your philosophers strive to speak wisely, for they talk with wise individuals. You, however, will have to talk mostly with the so-called fools, and you will not convince them with exaggerated wisdom and incomprehensibly wise words. You have to learn how to speak simply and even plainly, as John said. That does not mean, though, that the wise ones should not continue their work. That is necessary as well.

You attempt to explain the meaning of the word apple, but you were asked, "What is an apple?" After all, that is not the same thing.

_ ★ ★ ★ _

Santorino   04/23/44

Today I want to talk some more about love.

The people on Earth comprehend it so broadly that, in fact, they do not understand it at all. They toss the word love around like a football. You say, "I love pork and baked potatoes," even though you should say, "I like the taste of pork and potatoes." You say, "I love bright clothing," even though you should say, "I like bright clothing." A man quite often tells a good looking woman, "I love you," even though he should say, "I desire your body," because after what occurs he calmly puts on his hat and in five minutes has already forgotten his beloved. Here the word love has lost its meaning.

We, the spirits, understand love like this.

The foundation of love is sympathy, which unites Gods with the spirits and the spirits with Gods, and the spirits among themselves, hence also all living beings in whom spirits are incarnated.

This sympathy comes about from the admiration of the other spirit's nobility and beauty, mutual comprehension, and the feeling of kinship and friendship. The following feelings stem from it: constancy; sacrificing oneself for the sake of the beloved; giving up everything that might harm the beloved, even your love, if it gets in the way of his/her happiness; gratitude; and respect.

That is how we understand the word love. You, people, have to find a definition for it based on your point of view and essence.

I still want to talk about the so-called love in marriage. You consider marriage as the consequence of love, but is that always the case? I have already mentioned the mind-dazzling passion as one of the reasons. As the second one I will mention materialistic interests – marrying a rich and old, but unloved, man.

If prostitution should be condemned then that is understandable, and quite often it is not the woman who should be condemned, but your social structure. A marriage with materialistic interests, however, is the very worst form of this prostitution. Should [this marriage] take place with the blessing of the church, then it also means profaning God's name, for it supposedly takes place in the name of love and Christ, as if Christ and love recognize and bless this prostitution. Pastors who do that are committing a crime against Christ. Should a prostitute sell her body and receive money for it, then that is condemnable, but not anything else. Should a woman sell her body, though, under the protection of a sacred veil, that is already a hideous and punishable matter that cannot be justified and supported under any circumstances. An individual who does that in the name of love and God should be thrown out of society as a fraud and a blasphemer.

To continue: For the most part, you consider love as an egotistic means of acquiring and retaining for yourself the desired person. That is not love! That is something worse than the very worst! It is not possible to make someone love you by force, with threats, nor by other means. Is that love, if the loved individual is isolated from the world, and from other people and joys, in order to retain him or her only for yourself?

Those who beat their marriage partner, or kill him/her in the name of love, are the worst criminals. They should be thrown out of human society with the same disgust with which they are being thrown out of the realm of the spirits.

If you truly love someone, then do and wish him/her only good, even though you would have to suffer yourself, would have to give up happiness and love, and would even have to die because of that. Instead of where you now kill the other person, kill yourself if you can't [resolve the dilemma] otherwise.

With you, this entire so-called marriage is built on an incorrect foundation. Marriage should take place only because of love, and marriage should continue only as long as both spouses love each other. It has to be established so that both spouses would be entirely self-supporting and independent of each other, both in a material and a social sense; also so that concerns about children would not be a reason for continuing a forced marriage.

Whenever someone will love another only because he/she loves her/him as a person and will know that he/she can retain the other individual only with the power of love, then marriages will be genuine and happy, and you, too, my priests, will be able to bless them in my name.

With that I will conclude for today.

Otranto will talk with Mary, and after that Ilgya with all of you.

Be loving and kind!

Ilgya   04/23/44

Ilgya is speaking. We, the spirits, deceived you today. Only I promised to speak, but even the Divine spoke, for he was surprised by how strangely people treat the most sacred word in the world – *love*.

Now you, at least, comprehend what the spirits understand by this word, and what a superfluous and even entirely contrary meaning is attached to this word on Earth.

Then Otranto spoke, and I only after him. Still another surprise awaits you. Ali will say a few words as well.

We will have a talk now, my noble and dear friends.

One revelation comes to you after another. Christ selected His disciples from among uneducated fishermen. Omega has selected them from among the best educated people who have completed college. It seems that I do not have to explain to you why that occurred. I also do not have to explain why there is one among you who has not completed college, but the shadow of The Almighty's blessing falls on him.

→A difficult road lies ahead of you. That is the road, however, over which you have to take humanity – which is lost and yearns for justice – to The Almighty.

Christ's teachings turned out to be too divine for humanity on Earth. He asked the impossible of man – to love your enemy. That is impossible. One can keep from harming the enemy, can tolerate and even respect him, but man is incapable of loving him.

How can this situation be understood? Would you like to know?

It can be understood like this: Christ gave ideals to humanity that it must strive to achieve. Similarly, every youth is given ideals for his life, but are they achieved? No! Similarly, Christ's ideals are not being achieved either. They are, however, necessary as the ultimate goal. How will you know in which direction to travel unless you will see the objective of the journey? Therefore, many of Christ's teachings are impossible under the current conditions of humanity's development. These [would include]: love your enemy; do not sin, not even in your thoughts; do not look at a woman with lust in your eyes; and so on.

Well, that would be one point.

The other is that the disciples of Christ, as uneducated people, did not always write down the words of Christ in that sense, in which Christ had said them. He said, "Endeavor not only to not detest your enemies, but strive to even love them." His disciples shortened this instruction, intending to make it even more effective, and wrote down categorically and peremptorily, "Love your enemy." You know what came of that.

Yet even those teachings of Christ that can be carried out are not being carried out. Pharisees called themselves teachers and servants of Christ, and almost everything remained the same. People still pray to God in churches the same way, while staging theatrical performances there; they still slaughter and smite the same way – not only their enemies, but even their friends. Thus it turned out that by setting the demands too high for a human, so that he was unable to carry them out even with the greatest desire, the human does not carry out anything. Therefore, let us give humanity the same teachings of Christ, except without the modifications of the apostles, and within the bounds of realistic requirements. What Christ had to express in the form of parables, we will express in the form of scientific writings.←

Now, my friends, consider how you are going to accomplish this work. You have much to contemplate; how are you going to begin your teachings and with what? The adherents of all the confessions will ask you how their faiths differ from The Almighty's faith. You will have to respond to Christians, to Buddhists, to Moslems, and to many others. Therefore become acquainted with these faiths. For example, the people of India comprehended that the instinct of the body is hostile to the spirit and, in order to weaken this instinct, began to weaken the body in order to overcome it. That is one example for you that you have to know and which you have to be able to explain.

Now, what will you do with the priests of the existing confessions? Will you declare war on them, or else will you gradually include them in your faith? What will you do with the churches? How will it be with baptisms, marriages, and funerals? Will your priests perform them, or will judicial institutions? If you will perform marriages, then they will have to be given a legal basis as well and, if you will give that, then what kind of a relationship will you establish with the power of the state? Will it have to be separate from the faith, or will the faith have to subordinate and establish the power of the state as well? If you will base yourselves on legal foundations, then what will the courts, which will judge the quarrels and crimes of the citizens, be like?

On one planet, trials are conducted in this manner. The chief judge is appointed by the state. One judge is chosen – according to his choice, either from his friends or experts – by one of the litigants, and the other judge by the other litigant. The judges decide by a majority of votes. If it is a public or state case, then the town or village elects one judge. These two judges, the judges of the litigants, have been assigned some of the rights of your defense attorneys and prosecutors, for these do not exist here on the planet.

These would be some of the many questions which you will have to decide. Now you know why you have diplomas in your pockets.

I want to take leave from you. Ali will speak.

Ali   04/23/44

Your old Ali is talking. Well, how goes it with my wise brothers? You, yourselves, torment yourselves the most, but what can one do? Torment leads to paradise, but joys to hell; so then, just continue tormenting yourselves.

– ★ ★ ★ –

You are tired today, therefore I will conclude with two more examples of how trials are conducted on different planets, for Ilgya was very serious and abrupt with you today.

On one planet trials are conducted like this. A large bucket of water is placed in front of each litigant, and they are made to drink it. Whoever finishes drinking first has won.

On the second planet the matter is settled even more brilliantly. Both litigants are placed in jail, together in one cell, for three or six days. Since there [the inmates] are not fed in jail, one of the litigants has to bring along a salted ham, and the other a keg of beer. Generally, after three days both litigants go home singing and embracing each other and don't even glance at the courthouse door, which the doorman has politely opened for them.

Live soundly and cheerfully!

Ilgya   04/26/44

The Divine will talk in a few days about religion and science. You, too, should contemplate this subject.

I have to announce some sad news to you. Santorino talked with Omega today. Santorino said that he is ceasing to protect Latvia. We do not know whether that will take place today or later on, and we don't know why either, for we cannot read the thoughts of the higher spirits, and they remain silent regarding the fates of other nations as well. They only say that much will depend on the nations themselves.

The horrors in Europe have almost reached their point of culmination. Every day thousands of airplanes sow death among children and women, not to mention men. Thousands of towns and villages in Russia lie in rubble. The desert blows its sand of death across all of Europe; it buries people, the old culture, and the old gods.

You, here in Latvia, can't even imagine so far what other nations are experiencing. Multitudes of cripples, physical and spiritual cripples, roam the bloody ground. You hear the funeral bells for the dreams of many millions of people. Rows of corpses form giant stairs, but to where – to hell or to paradise?

You claim that Ortega, Karino, and The Almighty's other judges have arrived too soon, but can you count the harvest of death that occurs every day?

Santorino seeks the name of Christ in people's hearts, but it has gone out in them. Does humanity want to have it written there with a hot branding iron? All right! That will happen!

I conclude. Ali will speak in ten minutes.

Ali   04/26/44

Once again I come uninvited. What can one do with the force of habit? Today I will not tell you anything cheerful. Let us simply chat about this-and-that like old friends.

The salvation of Latvia and the entire world is in the awakening of the heart and the mind.

Let's talk a little bit about science now. Not from that point of view as the Divine comprehends it, but still some clarity will dawn for you.

Man has accumulated an entire herd of animals which he has supposedly domesticated for himself, has made them his servants, and exploits them. He is mighty proud of his work and of his mind. Yet is that really the case? Think this over well! Perhaps these domesticated and subservient animals think the same thing about you as you do about them, for they are also The Almighty's creatures and are no fools at all. It seems that these animals, too, have evaluated the ruler of Earth – dear man – rather well and have known how to exploit him rather well.

It seems that the horse and the mule are the worst off, for they have to work hard. Because of that, however, they can live in the cold Europe and other northern lands, where they would have starved to death in winter. The owner feeds them, cares for them, and keeps them warm. He pays lots of money for them – the Arabs even more than for a wife.

The cow exploits man really well – gives him milk, and leaves all cares to the poor master. The same thing is true of pigs, which give man even less than the cow. When these animals are eventually butchered, though, then that is no misfortune either, for the species of cows, sheep, pigs, and others not only do not become extinct, but even increase – and that is the goal of life, which they have achieved so sensibly. Out in nature they would have been killed and eaten by the same man anyway, and by animals as well, whom man now does not even let near them.

The dog and cat have established themselves very comfortably. One barks a little, and the other catches a mouse for its own amusement; and for that the master feeds them and protects them from the cold and the rain.

As you can see, wisdom is not nearly as one-sided as you think. Then there are still many animals who are altogether bossing over you – all kinds of mice and rats, fleas and crickets. Bedbugs, however, don't want to live without man at all and follow him faithfully everywhere, even to the North Pole.

Well, what are you going to say? Don't look all that proudly at the foolish cow. Perhaps it laughs heartily at you behind your back.

Would there be anything to ask?

[[We object, "Man has subordinated the animals, and animals don't think."]]

Oh, and how they think! Even a bedbug knows how to escape death, and just try to catch a flea.

[[We ask, "Don't they save themselves through instinct?"]]

Some mind is needed there as well.

We will talk again some other time. The laughter spirits now want to present a short poem about life to little Nick. Good-bye.

Laughter Spirits   04/26/44

Adhere to what is good
And avoid all evil,
Then your life will become bright
And your heart will be forever young.

Shota   04/26/44

I can see that you are waiting for something. What would that be?

[[We ask, "Could you tell us something good about Latvia?"]]

Nothing good, therefore I will remain silent.

Your nation has adopted too much from other nations; not what is good, but, unfortunately, what is bad. You expect some sort of sacrifices on your behalf from other nations, and [expect them] to care for you, expect them to stroke and to caress you, but what were you like with respect to others during your years of glory? Didn't you proudly deny the rights of others, and even their languages? All of a sudden you forgot how to speak Russian and German. You wanted other – old and large – nations to learn your language. This even though many of you, who were born and grew up in Russia or Germany, did not find it necessary your whole life through to learn the language of the state.

Then this arrogance and contempt! What mountains have you overturned and what wealth have you given the world, in order to at least have earned the right to do this?

This unnecessary and harmful contempt! All right, you felt no sympathy for the Jewish people. I understand that and agree. Was it necessary, though, because of that to have them write on their schools, Jewish School, because the word Jew [in Latvian] is a curse word for them, and every noble nation should have understood that.

You will in turn be weighed the same way as you weigh. The entire nation has to pay dearly, and will still have to pay, for the spilled blood of children. The entire nation is responsible for those sins which its sons commit.

I conclude. Be wise, but not overly wise.

Ilgya   04/29/44

Ilgya is speaking. Get ready for a conversation with the Divine. He will speak within the next few days.

Consider thoroughly [the following].

What are religion and science? What do they have in common, and how do they differ? Can they travel a joint path, or, else, are they incompatible and perhaps even hostile?

Consider the question regarding the church as well – what should it be like, and what icons should there be within it? How should praying to God be conducted, and what can one pray for?

Decide also the question regarding who are the Virgin, Christ's apostles, and the saints. How should they be considered?

All of you, in turn, will be asked these questions, and you will have to reply.

I will talk with you on Monday. Ali will also speak. Therefore all of you definitely have to be present, and summon me no later than ten o'clock.

Good-bye.

Chapter IX
May 1944 - Part 1

Santorino   05/01/44 1000

→Be seated. Today I will talk about religion and science.

Since you have not managed to delve sufficiently into these matters, there is no sense in debating with you. Therefore listen to what I will say.

Can science and religion be combined? No! Science deals with what can be researched, or, at least, can be understood and verified. Yet religion requires one to believe even without evidence. They both have common grounds as well. These would be: comprehension of the world, exploration of the unknown, striving to give humanity a happy life, freeing it from physical and spiritual suffering, and looking into eternity.

As long as science is incapable of answering all questions, it is powerless to satisfy man's thirst for omniscience and give him peace of the soul. Only religion is capable of that.

The people of science, while looking into the infinite space of the universe, seek therein their origin – God. Having failed to find Him, they will attempt to explain Him with their mind and ascertain Him with instruments, that is, [they will attempt] to comprehend The Almighty with them. The Almighty, though, cannot be found by these means.

It is not possible to place a sunbeam in a metal box in order to bring it into a laboratory and examine it under a microscope. It is not possible to stop the wind in order to see what it is. The wind, having been stopped, is no longer anything. You will be able to ascertain only one fact – the wind is either nothing, or something mysterious. Sunbeams and the wind have to be comprehended and investigated by other means.

Let us leave to science the explanation of everything that it is capable of explaining on Earth, and to the extent that its telescopes are able to see. Let us, however, leave The Almighty and the realm of the spirits to religion. The Almighty, Himself, reveals this to you through His spirits, Omega and me.

I am capable of speaking only through Alexander and Mary. When one of you will depart, I, too, will grow silent. Omega speaks only through Alexander. Once he will depart, the gates of Heaven will close to humanity for ever and ever. All those who will speak in The Almighty's and our names will be nothing but false apostles. And, oh, woe! what awaits them and those who will believe them.

Now, [I will talk] about the world and the universe. Your scientists have comprehended the infinity of time and of the cosmos. Yet, having acknowledged the infinite space, they now believe that the space which is filled with matter is limited after all – that it is not infinite. They claim that there are no straight lines in infinity. Rather, there are curved lines that return to the points of their origin, that is, close on themselves.

Therefore, they consider that the space which is filled with matter is not infinite and can even be measured. They have even measured it. Its radius is supposed to be 27,000 megaparsecs. However, even this world of theirs is so immense that it cannot be viewed even with the largest telescopes. Even if you will invent telescopes which are capable of that, you will still not have come closer to The Almighty, not even by one millimeter.

Science strives to understand and explain infinity, the infinity of space and time. That is a superfluous endeavor, for not even the spirits are able to explain and comprehend that. When did the universe begin, and when will it end? How can that be answered, and how can that be understood?

Let us suppose that previously there was "nothing," and then, at one time, The Almighty came into being out of this nothing, and from this nothing created the entire universe, with its infinite number of bodies. That is an absurdity, because nothing can come into being out of nothing, and nothing can be created from nothing. Therefore, The Almighty and the universe have existed, and will exist, eternally. They have never been created, but have always existed. You are not capable of grasping that, and will never be capable; you have to reconcile yourselves with that. Merely try to understand how that is.

You will understand that better if we will proceed and will seek the ending day of the universe. Let us suppose that the day has come, or rather the moment, when The Almighty and the cosmos cease to exist, and "nothing" sets in once again. How can you visualize that, and how is that possible? What happens to all these stars and planets? Will they turn into dust and gases? What will happen to the dust and gases, though? How will they be able to disappear completely, and where will they disappear to? How will matter be able to transform into the so-called "nothing?" Is that possible?

You are saying, "No!"

Therefore, only one possibility remains, even though an incomprehensible possibility – infinity, and a universe without a beginning and without an end. There remains infinite space, because one cannot visualize a boundary to it, and infinite time, for which one also cannot imagine a measurement.

Simultaneously with that, the question is also settled concerning the infinite and unfathomable Almighty, who rules in this infinity, infinitely.

Let us now turn to a second important question. How should one comprehend The Almighty's Commandment to the universe: Do not harm anyone.

Evil is a relative notion, because what is evil for one individual can be good for another. Who is more evil, a rabbit or a wolf? Both of them! The rabbit eats grass, and the wolf eats the rabbit; for that is how they have been created. The rabbit would gladly devour the wolf, and without any mercy, but it cannot eat meat. The wolf would gladly eat grass, particularly at times of famine, but it cannot do that.

An individual does good by cultivating his orchard, but if, in the process, he destroys an entire ant hill, he is evil to it. If man had wanted to avoid harming any living creature, he would already have died long ago. He would have been devoured by beasts and insects. He could not walk, for he tramples insects with his feet. He could not drink water and breathe the air, for with each sip of water, and every breath of air, he kills millions of living beings. Therefore, neither good nor evil, in the absolute meaning of the word, differ [from each other]. Good is evil, and evil is good.

God is Satan, and Satan is God.

We have only one way of looking at the concept of evil. Do not harm another human, that is with respect to you, people.

Many animals so far have understood and know this Commandment of The Almighty better than people do. Animals generally do not eat individuals of their own species, but only those of other species. They spare their own kind, and even defend them. Therefore, let us comprehend this word correctly.

The Almighty asks all living beings not to harm individuals of their own genus, species, or race – but not everyone – and to look after the welfare and existence of their own kind. The Almighty, Himself, settles the relationships between the living beings, and He lets the more capable ones live and rule.

Now [I will talk] about the relationship between The Almighty and the human being.

Pray to God only with good deeds. You may also turn to Him with the prayer which Christ gave to the people. It would be good if you, people, would turn to God with this prayer each morning. It would remind you that God does exist, and what your responsibilities are. Perhaps then this prayer will also be followed by good deeds, and they will reach the throne of God.

Do not pray to God so that others see it. Do not go to special buildings to pray to God. You may assemble there only for good deeds and discussions about spiritual matters and needs.

Pray to God with a bowed head, but do not fall to your knees; and never dare to pray to God while seated or lying down. One may pray to God only while standing on his feet.

Pray only to God, for He alone has been given the right to spare you and to help you. Pray neither to the Virgin, nor to the apostles, nor to the so-called saints. All [the saints] are your own creations and are incapable of helping you. Also, do not pray to icons, but respect them as depictions of the high spirits. Further, do not turn in your prayers to us, the spirits, but only to God. Do not turn to The Almighty either; He will not listen to you.

You may decorate your churches with the paintings of great masters that depict the high spirits, in Heaven as well as on Earth, and scenes of the beautiful world and of noble deeds. However, do not dare to worship them or to consider them to be sacred.

Now to continue. How to do good.

Do not give to those who ask constantly for something from you, merely because they ask and bother you. That is not helping. That is tossing a penny to a tiresome beggar and throwing a crust to an obtrusive dog.

You must seek out and see <u>on your own</u>, (I underline, on your own), who needs to be helped. Only then, if you will act like that and help from a pure heart, without expecting gratitude and praise for your help, you will have done a good deed, which will bring true blessing to your soul. Generally, those who need help the most ask the least, for they are high spirits and scorn begging. Begging is humanity's foulest profession, and you have to eliminate it.

Now let's talk concerning humanity's future.

Is work a blessing? No, it is a curse, and humanity will eliminate it, thanks to its science. Your people of science, however, claim that work is what has given culture to humanity and has taken it from the shack of the naked savage to palaces of marble. Struggle against harsh nature has forced man to develop ever more. Scientists claim that those nations which had achieved a high position, the position of mastery, have perished due to idleness and have been replaced by other, more industrious nations. Should humanity achieve a situation where it will not have to work, it will halt in its development and will even decline. This point of view simply proves the current narrowness of mind of your scientists.

Yes, humanity has achieved culture, thanks to work. That, however, is history. That is a child learning how to walk on his feet and to how talk. Yes, some cultural nations, or, rather, states, have perished because they had too many slaves, hence they did not have to work. Yet that occurred because the neighboring nations had to work, and they toiled and fought. If all the nations, though, if the entire humanity were to achieve this situation simultaneously, then it would not be threatened and could persist. Everything depends on the correct point of view and comprehension.

Work is man's most terrible curse. It makes him age rapidly; wears out the body; oppresses the spirit; deprives the individual of almost all his time; and does not permit him to become acquainted with the world, science, and beauty and devote himself to whatever he wants to do. In other words, it excludes the world with its beauty and significance. The day is spent in toil; the evening brings fatigue and drowsiness. The night covers him with the wings of death.

Science will liberate humanity from that work which is undesirable, unnecessary, and disproportionately heavy. It will give man work according to his choice and ability – light and pleasant work.

It will inure his spirit and body with science and exercise. It will make his life spiritually rich and physically perfect. [Science] will free his body from diseases and will preserve it, beautiful and young, until the day of death. If humanity's genius will be able to make this body immortal, The Almighty will only welcome this and will open the entire universe to humanity. From planet to planet, from eternity into eternity, humanity will be taken by its genius and by work; the work of a ruler, but not the work of a slave, which so far reigns on Earth.

I cannot complete [my tiding] today, for your spirits are tired.

Be alert, be bright, be strong.←

Ilgya   05/01/44

Ilgya is speaking. The Divine was particularly good to you today. Humanity would not have achieved in two eternities what he gave you in two hours. What he told you, however, is merely a tiny grain of sand from among those which lie on the shore of The Almighty's ocean of knowledge.

Santorino tried to talk with you in such a simple language that everyone could understand it. He strove to avoid foreign words with which the writings of your scientists, and even journalists, are overly abundant so that the poor reader feels that he is no longer a Latvian and has to reach for a dictionary every minute. Since man is a rather lazy creature, though, he generally lays down this wise book on a shelf and picks up some novel, which he is able to understand.

Your scientists should write not in order to demonstrate how many various foreign words they know, but, rather, in order to show that they know how and are able to express their knowledge in words that people understand.

True, you went to schools and hence you should understand these wise words as well, but do you remember them? No! Only those who subsequently have to deal with them remember them. They, however, forget that others have forgotten them.

If a scientist, in his paper, is unable to express some concepts without these foreign words, then let him explain them in parentheses, below the text, or after the text, but let him liberate humanity from dictionaries, for not everyone has them.

Should a scientist write some specialized work, which would be of interest only to specialists like he, himself – for example, the effect of the human shadow on the reflectivity of the Earth – then he might as well use nothing but just such words.

You will understand now why the Divine, when talking about scientists, used some words like that. Look up their meaning in dictionaries and put them in parentheses, if you are able to.

Let us talk about what might continue to interest you with respect to God and the spirits.

None of the sacred or religious books can give you anything. You receive

everything directly from God. Books of philosophy, too, with their speculations about what you already know infallibly, are entirely superfluous to
you. It is immaterial what Kant, Hegel, Nietzsche, and others have thought
about God and the spirits. You already know that which they were merely
seeking. They can only make you doubt your knowledge and delude your
mind. For the sake of interest you may, if you want to, familiarize yourselves
with them, providing you don't mind [wasting] the time.

The Holy Scriptures can be useful to you only for debates, because you
are neither Christians, nor Buddhists, nor Moslems, but are the bearers of
The Almighty's faith. This faith has not evolved from those religions but is
a basic faith, from which there may have been much in those faiths as well.
You are not permitted, however, to take anything from those faiths in order
to supplement The Almighty's faith.

If you can drink the water of cognition directly from the spring, then
don't go to drug stores for it. There it will already be stale and impure.

Utilize every moment for contemplation and questions, as long as Omega and Santorino talk with you.

The human mind has its limits. Therefore there is a limit to man's knowledge as well. An earthworm is incapable of seeing the stars and of determin-
ing the distance to them, no matter how brilliant it might be. The wise ant
will nevertheless be incapable of understanding that the Earth is spherical
and that the sun is a star. The human mind also has its limits, therefore, while
failing to understand much, man rejects whatever he does not understand.
Many people failing to comprehend God simply reject Him; just as a savage
would throw away a radio receiver which he has found in the woods, for
how could he make use of this strange box?

Similarly man, having failed to find the spirit anywhere, denies his existence and explains everything by the transformation of matter. He claims
that the brain thinks. Who has invented and formed this brain, though, and
why is this brain engrossed not only with material concerns but involves
itself with all kinds of abstract ideas that are not needed by the body at all?
[The brain] dreams of ideal beauty. It creates poems and novels. It writes
extremely thick books of knowledge about the stars and about justice. Why
is that the case? Why does matter, of which the brain is formed, take such an
interest in the immaterial, in the spiritual? How can it be explained that the
individual who has a large brain quite often is more of a fool than the one

who has a smaller one? Somehow that does not correlate with the materialistic understanding. A greater quantity of the same substance should also result in more wisdom or comprehension.

Yes, the brain is the laboratory of the spirit. Without the spirit, however, this laboratory is simply a worthless collection of instruments and materials.

Ali and Shota spoke with you Wednesday. Ali, as usual, clarified some concepts from a unique point of view. Therefore, you have to know how to differentiate between humor and scientific concepts.

Shota spoke about your nation, and you were incapable of understanding him. He did not justify other nations but only pointed out those bad characteristics which your nation had adopted from them. It became better than some of the large nations but, still, was not such an ideal nation as the noble Shota would have liked to see it.

To John. You may talk about some revelations, but only as your own ideas.

Shota   05/01/44

Shota is here. Argus cannot come to you and apologizes. He probably does not have anything new either.

_ ★ ★ ★ _

The Divine and Ilgya brought you pails full of gold today. What can I, a poor poet, toss into them? I will toss in only one tiny teardrop.

Do not torture animals, do not cause them unnecessary pain, and do not kill those which do not harm you. I will also add — love those which love you, are faithful to you, and serve you. With that you will not do as much good for them as for your own soul.

Do not forget that The Almighty, Himself, and the incomprehensibly great and noble Omega saved the mother of the helpless, young mice. Do you think that you were told that merely so that you would know what Omega was doing at that time on Earth? No, none of the words of the high spirits are uttered for naught, and only in order to satisfy your curiosity.

You have to learn from everything. You have to ponder everything, even the simplest point, and consider whether it has been understood correctly and completely. Did you, people, understand Christ correctly when He said to cut off the sinful hand and pluck out the eye which has succumbed to temptation? No, you understood that literally! Since you did not want to be without eyes and hands, you left them in their places as well, and since they had remained in their places you went on sinning.

Christ never spoke literally, though. He spoke figuratively. He did not speak of your physical hands and eyes but, rather, of the spiritual ones. It meant that the spirit had to withdraw the sinful hand from the sin and had to close the eye which was tempted by sin.

It has always seemed strange to me just how poorly you, people, have understood Christ and Buddha, how little of the teachings of Christ have reached you, and how you have utilized those teachings which have reached you. What did the priests, who bore His name, do? They acted exactly contrary to His teachings.

The Bible turned out to be the most harmful book for them, and they forbid to print and read it in the living languages of the people. Did the people, however, understand the dead languages – Latin and the Slavic language of the church? Thus only the name of Christ was left for the people, but not His faith.

The church cultivated only slavery – the slavery of the spirit and the body. May such servants of God be damned for ever and ever! They are the world's worst criminals, and the gates of eternity are closed to them; although they might call themselves Christ's deputies on Earth.

I conclude.

Otranto   05/03/44

I, Otranto, as instructed by God, am talking with you. I will talk about bringing [up children] and about pedagogy.

People will claim, "What business does God have in talking about such purely humanistic problems?"

Unfortunately He does, because you blame God for your own failures and for the consequences of your lack of knowledge. You claim, "We care so much about the upbringing of children and the teaching and education of the youth. We have built millions of schools and colleges. Man, however, remains the same, lousy individual he has always been. He cheats, steals, fights with others, murders, loafs, drinks, and acts rowdy – that is how God has created man, and nothing can be made of him."

That is what you claim.

Is God at fault here, though? [Perhaps] you, yourselves, might be at fault? Yes, you do bring up the children, but how do you bring them up? You have built buildings and have hung on them magnificent signs with the word school on them. You believe that because of that these building have already turned into schools. Billions of people, cultural people, stream from them into life. Yet what a surprise! This cultural man, who has put a tuxedo on his naked body of a savage and has put a bright top hat on his head, will – at the first real struggle, at the first serious war – throw this tuxedo and top hat into the bushes without hesitating for a moment; and the very same naked savage stands before you.

Now, what has happened to all of this humanity's civilization? Let us look for the guilty ones, and let us find the causes of the problem.

Your social structure and the upbringing of children are the cause of the fact that man's moral and cultural state of affairs is so pitifully low. This latter problem is also what I have been directed to discuss with you.

In order to form an ideal individual, in a spiritual as well as physical sense, he has to be brought up to be like that from the very first day of his life. He has to be brought up continuously and persistently until adulthood.

Who brings up a person during his childhood? The family – the father and the mother! How do they bring him up? Do they know how to bring up a child, have they been taught how to bring him up? No! Then how are they supposed to know that?

After all, you take pride in your schools. What then is being taught in them, if such an important subject as bringing up and caring for a child is not being taught? After all, the entire future of humanity depends on that! Hence the parents bring up a child without any knowledge, just as each one of them knows and can.

Just what can you expect from a gardener who has studied accounting? Deformed apple trees and infested currants! The least fool understands that. All your wise professors, though, have failed to understand that people have to be taught how to bring up children.

What is the result? Only a teacher who is good and capable, and who has been prepared for his work, is able to give good students to humanity.

What are your families like? There are good ones where the father and the mother lead a decent life and strive to bring up their children to be good people. Since they have not been given any prior knowledge, though, they teach while they, themselves, learn and make mistakes at every step. By the time they have finally learned, it turns out that life is already over as well. They either pamper their children too much or else fail to raise them as would be better and easier. However, if a child is being brought up by a family of drunkards or thieves, what do they instill in the child? Everything, except nothing good!

The child has to be raised according to a firm and resolute system. The main method is upbringing by example. The child tries to imitate his parents and grown-up people. Therefore, your child, too, tries to be like you are. He, too, behaves the same way as you behave. Therefore, in order for humanity to become ideal, the parents already have to be ideal.

The first and most difficult task for humanity, now, is to bring up these first, ideal parents. Only the state in its schools is capable of that. The parents have to be teachers and physicians as well. They have to follow the child at every step, have to guide and teach him while playing. He has to be brought up spiritually as well as physically. Under no circumstances should he be pampered to excess. He has to gradually become used to doing some work each day and has to learn to accomplish tasks and to obey.

The children have to be brought up to be spiritually strong, and also physically strong and hardy. Inure them, teach them to endure difficulties and hunger, teach them to suffer and to win. Protect them from adults and little ones of a negative nature. I repeat once more: Your children will behave according to the way you bring them up, and like you, yourselves, are. You, while behaving badly, are frequently surprised that your children have grown up to be bad. You claim, "After all, we taught them only good!" Yes, but did you do what you were teaching them? Those are the results!

You are not surprised that in a family in which Latvian is spoken the child also speaks Latvian, but not English, even though you wanted him to and are surprised about other understandable matters.

The upbringing of children and family life have to be instituted as the main subjects in your schools. Every young man and young woman, on leaving school, has to know fully how to bring up children and how to establish and carry on family life. The direct and main duty of the school is to teach the individual how to live correctly. It is not [to teach him] in which year Peter II died or what a deer's hoof looks like — is it split like that of a cow or, else, like that of a horse, and so on.

You will claim, "What business does society have with respect to my daughter or son? They are mine, and I can bring them up as I want to!"

No, that's not how it is! You do not raise them as much for yourselves as for society. After some twenty years they usually leave you, the parents. Quite often you no longer have any dealings whatsoever with them. The society, however, does, for you have blessed it with murderers, or with thieves and welfare recipients. Therefore it is the duty and the right of society to organize and direct the correct upbringing of the children and to take children away from bad parents.

Let us turn to schools, what they are like and what they should be like.

Your schools are overloaded with subjects that generally have very little significance, and even no significance whatsoever in the individual's practical life. The subjects are presented in a dry and appallingly boring manner. Subjects which are important in life are considered superficially or are not considered at all. The amount of human knowledge has grown tremendously, and the school is incapable of teaching all of it, and neither is that necessary. People have individual interests, and there are many occupations as well. It is foolish to teach everyone identically and for the same occupation.

This is what schools should be like.

The primary school is where children should be taught those subjects that everyone needs. Let's say sensible and practical grammar, which is essential for correctly expressing one's thoughts and for writing; mathematics, within the limits of the necessities of life for an ordinary person; and natural sciences to such an extent that the individual would know how to orient himself within the plant, animal, and mineral kingdoms on Earth. Then specialized knowledge that is necessary in life in order to comprehend it and make it easier. Much effort has to be exerted here toward the spiritual and physical upbringing of the pupils. They have to be given the correct idea about what life is; what it demands from everyone; and what are each individual's obligations toward himself, his spouse, his children, and society.

It is the duty of the teachers and the parents in this school to ascertain for what occupation the child has the greatest abilities and interests. Then send him off to college. This means a school with a specialized course of instruction, appropriate for the student's abilities and interests – a college in which professions are taught.

In these colleges one can explore the very depths of the necessary knowledge – either higher mathematics or a complete and detailed history, botany, zoology, theology, law, and so on.

The most important consideration in all schools is to teach only what is essential and to teach in an interesting and lively manner. Schooling has to be continuous. The school has to be well illuminated and attractive. Its walls should be decorated with the paintings of great masters. Only whatever is artistically valuable may be located within the school premises.

There have to be libraries with worthy books in the schools, [as well as] gymnasiums, playgrounds and rooms for play, stage and movie theaters, laboratories, and various workshops. The schools have to have swimming pools, gardens, vegetable gardens, and various athletic fields.

Instruction has to take place as much as possible in the open air or in bright rooms that are full of fresh air and well ventilated.

The pupils have to live next to the schools under the constant supervision of a teacher, winter and summer. The summer has to be spent in field work. In general, all instruction should be presented as much as possible in a practical manner. All that can be taught theoretically is that which cannot be presented otherwise. Teach botany in gardens, fields, woods, and botanical gardens. Zoology – in zoos. Whenever and whatever cannot be taught like that, use the aid of movies. The students should go on field trips. Teach geography from the windows of airplanes or cars. Chemistry – in laboratories. Physics and mathematics – as much as possible by means of practical assignments as well. Many problems in physics can be solved by practical means. Similarly, many laws of geometry can be demonstrated in nature. The triangle – consider a tree in a field and its shadow. A mountain on the other side of a river – measure the distance to it without crossing the river, and so on.

The book for teaching geography has to be short and interesting, like an adventure novel. Illustrate it with the help of movies. Do not teach geography and history primarily in classes, but by having the pupils read adventure novels written by good writers. Novels like that have to be written for other subjects as well – such as for botany, zoology, and so on. All of the world's best writers and scientists have to be involved in writing these novels. They have to be worthy as science and as literature.

With the help of these books and movies, you will ease class work to such an extent that it will become easy and an enjoyable pleasure, and a game for the pupils as well as for the teachers.

The basic principle of instruction is: Teach interestingly, teach so that [the pupil] will want to learn. Teach so that the pupil will await his teacher impatiently and with love.

Let us summarize now.

Bring up a child from his first day of life at home, and in the school, until adulthood. If you, people, will raise your children like that, then humanity will achieve bright days of happiness. The lazy, drunkards, thieves, and murderers will disappear. You will claim, "How beautiful and noble is man whom God has created!"

The Almighty has given you a wonderful, ideally formed body for your spirits. You only have to know how to utilize it properly and how to control it.

Ilgya   05/05/44

_ ★ ★ ★ _

Janoss and the rest of you do not understand clearly the relationship between the living and the souls of their deceased relatives. You think that your mother and father always remain your mother and father eternally, but that, after all, is completely absurd. The Pharisees already posed the question to Christ regarding the wife of the seven brothers. Do you remember what Christ replied?

Similarly, you also know that Alexo was once Mary's father. Those feelings and bonds of kinship which you have established on Earth do not continue in the realm of the spirits, or else continue only for a short time; except in those cases where they have been and remain kindred as spirits, as in this case where a long and friendly past binds Janoss with Alexandra, but not Alexander U. with Ann. They met for the first time on Earth, and learned only on Earth to admire and love each other. Still, they are infinitely more alien and more remote than the spirits of Alexandra and Ann. Ann undertook to care for Nicholas, who is very intimate and dear to Alexandra's spirit, only at the request of Alexandra.

Think about Otranto's tiding and prepare your questions for Sunday. John has to prepare an answer to the question, "What is time?"

Do you have any questions?

[[We reply that we do not.]]

Too bad! I had so much to answer you, and you have nothing to ask. Can't be helped. Let us part.

Ilkansito   05/05/44

Don't talk! Be silent! Time, time, what is time? Can death be called life?

Why does the brain think, but a sewing machine does not?

What is the mind?

Who has created what, the brain – God, or God the brain?

People once asked each other foolishly, "Which came first – the chicken or the egg?"

What is stupidity? Why is the devil evil? Why does an individual scratch himself while asleep?

Why are your prayers not being considered? Thousands of ministers prayed for Nicholas – the Czar of Russia – but to no avail.

Why do you ask the spirits?

What is heavier – lead or a guilty conscience?

Ilkansito has spoken.

Nakcia   05/05/44

[[We ask for explanations about Ilkansito.]]

I am not allowed to [explain that], for he came from infinity and returned to infinity. He is the good and the evil. He wanted to say [that you have to] think, combine the incompatible, and comprehend the incomprehensible.

Get together on Sunday.

Ilgya   05/05/44

Alexander, Ilgya is speaking. The Almighty's will is unalterable. Do not refuse to concur with it this time, because the foundations of Earth are weaker than those of Heaven. The shadow of Satan, through which the Earth has to pass, is harder than steel. Only the fire of the hearts of all people can melt it. Do not stand between God and Satan.

I conclude. Do not talk any more today.

Santorino   05/07/44 1100

I, the ruler of the world's love, God's sunshine, Santorino speak unto you, the people on Earth.

You are faced with a critical decision. You, The Almighty's chosen ones, have to give me an answer with pure hearts and a keen mind.

Listen and reply.

The Almighty's decision was announced to Alexander. He raises justified objections to it, for he has a right to do that since this task was not announced to him when he was being sent to Earth. He tells The Almighty that he does not agree with His actions because of these reasons:

1. He does not believe that humanity will, through these horrible evaluations of suffering, awake and understand God and justice.

2. He does not believe that the religion which has been promulgated by The Almighty will conquer the world, for the ignorant people will not believe in it because there are no miracles in it; and the educated people because the existence of God and the spirits has not been proven.

3. He claims that The Almighty's chosen envoys are too weak for this task. They worry all the time more about their bodily needs and ask [questions about] what will happen to them tomorrow. Heaven has become distant and alien to their spirits. Neither do God's bells toll in their hearts. A superhuman task has been assigned to them, good people, and that is not fair.

4. He claims that he, too, while coming to Earth, was not prepared for this task, which now will require all of his spiritual and physical strength and will result in the greatest suffering for him. Therefore he asks The Almighty to release him from carrying out the task and to assign it to someone else or have the four others continue it.

The Almighty has not given an answer yet.

All the Gods and spirits oppose his refusal, but Ilgya agreed with him yesterday and, turning directly to The Almighty, asked Him to note this request. God ordered me to announce this to you, and since you have been given a free will you have to decide and reply. Do you support Alexander's request and agree with it? With his departure, you will have to accomplish the work by yourselves. Neither I nor Omega will talk with you [any longer]. The Almighty refuses to send another envoy, in lieu of Alexander, to Earth.

I will give you an hour for your reply. Consider everything calmly and cordially, without hatred and accusations.

[[After an hour. During the discussions it turned out that we do not support Alexander's request.]]

With your decision, you are taking on the heaviest burden that a human being can imagine. You are also assuming an unimaginably great responsibility.

The Almighty announced that this evening He will give His answer – through Omega – to Alexander and you.

Let us continue now the series of God's tidings.

Have John give his answer.

[[John gives a reply regarding the assignment, "What is time?"]]

When talking to the high spirits, an individual should stand up, for the spirits speak while standing.

I thank John for the beautiful definition of time. We will be satisfied with that. John, please be seated.

Let us consider time from another aspect, and altogether simply.

→You have acquired the notion concerning time, thanks to reference points which phenomena of nature have given you. Earth's rotation about its axis gave you the concept of day and night. This you were able to, then, divide into hours, minutes, and seconds, and to measure them with the help of clocks. You obtained the concept of the year from Earth's orbit around the sun. Yet all these concepts are relative, are imagined, and are not entirely correct mathematically.

For example, Earth's rotation about its axis is not constant, is not rigidly or absolutely the same. For a while Earth rotates faster and then somewhat slower. This difference is measured in seconds, but it does exist. Therefore, your measurements of time are not absolutely correct, with respect to those foundations on which they are based; that is, on which the designation of time is based.

Now let us imagine different conditions. Let us say that you live on a planet which is illuminated by a source of even light, even and immobile and so bright that you are unable to see any heavenly bodies. How will you acquire the notion of time, not to mention its measurement? Now, perhaps you will claim that it could be determined by inventing instruments, such as a clock. However, I cannot imagine how you could do that. How will you tell the height of a mountain without seeing its summit or, at least, the mountain's shadow?

Let us proceed. You have been placed inside a room that is completely isolated from the world and does not contain any clocks. In a few years you are asked, "What is it now, daytime or night, and how long have you been within this room?"

Will you be able to answer even approximately? No!

You are awake for eight hours, you work, rejoice, grieve, and enjoy yourself; and then you go to bed. On awaking, you reach for the clock immediately. Why do you do that? Simply in order to know how long you have slept, because you are unable to tell whether you have slept for one hour or a thousand years.

What happens to time when the individual is asleep? Does it exist at all, and does the entire world exist at all while you are asleep? Answer yes or no, but, if it did exist, then prove its existence with facts, with experiences. No, you are unable to! Therefore, the world and time exist only for those who live and do not sleep. They do not exist for the dead and those who are sleeping, or, rather, those who are asleep. Only nothing exists, immeasurable by any methods.

Let us, now, consider time from still another angle. Is the measurement of time – the factual, not the imagined one – always the same, even when you are not asleep? Let's say you are playing cards, your favorite means of killing time. You play for ten hours. Then, again, you are standing on a street in the rain and wind and waiting for a streetcar. Every minute you reach for your watch impatiently. The streetcar does not come. Somewhere, in a warm room, a young lady awaits you, but the streetcar does not come. You chew your fingernails, you say, "An entire eternity has already passed, but this cursed streetcar does not come."

Finally it arrives. You get on it, look at your watch once more, and exclaim in surprise, "Only half an hour, and I thought that the entire day had already passed!"

Is the time spent at a card table, or some other "better place," equal to that spent while waiting or suffering? Yes, with a watch in hand it is the same, but without a watch it is incomparably longer or shorter. Therefore, time is something completely relative, and even unreal. Time loses its concept on leaving Earth. If no changes were to take place in the human organism – and also none in the world, that is, on Earth – then the person who would have slept one day would feel just the same as the one who had slept for millions of years. They would not feel any difference, for they would be unable to tell the time which they spent while asleep.

You are also trying to transfer your Earth time into the realm of the spirits and measure the universe with it. That is the same thing as to drive an ox cart on the rainbow. A million years in the realm of the spirits are a million times shorter than a second on your Earth. What then do you want to measure with your hours, years, and centuries? Perhaps only a zero, if it could be measured.

Your scientists on Earth claim that the speed of a ray of light is the fastest speed that is possible in the universe, something around 300,000 kilometers per second. Within the boundaries of your solar system that is fast and sufficient. With it, you can reach the sun from Earth in eight minutes, and you can cross this entire system as well with only the help of minutes. Therefore, this space is realistically accessible even for the old, winged angels, not to mention the spirits. They could even be transported from one planet to the next in a manner which even your skeptics – your scientists – would acknowledge.

They claim that the force of the pressure from a ray of light is proportional to the surface area of a body. The force of attraction, or gravity, however, is proportional to the mass of the body. Therefore, the force of the pressure from a ray of light on a large body, as for example the Earth, is minute. However, as the body becomes smaller, this situation changes ever more. The force of the pressure from a ray of light on a tiny body as, for example, a bacterium is already much greater than the force of gravity. A sunbeam can carry this bacterium, or an infusorian, from the surface of the Earth into infinity, with an ever-increasing velocity.

Yet how would it be if Hell is not at the center of Earth, and Paradise is somewhere beyond the stars? It is 260,000 times further to the closest star, the star Proxima Centauri in the constellation Centaurus, than it is from Earth to the sun. So then, as you can see, somewhat too far even for a spirit who rides on a ray of light.

As your scientists tell you, one has to travel approximately four light years to the nearest stars. Yet the distances to the more distant ones cannot even be measured in light years; one has to use megaparsecs. However, even these, the most distant visible stars, are more distant from the Deoss Temple than the human mind can imagine. Your scientists cannot imagine anything faster than a ray of light, just as they cannot imagine the speed of thought. There is still much in the universe that you do not see, do not know, do not understand, and can't even imagine. However, simply because you are incapable of all that, all of it must not exist either? That would be an outrage against The Almighty's omnipotent spirit, and an idle conceit.

Your technology has reached such levels that it could already be called a miracle. It is capable of much more than the god of the poor savage was capable of. Yet is that any reason for you to no longer have God? Most recently, your technology has invented a small cylinder which, loaded with explosives – by itself, without man, without a pilot – proceeds to the target and reaches it, guided with the help of invisible rays or waves.

Just because this container is able to move forward and accomplish its task without man, though, does that already make it a man? No, nothing has changed in essence, and no one, not even the greatest fool, will claim that it is not the same machine, except more brilliantly constructed. Without human guidance, visible or invisible, direct or from afar, it is simply a senseless metal cylinder, with valuable and wonderful mechanical achievements and formulations.

The same holds true of the human and his brain. Just because one cannot see and cannot feel God, or a spirit, within oneself, does that already mean that the cylinder moves forward by itself and without higher guidance? You, too, would call that an absurdity. You claim that the brain does everything by itself, and that people's different abilities and talents depend on the structure of the brain, on some sort of bumps and furrows. Who has formed these bumps and furrows? The brain itself?

Will you claim that a ditch has formed in a well-drained meadow because the meadow is well-drained? No, after all, you will claim that the meadow is well-drained because you have dug a ditch across it and that only a lunatic can claim that the meadow has created the ditch, or the ditch has created the meadow.

Why is it that, when considering your human affairs, you reason so logically, but, once you start talking about the spirits and God, you are no longer able to understand and acknowledge anything?

With that, I will conclude for today. Await Omega at seven. Do not carry anything out of the room, merely arrange the prescribed lighting.←

Chapter X
May 1944 – Part 2

Kolinto   05/07/44

Kolinto is speaking. Greetings! Do you have any questions?

[[We reply that we do not.]]

I want to talk with you a little bit. While talking with the spirits you are not ideal communicators of the spirits' thoughts. Therefore all kinds of errors crop up, starting with spelling and ending with syntax. Hence they have to be corrected according to your rules of grammar, and improper structure of the phrases has to be eliminated. You can do that as long as the correction does not alter the meaning of the sentence. Should some sentence be incomprehensible, then extract it and ask Astra. John has to assume the supervision of the editing.

Therefore, do not adhere to the letter, but to the idea.

Since the High Ruler of Death will talk with you soon, we, the spirits, will leave you.

Santorino   05/07/44 1900

The highest chief spirit in the universe, the promulgator of The Almighty's thoughts, the Ruler of the Future and of Death, the almighty Omega will speak with you momentarily.

Invite the three remaining persons, and wait standing up until Omega arrives. Then seat yourselves, and do not utter a single word, only listen. Wait for ten minutes after Omega beams away. Another spirit will talk with you then.

Stand up! The Almighty's spirit Omega approaches.

Omega   05/07/44

→I, the Ruler of the Future and of Death, am talking with you in the name of The Almighty. Listen to the words of The Almighty, you, His high spirits and envoys to Earth:←

"I, the creator and ruler of everything that exists and does not exist, I, The Almighty, am telling you: Alexander, your request has reached infinity and is heard in eternity. I hear it and reply to you, My high spirit. You were right, and you have the right to speak with Me. I reply. You will understand Me if I will tell you that My decision has been made because only you can carry out that which I desire. You have the right to wonder whether your mission might [not] end the same way as it did in the land of Maya. Yes, I cannot promise you that. However, you, and the six of you, have to help Me save humanity on Earth from the fate of the Mayan people. Do you refuse?"

[[Alexander replies, "No."]]

"Do [the rest of] you refuse?"

[[We reply, "No."]]

→"I gave a free will to the people, but they did not know how to utilize it. Should this situation persist, there is no sense in My prolonging the days of Earth. I will turn it into the dust of cosmos, for I want to — you must understand, I, The Almighty, want to — open the gates to the universe to man and hand him the key of science for opening these gates. I want to give him the wings of eternity for flying into infinity. But he has to be worthy of receiving this key and capable of spreading the wings of eternity.

"To you, too, I gave a free will of choosing. You followed Me freely. I bless you and your work. All the spirits in the universe will congratulate you along the way to the Deoss Temple, and the brilliance of the rays from My Cross will illuminate your way to Me. Follow Me!"

You heard the words of The Almighty. I, Omega, also want to tell you: That honor, which The Almighty has bestowed on you, is unprecedented. In all eternity, His words have come from infinity only a few times in millions of years.←

Alexander, you did right by turning to The Almighty with your request, but did even better by agreeing with Him.

→You, people, do not realize how difficult it is for the chief spirits to find amongst you a sufficiently high spirit who would be capable of bearing the luster of a chief spirit, and could establish contact of the souls. I will speak in your language. It is not possible to find a sufficiently tough metal on Earth that would not melt under the extremely great tension of the spirits' energy. Therefore, The Almighty tasked you, Alexander, to undertake this difficult mission, because all of us can talk through your high spirit. Only three times has The Almighty sent to Earth spirits who were capable of withstanding The Almighty's breath.←

I understand what you said and, even more, that which you did not say.

You are a spirit who strives neither for fame nor for the degree of divinity. You seek only justice and reach only for love. On Earth, too, you were tempted neither by the fame of a priest of God nor by the power which Satan offered you. God, as well as Satan, has allowed you to travel your own path and has neither rewarded nor judged you. Therefore I understand why you told The Almighty that He has placed a superhuman burden on His envoys, for they have been torn away from Heaven. I heard, however, that you thought that you are not worthy to lead these high spirits who, here on Earth, are more distinguished than you, thanks to their age, education, and hearts. The Almighty heard that as well, and He wants all of you to hear it as well.

Mary, John, Janoss, Alexo, and Nicholas, I bless your hearts for good thoughts and deeds. I bless your minds with the blessing of omniscience, and I bless your bodies with the strength to overcome and endure everything. You are The Almighty's chosen ones. You can invite those to join you who are worthy and are capable of helping you by asking for the spirits' consent in each case. Do not ask, however, whether your mission will succeed or not – that depends only on The Almighty's trend of thoughts, which no one knows or comprehends.

Just remember one thing – that which The Almighty told you today – and carry out your task, because now you know what has been destined for you here. That is something that cannot be weighed or measured with any measure on Earth and cannot be bought with all the gold and jewels on Earth.

I, the Ruler of the Future and of Death, am telling you, "May The Almighty's blessing be with you and may His mind be with you."

Ilgya   05/07/44

I, The Almighty's and Omega's envoy, Ilgya, am talking with you.

I congratulate you on [having received] The Almighty's blessing. The moments of doubts are behind you. Along with Alexander, I declined my mission, and now I come to you as Omega's envoy to Earth. The Almighty has entrusted me with the destinies of the nations on Earth, and all spirits who have been sent to Earth are subordinate to me. I will travel with you, for the destinies of the nations on Earth depend on you as well. Let us travel the road which The Almighty has indicated to us, and let us sacrifice our bodies and, if necessary, also our spirits for humanity. May The Almighty's mind cover the Earth.

What The Almighty wants to give to human genius is unprecedented and unimaginable in the universe. The Almighty seeks new pathways for His eternally-seeking spirit, if one may express oneself like that.

Alexander, I am extremely happy that He has comprehended you and that you have understood Him. I, Nakcia, Otranto, Aksanto, Ali, and Shota congratulate all of you and express the joy of our good fortune, because the blessing which you received fell on us as well.

Let us travel our roads and not think about what will happen to us and to our work. This time, let us allow The Almighty alone to bear this burden of responsibility, because His goal is infinitely distant and His burden is too heavy for all the strength in the universe. Let us bow our heads before Him, even if we will not understand His deeds. Through life He gives death, and through death eternal life. Through torment He gives bliss, and through happiness He takes us to torment. Through wisdom He takes us into incomprehension, and through incomprehension He takes us to wisdom. Such are the roads of The Almighty, and only those who do not doubt and who believe can travel them. Only those who, while stepping into an abyss, believe that a bridge will form underfoot, will walk across the bridge, even though it may be only as real and as strong as the rainbow.

Nicholas, I congratulate you, too, in our midst. Place The Almighty's burden on your shoulders, and bear it as the highest blessing. Ask your elder brothers how you can help, and help them.

John, I will give you additional headaches. Take over the leadership in compiling the books.

Janoss and Alexo, continue your task.

Mary, continue your task as well.

Little Nick will have to continue your work.

I will conclude with that, and bless your work on Earth.

Ilgya   05/10/44

The high Otranto will speak today at eight.

I want to talk with you a little bit now about important trifles. To begin with, don't misunderstand our words. If one says that someone is next to Santorino, that does not already mean that he is as great as Santorino but merely that he has earned the high honor of being received by Santorino.

_ ★ ★ ★ _

I will not talk about Alexander but will mention that he possesses one characteristic of the spirit, which precludes The Almighty from finding a substitute for him on Earth. He is capable of preserving any secret which The Almighty has to announce only to His envoy alone. The Almighty can be sure that people will find out only that which they need to know, and not one letter more. In the excitement, even Christ said a few words that were not intended for the people and that they did not need to know. Immense problems arose from that.

_ ★ ★ ★ _

Your beloved Ali will talk with you within the next few days. Since he knows that you now have extremely vast knowledge about all kinds of infinities, he asks you to help him solve a problem which Satan has assigned to him. The assignment is as follows, "A road has been drawn around the globe so that its end coincides with its beginning. One has to reply now whether this road is infinite. If it is not infinite, then where does it begin and where does it end?"

The second question, "What would this road be like from the point of view of someone driving a car, someone riding a horse, a pedestrian, or a snail?"

Then still consider this. A pedestrian walks along this road so fast that he completes this road at least once. A pedestrian walks so slow that only his children, or even his children's children, complete this road. In addition, these travelers do not know anything beforehand, such as what kind of a road it is and where it goes to.

Ali puts all his hopes in you. Therefore don't disappoint him. Are there any questions?

Say that God has proclaimed that to you. One is punished only if one does not do anything. If, however, everything is being done that is within the individual's abilities, then that means that God has assumed the responsibility.

Excuse me for leaving you, but I am being called to England. Until we meet later on.

Otranto   05/10/44 2000

I, Otranto, continue my conversation with you regarding upbringing. Have you thought anything over, and what are your questions?

[[We ask about the first people who would raise children, and when would the teaching of religion start.]]

I want to tell you how the bringing up of children is being accomplished on the planet Iyalaga.

The bringing up of a small child there takes place in the family and in solar palaces, or only in solar palaces if, for some reason, the parents cannot bring up their children. Your kindergarten can give you a vague idea regarding the solar palace.

It does not make sense for one person – the mother – to devote her life to raising children, as is done by you. This cannot be justified from any point of view, this practice of one individual devoting the entire or the greater part of life to another, that is – the mother to her child. After all, the mother, herself, has to live as well. It would be foolish to justify her life as only the life for someone else; everything loses its meaning then. One person can bring up many children. Therefore your system – to have a separate individual for raising one child – cannot be justified and is criminal.

On the aforementioned planet, whose inhabitants have traveled somewhat further along the pathway of culture than you have, they have worked out a system like this:

Everything in the solar palaces is ideally established for bringing up the children. In sunlit halls, which are illuminated by electrical suns on cloudy days, there is a constant circulation of air, which is evenly heated and filtered to remove dust. Open and covered gardens surround the palaces. The children are usually naked in these palaces. They are under the constant supervision of nurses – educators – and physicians. Their food is ideally combined. Milk is kept in containers in which it is exactly as if it had just come from the mother's breast or from a cow. The smallest children sleep in small beds which convey to the nurses each movement and need of the child by means of sound and light signals.

The children generally spend their time in these palaces. The mothers, on their way to work or for other reasons, drop them off there. Other mothers do not take them home at all, if the conditions there are not ideal for the children. They come to the palace to play with them and that is all. No child may be kept in the room of adults at night, so as not to poison him with the adults' breath. The bodies of the little ones are gradually inured in these solar palaces and become so hardened that later on they do not fear anything and can withstand everything.

The adults on this planet, also, are not such fools that one person prepares meals for two or three people. They eat in clubs, while simultaneously watching performances and listening to music and singers. Anyone who wants to eat at home receives food from the club through air tubes in rockets, [which are propelled by] air pressure.

Overall, everyone there has to work four hours a day. Two hours are for mandatory, state social service and for sport, as well as half an hour for school, since one learns there during his entire lifetime.

On leaving your schools you forget soon everything that you have learned there. How about the new knowledge that humanity acquires during your long lifetime? So it turns out that each of your most recent graduating class is smarter than the previous one. You are very ignorant in your old age, when compared to your children – the students. That is not the case on this planet. There you are in the first ranks for your entire life, because nothing new bypasses you; and you do not forget any of the old.

The children are taught from the first year of their lives, obviously, while playing. Letters formed from large figures of the alphabet are [located throughout] the palace and the garden. The children see them constantly in front of them and learn from each other imperceptibly and without being taught by the adults. Later on, individual short words appear, and the children, again, learn to read them on their own. Then they learn, while playing, to write letters in the sand with sticks. Eventually the children have learned to read and to write without realizing it themselves, and without any difficulties for themselves or for the adults. Then the educators continue teaching them. I will give you examples concerning the manner in which this is done.

The first example. The children are taken into a garden or a field and everyone is instructed to pick several flower blossoms, to examine them closely, and to tell what they have in common. The children discover that, and tell you such-and-such. You explain that this component of the blossom is called a petal, this an anther, and this a pistil.

"What are they for?" the children ask.

They are not given an answer immediately. Instead, let's say, a bee is located, it is caught, and the children are told to examine what this bee has on its feet.

"Pollen," shout the little ones. Then the rest is explained to them.

A plant is then examined. It is pulled out, and the roots are examined; the functions of the leaves, stem, and the roots are explained. Later on one turns to bushes, trees, and microorganisms. If you visualize the plant kingdom on Earth, you will have so much to tell that is interesting – from the hundred and fifty-five meter tall eucalyptus to the tiny, flu bacteria, half a micron in diameter.

The second example. The children are taken to the zoo, are divided into small groups, and each group is assigned to closely observe some animal; let's say a lion, bear, and so on. Having come back home, one of the children is asked what the lion looked like. The child relates that. The adult turns to the next one and asks, "Is the lion such as, let's say, Johnny depicted it?"

Little Peter will have something to supplement and to correct. Thus, proceeding through the entire group, the lion grows as though alive in the memory of the children.

That is how the little citizens on this planet are brought up. Probably no worse than how you do it, and perhaps you could adopt something from them as well.

Let us rest for half-an-hour before turning to a description of their schools.

Ilgya   05/14/44

Ilgya. Verily I tell you – man is incapable of comprehending pain until he has endured it [himself]. He is incapable of comprehending someone who is starving until he, himself, has been pushed to starvation. Verily I tell you – it is not possible to make someone who is blind from birth understand that milk and snow are the same color.

You live here in Latvia like people live hardly anywhere else, and what do we see? You are blinder then the blindest! You do not understand what takes place in the world. Every day, even every hour, shapes the destinies of nations, and you keep yourselves busy with your everyday concerns. At a time when entire cities crumble, you howl because there is a hole in your sock. You shout that there is not enough butter to spread on your slice of bread, when millions of people dream of a crust of bread, dry bread.

You claim that you are tired of the war. Well, all right then, watch how your cities burn and listen to how those who are dying beneath the rubble moan. Verily I tell you – the deaf and the blind – you do not see anything, and you do not hear anything. Do you want the lightning of heaven to cleave your silence and set the ground beneath your feet on fire? Perhaps then you will understand what is taking place in the world and who you are.

Verily I say – The Almighty's cup of patience is full, and your ungrateful hand knocks it from His hands. Do not cry, and do not scream if fire and blood will rain on you. Verily I tell you – there is no greater sin than the sin of ingratitude.

I am telling you – a crowd of people once walked along a road. Suddenly a storm started, it uprooted trees. Lightning split and thunder rumbled between heaven and earth. Sheets of rain turned the roads into rivers. The people sought shelter in castles, but the castles crumbled under the strikes of lightning; and the people from the castles wandered around seeking shelter. Then these people noticed a shabby shanty at the edge of the woods. They knocked at its door asking for shelter and for bread.

The host opened the door politely and said, "Come in. I can offer you only a roof, a hearth for heat, straw to sleep on, bread for lunch, and water to drink. If that is agreeable then come on in."

The people pressed into the shanty while muttering words of gratitude.

Days passed, but the storm did not subside. The surrounding fields turned into a wasteland, and the nearest cities into graveyards. In the shanty, however, everything was the same, except the host began to hear ever more often that the straw is too hard, the bread too dry, the water is muddy, and the windows are too dark. Then the wind tore some shingles from the roof and the host asked the people to help him repair the roof. They replied that it is not their shanty, and therefore they had no concern for it.

Then came the day when the hospitable host's patience gave out. He opened the door and told the ungrateful guests, "Leave my nasty, dark shanty and go on to seek bright castles and roast birds for yourselves."

He closed the door behind them.

Verily I tell you – those who have ears – hear, and those who have eyes – see. Danger, death, and starvation stand outside your door. Thus say I, Ilgya, The Almighty's envoy to Earth.

You heard my words. Tell the blind ones to see and the deaf ones to hear.

God's anger will strike with inexpressible harshness those who, during this time of evaluation, think only of amassing worldly goods. They will lose everything in this world as well as in the other, for they are the blind ones who are not worth healing.

The long-awaited moment approaches, but did one have to wait for it? You now begrudge to give a worn-out shirt to someone who is naked and a crust to someone hungry, but the day may come when you will pray to God in despair, "Oh, Merciful, take all my possessions. Leave me naked and hungry. Just preserve my life!"

Will God, however, be able to hear you then, when in the noise of death you will be unable to hear your own voice? Will He be able to spare you if you, yourselves, will not have spared your brothers and sisters, if not one prayer regarding you will have reached Heaven, but only curses and tears?

This is what I am telling you – the nations on Earth – I, The Almighty's envoy and judge for Earth. My ears hear only the voices of the hearts, and my hand reaches out only after good deeds. My judgement is just and, therefore, merciless.

You, Alexander and Mary, have been burdened with the heaviest load which the world knows – the burden of The Almighty's thoughts. Your spirit is on the brink of endurance, and the strength of your body burns up in the fires of Heaven. I do not know how long the body will be able to endure, because one hour of conversation with Santorino costs you a month of your life – and with Omega, even an entire year. Only the smallest mistake is needed, the least interruption of contact during the time of the conversation, and the heart will break. We attempt to help your spirit, but you, yourselves, have to help the body. Only you, yourselves, realize the weight of this burden, which seems like a child's play to others.

In order for The Almighty's chief spirits to be able to establish contact with you and talk through you, they have to utilize all your spiritual and physical capabilities. These are not infinite, but those of The Almighty's chief spirits are infinite. Therefore your strength has to withstand a tension which would melt even a stone.

I announce to you – Otranto will speak in ten minutes, and Ali in the evening.

Otranto   05/14/44

As directed by God, I, Otranto, continue my tiding. First, however, let us linger a little bit on your Earth.

The previous time I had a conversation with Ali, who is observing our course. He said, "Yes, a human child has to learn so much in order to become a fool like the adults are."

That sounds paradoxical, but these words do encompass some truth.

You teach your children to lie, to loaf, and much else that is completely superfluous for them. Formerly you paid attention only to the development of the spirit, therefore the flesh was crippled, or, rather, the bodies. Now you only look after the bodies and have instituted sport as a god. The results – an empty and rattling body, and only a bad stench of the spirit.

The most important consideration is a harmonious development of the spirit and the body.

Then still, as I already said at the beginning of the tiding, your methods of teaching are boring, lifeless, and appalling, as well as entirely incorrect. For example – you have the pupils learn the myths of the gods and heroes of the ancient Greeks. What do these myths give to young heads that are thirsting for knowledge? Examples of brutality! [Examples of] how fathers kill their children and even eat them and how children destroy their parents; how gods deceive maidens by turning into bulls, swans, and clouds; how gods envy and fight with each other; and so on! Consider that for yourselves! Do the unsure minds of the children gain something positive or negative from these myths and fables?

They should be taught, if they are to be taught at all, only in the higher grades, once the young people are already capable of critically examining matters and life. Similarly, humanity's history in its complete entirety should be taught only in the higher grades. Only a brief and interesting overview of history should be given in the first grades, while avoiding everything that is base and that would have a negative effect on the child's psyche.

Your adventure novels have been written only by writers, without the participation of scientists, therefore they contain very many scientific errors.

Then still, one of the more important subjects, which is most potent in unleashing the spirit, is astronomy. Take the child from the very first years of life into the infinitely marvelous space of heaven, so that he could inhale the breath of The Almighty from the very first days of his life.

We will now return to the planet that we left behind on Wednesday and observe how they teach in schools there.

There are general schools there, and colleges which teach professions, in a form as you have already been told. These schools use hardly any books at all. They are useful only for reviewing subjects. All knowledge is presented in a practical manner and with the help of movies. Instead of classrooms, there are large, bright halls with screens in the schools. The technology of movie-making has advanced so far there that the screen shows everything in relief and in natural colors, so that it is not possible to differentiate between what is shown on the screen and what you would see by looking out the window. Besides that, the movies are shown in full daylight.

The day will come when your scientists on Earth will accomplish the same thing as well.

The duties of teachers are minor there. They merely have to direct the instruction and upbringing, for the world's best professors read lectures on the screen in their stead. You will understand that if a genius teaches even the most boring subject, while illustrating it immediately on the screen with three-dimensional examples, then all of these lectures become very interesting.

You will claim that the school deprives children of their families. That, however, is not the case there, because the children are dismissed for a few hours to go home, which depends on their preference and the conditions at home. Special evenings are organized in the schools with theater performances, singing, concerts, reciting of poetry, sports events, dances, and so on. These evenings are organized by the teachers and by the pupils, and each of them can display their physical and spiritual abilities during these evenings.

The parents of the children – their bothers, sisters, relatives, and friends – are invited to these evenings. Therefore everyone breathes the same air and participates in the same activities. Every child wants to show his family what he is capable of and what he has achieved. The parents with tears in their eyes, tears of joy, follow the storm of applause which rages above the heads of their loved ones.

A joint meal follows these evenings. Then the children accompany their guests home and, chatting joyfully, return to school. There, after a refreshing shower, they throw themselves into their air nets and fall asleep.

Besides that, exhibitions are also organized in the schools. Tools, furniture, and other objects which have been made by the pupils are displayed, as well as fruit which has been grown by them – or newly developed plants and animals.

The pupils receive prizes in each school and in every category. The top winner each year receives a prize. The names of these winners are engraved on the golden plaques of the schools for ever and ever. One winner of the planet [is selected] from the top winners in each school. A statue of the planet's winner is placed in the planet's temple of honor, also for ever and ever. These winners are awarded silver and gold wreaths. The respect of all citizens accompanies them for their entire life, and the youth dream of them.

This method is that potent incentive which raises this planet's culture and technology to unreachable heights.

With that I conclude my brief tiding and bid you farewell.

Ali   05/14/44

Greetings, dear children of the Earth! It is almost awkward for me to talk with you; you have become so smart. Nevertheless you have not solved the assignment which Satan gave me. Your inbred sin – laziness – is at fault here.

First [you have to] understand the correct meaning of the word, and only then talk. As I recall, even your human courtesy required that one speaker not interrupt the other. Perhaps I have been away from Earth for too long, though, and in the meantime you have "advanced" considerably.

I wish to talk with you a little bit, and in a friendly vein, about the same topics about which the high and divine Santorino spoke.

Infinity. After all, do you, and do we, understand it? No, but let us attempt to, at least, approach its comprehension.

Please tell me, "Which is older – a ten-year-old dog or a hundred-year-old turtle?"

[[We reply, "The dog."]]

Correct, even though not from the point of view of time.

Then still, "Which one has fulfilled its life's task more successfully – a one-day butterfly or an elephant?"

[[Our answers vary.]]

The butterfly has accomplished a greater deed in one day than the elephant has in over a hundred years. The number of the butterfly's offspring, during the lifetime of the elephant, exceeds the number of the elephant's offspring a billion-fold, and that is the task of their lives.

Let us turn now to the challenging road around the globe. By examining this assignment mathematically, it would seem to be easy to solve, and even the length of the road could be measured. Therefore the road would not seem infinite, but subject to measurement. Let us now start to enlarge the radius of the globe a hundred-fold, a million-fold, a billion-fold, and so on. What will happen to the road now, and what concepts will we acquire regarding it? The moment will come when this road will no longer be measurable by any exertion of the mind. It will become mathematically infinite as well.

Let us return to the road with the dimensions of our Earth and imagine that a traveler walks slowly, stops, and rests while walking along this road, which is unfamiliar to him. Then he will reach places which seemingly he has already seen. Would he have come back, or do things repeat themselves on this road? How can he tell the difference? It is not quite as simple with him as it would seem to you, for much will have changed during this long time; and the people will have changed as well. Should we, however, assume that only this traveler's children, or his children's children, complete this road, what will occur then? Will they be able to tell that this road repeats itself? Perhaps they will claim that history repeats itself.

Consider these seemingly simple questions. You will see just how relative everything is.

The other day I observed Janoss. He was standing in the stable and, with a joyful heart, watched the beautiful swallows and thought, "How beautiful and good they are, for they catch flies and free my dear cows from torment."

The swallow looked askew at Janoss and thought, "That seems to be a rather kindhearted walking post."

Lucifer, having glanced at Janoss's happy and joyful face, told me, "I will turn Janoss into a fly, then we will see just how happy his face will be and how enthusiastic he will be about the swallow."

I talked the kind gentleman out of this pleasant pastime, and Janoss returned home in a delightful mood.

So, we have chatted a little bit. I did not tell you anything particularly important, but you were not much better either. Still, I hope that you will be capable of finding the correct solutions to this day's examples.

Permit me to take leave from you. Now, in ten minutes, Ilgya will talk with you.

Ilgya   05/14/44

I, Ilgya, announce to Alexo that, by request to Omega and Alpha, I have obtained permission for Nakcia to tell him about their joint life on Earth – many centuries ago in Central America. Within the next few days Nakcia will talk with you, and Alexo will be able to satisfy his desires of the heart, except the story will not be about Atlantis.

_ ★ ★ ★ _

I conclude. The Divine will talk very soon about the social structure. Your series of tidings approaches its conclusion.

Ilgya   05/17/44

Ilgya is talking with you. Alexo, Alpha noted Alexander's request, and he, himself, will, in an hour, relate to you your and Nakcia's earthly course in the northern [part of South] America several centuries ago. Lower the curtain and close the door, prepare the lighting as though for Omega. Do not ask anything, and do not talk. Merely read and write it down.

Mary refused to talk with Alpha. Does the refusal remain in effect?

[[Mary replies, "No."]]

Then have Alexo write down [the tiding]. Only three people may be in the room. The rest have to see to it that nothing disturbs you. You know why.

I conclude. Get ready to receive the high ruler of the universe, The Almighty's Chief Spirit Alpha.

Ilgya   05/17/44

The high ruler will talk about the Chibcha people. They lived in Colombia and were divided into several states. The largest was Bogota, and the most brutal one was Sogamoso. There were others as well. Back then Alexo and Nakcia lived in the state of Bogota. Their fate was horrible, and you will hear about it immediately.

Santorino   05/17/44

Santorino is speaking. Stand up! Welcome the high chief spirit.

Alpha   05/17/44

Astra, Astra, Astra. Ilgya, Ilgya, Ilgya. Santorino, Santorino, Santorino. Alpha, Alpha, Alpha.

Alexo, close your eyes for a moment, and follow me in spirit.

It is the evening of the festival night of the sacred goddess – the moon goddess Chis, the wife of the sun god Bucik. You *guechas*, in your magnificent costumes, have set out to enjoy the pleasures of the beautiful goddess's orgy. Many beautiful girls await you. Your eyes, however, have noticed the daughter of the great and rich Kacik. Her beauty has captivated not just only you alone, and you know what handsome and noble rivals stand in your way.

The festival has begun. Intoxicating music can be heard. Then you see Nakcia, we will call her that, who has come out into Kacik's garden. Your heart starts to beat hard, so that it seems that the large crowd of rivals hears it as well. You break through the crowd and stand before the beauty. She is so near, and yet so infinitely far. You, the brave soldier, are scared like a boy. The dark eyes of Nakcia, though, fall on you, and she smiles at the dashing *guecha*, whose lower lip is adorned by several small, gold bars. She begins to count – yes, so young, but he has already killed six enemy soldiers. An enchanting smile appears on Nakcia's rosy lips. Your rivals retreat slowly. You approach Nakcia, and she disappears with you into the night shadow of the garden.

The whole night long she lies in your arms, and your eyes shine from love and happiness, like the stars. You both sense that you have been born for each other, and your lips whisper a silent oath – to belong to each other for life and to allow only death to separate you for a moment. You turn to all the good spirits of nature with a prayer to bless your love. At the break of dawn you proceed to the sacred lake to also pray to the great water spirits – gods – to bless both of you.

The sun casts its golden rays on the distant summits of the mountains, but you are still on the shore of the lake. Then both of you stand up and leave the sacred lake, in order to head home. Along the way you meet old Kacik and stop.

At that very moment the king passes by. Having noticed you he stops, comes closer, and asks Kacik, "I have been told that she is your daughter.

How dare you to hide from my eyes the most beautiful daughter of Chib-cha? I will bestow a high honor on you and take your daughter as my one hundred and eighty-third wife, but despite that she will be my first and dearest wife."

You feel how your body and spirit stiffen. You see how pale Nakcia becomes, but you also see how happily smiles the old and inflexibly natured Kacik, who has finally achieved the dream of his lifetime. You know that there is no salvation, that there are no ears which would listen to your pleas, full of despair.

A few days pass, and the day has come when Nakcia is to become the king's wife. The king's massive castle, decorated with slabs of gold and with jewels, hides Nakcia behind its sturdy wooden walls. You are a soldier, though, and you have friends who know how to die for you. They organize a strong squad and, also, do not spare plates of gold.

Somewhere in the darkness of the night stand llamas, loaded with supplies. Hours pass, and you succeed after all. Nakcia has been rescued, and your squad disappears into the darkness. You have a good guide, and you plan to proceed to the good king in the north. Only a few days on the road and you will be saved. The good spirits, however, do not protect you, and the evil Cia haunts you. The castle guards pursue you and you have to change directions.

<u>Your second ray</u>. Instead of a few days, days have passed whose number is large, very large. You are sitting on the shore of the beautiful lake of sacrifice. Nakcia lies next to you. She is pale and exhausted, but almost even more beautiful. Your bodies are scarred, and your clothing is torn. You are sitting, looking at the tired and sleeping Nakcia and recalling the long and difficult journey.

While eluding the persecutors you traveled through distant lands and even reached the world's largest lake, whose other shore no man has yet seen or reached. You walked across snow-covered mountain paths under the keen observation of condors. You hid in the moss in a dark forest, where, in the wind, ghostly beards of moss swayed from the branches of the trees above your heads.

Then one day you heard the terrible rattle, which was followed by a death scream. Your guide died from the bite of the dreadful snake. You wandered on without a guide and without knowing the way. A jaguar tore to pieces your youngest companion. Two died from fever. The enraged herd of wild boar trampled one. Two others disappeared without a trace. There were only three of you left.

Thus you reached a tropical region. The beautiful hummingbirds shot around like sparks in the branches of the trees while drinking the nectar of the flowers. Fiery blossoms hung in Nakcia's hair. Then you climbed, along the vines and in-between the dark shadows of the trees, to the sun. There, above the treetops, in the rays of the sun swayed a beautiful garden of orchids through which flew swarms of wonderfully beautiful butterflies. You picked the most beautiful blossoms and brought them down to Nakcia, for she loved them so much. You also remember that in the blossoms of the flowers she, herself, looked like the most beautiful blossom. You both laughed at the monkeys who stared incomprehensibly at this living bush of flowers. And you particularly laughed at the funny pepper eater with a large beak.

Then before your eyes appeared the jungle river, full of caimans. In envy you observed the monkeys with their tails, who formed a living chain by grasping each other's tails. This swung back-and-forth and flung over to a tree on the other side. A living bridge had been formed. All the monkeys crossed over on it while laughing at the caimans. You, however, had to take a chance. This time your last friend sacrificed his life for you. The disgusting head of a caiman appeared in your way as well. The sharp teeth were about to split Nakcia's slender body, but then you still managed to stick a sharp stick into this dreadful jaw – and the caiman was defeated.

You remember the loathsome dry-land leeches which stuck to your feet and the lightning-fast blood flies.

Yet even now you turn cold whenever you recall a dreadful night in the forest. Nakcia slept on a bed of leaves, and you dozed while leaning against a tree. Everything was silent. Then you suddenly noticed that a strange shadow fell on Nakcia's face. You waved your hand and something dark disappeared silently in the bushes. You leaned over Nakcia and screamed in fear – a stream of hot blood flowed from behind her ear.

"A vampire, the horrible bat," you shouted as if insane, "this evil spirit of the night wants to rob me of my Nakcia!"

It was extremely difficult to stop the bleeding.

Thus you wandered through forests and deserts. Finally some good people helped you, and now you have been saved on the shore of the sacred lake.

You raise your head from memories and look at the lake. Nakcia, who has awakened, also looks at it. A large multitude of people has gathered on the shore of the lake. A large raft, loaded with gold and jewels, undulates by the shore. The young king comes to the shore. The priests start to undress him. Once the king has been undressed, the priests anoint his body with something and then begin to dust him with gold dust. Sacred music resounds. Fragrant incense burns. Four noblemen, and the king shining like a golden sun, head on the raft toward the sun. In the middle of the lake the king begins to toss gold and jewels into the lake, sacrificing them to the water spirits – gods. People dance on the shore.

After the ceremony of the festival has been concluded, you approach the young ruler and relate to him who both of you are, how you got here, and what you desire from the high ruler.

He listens to you patiently and tells you mercifully, "Yes, you will not be disappointed, because a noble soldier like you has a place in my legions as well."

You are taken to a new life – to the bright happiness of love.

Your third [ray]. A few years of happiness have passed. You have achieved a high position in the king's legions. Today you have to lead them against the terrible eastern king, where mercilessness prevails and where the priests sacrifice young men to gods by tearing their hearts from their chests. Today you have to travel this road toward a dark future, and the worst of it is that Nakcia wants to travel this road along with you. Neither your begging nor the king's command are capable of holding Nakcia back from her pathway of love, and she comes along with you, being hidden by the dust of the road.

Your fourth [ray]. A dark day lies over the Earth. You have been thrown in prison. The battle has been lost. The worst of it, though, is that Nakcia has been lost as well. The merciless king has taken her for his wife. That, however, was also his – the king's – wedding and death night. Nakcia killed the king with his own sword. Today is the day of the king's funeral. The guards come and take you out as well, to observe the funeral. You see the king's corpse in the middle of a meadow. A throng of women is being taken to it. Among them you see Nakcia as well. No, not among them, but in front of them. The priests and the executioners approach. For the last time you meet Nakcia's eyes. Infinite love radiates toward you. These rays dazzle you. When you open your eyes again, Nakcia's spirit has already set herself free from earthly bonds.

The king's corpse has to lie among his wives and a mountain of jewels. Soon a large mound of earth grows over the king, and everything is over. You are taken back to the prison. That is, the guards think that they are taking the great enemy hero, but they are taking only the unhappiest man in the world, whose chest is fire, and mind – despair.

Your fifth and final ray. The morning approaches. High above the lake, you are standing tied to a cliff. Priests, with knives in their hands, stand around you and look toward the east. They await the first rays of the sun – the harbingers of your death. The sky turns ever lighter.

You cast your glance across the wide and silent lake, the curious crowd of people, and the distant meadow, where the fresh burial mound is barely visible. Within it lies your love and your world – Nakcia. Your eyes turn dark from tears, but then you remember who you are and that the crowd might misconstrue your tears. You raise your head proudly and smile at the empty world, which has already died for you.

You smile at the first ray of the rising sun. The blades of the priests' knives split your chest. Your blood, burning like red gold, flows over the edge of the cliff into the cool waters of the lake, bringing the gods the greatest sacrifice of the people on Earth. Your head droops, and your spirit meets her who was waiting for you.

I conclude. Be bright, be pure, be true!

Chapter XI
May 1944 – Part 3

Ilgya   05/21/44

Ilgya is speaking. Wednesday was a difficult, but interesting, day for you; an evaluation of the spirits and the bodies. The high Chief Spirit Alpha gave you the opportunity of looking into the land which had been created by the god Ci-mi-ni-ka Ga-gua. You walked through the large state of Bogota, the noble state of Guatavita, Sogamoso – the state of the dreadful mountains and [terrible] people – and many other states, and inhaled a different air – the air of Earth and of infinity.

As I can see, you do not understand why your previous lives are being revealed to you. You approach that from a narrow, personal point of view but fail to comprehend the main reason. How could you imagine that the high chief spirit would waste his valuable time in satisfying your egotistic interests?

With these revelations, humanity and you are being given the opportunity to comprehend the means of the spirit's movement, his growth and transformation. You can see that the spirits engage in a struggle for their further development, and can see how difficult this struggle is. However, [these revelations] also give you the opportunity to see the sense and justification of this suffering. You can also see that every nation, no matter how far from your current level of development it might be, gives an opportunity for the existence of noble and high spirits – people. You can see that, under the stroke of fate, earthly mud falls from a noble spirit, and he gleams in the eyes of people like a bright sun. You can see as well what occurs if two noble spirits manage to travel their earthly course together. You also saw alien planets, and one with an old and high culture but a cold soul of the people, who do not know mercifulness and God. These people have not achieved happiness, despite them having achieved everything that is capable of giving happiness.

You also saw how merciless the people are and how insignificant is the power of death. To an individual with the vision of a broad mind these revelations are capable of revealing another world, are capable of opening his eyes toward the cosmos, and also of giving him the opportunity to return to his lost soul, not to mention the historical and geographical wealth which they provide. Thanks to these revelations, you can also see yourselves here on Earth, and you can evaluate yourselves. These revelations are a gate to the unknown, a gate which The Almighty never opens. These revelations are such a bright sun that all of you should fall to your knees in front of its rays, because these rays come to Earth only for the third time.

_ ★ ★ ★ _

Otranto   05/21/44

I, God's Envoy Otranto, am talking with you for the last time, prior to taking leave.

I will talk a little bit more about the problem of upbringing. Perhaps what I will tell you is not exactly the problem itself, but it, nevertheless, has to be considered as such, for it is almost as important.

I will talk about matters about which, as it seems to you, it would not be becoming for the spirits to talk. Do not forget, though, that The Almighty is the creator of the body as well. So then, listen!

Many marriages fail because the spouses are not prepared for married life and simply do not know how to get along and how to understand each other. There is, however, one more consideration due to which the happiness of marriage fails, and the spouses seek it outside marriage. The basis for this is the very same human egotism and ignorance.

As you probably know, people possess different temperaments, and they are not always the same in both spouses. One catches on fire quicker and also achieves pleasure sooner than the other, who catches on fire slower and, therefore, remains unsatisfied in his/her pleasure – hungry, if you will.

You will say, "So, what is the problem?"

The problem is large, however, because the hungry one goes to someone else to satisfy his/her hunger. Thus all the happiness of marriage fails.

You will say, "But how can that be helped?"

There is very much that can be done to help if the individual gives up his/her egotism and knows how to love. If he/she really wants to, the one who catches on fire sooner can delay his/her burning sufficiently long until the flames of both reach heaven, and then they both will simultaneously drink the universe's sweetest cup.

What should be done then? Very little, merely such a trifle as a slight instruction in a locked book, which would be given the young people on completing school or getting married. The art of love is a great and high art as well, and everyone who wants to love and wants to be loved has to know it. There is no place here for any excessive modesty, because it does not cover up anything, but only makes everything dark and repulsive.

I conclude my tidings with that, and also take leave from you, while departing from you with The Almighty's consent.

Along with me, Ann bids you farewell as well, and wishes Alexander and all of you, particularly little Nick, a happy and bright future. She says that little Nick is a very good and smart boy, and that with the right upbringing he will not only live up to all the expectations that have been placed on him, but will even surpass them.

Both of us are heading for distant planets.

Be strong, be wise, be fearless!

Santorino   05/21/44 1800

I, Santorino, am speaking unto you. Listen and remember!

An individual is born only through his mother's torment. Similarly, new ideas are born only through the suffering of prophets. Note these words, and do not be surprised that one has to suffer.

I want to talk with you now about the social structure. In essence this topic does not belong in the series of the spirits' tidings, but, because of your request, I will examine this subject, even though not as you expect it.

To begin with – what do you, yourselves, understand by social structure? Is it something permanent or changeable?

[[We reply, "Changeable."]]

[In that case], exactly to what should I respond? Social structure during the cave era, in ancient historical times, during the Middle Ages and now, or in the future? You will understand yourselves that the social structure was not permanent during all these periods. It depended on the level of the spiritual development of the people, on materialistic circumstances, and on those of nature. Therefore neither time nor space will permit us to examine this topic in its entirety, and neither is that necessary.

Let us talk about the future. Let us talk about what kind of a social structure would be best, so that humanity would feel satisfied and happy. The main consideration is the nation, itself. Good nations have good social structures, bad ones have bad ones. Therefore, we have to first get the nation to become good. How can that be achieved?

To begin, with the help of science, humanity has to be liberated from superfluous and hard work. Everyone has to be given the opportunity to readily obtain [everything that is] essential for life. One could not talk about happiness when people had to spend entire nights threshing grain in barns and spinning yarn on a spinning wheel by the light of a taper. Threshing machines have now transformed this farmer's scourge into almost a festival; similarly, weaving mills in factories.

Technology liberates man from the work of a slave. Previously one individual could accomplish – only with difficulty, by working from morning until night – the work that was capable of feeding only two or three people. Now the same person, while working with the help of machinery and only for six or eight hours a day, is able to accomplish work that feeds tens, and even hundreds, of people. With continued development of technology it will suffice to work supervisory work – that is, the work of supervising machinery – for only three or four hours a day in order to supply all of humanity with everything that is necessary and unnecessary; and in order to give everyone the opportunity of obtaining for himself everything that is essential for life and for enjoyment.

The foundation of the social structure is to establish human society so that the benefits from this genius of technology will be enjoyed as much as possible equally by everyone, but not merely by a few who do not do anything themselves. Those who do more and are more capable, obviously, have to be given more as well. All the others, though, have to be placed in a position where they will not lack anything that is essential for life, and for enjoyment during periods of rest. The duration of work should not exceed six hours a day. Besides that, it would be good if community responsibilities, sport, and time for school could be included in this time. It would be desirable to give a day of rest after every three days [of work].

Why do burglaries, murders, and fraud occur? Because the individual has either nothing to eat or to wear. Should everyone, however, have enough to eat and also have sufficient resources for clothing, a good apartment, the theater, some travel, and so on, then all these crimes will disappear on their own, without any judges, lawyers, and jails. Other evil characteristics – such as "brown-nosing," slander, flattery, envy, and greed – will disappear as well.

Therefore technology is the first and foremost consideration in shaping the social structure.

The second, equally important consideration is the upbringing of children. The high Otranto, Omega's assistant in the formation of the universe, has told you about this very thoroughly and beautifully. Therefore it would be superfluous for me to examine this topic. Only it will be difficult to institute this upbringing, for, seemingly, a vicious cycle forms here. Good people are needed in order to bring up good people. This stumbling block has to be gradually overcome though.

These would be the foundations then. You, however, are probably interested in the form – what should the government be like? Here, again, we reach the very same relativity. You are familiar with monarchies whose citizens feel quite happy, and with republics whose people feel worse than in hell. As you can see, the form does not have a decisive significance, but rather the people who structure their government.

There are planets with a high and ideal social structure where the most difficult task is to find rulers, for everyone avoids this difficult and responsible position. To you, who strive for power so much, that seems strange, because, to you, power gives what you lack – prosperity and happiness. There, however, where everyone has more than enough of this prosperity and happiness, these positions of power are simply superfluous and difficult work, for no citizen there is so irresponsible as to – having accepted a position of respect and responsibility – not carry it out according to his best conscience as well. Therefore the rulers there are shown an almost divine respect.

There are also republican structures, and many others, but it is not worth examining them. The Almighty wants man's free spirit and genius to find and establish, for himself, the most ideal system of governing. That can be achieved easily, because you lack neither science nor mental giants.

Do you have any questions? I will answer in ten minutes.

[[We ask about the start of this ideal structure of the state and about settling of private property.]]

I am sorry, but you, yourselves, will have to find the answer to your questions.

Now close your eyes for a moment, and look into the history of humanity.

The cave era. Which of your poor people would want to trade places with a king of that era? None!

To continue. Let us consider the bleak Middle Ages with dark and cold castles of stone. Knights clad in iron and infested with lice and fleas wandered through the gloomy halls. What comforts did they have, and what did life give to the people of that era? Work, fighting, the tavern, the market, and – that's it! Doesn't your middle-class individual live better, more comfortably, and more interestingly now than did the highest class back then? It would seem to me that any one of your working people or bureaucrats, had he accidentally entered into the skin of a knight, would [try to] escape from within it after just a few days. As you can see, you have already come very far in forming your social structure.

Workers in North America earn more and live better than your bureaucrats; except they have succumbed to extremism there, but this will be easy to eliminate.

The more capable nations will form their social structure better, and only better. There is, however, a particularly large obstacle to achieving the goal – that is war. There are two ways to eliminate it. The states can join in one friendly community, but it is doubtful whether this means will be within your abilities. The other way remains – war until the moment when only one state remains in the world, the victor. Then there will no longer be an enemy. Then there will not be anyone with whom to wage war either. The nations on Earth will be able to devote themselves to the work of forming their peaceful future, because after some time all nations will merge into a single nation, and all quarrels will end. The sun of peace, happiness, and justice will rise for everyone. Man will then turn his eyes toward the stars, and The Almighty will give him wings and will say, "Planets which are void of My spirit orbit your sun. I turn them over to you. Become a ruler within the entire solar system, for I have given you My creative spirit, which has neither time [limits] nor boundaries."

You argue much about the word *work*. There is work – God's blessing, and there is work – God's curse. The work which serves the development and happiness of humanity and of man's spirit and body is beneficial and necessary work. That work, though, which oppresses the body and the spirit is a curse, and humanity has to eliminate it, as our great poet Shota said. You will claim that, only thanks to work, humanity has become humanity and surpassed the animals in development. Correct! You will claim that, should man stop working, he will regress again, or else will degenerate. Incorrect! That will not happen, because some work will always remain, and man will achieve a level of development where he will not permit his body and his spirit to degenerate. He will replace the missing work with mandatory sport, and there certainly will not be any lack of mental work.

What should be the relationship between the state and the church? They both will have to merge, for they have the very same goals.

You ask, "How will it be with the teaching of religion?"

Otranto has already told you that a child has to be familiarized with astronomy as early as possible. It is the pathway to God and to The Almighty. Since one can pray to God only with good deeds, then services, prayers, and all religious ceremonies become unnecessary.

Originate new and beautiful ceremonies for funerals, baptisms, and weddings, and nobly and respectfully mention God in them.

Teach the Lord's Prayer to children. Teach them the noblest examples from history of good deeds, of God's love and justice, of self-sacrifice, and of heroism – not only in war, but that of explorers and rescuers of people as well.

With that, I will conclude for today. Be clear, be noble, be polite!

Ilgya   05/29/44

I greet you with the summer's lovely festival. This wonderful weather is the Divine's gift to Latvia and to you. It is also God's appreciation for the tasks which have been accomplished well.

Today at three, the divine Santorino will talk with you about Gods, spirits, and other important topics, without which your work cannot be complete.

A task which is immeasurably difficult and too heavy to be weighed lies ahead of you, for whose accomplishment days are shorter than seconds, and years shorter than minutes. That is the work of a lifetime, not just for you, but also for those to whom you will pass on its continuation. That is the work of generations and generations.

It was begun at a moment when clouds of death covered the Earth, and the Earth moaned and groaned under the mad storm of a war. It will end when the eternal sun of justice and love will shine above the Earth, and the Earth will repose in the lap of fragrant flowers.

_ ★ ★ ★ _

I will talk about the three books which you have been assigned to compile. Janoss and Alexo have accomplished their tasks [to draft the introductions for the first two books] well, but their work should be considered as secondary.

You should initially compile a single book of the spirits' Tidings. All the Tidings of the spirits should be collected in it in chronological order, except for the Tidings of the third book and, for the time being, omitting tidings of a political nature. Note in the book, however, that the tiding of such-and-such a spirit, based on the spirits' instructions, will be included later on.

Let us rest now until the moment of the Divine's arrival. This time Kolinto is satisfied more than he was during the last holiday. He is particularly satisfied with Janoss, who has improved quite a bit in his view. Obviously, it is not worth talking about those who did not sin the last time either.

We will talk some more after Santorino's tiding.

Santorino   05/29/44 1500

→I, Santorino, as directed by God, am talking with you, The Almighty's envoys to the nations on Earth.

Man is permitted to look into the face of God. Listen, and announce to everyone, once the time for dissemination will come.

People should never needlessly endeavor to comprehend The Almighty. That is not destined for mortals, nor for immortals. He is neither visible nor comprehensible. The only perceptible and visible sign of His existence is His Living Cross above the Deoss Temple. [This Cross] changes its brightness and color continuously and, thus, gives the spirits a sign indicating the course of His thoughts. The Cross has grown dim three times, and the world, the entire universe, froze in the foreboding of death. Yet The Almighty's anger vanished at the last moment, and the universe could, to put it in human terms, breathe again.

The Cross is surrounded by a sphere of an invisible element. Every spirit who attempts to approach The Cross, strikes a seemingly infinitely hard, but invisible, wall – and breaks up into dust.

The Deoss Temple is located in the center of the infinite universe, far from the closest stars. It is extremely beautiful, for it glitters like the most magnificent jewel. It is so immensely huge that your entire solar system can be readily placed within it. It is real, and simultaneously unreal, for it is formed from rays of inexpressible beauty and brilliance. Its stairway resembles a carpet woven from the rainbow.

There are two thrones in the rear of the Deoss Temple. On the right is that of God; and on the left, that of Satan. Behind the throne of God is a lustrous white, glittering background. Behind that of Satan — a fiery red background. The scale of fate is between Them. The rays of Chief Spirit Alpha fall on its pans; two rays, a white and a red one, and the pans of the scale rise and fall due to the weight of these rays. Alpha, himself, never leaves his temple. Just as with The Almighty, no one has ever seen him, nor do they comprehend him.

God and Satan have a human form. They have the appearance of extremely stately, handsome, and noble young men, without beards and mustaches. Their height is five times greater than the diameter of your sun, and They are visible from the most distant corners of the Temple.

God's face is bright as the sun, and His smile fills the world with light, love, and happiness. His smile lulls all sorrows and pains, as a mother's arms lull a sick child.

The face of Satan is dark and hard as a rock. The rays of death and ice radiate from His eyes. Your scientists, nowadays, call them cosmic rays.

High above, and in-between these two thrones, is located the throne of Chief Spirit Omega, against a blue background. The high chief spirit, himself, is not visible on his throne. Only his black shadow falls on it, and his voice comes from there.

A stream of spirits flows constantly in the Deoss Temple, flows into it and out. There is a complete void around the Temple itself, and not one spirit can be seen approaching or departing. That seems strange and incomprehensible to you, but that can be explained very easily. A spirit relocates with the speed of thought. This means that he arrives instantly wherever he wishes to be. Therefore, he does not see anything along the way, and neither does anyone see him. At the Deoss Temple the spirits fall from infinity like snowflakes from a cloud, within which it would also be a futile attempt to locate even one snowflake.

My throne is located at the stairway to God's throne. God's high envoys gather around me. Among them are Zoroaster, Buddha, Confucius, Mohammed, and others. You seek Christ in vain, for He was the Son of God, and returned to His Father.

You have already been told about the spirits and their essence. I will relate only what you do not know yet. The spirits converse among themselves in the form of comprehension, besides which the higher spirits can read, to use your terminology, all the thoughts of equally high and lower spirits, whether they are incarnated or not incarnated. The lower spirits, however, [can read] only those thoughts of the higher spirits that are intended specifically for lower spirits.

The spirits do not see in the same way that you see. They see everything in the form of fog, a dark fog. This is because they see not only the bodies, but also the atoms which form them. Thus they see through everything. They see the sun and the stars through the Earth. The walls of your homes, and even of your prisons, are like a thin, transparent veil to them. However, on arriving on a planet, if they desire they can condense the atoms and acquire exactly the same abilities of sight as the inhabitants of that planet have.

Now rest for twenty minutes, and then we will talk some more about matters of Earth in the light of God.

[[After twenty minutes.]]

Now I will talk about religion on Earth.

To begin with, [I will talk] about the existing houses of prayer. Until now, man had not yet achieved a level of spiritual development where he was able to believe in something invisible, beyond his understanding, or even intangible. Thus savages carved gods of stone and wood for themselves. Later on, God's envoys brought the notions about The Almighty, God, and Satan to humanity. However, man was capable of comprehending little and preserved in his memory very little of what had been revealed to him. The remainder he modified according to his abilities to understand.

Your houses of prayer are full of images of gods and the saints. Thanks to these images, gods become real, visible, and even tangible to the people. The only problem is that you transform these images of gods into gods themselves, even though the Commandments prohibit this.

The other problem is that humanity's priests have transformed prayer into a theatrical performance and have killed it completely. What are these services in which, according to a strictly prescribed ritual, the very same prayers are being recited, mechanically and coldly, without the warmth of life? Similarly, people do not pray to God with words which come from a hurt or a joyfully rejoicing heart, but pray with memorized, dead, cold words taken from the pages of moldy books.

In your thoughts, assume the place of God for a moment, and listen to this stream of prayers. A stream of monotonous and lifeless prayers flows to God from your houses of prayer, from your lips, and from your prayer mills. Could you endure for long this racket of the flood of empty words? Would you be able to recognize a true prayer of the heart, to hear it, among these mechanical prayers? I don't think so! If a pauper were to beg you constantly, with the very same memorized words – whenever necessary, and also whenever he did not need anything – wouldn't you send a beggar like that off with the dogs, even though you had the very best of hearts?

Services are not intended for God, but only for the people and, particularly, for the priests. In order to dazzle the mind of a simple individual, these services are held in an unusually splendid form and within halls decorated with paintings and statues, frequently of an awesome form. Thus the commandment of Christ – to pray to God in solitude – is being transgressed.

What should the churches be like? Anything but what they are currently! Their task has already been explained to you. The churches have to be the bearers of love, compassion, and the light of science. They have to be beautiful palaces, decorated with the paintings, sculptures, and statues of great artists, which depict God, the high spirits, humanity's geniuses of the spirit, and good deeds.

On gathering there, bow your heads before God and silently recite the Lord's Prayer, and a prayer of the heart. This would be followed by lectures of highly talented people about life, good and evil, and scientific presentations as well. Concerts would follow in which the works of musical geniuses – dedicated to God, to the good, and to the beautiful – should be performed. Theatrical performances and movies, with a religious and educational content, should be presented as well. Then matters of everyday life, spiritual upbringing, and assistance should be discussed.

This is what a service should be like in a true house of God.

The specific task of the church has already been discussed, but how should one convert to this new church? Very easily, for within it, side-by-side, will stand Christ, Buddha, Mohammed, and other of Almighty's envoys to the nations on Earth. It will be difficult only for the current priests. The true priests of God will understand their delusions on their own and will come to you. However, the false ones will die out gradually and slowly, and will return to the realm of dust.

Do not call on the people to desecrate and smash their gods. Rather, place them reverently in a single hall of The Almighty, as the different images of the one and very same God that have come about only due to the different forms of comprehension and fantasy of the nations. Christ, Buddha, Mohammed, Zoroaster, Confucius, and the gods of other nations will stand side-by-side in the temple of God. They will remind humanity of the future of its spiritual essence and of God's endlessly different depictions in the hearts of the various nations.

The new faith does not come to destroy the old gods, but to unify them in a single, true God who will rule all the nations and all the lands. This faith will not conquer the world by force, harshness, and lies. Rather, it will conquer the world and the hearts of people with justice, love, omniscience, and the demonstration of humanity's goal of happiness.

This faith does not ask man to obey God because He is harsh, but only because He is just and obeying Him means serving yourself, the nation, and humanity's happiness. This faith does not summon slaves to it, but rulers of the spirit, like man with a free will has to be.

The Almighty does not punish people in order to avenge them for their sins, but in order to purify them and elevate them next to His spirit. The Almighty does not force anyone to live in the world which He has created, but permits the discontented ones to pass into nonexistence.

With that, I conclude God's high tiding for today.←

Ilgya   05/29/44

The Divine revealed God's face to you today. Humanity should celebrate this day as the greatest festival; this day and the day when Chief Spirit Omega proclaimed The Almighty's Commandments to humanity [[02/23/44]]. The third festival day for humanity will be your – The Almighty's heralds – remembrance day. It will coincide with the day when The Almighty will recall from Earth His primary one of you [[03/10/71]]. The Almighty commands humanity to celebrate these three days for ever and ever.

You should compile initially a single book of the spirits' Tidings, in which all the Tidings of the spirits should be combined in chronological order. Provide an introduction for this book, and combine the Tidings of the spirits with explanations of a chronological nature.

From this book of the Tidings of The Almighty's spirits to the people on Earth all your subsequent followers will be able to derive all the necessary knowledge. Based on it [they will be able] to create various books of broad – as well as narrow, specialized – scope.

Your next work will be to compile, from this book, those two books whose foundations you have laid today.

_ ★ ★ ★ _

Chapter XII
June 1944 – Part 1

Ali   06/01/44

You have gathered today in fewer numbers than usual; even my Alexo is missing. You expect some joke from me again, but this time I will disappoint you. Then you will expect me to tell you something unusual, and, for the second time, I will disappoint you again. I have decided to talk with you today about matters that you, yourselves, could understand, but unfortunately you are too indolent for that. I will talk about problems that your high spirits of science have discovered and have written into books but you, unfortunately, are too lazy to read them. Hence old Ali has to use his old feet again. I will talk only about what your science has already achieved and understood on its own, so that it would be possible for you to verify the accuracy of my words. So then, let us begin our trip along the roads of the spirit.

First for an introduction. Permit me, my high spirits, to pose a simple question to you. If you were to sow clover next to your house, would your house cat have an effect on the yield of clover seed?

[[We reply that it would not.]]

Too bad, and I considered you to be good farmers! You probably know that bumblebees are essential for the pollination of clover. The more bumblebees, the better is the yield of clover seed. Fine! Bees and clover blossoms – that is understandable, but the cat? What say does it have here? It turns out, though, that it does have, and even a very significant one.

Bumblebees live in borrows and keep their honey in them. The honey, as you also probably know, is very tasty, and besides you the mice know that as well. They destroy the borrows of the bees and thus the bees themselves also perish. Should the mice breed extensively, they can completely wipe out all the bumblebees, and your harvest of clover seed will come to naught.

Wasn't that simple? Let that serve as the introduction to our conversation.

"The world is strange," claims one individual.

"The world isn't fit for anything," says another.

"The world is brilliantly created," the third one says.

Which one of them is right? Let us, too, try to look into this world. Does everything in it proceed as it should, is there something that could be improved? Let us look around thoroughly and let us try to find an answer with your, human, mind and knowledge.

The plant kingdom covers the surface of the land. The plants, it seems, could get by beautifully all by themselve without the animal kingdom. Could they? They could if they did not have to breathe! That is the main point, let's not dwell on trifles. Could, however, the animal kingdom [get by] without the plant kingdom? No, that is clear to everyone! Yet could one get by with only herbivorous animals, because then true paradise would reign on Earth?

[[We reply, "No."]]

Yes, the herbivores would then multiply to such an extent that there would be a shortage of grass and leaves, and starvation and misery would set in. The Earth would turn into a desert and the animals would die out. Here the law of maintaining a balance comes to light. So that the carnivorous animals would not multiply excessively and kill off all the herbivores, and again everything would die out on Earth, it is essential that these carnivorous animals also regulate the numbers of each other by eating each other. That is how nature maintains the necessary balance – everyone can live on each other's account.

Why would all these microorganisms and disease bacteria be needed, though? For the same purpose as well! The large animals, being safe from threats by other animals, would multiply very extensively and would live long, thus annihilating all the weaker ones. Here, however, the bacteria terminate their dreams and kill the proud lion and tiger more readily than they would kill a hare.

You will claim, "For what reason, though, have these dreadful mosquitoes, flies, and other insects – bugs – been created? After all, one can get by without them, and then in the summertime one could doze peacefully underneath a bush and could enjoy the beautiful songs of the birds without being bothered."

Yes, perhaps one could doze after all, but probably nothing would come of the beautiful songs of the birds. Where can the bird gain the strength for singing if its tummy is empty? Thus Janoss could say good-by to his friend the swallow. The sky would be empty and silent.

Besides that, insects are also necessary in nature, for they have a very significant role. Unfortunately, though, I cannot deliver you a lecture on natural science. You know that insects destroy each other as well. If aphids multiply excessively, then ladybugs start to multiply as well, and equilibrium sets in once more. Should the ladybugs destroy all the aphids, except for a few, then they, themselves, would also be destined for death by starvation. When new aphids would start to multiply from the two or three remaining ones they would destroy all the plants. Therefore, in order for ladybugs to exist, aphids have to exist as well. As you can see, a wonderful law governs in the world – the law of equilibrium. The Almighty gave it to Earth, and He allows human genius to adjust it, except this has to be done carefully and within the bounds of reason.

Let us turn to another subject now. You will say, "Perhaps God is right after all, and His world has been created rather logically and is being, perhaps, managed sensibly as well. One thing, though, is completely incomprehensible as well as unjustifiable, and has been instituted with an evil intent – that is pain and the suffering and torment that it causes. God could, after all, free man and all the living beings from that."

It would seem that it will be difficult for God to justify Himself. I will attempt to justify Him. Could you live if pain did not exist? To begin with, tell me, what is pain? Without the sensation of pain your organism would be insensitive like a stone. A streetcar would sever your foot while you were walking along the street. You would continue to walk along while laughing and would wonder why the street has become so uneven. Gradually your blood would drain, you would turn white as a sheet, and would cease breathing.

A poisonous insect would bite you. You would not feel that and would calmly return your soul to God, while wondering how come that you have gotten rid of your body so quickly and unexpectedly. Somewhere in the body something is not in order, the help of a physician is needed. Yet how can the body alert you that it is in danger? If you are endangered then you either scream or else call the fire department. Pain is an alarm bell like that in your organism; without it you would perish very quickly. Pain is that guardian angel whom God has given to your body, but you want to run him off with all your might.

In the last, desperate struggle against God's mind you will claim, "But, dear God, if pain is essential then You, The Almighty, could have, after all, invented some other alarm signal instead of it; one that would not be as painful."

God would reply to you, "Dear human child, that could be done, but you are so indolent that it is possible to force you to take care of your body only with the help of severe pain."

It seems to me, Ali, that I have accomplished my task after all, even though it seemed to be impossible. I remember that, while being a human, I screamed [in pain] night after night but did not go to the dentist. What's there to say if the tooth were to simply announce, "Treat me, I have a cavity!"

Quite probably it would not see the dentist its entire, hollow life.

I do not have much time left, for you were late today. Therefore, I will turn to the third and final topic that I wanted to examine with you.

The Divine told you on Monday about God and other matters in Heaven, which may seem strange to you, people. First of all, many of you will be surprised by God's size – seven million kilometers. That, after all, is an impossible height! Yes, impossible on Earth but insignificantly tiny in the universe.

Let us tear ourselves loose from the Earth for a moment, and let us look into the space of the universe with the eyes of your own astronomers. You know – rather, you should know – that somewhere in heaven there is a sun that is slightly larger than your. Let us say, so slightly that if it were to replace your sun, your Earth could float on its surface like a [beach] ball or a boat. Let us, however, consider another sun, still slightly larger than the former. There would no longer be any floating whatsoever now, it would be necessary to submerge, but Mars would now float. What miracle is there, if your astronomers have measured that the star Alpha Orionis, in the constellation Orion, is three and a half million fold larger than your sun. Yes, only now, looking through an eye armed with science, does man discover in surprise phenomena that seem impossible to the mind.

In the Southern Fish constellation there is a star that is 600,000 times brighter than your sun. There exists a star with such a dense mass that if it were to be poured into a teacup, your strongest fairy tale hero would be unable to lift this cup, for it would weigh merely 12,000 kilograms. That's still not all, though. The mass of another star, having been poured into this cup, would weigh even slightly more – around 80,000 kilograms.

What does your mind tell you about all these simple matters that you could find in your books, if only you weren't so lazy? On your Earth, too, the differences between different beings of the same kind are unimaginably large. The tallest tree on Earth is 300 million fold taller than the smallest bacterium, which you can see in your most powerful electron microscopes. A eucalyptus would probably seem no smaller to this bacterium than God does to you. Therefore do not be surprised, because what you know of the wonders of the universe is still nothing compared to what you will still have to learn, and what you will never learn.

I have run out of time. Until we meet another time. [[1900]]

Santorino   06/01/44 2000

→I, Santorino, am speaking unto you, The Almighty's envoys to the nations on Earth.

The most important moment of fate for the nations on Earth approaches. I proclaim to you an immensely joyful message. Out of all the people in the universe, The Almighty has selected the ruler of Earth, man, as His first bearer of the spirit, and the ruler of the universe. In conjunction with this decision, I proclaim to you the following:

The Almighty has listened to the thoughts of Alexander, has considered them, and has agreed with some of them. Simultaneously with that, I can announce to Alexander that the first stage of his mission has been concluded. He had been sent to Earth to evaluate the human spirit. That has been accomplished and a decision will follow.

I am also announcing to you the trend of Alexander's thoughts, thoughts to which The Almighty listened. They are as follows:

"The Almighty has given man His eternally restless spirit, searching and thirsting for omniscience; a spirit who is capable of extremely great and good deeds, and of most horrible, evil deeds. Man has now reached the crossroads of his fate. He has abandoned the old faiths and comprehension of the world, and in their stead, currently has gained only doubts, and the dreadful sensation of not finding the goal.

"He is no longer capable of believing in the bugbear of children – hell – for he realizes that it was merely an allegory. [He understands] that there is no place for hell, neither in the center of the Earth, nor elsewhere in the universe; that as a place of punishment it does not belong in the world in which God's love has been proclaimed, and that the devil is a nasty and long-since unreal creature. He understands that hell was the whip of a slave. Yet now that he and his spirit have shed the shackles of slavery, this whip has decayed in the dust of time.

"He understands that paradise, a paradise like it had been proclaimed to him, does not exist. It does not exist, not because it would not have a place in the universe, but because this paradise would not be Paradise, but rather Hell. There is nothing in it that would allow a high spirit to feel satisfaction and joy, that would give him something eternally valuable. This paradise does not have a goal. This paradise promises the spirit only eternal stagnation, that is, a dreadful, eternal death.

"The Almighty has comprehended that the time has come to take the childhood book of fairy tales from man's hands, and give him, in its stead, the book of intellect and scientific truths. Having comprehended this, The Almighty has revealed His new faith to man. Yet what has been revealed [so far] – no matter how new, truthful, and important it may be – is still not capable of giving man that for which he craves.

"He wants to know who has created him, has created him for what purpose, and what is the sense of creation. If man knows the goal of the labor, and the sense of the work, then he will accomplish the most difficult work patiently and with joy. If, however, he is given even the easiest work, but work whose goal and sense he does not know, he will never complete this work, unless he will be forced to work.

"If The Almighty wants man to accomplish, and [wants him to] want to accomplish, the tasks which The Almighty has given him, and wants man to follow – joyfully and with a free will – His laws and abide by them, then it is essential for The Almighty to reveal His face to man, and to announce the sense and goal of the work of His creation. Otherwise, the same fate awaits the new religion, as that of all the other former and current ones."

These were the thoughts that The Almighty considered. Once He had decided about the capabilities of the people on Earth to follow the call of His spirit – as the first ones in the universe – an obstacle arose, with the possibility of overcoming it bordering on the impossible. In order for it to be possible to announce to the people what they desire to know, both Chief Spirits, Alpha and Omega, have to speak simultaneously.

That is unbearable for a spirit, even for the strongest one. That is almost unbearable, and only one spirit on Earth has a chance of enduring that. Yet even if he were to endure that, he will lose his strength for continued work for a prolonged period of time. He has to sacrifice extremely many years for these minutes. No one could have been assigned this task, but Alexander undertook it, even though he had to turn down his great task on the planet Ometo.← The missions that were intended for you there disappear at the same time as well. Only the question remains now, whether Alexander's spirit will be able to withstand this unimaginable pressure, for Mary is capable of withstanding only one quarter of the pressure of Omega's spirit. This time she will have to attempt to bear one third of the pressure. That will cost her infinitely much, but I, Santorino, knowing her willingness to sacrifice herself, gave The Almighty a reply in her stead. Therefore, Alexander will have to withstand two thirds of the pressure of Omega's spirit and all of that of Alpha's spirit.

The Almighty will still evaluate his strength until Sunday, and then – we do not know what then....

→Now listen. Sunday at five o'clock, Omega and Alpha will herald to Earth about The Almighty; about the creation of the universe; about the course, sense, and goal of that creation; and about the purpose of creating man and the goal for human life.

What is not yet known to any creature on the planets, will be proclaimed, and to you, humans, will also be revealed what even the high spirits have not heard so far.

You must realize what an event, in the eternal flow of time, approaches the universe, not to even mention humanity.

At three I will explain what has to be done. You have to be present, and invite still three more selected and worthy people, so that there would be three times three.

Sunday at three I will announce who can be admitted. Pray to God to invigorate your strength.←

Ali   06/03/44 1700

I summoned you again today in order to discuss what we did not get around to on Thursday.

Man possesses a characteristic that is not particularly desirable. Quite often he considers many important phenomena rather superficially, or else does not seek the causes of the problem where they are located. My high ruler, the sultan, usually told people like that, "If you have a cold, then stick your feet into a bath of hot water, rather than your nose."

You complain about different mishaps, and generally only because you do not know how to find and avert their causes. You do not believe in the spirit and in God because you cannot see and understand them; because they seem to you – rather, to your mind – incomprehensible and amazing. The previous time I told you enough about wonders. There is, however, a wonder that is unimaginable to the human mind. This wonder flies around you all summer long, and you curse it with every step. This big wonder is the insignificant mosquito.

Tell me, why? You know that the mosquito flies. Do you know, however, that in order to fly it has to move its wings? It moves them at a speed that your mind refuses to grasp – more than 500 times a second. As you can see, if even a mosquito can provide you with such wonders, what wonders then can God provide for you? Therefore, for once, let us cease wondering and not believing merely because we do not understand something.

Hasn't current humanity, with the help of technology, exceeded all the dreams of former generations? Was their fantasy capable of achieving what reality has now achieved? They dreamed of flying on a magic carpet, or with the wings of a bird. You are now flying in magnificent and comfortable cabins, that is – are flying with the entire house. Wouldn't your ancestors consider an individual to be mad if he were to claim that someday a person, while standing in Paris, will speak and sing so loud that everyone on the entire globe will hear him? This miracle has come true, and to you it seems so simple and commonplace for, after all, it is the ordinary radio.

Let us now turn to an important concern. A part of humanity acknowledges only matter, and denies the existence of the spirit. They claim that matter transforms by itself; develops, thinks, and directs itself. Do they understand the essence of matter, though? Let us examine the laws that govern in the realm of matter. You know that matter consists of atoms. The atoms consist of positive and negative electricity, of the positive nucleus and the negative electrons. The objects that have been formed from matter are inert. A stone will never consider moving on its own, but having been set in motion it will not stop on its own.

You can observe extreme variety and even wonderful beauty in the plant and animal kingdoms – much that exceeds the bounds of necessity. Matter could not be enticed to such things strictly on its own, [it could hardly be enticed] to the most necessary ones. The plants could get along quite well without blossoms – division [of the cells], and spores, would suffice. The animals, too, could be much simpler, more primitive. Who drives these animals to change their shapes and appearance, and to strive to achieve some sort of an ideal perfection? Who plants beautiful gardens around the house, and tries to create ever more beautiful flowers and more beautiful animals?

"The owner," you will say.

Yes, an owner like that, who attempts to make His world more beautiful and ideally perfect, has to exist in the universe as well, and this owner is God. Only those who are completely blind are incapable of seeing that, and only utter fools are incapable of understanding that.

Should a savage see a car for the first time, and the driver sitting in it at the wheel, he would probably claim that this monster – the car – has seized this unfortunate individual and is dragging him to its cave to devour him. As a minimum, it would appear to him that the car guides and carries the person, rather than that the individual drives this monster with huge eyes. He would judge with irreproachable logic from the point of view of his mind's development. That is understandable, and none of you would be surprised at the savage. Should there be, though, among educated people, and even professors, people who consider matter – the car – as a being that is independent and conscientious, and capable of molding and guiding itself, then....Then what can one say about people like that? It will be better not to say anything.

Let us turn to man, himself. Why does man, if there is no spirit within him and if he consists of only matter, reach for things about which matter doesn't even have any inkling, because they are entirely alien and in their essence even hostile to matter? Why has this matter, in the shape of a human, created the spirits, its soul, and gods in heaven, starting with the very first steps of its history? Why have they, these children of Earth, created immortality for themselves, and sought and found heaven and hell for their souls? Why does this product of matter strive so much for perfection and beauty? Why does it invent so many objects and instruments that serve more its spiritual interests rather than the needs of the body? Why does it, with the help of telescopes, seek an answer in heaven to questions that can be of interest only to the spirit? Why does it fly in a dream, and see things that are unknown to it in life? Would it not be simpler and more sensible to confess that matter is not the master and guide of man and of the universe, but rather it is the spirit, and the spirit's highest substance – God or The Almighty?

The most important day, not only in your lives but also in the life of the entire humanity, lies ahead for you tomorrow. We, the spirits, are with you. With bated breath, speaking in your words, we await this moment. The Almighty also places an extremely heavy burden on the strength of a high spirit like Alexander. We will not be surprised if we will be able to welcome him tomorrow in the Deoss Temple. Mary's burden is also heavy, but Aksanto took on himself half of it. He will share his spirit with Mary's spirit tonight. Superhumanly heavy burdens will lie on the spirits of John, Janoss, and Alexo as well. All the others, too, will be co-bearers of this extremely heavy burden, even though their bodies and souls will perhaps not feel this at the moment.

Today is the final day of the evaluation of the spiritual strength. Let us hope that The Almighty will do everything so that what has been promised will come true.

- ★ ★ ★ - [[1845]]

Ilgya   06/03/44 2039

You had to wait. Excuse me [for that]. The destinies of the Eternal City delayed me. The Eternal City trembles under the roar of cannons and counts its last fateful minutes.

With a sad gaze, Shota observes the suffering and destruction of the divinely beautiful Italy. He is resting at the moment on the summit of his beloved Mt. Elbrus. His gaze, however, wanders across the plains of England, where army regiments roll like a black, dreadful wave, and a man raises his arm for the fateful signal.

The bright sun of the future – tomorrow – will light up during these, the Earth's darkest days. [It will be] the lighthouse which The Almighty will light for humanity's spirit, intellect, and happiness – an infinite, inexpressible happiness – compared to which the current horrible nightmare will seem to be trifling and insignificant. As of this moment I will be with you, particularly with Alexander. My prayer before The Almighty is ardent, and I believe that it will overcome the space of infinity and will reach The

Almighty, and that The Almighty will give His blessing to you and to the strayed nations of Earth.

Alexander, I cannot help you to bear your burden. That is almost unbearable for me, but we have to endure that. Neither Santorino, nor God, nor Satan, nor Alpha, nor Omega can help you. Only The Almighty can help you and He, as usual, remains silent. His Cross above the Deoss Temple burns evenly and brightly, and only at the last moment bolts of shadows begin to flicker among the rays. The face of God becomes serious and hard. The gaze of Satan is turned toward infinity, and He is gentle and sad.

I will stand next to your bed tonight, and will pray to The Almighty for you, and for all of you – children of the Earth. Be steadfast in your faith in The Almighty's merciful justice, in God's love and helpfulness, and in the righteous justice of Satan.

Be alert and strong!   [[2100]]

Santorino   06/04/44 1500

→I, Santorino, am talking with you. The creator and ruler of the universe, The Almighty, will speak, through His Chief Spirits Alpha and Omega, unto the nations on Earth at five [o'clock].←

The room has to be darkened so that the light falls only on the table. The following objects have to be in the room: One round wooden table with the circle of the alphabet, nine wooden chairs, nine paintings, and nine people. I summoned ten people today, because one has to be at the door of your room as the guard between the worlds of matter and of the spirit. I permit the four guests to select from their midst the worthiest one for this high assignment.

Alexander and Mary will talk with the spirits. Two of you and one guest will write down [the conversation]. The rest have to conduct themselves calmly. No question may be asked, and none of those present in the room may react with any movement to anything, no matter what might occur in case of a catastrophe, for it, perhaps, will be overcome. Those who will write have to group themselves around the table. The remaining five in a semicircle behind them, but no closer than half a meter. Those who will be present have to remove all metal objects from their pockets and leave them in the outside room. Those who have crosses have to remove them from their chests, and place them together with gold rings in a saucer, which has to be placed underneath the top leaf of the table.

At five o'clock have all those who are present, except those talking, rise, and seat themselves only after the first word has been read off.

After the tiding has ended, have everyone stand up for a minute, in order to bid farewell to The Almighty's high spirits.

I conclude. Be strong and you will overcome.

Alpha and Omega   06/04/44 1700

→We, The Almighty's Chief Spirits; I, Alpha, Ruler of the Beginning, the Past, and the Present; I, Omega, Ruler of the Future and of Death, and the promulgator of The Almighty's thoughts; speak unto you, the nations on Earth, in the name of The Almighty.

At one time only the immaterial spirit of The Almighty existed in the space of universe. The Almighty [existed], and matter, which, like fog, immobile and dead, filled this infinite space – immobile matter, within which lay equally immobile energy.

Intolerable tranquility and unbearable silence reigned in the universe. This tranquility and silence had neither a beginning nor an end. This tranquility and silence had neither a purpose nor any sense. They were hostile and unbearable to the living spirit of The Almighty. The Almighty's spirit felt inconceivably lonely in this dead universe of matter. It was intolerable for The Almighty's immortal spirit to live in this immobile and aimless universe.

Overcome by inexpressible despair, The Almighty, in extreme anger, shattered the universe of matter. A cosmic storm arose. Matter was perturbed and began to move. The dormant energy within it arose, and maelstroms of matter started to whirl in the space of the universe. The transformation of matter began.

Once perturbed, matter could no longer stop and calm down. Nebulae came into being, these condensed still more, and the so-called suns formed, which rushed through space with enormous speed. They collided and caused huge conflagrations of the universe. They rushed past each other, extracting huge tongues of fire from each other. They parted in the space of heaven, but new, small stars – suns – were left behind them. On cooling down, these became hard and dark. Thus planets came into being.

The Almighty bound matter within His laws, and began to investigate and form this universe. As helpers for Himself, and so that He would not be alone, He created the spirits from His spirit. Yet He failed to achieve the second goal. He remained lonely, for the spirits whom He had created were the very same He, simply split into many parts. Imagine, if you humans could split yourselves into several parts, would that save you from loneliness? All of your parts would think, talk, and act the same way as you did. Simply put, you would see yourself, multiplied innumerable times, [reflected] in a mirror with a cracked surface. In order for you to preserve yourself, and find a friend, you have to use other means; you have to bear children.

On many planets the conditions arouse where matter on them had hardened into rock and soil. Clouds floated above the ground, it rained, rivers murmured, waterfalls roared, seas billowed, and winds howled. It seemed that matter was alive, but it only seemed like that.

The spirits turned to The Almighty and said, "You had us rule over stars and planets, but this rule has no purpose and no sense. Why does it rain on ground that is lifeless and empty? Why do rivers flow into seas, which are empty and meaningless?"

Once again The Almighty felt alone and despaired. Yes, the space of the universe glittered with stars. Yes, there was eternal noise and movement on the planets. Yet all that was and remained the very same lifeless matter – the hostile and intolerable, dead matter.

Time passed. Then The Almighty undertook an inconceivably great and difficult labor. He undertook a struggle with the very essence of matter. He decided to create living matter. After long, endlessly long, struggles, the great moment arrived when matter began to live. Atoms created the first molecule, and the dead matter began to live and to breathe. Living beings came into being. The ground became covered with grass and trees. The water became filled with fish, the surface of the ground with animals, and even the air with insects and birds.

Now The Almighty and the spirits faced a new task – to form this living matter in a way that it would attain an ideal perfection, would be capable of comprehending the spirit and of ascending to him, and, having comprehended the spirit, would cease its hatred and would merge with the spirit to realize the loftiest goal – the creation of the most ideal universe.

One goal still remained, though – The Almighty's desire not to be alone, and to acquire spirits for Himself who would be capable of understanding Him, and of helping Him in forming the universe. This goal had still not been achieved.

Then The Almighty began His second gigantic work of creation. He had given the animals a brain, that is, a complicated nerve center, because the animals had to move and had to seek food for themselves. They also had to fight and adapt themselves to the demands of life and nature. With His spirit, He spiritualized this nerve center, which so far had been guided by instinct. He created man on Earth, and other beings, similar to him, on some other planets, but not many. He formed a wonderful brain for this man, and turned this wonderful thought-laboratory over to the spirit.

The cycle of loneliness was concluded with that. The Almighty's spirits, on incarnating in human bodies, engage in a struggle therein against the living and hostile matter. However, this is not a struggle of destruction, but a struggle of resurrection and transformation. The spirits give much to matter, and they, themselves, also receive much and transform, thus helping The Almighty to form an ideally perfect universe and conquer the inertia of matter – [its desire] not to live and its hatred for His spirit, for having forced it to live and to move.

Man's task is, by combining the strengths of the spirit and of matter – the body, to rise above the currently existing laws of nature and to create an ideally perfect and eternal being, who will ascend to the level of divinity, and jointly with The Almighty will undertake continued formation and ruling of the universe. This is what the goal and sense of human life is. For the time being, while it still has not been possible to overcome matter and to form an immortal body, the spirits have to travel from one body to the next.

To you, the goal of humanity's life may still appear to be unexpectedly great and unachievable. However, that may only seem like that, for man is guided by The Almighty's all surmounting and immortal spirit.

With that, The Almighty achieved His second goal. He, the father, with the help of matter, the mother, has created for Himself a son – man, who will be He, and also not He.

You have to keep one thing in mind, though. You have now been given the opportunity to understand The Almighty and the universe which He has created, to understand the Almighty's sense of creation, and the goal and sense of human life. While understanding all this, you have to comprehend on your own what you have to do, in order to achieve this goal.

To those who do not wish to heed the call of The Almighty, He leaves only one alternative – the road to nonexistence. All those who do not wish to heed the call of The Almighty – to form the world and to reach the heights of the spirit, The Almighty – to them The Almighty promises neither Paradise, nor threatens them with Hell. He merely allows them, as unnecessary [specks of] dust, to drift through the window of the universe into the darkness of nonexistence.

The Almighty divided Himself into two high spirits – God and Satan. They are visible to the spirits, and They are accessible to them. God has the right to uplift the spirit of living beings and of man, and to illuminate him with light and love. He has been given the right of listening to man and of helping him.

Satan has the right to evaluate man, to punish and to destroy him. Observing from the human point of view, God possesses only everything that is good, and Satan – everything that is evil. Therefore, pray only to God, for The Almighty will not listen to you. Do not pray to God with words, but with good deeds.

We, The Almighty's Chief Spirits, Alpha and Omega, bring to you ten, and to all the people, The Almighty's blessing and the love of God.

May you be bright as the sun, and strong as steel.←

[[1845]]

Ilgya   06/06/44 1615

Ilgya is speaking. After the fateful day, I am glad to be talking to all of you, particularly to Alexander. I want to talk to you about our personal concerns. This time, however, these personal concerns lose their narrow, personal aspect and encompass the destinies of the entire humanity.

When Aksanto and I learned of your bold request to The Almighty, and that He had consented to it, we felt entirely crushed and lost, for how can man's spirit withstand the pressure of The Almighty's spirit, if none of the higher spirits are capable of that. That is why The Almighty does not speak directly to any of the spirits.

Aksanto turned immediately to Santorino and God, and received permission to help Mary – by sacrificing his own spirit. My path, however, turned out to be much more difficult, because for me remained only the possibility of turning to The Almighty through Omega. I implored The Almighty not to place this burden on Alexander's spirit, for it cannot be borne and will kill him.

The Almighty's reply came, "Alexander did not obey Me in the land of Maya, why then should I listen to him today?"

I replied, "Almighty, it is not he who implores You, but I implore You on his behalf and my own. At least permit me to share with him in bearing this burden."

The horrifying reply came again, "Ilgya, you also did not obey Me. Why should I listen to your request?"

Then I turned to The Almighty for the third time and said, "Almighty, we both sinned back then. Therefore, place this burden on both of us as well, but not only on one."

The Almighty's final reply came after a prolonged period, "Your words have truth to them, and even I, The Almighty, am not allowed to disagree with the truth. I have to give you an answer about why I act like this. Listen!

"I listened to Alexander's thoughts and accepted his offer not because I want to punish him, but because I love him more than you – Ilgya, an insignificant spirit – are capable of. While loving him, though, I give him the opportunity of doing what other spirits are incapable of, so that he, himself, could ascend to Me, for he will never permit Me to elevate him. That is one motive of My action.

"The other is to save humanity on Earth, and to ascertain whether the human spirit and body – matter – by supporting each other, have already achieved a level where they are capable of withstanding what neither of them can withstand individually. Alexander's high spirit has achieved a high level of cooperation with matter, and matter follows the leadership of the spirit and does not reign over his spirit, as is still the case with a large majority of people. Therefore, should this spirit, while drawing strength from the living matter, withstand the mightiness of My spirit, then it is clear that man has lived up to My expectations, and his future becomes My future. All objections disappear, love is extinguished, and tears dry off in front of this important goal.

"You understand now which of us, you or I, will lose more should Alexander's spirit break. Your question will not ease your concerns, but will bring you inexpressible sorrow. I still have to tell you that in order to achieve My goal, Alexander's spirit and the strength of his body have to withstand the mighty pressure of My spirit by themselves. Therefore Aksanto will not share with Mary. She will bear one eighth of the pressure only for a moment, and then the entire pressure will gradually transfer to Alexander alone. The pressure will be dreadful until contact will be established, and then it, the pressure, will spread throughout all nine people. If Alexander withstands the pressure, then nothing will threaten him any longer, but if he will not withstand, then.... Of all the spirits, I permit you alone to be with him, in order to escort him into nonexistence."

The Almighty's voice grew silent. I also remained silent, for what could I say after that?

The fateful moment approached. I looked at God and Satan, and.... I don't know, how can I explain this to you? I could not differentiate who was God and who was Satan. Their faces had become equally hard and sad. The background behind Them had disappeared. Neither did Alpha's rays radiate, and both pans of the scale dropped simultaneously. Omega's shadow rose above his throne and covered the entire universe. Even The Almighty's Cross barely shone through this deadly, dark shadow.

Then I understood what man means to The Almighty, and what expectations He has placed on this creature of His. I understood how insignificant are my sorrows and I, and how correctly Alexander has acted by devoting everything to the future of humanity.

I came down to you. Blood of sacrifice flowed in the streets of the Sacred and Eternal City. You sat in the dark room, and seriously and with reverence awaited the moment. None of you, though, sensed even remotely the drama and significance of this moment. Not a single spirit was any longer on Earth. Aksanto was the last one to leave it.

Chief Spirit Omega began by drawing his sign. You withstood the pressure of his spirit wonderfully easy, and a ray of hope arose in me. Then the pressure of Alpha's spirit began to arrive, and I observed in horror how Alexander's spirit began to bend. The energy of matter, though, hastened to his aid with inconceivable strength, and Alexander began to lift his head up again. Then, however, came the final pressure and I felt that Alexander's spirit was bending and was getting ready to break.

I could not bear this and cried out, "Almighty, what are You doing? Stop!"

At this moment the energy of matter rose for the second time, and by merging with the spirit opposed the immeasurable pressure. This gigantic struggle of strength, of the combined strength of the spirit and of matter against the pressure of The Almighty's spirit continued for several seconds. When it already seemed that the struggle has been lost, contact was established and The Almighty's words began to sound.

Forgive me, but I left you. I could not retain tranquility and headed into infinity again.

The voice of The Almighty met me there, "Ilgya, are you able to express how happy you are?"

"No, Almighty," I replied.

"And what is most unusual," came the voice once more, "is that I, The Almighty, am also incapable of that. My greatest goal will, after all, be achieved eventually!"

I asked softly, "What will happen to Alexander's spirit, though?"

"Let us allow him to live on Earth, as he wishes, as an insignificant, according to his thoughts, individual."

"Yet after that," I asked.

"After that? He undertook this unexpected mission on his own, without asking for anything, rather – without any conditions. I, too, did not promise him anything, so then – My hands are free. Neither do I promise him anything now, except for one thing – you will follow him to Me."

"And Mary?" I asked.

"Mary is God's spirit and God, Himself, will know what to do."

"But the rest?"

"The rest? Without them knowing it, they have given Me much, but you know that whoever gives Me something receives back a thousand-fold, and that whoever takes something from Me pays back only a hundred-fold."

The Almighty grew silent, and I returned to you.

Alexo's poor Nakcia, just as I, wandered through infinity. I calmed her down. Alexo had sat down outside the semicircle and received much more pressure, but if one recalls The Almighty's words, then Nakcia can congratulate him.

Argus will speak in half an hour, and the Divine following him. Get ready!   [[1750]]

Argus   06/06/44 1820

I will speak very briefly. As you can see, what had been announced to you is being realized, because we announce to you only the unalterable. [[This refers to the D-Day invasion.]]

I have to conclude, for the Divine will speak immediately.

Santorino   06/06/44

Those of you who are talking do not have to stand up. Greet [the spirits] only on parting.

Since Ilgya has already told you about the great moment in the universe, then I have nothing else to say about it. I can only congratulate heartily all of you and the entire humanity.

I want to talk about something else, yet something that also may relate to this moment.

The Almighty expressed a desire, not an order, for humanity to celebrate three festivals – the festival of your remembrance, the festival of the anniversary of the day when the Commandments were given, and the festival of the anniversary of the day when God's face was revealed. He wants humanity to combine the latter festival with the festival of The Almighty, by celebrating it for six days. This festival should be celebrated as follows:

The first three days should be dedicated to the recollection of humanity's past. During these days people should dance the dances of old times, and should perform the best musical works of the best composers of the past. The works of the best writers of the past should be performed in theaters and on television, the poems of the great poets should be recited, and lectures should be read about the geniuses of the spirit and of science. Scenes from humanity's history should also be shown in theaters and on television, scenes from its very first days until the present day. Life should be shown as it was. People should be shown slavery, poverty, war, the Inquisition, torture chambers, and the churches and gods of all religions, by conducting services in the churches and by opening all museums. In a word – have the people live for these three days only in the joys and sorrows of the past, have them remember humanity's difficult road to justice and to happiness, and have them remember those who have led humanity along this road.

The last three days should be dedicated to the present and the future. Let unlimited joy and beauty reign during these days. Dedicate these days foremost to The Almighty and to God. The year's best plays, television films, and shows should be shown during these days in theaters and on television. The best composers should perform their best works in concerts, a competition. All poets, writers, musicians, composers, artists, scientist, gardeners, craftspeople – in a word, everyone who functions in the field of humanity's culture – should show, during these days, the people their best works and achievements of the year, that is of the year which is being celebrated.

On the last, the sixth, day the winners of the competitions should be awarded prizes, and this day should be dedicated to them. Every school, every city, every district should dedicate this day of the festival to their prize recipients. All the people [should dedicate this day] to humanity's brightest spirits – humanity's geniuses. Those who have received prizes should go to the temples of humanity's geniuses during the evening of the last day of the festival, in order to meet there in spirit with the mental giants who have departed, and in order to hang their wreaths on the wall next to them, in the place of the wreaths of the previous year.

This festival should be a motivation to humanity for the achievement of the ideal, and a gift of gratitude to the departed spirits who have built humanity's temple of the sun.

→Let's talk about The Almighty now. You expect everything from Him, even the impossible. You ask it of Him, and are disappointed if your requests do not come true. Frequently you reproach The Almighty because He has given humanity laws of nature, and other laws, which bring not only happiness, but also misfortune and misery. You have to understand that quite often The Almighty cannot fulfill all your requests, or rather – is incapable. Why? You have to understand that, because many of you claim that in such case The Almighty is either not almighty, or else is evil in essence. Yet is that the case? No!

Let us say, could man manufacture a knife that would slice bread and meat, but would not cut his finger? You will respond that it is obviously foolish to ask for this, not because man's genius would not be up to this task, but because this task in itself is absurd. When things like that occur with The Almighty, though, then that is no longer absurd. Think [about that] for yourselves, could The Almighty create a fire that would burn wood in a stove, but would not burn it in the walls of a house? Could He create water, which would moisten the thirsty soil and wash the dust from its face, but would not soak the young lady's expensive dress and would not rinse the perfumed powder from the beauty's face? Could He create a sun which would shine in the daytime for one individual, and at night for another? No, and once again, no!

He has given man a mind in order to control and exploit the fire. If man has turned this fire into a monster which now devours his cities and culture, then the fault here probably lies not with The Almighty, but with the confused man himself.

The Almighty has given man a mind in order to protect himself from the wet rain by means of an umbrella or a cape. The day will come when man will be able to control the rain clouds in the sky as well.

Although He could, The Almighty does not give continuous sunlight, day and night. Instead, He again gives man a mind. This mind, starting with a torch and a candle, now lights electrical suns in his homes and streets. God has not given man a body which would be immune to germs. He has, however, given him a mind, with whose help he will destroy the power of these germs to effect him.

He, The Almighty, has given man His spirit and a mind. With the aid of this mind, man will be able to light suns for himself in the daytime as well as at night, as needed. With the help of this mind, man will overcome everything and will become the ruler of the world.

Have you considered that what The Almighty has created in the universe surrounding you is not a miracle, but that the greatest miracle of His creation is the brain, which He has created and given to man.

With that, I will conclude for today.←

The high Shota will sketch a magnificently beautiful scene for you within the next few days. [[1945]]

Santorino   06/08/44 1700

→I, Santorino, am talking with you.

The world is experiencing its most fateful and most painful moments. At such moments the transformation of all ideas usually takes place, and new ideas are born. At moments like that God, too, has to come to the aid of humanity, by bringing it hope and a new religion.

I would like to return somewhat to the more important problems which have been considered recently. Alpha and Omega gave you a feel for the mightiness of the epos of creation by The Almighty. You could comprehend the despair of The Almighty's immaterial spirit, in the universe of the dead and immobile matter. This universe was something, but this "something" was inexpressibly more ghastly and unbearable than "nothing." After all, "nothing" does give peace; it has a goal. Yet this "something" did not give anything and did not promise anything, except only eternal tranquility, stillness, and a loneliness full of despair. Is it possible to imagine anything more dreadful? And from this ghastly "something," The Almighty started to form the universe which you see today.

Contrary to what many of you think, The Almighty's toil of creation has not ceased. It has merely begun. All the spirits and all living matter are involved in this work of creation.

Man's task is, with the aid of the wonderful laboratory – the brain – given to him, to help The Almighty in this gigantic labor, [while man is] simultaneously uplifting himself, and matter with the spirit, to the heights of immortality and ideal perfection, alongside The Almighty.

Man, consisting of two substances – the spirit and matter, must strive to unite these substances into a single one, which will be sovereign and almighty. In most cases man finds himself, so far, only at the beginning of this road, and is a slave to matter. Only individual people, in whom a high spirit has fortunately met extremely progressive matter, pull humanity forward and elevate it – despite its strong power of inertia.

The spirit is creative and cannot endure tranquility or standing still. He is active and a seeker.

Matter is inert. It adheres to tranquility. Once set in motion, it can no longer stop again. Therefore, it is hostile to everything that disturbs its state of inertia.

The spirit has to engage in an inconceivably difficult struggle against this tendency of matter. Therefore, so far there are few people in whom the spirit reigns over matter. Yet there are very many in whom matter reigns over the spirit, for, despite the thousands of years that have been lived so far, the road has just begun.

What would be the indications of the spirit, and of matter, in the individual?

Indications of the spirit are: kindheartedness and mercy, love, ignoring material interests, a sense of justice, undying thirst for knowledge and omniscience, a tendency to sacrifice oneself, a conscious belief in God – the creator and guide of everything, and a sense of immortality.

Indications of matter are: egotism, greed, ruthlessness or hard-heartedness, laziness, a lack of interests, the worship of peace, sensuality, and either a blind and formal belief in God, or atheism and lack of a sense of immortality; [as well as jealousy, and its sister – envy].

According to these indications, you can evaluate readily each individual and tell whether the spirit or matter rules within him. [You can tell] what the relationship of these substances is, their mutual relationship. (Ten minutes for rest.)

These indications are not as important for understanding another person as they are for comprehending yourself. They emphasize the problems against which each individual has to struggle ruthlessly.

Now I will talk some more about nonexistence, which you are somehow incapable of understanding.

The amount of spirit and of matter that fills the universe is constant. Nothing can be added on and nothing can disappear completely. It can only transform.

There is only one Almighty's spirit, and He can only divide Himself. He divides Himself into the spirits. A spirit acquires individuality either temporarily or eternally. Those spirits who have lived up to The Almighty's expectations of them, acquire eternal individuality. Others, again, lose it and merge with The Almighty's spirit. That is the nonexistence of an individual spirit. I will attempt to explain that, at least approximately, with an example.

Let's assume that water is The Almighty's spirit. With The Almighty's blessing, or heat from the sun, some water turns into vapor. The vapor condenses and forms water again, but in the shape of an individual drop. This drop of water now exists separately from all other masses of water. It falls to the ground. It drops on a tree leaf and sparkles in the sunlight like a jewel. Or else, it is absorbed by a tree or a flower. For a while, it becomes part of this plant, or even part of an animal. Another drop of water falls into a river, a lake, or the sea, and again merges with the mass of water. It has not disappeared, but it no longer exists as a drop. It will never again exist in exactly the same composition. Something similar to that happens to the spirits who were unable to retain their individuality. They pass into nonexistence – merge with the ocean of The Almighty's spirit.

With that, I will conclude for today. ←

_ ★ ★ ★ _

Ilgya   06/08/44

Ilgya is speaking. I just came from France. If you were to see what human genius is capable of, in this case, unfortunately, only in an evil sense, you would be struck dumb. It seems as if the Earth itself will break apart, the air will be torn to pieces, and fog will envelop not only ships but also man's intellect for ever and ever. Fortunately, however, he, himself, will be scared by this fog that he has created, and will start to seek the sun and a clear sky.

Humanity pays dearly for the awakening of its spirit, it pays with blood and destruction. Generally, though, one preserves only that for which one has paid most dearly.

→Today the Divine enumerated for you the indications of the essence of matter. Unfortunately he forgot one indication, a very important one, and it is – jealousy, and its sister – envy.←

_ ★ ★ ★ _

Ilgya   06/11/44 1130

Let us talk some more about man. Doesn't it seem strange to every thinking human that The Almighty has not given His chosen creature – man – such a mighty body, such a body that is capable of fighting, as [He has given] some of the animals. Rather, He has given man a body that has neither horns, nor claws, nor sharp teeth, nor the thick hide of a crocodile, nor the swift feet of a deer, nor the wings of a bird, so that he could fight successfully against the other animals and overcome them, or at least run away from danger. The Almighty, however, has given His chosen creature only a naked and not particularly strong body, which is not even protected from the cold and the wet by fur or by feathers. This body is completely incapable of fighting the beasts of prey, and cannot run away even from a hare. Tell me, why is that the case?

[[We reply, "So that the mind would overcome the shortcomings."]]

You have become quite educated, and it is already interesting to talk with you.

When the first human appeared, the beasts of prey were pleasantly surprised that a ready prey like that had been provided for them. The other animals decided that this naked and helpless animal will disappear very soon from among their midst, for while being physically helpless it was not armed with the ability of rapid reproduction either.

It was difficult for the first human in the world. It was relatively easy to obtain food from fruit, but he had to flee from every larger animal or else climb a tree. He had to take shelter from the rain and the cold in hollow trees or in caves. Danger lurked from all directions, but something occurred that surprised all animals.

Not only did this helpless creature not consider becoming extinct, but it began to destroy them – the stronger ones. How could that have occurred? That happened because The Creator had given this human something in-visible – a wonderful brain, this strongest of armaments. This brain began to function, and the results of this functioning were, initially, the utilization of stone. Then that continued long enough until the poor rhinoceros and crocodile felt that their armor no longer protected them from the teeth of this beast. The lion and the tiger, though, found it more sensible to give way to this fire spitting animal, and not stick their heads out of the bushes when this human walked along his paths.

The more sensible animals understood the danger that had arisen and began to make up to man and serve him. Those, however, which did not understand that began to disappear from the face of the Earth. Thus this helpless and pitiful creature became the ruler of Earth.

Not only does he transform the animal and plant kingdoms, but he also begins to transform the appearance of the entire Earth and to turn the laws of Earth into his own laws. He starts to exploit the air, water, and other ele-ments. He creates new rivers and even seas. He deprives the sea of entire plots of land, and will soon make the Earth like he wants it to be, rather than like it was once created.

That was achieved by the human brain, guided by The Almighty's creative spirit. The Almighty deliberately gave man such a helpless body in order to force the brain to find the means for the opportunity to exist.

You will ask, "Why is this long road of development needed, because The Almighty, after all, can create immediately an ideal man and ideal conditions for life?"

This question would be thoughtless and illogical, though.

→You should remember from what The Almighty created the universe. The Almighty did not have, and does not have, anyone whom to ask for advice. He has no model; He has to create everything all by Himself. He has to undergo a huge process of development; He has to seek and discover the best. What He has achieved so far is inconceivably great and wonderful. Just examine the laws of nature and the incredibly diverse plant and animal kingdoms! It is easy to criticize His work, but He alone was capable of accomplishing this work.

His latest brilliant work is your brain. It permits you to rise above all other creatures, and become the rulers of the world and of yourselves. It gives you the ultimate opportunity, one that has not been given to any other creature. It gives you the opportunity to understand The Almighty and His goals, and to combine your own, humanity's, goals with the goals of The Creator.

Can you grasp and perceive all this at once? These are such heights as to take your breath away. Your current war is only a trivial episode, a very dark episode, but still only an episode, compared to what the future brings to humanity, and those days during which The Almighty's voice was heard on Earth.

So far you can evaluate The Almighty's miracles of creation only on Earth. Yet there are worlds with entirely different conditions for life. Even on these planets, The Almighty seeks means for creating life.

There are many suns in the universe which shine only for themselves. There are many planets which are numb with the embraces of cold, or suffocate in a hell of heat. The Almighty, however, does not stop even there. He fashions forms of life that can overcome the cold as well as the heat.

The Almighty has created laws for all elements and forces, both the living and the lifeless ones. He does not tolerate miracles, for miracles undermine these laws. He gave equal laws to everyone. What would you say about a ruler who does not obey his own laws? How can you expect The Almighty, who recognizes only fairness, to violate these laws in order to help some of His creatures?

Therefore God appears merciless to you. He rewards you only in the realm of the spirits, where different laws govern.

He, The Almighty, gave one law to man, "I gave you a brain and My spirit. With the help of these you can alter all laws which are unfavorable to you, and can achieve ideal happiness for humanity. Everything will serve you, once you will have learned to serve humanity, and only humanity. The entire world was created for you, and you were created for Me."←

Allow me now to conclude with that. If time will permit, I will speak [again] after three o'clock, or else Shota will talk.

Shota   06/11/44 1700

A promise has to be kept, even though I was not the one who made the promise. It will be particularly difficult for me to carry it out, for the Divine promised you such beautiful things as are not within my, a poor poet's, abilities. Let us try, however!

Just as the high Chief Spirit Alpha, I will ask you to close your eyes and follow me in spirit. It will be a long journey. I will not say whether it will be a journey in time or in space, but nevertheless it will be a journey – a journey away from this day and this place. Well then, let us begin.

So, we have arrived! Open your eyes and look around. What do we see? Yes, it seems to be the same old Earth, and yet not the same but a different one. Wherever we might look, everywhere we see nothing but wonderful gardens. Incomparably beautiful flowers and trees bloom. Fruit ripen on other trees. The flowers and trees remind us of something that we have seen before, but they are much more splendid and the fruit are unusually large and juicy. One sees hardly any fields of grain or herds of cattle. What does that mean? On what do the masters of this planet subsist?

Let us continue our journey, on the planet itself now. Let us walk along a paved path, which meanders through fields of flowers and gardens. We reach a river, but the river is enclosed in a concrete channel. The power of its water is harnessed and drives some sort of machinery. Cheerfully murmuring brooks weave from the river, though, and everywhere, wherever we cast our eyes, wonderful, multicolored fountains rise into the air. Invisible rays illuminate their waterspouts, and a rain of jewels falls from the air.

We see the figures of two people next to a fountain. Let us walk over and get acquainted. They are the beautiful Livia and the dashing Antilio. They speak our human language, but it is much simpler and more sonorous. We will ask these young people to be our guides. They accept gladly and initially take us home for some rest. They rise into the air like butterflies and, since we cannot follow them, take us by the arms and carry us. We fly above the trees and fountains, and are home soon.

The house is located in a garden, but it does not look like a house on our

Earth. It is constructed of some transparent material, which is opaque from the outside but is brightly transparent from the inside. For that reason the houses have only doors, but no windows. Neither do they have the regular roof and ceiling, but only the same, let us say – glass, because what else can one call this transparent construction material. You can see the sun during the day, and at night the moon and stars look into your bed. By pressing a button you can regulate the transparency of the walls and ceiling as you desire, to the extent that you can even make them completely black. The rooms are surprisingly large, bright, and clean. Fresh air circulates through them continuously. It comes out of the walls, and the walls absorb it again. You can also regulate the air temperature as you wish, you simply have to press the appropriate button on a thermostat. The furniture is elegant but simple. There is nothing extraneous in the rooms.

The main room is the combination bath, shower, and exercise room. Everyone has their own. There is a radio receiver and a screen in the room that serves [as the place] for gathering. You may, if you want to, view the newspaper – yes, view it – for you can see all events with your own eyes. You may view the famous writer's latest novel. You may listen to a great poet's latest poem from his own lips; may listen to a composer's latest dance music, and may dance as well, if you wish. You may listen to the best orchestras, or view a theater performance from the capital. Should you not like that, switch over to an opera or a musical. If you don't like that either, then switch over to a sports event, or else to the lecture of some scientist. Everything in the world that you want to see is reflected on the screen in your room.

Should all that not satisfy you, then you can walk over to the bookcase and pick out a novel by the writer of your choice. It looks like a roll of film. You put it in a device and, having relaxed in a chair, view and listen to this novel which lives on the screen. You will seek books and newspapers, as we know them, in vain throughout the entire house. You will find them only in museums.

The gracious hosts ask us to the table now. We sit down and wait for the servants to bring a tasty lunch, because we are rather hungry, but the table is bright and empty. Neither do any servants appear. While smiling politely the hosts ask us what we would like to have. We are confused, though; should we ask for stew or for roast duck? Perhaps these foods have not been prepared today. We ask the hosts to serve us the same food as they have chosen for themselves.

With a polite smile they bend over some sort of a list in front of them on the table. An entire row of buttons can be seen there. They push a button next to them and then next to us. A round hatch opens in the table in front of us, and the next moment there is a plate full of delicious soup in its place. Once it has been eaten, the hosts push another button. The empty plate disappears and there is a wonderful roast in its place. Dessert and various fruit follow it. Glasses with different juices and a light, aromatic wine appear on the table as well. Gentle music plays all the time.

Once lunch has been finished, the hosts invite us to rest on billowing couches.

They tell us, "We generally eat little and simply. All our food is made from fruit, their juices, and chemical substances. We have long since stopped using meat; therefore you can find animals only in zoos and in nature preserves. These are areas of land where the flora and fauna of old times have been preserved. You can still see there the funny cow, and the beautiful but useless horse. It is hard for us to understand why they were so essential for our ancestors. A barking animal can be found there as well, one that once had been man's friend, and a guard against some sort of mysterious beasts by the name of thieves and robbers. For some reason there isn't a single bone left from these beasts in the anthropological museums. Therefore our scientists cannot tell what they looked like, but we think that they had to have been repulsive and hideous."

After a brief rest we fly out for a stroll. The gracious hosts have lent us their clothing. It is made from some sort of elastic and soft material, which is interwoven with a mesh of electric conductors. The outfit has several buttons again, and on the belt there is a small, elegant case that conceals an extremely powerful battery and a motor. By pushing the appropriate button the outfit produces a temperature of the desired warmth or coolness. By pushing another button your clothing acquires the desired color. Women have very many of these buttons on their clothing, and they change their attire hundreds of times a day without taking off their clothing. Isn't it a paradise for the fair sex? Men here are plainer as well, and use only twenty-three buttons on their clothing.

Our attire is finally in order and we can fly. Let's push a button again.

What a surprise! Our bodies have lost their weight and we rise into the air readily. We push another button and we start to move forward. In order to change direction it is merely necessary to change the direction of your body.

(Let's rest for half-an-hour, and then if Mary wants to, she can change places with Alexo.) [[1835]]

We are flying now. The planet looks like a large, magnificent garden, throughout which very many houses have been scattered. Cities have disappeared, for the entire planet is a single garden – a city. Our eyes notice a larger concentration of buildings only occasionally. They are centers of government and factories; factories whose stacks do not emit any smoke. In general, this planet no longer knows the pungent and dirty smoke. We don't see any railroads either. They have long since disappeared. Highways and airplanes had replaced them, but these, too, have already disappeared. Their place was taken by moving highways that transported people and cargo like the escalators that you already know. However, these highways begin to disappear as well, for people have invented powerful motors and have learned to acquire and utilize the energy from matter. They fly now more readily than a bird, and huge loads fly through the air accompanied by an individual with a small case, which could be confused with a cigarette pack or case, if the people here smoked. I have already told you, though, that they do not tolerate smoke.

In order to preclude collisions in the air, the so-called air highways and air spheres have been instituted. As we already saw, the rivers have been enclosed in concrete shackles. Seashores have been enclosed in the same shackles, for the free sea now also serves the master of the planet. He utilizes not only the power of the wind, but also that of the waves to drive his machinery. The warm water of the ocean's tropical regions is used as well. It is driven to the north and the south and heats these once cold regions. Therefore, ice regions have disappeared and there no longer are any uninhabitable, white deserts. Neither are there any sand deserts, for man has learned to control the rain clouds as well. There are huge plants on the sea and on dry land. These plants force the sea to evaporate and give the necessary amount of water vapor to the land. The power of electricity, too, has been harnessed. It rains on the land every day at a set time, and rains only in the necessary amount. Man has grabbed in his mighty hands the wind as well, and regulates its path according to his needs. Man obtains heat not only from the sun, but the heat from the center of the planet also heats his homes. That, however, is the least of it. Man has taken into his hands the energy of matter, and with this key he unlocks all the doors in the world, performs all work, and acquires everything that is desirable.

Your astronomers scare you that the Earth will some day become numb with cold. When we tell that to our gracious hosts, they just smile and reply, "Call on us to help you then. We will warm up your old Earth once more, and you will be able to live on it peacefully and happily until you get tired of it."

We proceed along. We look over the huge and bright factories, beautiful as palaces, in which this planet's masters work. They work only four hours a day. Can this work, though, be called work? Probably not! We inspect factories in which foodstuff is manufactured. Only machinery hums there; and prepared meals, pressed into a cube, flow into the room. No raw materials can be seen.

"Do you really obtain all these wonders from the air?" we inquire.

The plant supervisor merely smiles and does not reply. "You can also visit the plants in which fruit juices are being processed," the plant supervisor tells us eventually.

It is not possible, however, to relate everything that we can see here. We proceed now to the schools and to the solar gardens, or palaces. We already know them, thanks to the high Otranto, and we will not stop in them. Neither will we stop in the government buildings, for they are too bright for our eyes.

Let us drop in for a moment in The Almighty's temple. We can feel The Almighty's breath in this magnificent edifice, and our eyes view in surprise the huge statues whose faces seem so familiar to us. We observe in amazement how the heads of the proud masters of the planet bow before us respectfully, and deeply moved we leave the sanctuary.

We fly along. Our eyes meet only beauty and happiness everywhere. Nowhere are there any beggars or poor people to be seen. Nowhere can be seen any cripples and sick or old people. Diseases and old age have been overcome. Nowhere do our ears hear moans or curse words, because hunger, pain, and misery have disappeared. We do not meet any sad faces. A cordial and polite smile greets us everywhere. Happy laughter, music, and songs can be heard everywhere. It seems as though an eternal festival reigns here, but that's not the case. Man's mind and the genius of the heart reign here.

We reach now a peculiar, magnificent building. We enter it. Unusually dressed people with energetic and hard faces and dreamy eyes meet us here. They show us around, and we reach some strange and shiny objects. The door of one of these objects is open at the moment, and a young woman of a noble but energetic appearance is climbing into it on a ladder.

She notices us, stops for a moment, smiles, and asks in a sonorous silver voice, "Would you care to come along with me?"

"Where to?" Janoss asks.

"This time only to the moon, but should you wish we can proceed to our nearest neighboring planet as well."

I take Janoss gently by the arm, and the beauty has to fly away by herself.

We turn to the commander of the airport, and he explains that there were unbearable conditions for life on the nearest planet, but that by now they have managed to restore the moon's rotation around its axis and to create air on it. It was much easier with the neighboring planets that man reached.

"It seems that man has now achieved everything that one may wish for, but there are many young people who are not satisfied and have begun a struggle with the more distant planets, where the conditions of life are almost insurmountably difficult. Some of us already feel in our solar system like in a prison, and set their sights on other suns, but they are fantasists whose dream is impossible."

Then I, Shota, tell the commander softly, "Don't be rash, my dear friend. On that planet from which I have brought you the visitors, people say the same thing about those who dream of a trip to the moon or Mars."

The evening has come, but even though the sun has set, it has not turned dark. Some sort of a soft and pleasant light spreads across the planet.

"That is the day which we have created," the gracious hosts tell us, "and also night, if you wish. We can get some rest if you are tired."

We thank them and tell them that it is time for us to take leave from the noble and hospitable masters of this beautiful planet, and return to our dark and unhappy Earth.

While parting, Mary still asks the young woman, "You have shown us everything, but perhaps you could still tell me how you have instituted love and marriage?"

"Real simple! We love just as you do, but we probably love for real, with a pure love. All of us are beautiful, healthy, and rich – extremely rich with happiness. Therefore we love only for the sake of love, we love as long as love lasts, and then part as dear friends. Our children are provided for and their fate does not influence our love. You will claim that in such case our marriage is merely a brief living together, and we [turn from one lover] to another. That's not the case at all! Our love is strong, because each of us can retain the other only with the strength of love, therefore we do not know transgression of marriage, because when love has ended marriage has ended as well. Tell me, are all husbands and wives on Earth faithful [to each other]?"

Mary replies, "Probably not. Our marriage possesses only a mostly formal characteristic, and every husband usually has many secret wives, and wives – secret husbands."

"How ugly and illogical," the beauty says. "We love, and no one has any business regarding our love, neither the state nor the church."

We take leave from the gracious hosts, put on again our ugly and uncomfortable clothing of Earth, and leave the house behind. The air envelops us in a fragrant wave. The fiery flowers of the fountains rise into the air, and a rain of jewels falls from them. The stars shine dimly in the sky; ethereal music sounds. With sadness, we take leave from the happy people and the beautiful planet, and close our eyes.

Open them. We have returned from our journey, and I, too, take leave from you.   [[2055]]

Chapter XIII
June 1944 – Part 2

Kolinto   06/15/44 1700

Kolinto is speaking. A prolonged period of time has passed. A high spirit joked about me, he said that I want to scold. I do not have any particularly big desire to scold. I would gladly praise and laugh but, unlike Ali, I do not know how to make laughter out of tears.

God had once sent to you on Earth a wonderful, noble, and great spirit, who wanted to find only good and pleasant characteristics in man, but very soon this spirit had to laugh through tears. He looked into the human soul while seeking sunshine therein, but found such a horribly dark night there that he become disgusted with man. He burned his latest, brilliant work and returned to God, with a request to never ever send him to Earth again, to the people. This great spirit, this one of the greater of humanity's geniuses, departed from you without fulfilling even one fifth part of what had been envisaged, and you lost such treasures of art that one wants to laugh with the tears of despair. Do you know who this genius was?

[[We reply, "Gogol."]]

Nikolai Gogol.

I, too, just like he, came to you with the intent of acquiring something noble and high, of being a cheerful friend to you, but, forgive me, I cannot, just as Gogol could not. Was it only he alone? Leaf through [the pages of] the history of literature, and you will see how many geniuses have run away from you rather early. Would that be a reason for despair? No, but that does mean that a long and difficult struggle still lies ahead for humanity, which will require still many, many sacrifices.

There are very few of those among you who lead humanity. Neither are there many of those who support them and follow them. There are, however, endlessly many who detest them and oppose them, for there are many who have been summoned but few who have been chosen.

The battle that The Almighty wages for the world's happiness and for the ideal of the beauty of perfection is mighty, and difficult without an end. The spirits whom He has created fall in this battle in untold numbers. The

Almighty, though, does not grieve if [only] one out of a thousand survives this battle, and is happy if one out of a million wins it.

The other day I accompanied Alexander along the streets of Riga. As usual, he walked along while absorbed deep in thought, and did not notice anyone and anything. Then he stopped suddenly. Something alive was rolling at his feet. He took a look – it was a round and lifeless cigarette butt that the wind was blowing along the sidewalk. He raised his eyes then and looked at the crowd that, while shoving and talking, swarmed on the street. Where were these people rushing to while shoving and cursing? One to the market, another to a movie, the third to a date, the fourth to pile wood, the fifth to lunch, the sixth to an accountants' meeting, and so on. These were the important tasks that drove these people along the street in senseless haste. That was the wind which blew the burned-out cigarette butt along the street. Verily – the vast majority of these people were deader than the cigarette butt, for not everyone who lives is alive, and not all those who are deceased are dead. Hardly anyone of those whom [Alexander] met that day was alive, and Gogol or Koch will never die.

What is death? For a human, death is the parting of the spirit from matter. A man whose spirit served matter dies simultaneously with it. A man whose spirit ruled matter never dies. The man who lives without any spiritual goals is a zero – without a past and without a future. He does not differ in any way from an animal, whose only goal is to eat, sleep, and preserve its life.

_ ★ ★ ★ _

I will tell you a little story. There once lived an owner of a large estate. One day a rainstorm came and water washed away the little bridge that was used not only by all the people on the estate but also by many of the neighbors. The estate owner summoned his servants and tenants, and ordered all of them to go early the next morning to repair the bridge, while also setting the wages for the day.

The morning came. One servant did not go claiming that the pay was too low. Another claimed that he had more urgent work. A third one was all set to go, but his son fell from a ladder and he had to take him to a physician. The rest went.

Around lunchtime a servant who was on vacation happened to walk by. Having seen what had happened, he hastened to help with the work, even though those who were working said that he did not have to work, because he was free, and since he had not been hired he will not receive anything for his work.

After a while, a poor neighbor passed by on his way to a party. He stopped, took off his dress jacket, and also set to work.

The servants laughed, "You will only forego the party dinner and enjoyment, and will get your dress pants dirty, of which you only have one. You will not, however, receive any wages, for you have not been hired and arrived late. Besides that, neither is this bridge on your property and you do not have to repair it."

"Yes," the neighbor replied, "there is much truth to your words, but I and other people, too, use this bridge, therefore it is my duty to help a neighbor even without being asked and without any compensation."

The evening came. The estate owner summoned all the servants and paid their wages to those who had worked. The first two, however, he threw in jail as criminals. To the third servant he paid the same wages as to the rest, while saying, "The desire to work is important, and it is just as important as the work itself, if failure to accomplish the work depends on insurmountable circumstances, or at least on circumstances that are more important than the work."

He rewarded the servant who was on vacation a hundred-fold. Then he had the helpful neighbor summoned, rewarded him handsomely, and appointed him to be the overseer of the estate.

That concludes this little story. Contemplate it thoroughly! Doesn't The Almighty act even more fairly than the estate owner acted?

Permit me to conclude our conversation with that, and to take leave from you.   [[1830]]

Ilgya   06/18/44 1530

_ ★ ★ ★ _

The high Ali spoke wonderfully with you about pain, but do you know that a spirit can overcome all pain and not feel it? You have heard about people who laugh on a torture rack, and about fakirs who sleep on [a bed of] nails. Why don't these people feel pain? Because pain, in fact, does not exist. There is only a signal sent by the nerves, and a strong power of the spirit can turn this signal off, it is only necessary to want to and to believe in oneself.

An individual is sick not because he is sick, but because he is a "wet rag." He succumbs to his disease, fears it, and does not struggle against it. Anyone who does not believe in medicine and the physician cannot be cured. Whoever does not believe in himself is already dead. Only faith and an unbreakable resolve perform miracles. You do not know at all what can be achieved by the power of will and faith. I will say – almost everything; I will say "almost everything" simply because only The Almighty is capable of everything.

_ ★ ★ ★ _

The Almighty granted my request and bestowed a particular honor on you, by sending to you one of His higher spirits and Alexander's good friend, Indra. Welcome this high God with a particular respect. He will talk with you in half-an-hour.

Permit me to take leave from you now. [[1600]]

Indra   06/18/44 1630

I, The Almighty's high envoy, Indra, am talking with you, the children of Earth. Greetings and a blessing to you!

My name is not unknown to you. The ears of all educated people have heard it, because the people of ancient India considered me as God, and my task was to lead this noble nation and shape its destinies. I seldom visit Earth nowadays, for other people and other gods rule here now.

I greet Alexander as my old friend and a mutual comrade in arms on several planets. It seems strange to me to see him this time in the role of an observer of the people's fate on Earth. I am particularly pleased that this time The Almighty has played such a fine trick on him. He deserves that, for a high spirit is not entitled to any rest and any role of an observer.

The Almighty has so much work that no spirit, not to even mention the high ones, may dream of some sort of a rest, or the Solar Fields. For millions of Earth years already I have not known a moment of rest. I was grieved and surprised when, after the catastrophe in the land of Maya, Alexander had decided to turn down for a while all high assignments and return to Earth as an observer. I was incapable of condemning him, for neither did The Almighty do that, but I did feel painfully disappointed, because I expected the impossible from him. Then, when I heard his voice in The Almighty's infinity and heard his proposal to evaluate man's worthiness, while risking nonexistence for himself, I understood that I have been disappointed again

– except this time with myself, because I had comprehended neither The Almighty nor Alexander.

When I heard Ilgya's request to The Almighty today, I also turned to The Almighty with a request – to permit me to return to Earth for a brief period and be with you. After a prolonged period, The Almighty gave His consent after all, and I came to you. Undoubtedly you do not remember me, for such is the law of the human spirit – to forget the past.

– ★ ★ ★ – [[1730]]

Indra   06/18/44 1830

– ★ ★ ★ –

With respect to war, this calamity of mankind, one has to say, after all, that it does possess positive traits as well. Thus war advances technical inventions at an extremely brisk pace. These bring destruction and death during the war, but after the war – happiness and life. Lack of time does not permit me to examine this topic closer.

Let us turn to our subject – the spirit and matter.

You already understand somewhat what the spirit is and what matter is. Are all the spirits, however, created exactly identically, that is – with equal abilities and characteristics? No! Why not, though? Because the spirits do not have similar tasks. Here again The Almighty's mightiness is manifested – to create spirits with varying abilities, from His very same spirit. This principle is being adopted on a broad scale in the entire universe.

Let us consider your planet – Earth. Why are the people so different? Let us assume that a high prophet, philosopher, or genius is born on Earth. Good! One of them is born – good! Three of them are born – good! A hundred of them are born – good! A thousand of them are born,… Would it be good, though, if a million, a hundred million, every one were to be born like that? What would happen then? Who would manufacture clothing and shoes, build houses, sow grain, bake bread, fire the furnaces, and clear refuse from the streets? After all, not these philosophers and writers, for they have to write and think. Neither would this work attract them, because their mind dwells elsewhere.

Therefore people who are interested in other things and other work are needed for the existence of these leaders. We see that someone likes to raise cattle, another to sow rye, the third to drive a locomotive, the fourth to bake cakes, and so on. Such diversity is essential and logical, so that humanity could exist and could travel the pathway of culture, and so that the leading people would be given the opportunity to take humanity forward. The more humanity will grow in the spiritual and technical sense, the more people will be able to come [to Earth] who will uplift humanity and will take it to the ideal perfection of happiness.

Once all hardships will have been overcome, and everything that is achievable will have been achieved, the great diversity of the spirits will also disappear on Earth, even though it will never disappear completely and must not disappear. Therefore, do not be surprised that one individual is able to write poetry as readily as the nightingale can sing, and for another it seems easier to unload an entire carload of coal than to compose a single verse for his sweetheart.

[I will talk] now about matter. The basic law of matter is the state of inertia. The Almighty gave the living matter, which He had created, the impulse to live, the urge to move and to transform into ever more ideal forms, up to the level of the spirit. The blind matter began this unstoppable journey. In order to carry out the law of inertia, it began to fight blindly and brutally for the opportunity to live and to develop. Every body, living body, began the fight for the realization of this law. The body strives for good food and for security in order to realize this law better. Therefore one has to eat the most nutritious food and has to destroy everything that hinders or threatens the development, propagation, and existence of the body. We can call the manifestation of this impulse by a simple word that everyone understands – egotism.

The lower man stands, and the less he has distanced himself from his cradle, the stronger is this egotism in him. The less spiritually developed a person is, the more egotistic he is. Take, for example, many of humanity's physicians, scientists, and writers, to whom egotism seems to be completely incomprehensible. On the other hand – others of these same people are egotistical after all. How can that be explained? With the proportions of the strength of the spirit and of the body – matter. You probably understand that for yourselves.

I will go on. Which is more ferocious, a tiger or a rabbit? The rabbit, even though that seems strange! The tiger is a beast of prey and subsists on meat, therefore his ferociousness is not evil – it is a necessity. The rabbit of a peace loving appearance, though, the herbivore, is significantly more merciless and ferocious. If you don't believe me, then place two male rabbits in the same cage for a brief period. Quite soon, you will find one of the rabbits dead, with its stomach torn open. Not everything that seems to be gentle and kindhearted from the outside is like that in reality. Some young woman with the face of an angel can stick the most evil devil in her belt. Don't be guided only by external appearance, for quite often that is merely a clever means of disguising oneself, and a means of establishing oneself better.

For a brief conclusion now. What is the duty of every human being? To struggle against the egotism within himself, not harm another individual, struggle against all the evil that is within others, and fight all manifestations of evil, if only they have been observed and can be fought!

Whoever sees a thief stealing and does nothing to delay him is a thief himself, and will receive no lesser punishment. Anyone who sees that someone weaker is being wronged and does not try to help him is an oppressor himself, and as such will be punished as well. Anyone who tries to close his eyes in order not to see injustice will be punished as an evildoer.

It is not at all as easy and simple to live as it might seem. Yet how should one act now, when your entire life is based only on lies, injustice, and egotism? Yes, humanity has wandered into a substantial swamp, one whose shores can't even be seen. A long and difficult road lies ahead for you, people. Otranto has already endeavored to show you the road for getting out of this swamp. Travel it, there is no other, no matter how difficult and long this road might seem.

Allow me to conclude with that for today.

- ★ ★ ★ - [[1945]]

Indra   06/21/44

I, Indra, am talking with you, my children of the Earth.

I will initially say a few words again about our personal concerns.

The great moment, when you had to take on the mightiness of The Almighty's spirit, has passed, but the consequences of this mightiness have not passed. To a larger or smaller extent all of you feel them. In a physical sense, too, your bodies have been considerably weakened in their strength, and fatigue, apathy, and all kinds of weaknesses beset you. Specifically, with respect to the spirits, you are unable to feel the major weakness that they have, and will still have to overcome. It seems strange that Alexander in particular, who had to endure the most, is more robust than [the rest of] you, who had to endure incomparably less. Here again is the miracle in front of which we, the spirits, have already stopped in incomprehension several times.

Alexander's spirit and The Almighty are a riddle that we are unable to solve. It seems to us frequently that they are hostile to each other, but it turns out later on not to be the case at all. We do not know, however, what the case is, for none of the spirits act like the spirit of Alexander occasionally acts. My duty is to talk with you about this to some extent.

Alexander's spirit, and this is the most surprising part, is one of the younger great spirits. When The Almighty created him, I was already a gray old man, speaking in your language, and speaking in our language – several billion Earth years old. Back then the Earth was still a ball of liquid and, obviously, uninhabitable.

The first surprise came immediately after the creation of Alexander's spirit. The Almighty had him incarnate on a planet in the body of the ruler of the people. That was an unusual occurrence – to assign such a high task to a new spirit. We had to confess, this task was accomplished blamelessly well. Thus all of us expected this new spirit to climb higher immediately. When the ruler died, though, came the second surprise. Alexander's spirit refused rest in the Solar Fields, refused a new high mission, even refused to stop by in the Deoss Temple, but immediately turned to The Almighty, through Omega, with a request to permit him to return to the planet Anos, which he had just left, and to permit him to incarnate in one of the lowest slaves. The third miracle followed – The Almighty agreed.

We did not understand anything. Since Alexander had departed rather quickly even from the body of a king on this planet, why then did he want to return there in the body of a slave? Yes, he returned and lived in it for a long time.

When the slave died, Alexander told The Almighty, "Almighty, send me back now as a king, for only now will I be a [true] ruler of my people, because I have been this nation's slave and know what has to be done so that a slave would not be someone else's slave, and the ruler would not be a slave to himself. I know now how sweet bread is and how painful is the whip. Now I know what is justice and what is injustice."

The Almighty said through Omega, "My son, you want to teach your Father! That is not good! It is good, however, that you dare to tell your Father that He occasionally makes mistakes. Return, but not to this planet, rather to Ortis, where a good ruler is needed."

You had to go.

I also remember the time when you engaged in the difficult struggle for the Mayan culture and people. You lost this struggle, and none of us, Alexander, knew how that would eventually end. You did, however, gain Ilgya's love with that, and the sympathy of all the spirits. The fourth miracle – The Almighty is favorably disposed toward this sympathy.

I also remember the time when you came to my people in India as the lowest of people, and endured all the unbearable suffering that a pariah is capable of enduring. Then you came again, dressed in the bright clothing of a teacher, and all those who had suffered followed you, and all those who did not know how to suffer bowed their heads before you. Then you departed from my people, who are beginning to forget me as well.

Now comes the fifth and final miracle. You, Alexander, returned to Earth, and for the first time without any mission. I was so surprised that I even tried not to think. What followed that, however, surpassed everything that could have been imagined. You offered your spirit to The Almighty for the redemption of the people on Earth from ignorance, from a spiritual death. That was insanity. That was guaranteed nonexistence, and even the words of Santorino left you no other hope than only the hope for an impossible miracle. We hoped up to the last moment that The Almighty will alter His decision. That did not happen, though.

Instead, a miracle occurred – you endured. You and The Almighty understood and knew each other better than all of us did. Not only did your spirit endure, but your body withstood as well. We felt very insignificant when faced by the manifestation of this inconceivable mightiness.

I can no longer read your thoughts, and none of us can read them. Therefore tell me, should you find that possible, "Why do you believe so much in the people on Earth? Why don't you give them your works of poetry? Why do you ignore your body like that? Why did you reject The Almighty's intervention on your behalf, and want to continue the path that you have begun?"

I ask you to answer me, your old friend, if not today then some other time.

– ★ ★ ★ –

Let us turn now to another subject. We will talk about the concerns of Earth.

Two countries start a war. The inhabitants of one of the countries pray to God to help them. The inhabitants of the other country do the same thing. Both believe and hope that this will happen, that God has to specifically help them, but not the enemy, because each side believes that they are the true ones and that justice is on their side. The losing side feels deceived and feels a sense of injustice. Have they considered, though, what God can do? Imagine that you are a father and that two of your sons have started a fight. Each of them thinks that you are on his side and will help him. Yet what will you do? You will probably thrash both of them, and rather thoroughly.

That is why it turns out so sadly for all those who wage a war. God does not side with anyone. It is ridiculous to pray to God for Him to help you slaughter your brothers, only because they live in another country. The same thing holds true of the struggles and quarrels of individual people. The trouble is that to every one of you it seems that justice is on his side and that he is the wisest one. You, people, forget that all of you are the children of God, and that all of you are dear to Him. You want God to always side with only you, and if that does not take place then you complain about God's injustice, or else deny God altogether. Poor man, how childish and naive you still are! You want God to share with you your hatred for some individual or nation that you dislike. You want the Father to acknowledge only you as His son. Isn't that ridiculous? You ask for that, though!

Should some nation seem bad to you, then you want it to seem bad to God as well, and you want Him to destroy it. Do not ask that of God, though! Should everyone except one person be evil in a nation, then God will not destroy this nation but will destroy and punish only the guilty ones. He will, however, reward the one a hundred-fold, for he alone was capable of remaining good when everyone else was evil. Should everyone except one individual be good in a nation, then God will not send happiness to the entire nation but only to the good ones. He will punish the evil one a hundred-fold, for he alone among the good ones has, after all, remained evil. That is how God judges, and His judgement is fairer than your human judgement.

Should you detest an individual or a nation, then you no longer see anything white in them, only black. God recognizes as a true human only someone who knows how and is capable of seeing and acknowledging also the good characteristics in his enemy. Whoever is incapable of that is a blind villain, rather than a man worthy of God's spirit.

Every country thinks only about itself, and each citizen only about his country. One can commit the worst atrocities on behalf of his country. Atrocities and injustice always remain merely atrocities and injustice, regardless of in whose name or for what purpose they might have been perpetrated. Never and under no circumstances is someone permitted to beat someone else to death with the holy cross.

Every state and nation has a desire to be the first and to rule others. If a small nation comes under the power of another nation, then it sees and condemns all the wrongs and injustices that the ruling nation inflicts on it. When this small and oppressed nation, though, itself becomes accidentally a ruling nation, then it immediately forgets everything and acts just like its oppressor acted.

Every nation strives for power, but while not denying it to itself, it denies it to other nations. The Latvian nation is a small nation, but one of its leaders claimed that it is a great nation, and all of you were ready to rule almost the entire world. All, almost all, nations are like that. Somehow I can, after all, understand that. I cannot, however, understand that you are surprised that one of the nations which you detest also wants to rule the world. You may fight with it for power, but you may not deny it the right to desire that which you may desire. After all, it is not known at all yet which nation is the better one. You see a new nation nowadays, the people of the United States of America. This nation is a single nation, even though it consists of people from the entire world. A German of this nation is not a German now, and fights against Germany. Someday the entire world will be a nation of united states like that.

It is the essence of matter, which fights only for its own good and its own justice. Individual people as well as individual nations have to overcome this blind egotism. It can be good only if everyone is well off; and no one can feel truly happy if everyone around him is unhappy.

Humanity has to overcome this erroneous view. How can individual people or individual states be happy? Sooner or later the unhappy ones will impose their unhappiness on others. One should not look to others and wait for others to be the first ones to begin the work of redeeming humanity, because then this work will never get started. Everyone has to begin, regardless of how puny his strength might be. A single brick is nothing, but if no one will come forth with this first brick, then no palace will ever be erected, even though the entire humanity were to talk about it.

With that, I will interrupt my conversation with you today, in order to continue it in a few days. [[2115]]

Nakcia   06/25/44 1135

Nakcia is speaking. I greet my friends – I have returned to you.

An almost unavoidable danger threatens you and your nation, and not just your nation alone. Only a miracle can save you. I do not know whether it will take place this time, for Omega and Santorino remain silent. Believe in and hope for a miracle. You will claim that miracles do not happen, for The Almighty is against them, but they do take place after all. The entire Latvian nation knows that.

Miracles happen more frequently than we want them to and than you know. You know only what has happened, but not what had to occur. You go to work and in the evening return home calmly, for nothing happened. You do not know, however, that you were destined to be run over by a car today, but you crossed the street a second too soon. That was not a miracle, you were just lucky. It is a good thing that you were lucky, and why were you lucky? You are sick. There is no hope of getting well, but a physician comes along who, contrary to his own expectations, cures you after all. That, after all, is not a miracle either, that is the physician's skill and the capabilities of your body. What a surprise, though! Your friend had caught merely a mild cold, and you receive the unbelievable word that your friend has died.

We, the spirits, try not to help you, if this help does not coincide with the task of your life, or else benefits only the body. Therefore, those miracles that one expects seldom take place, for then you would know that they are miracles. Man should not rely on the help of miracles, but only on his own strength. Miracles occur if The Almighty, for whatever reasons, changes His previous decisions. That happens if you have either surpassed the expectations that had been placed on you, or else have failed to live up to them.

– ★ ★ ★ – [[1225]]

Santorino   06/25/44 1500

I, Santorino, am talking with you. Much has been proclaimed to you. What the church should be like has been proclaimed to you, but nothing has been said regarding what the structure of this church should be. As instructed by The Almighty, I will talk with you about that today, and will express our, the high spirits', thoughts. First, though, I will permit myself a brief remark. It is not good that some of those who should be here fail to come without valid reasons. Let us begin now.

A priest is essential for the church. Who might be appointed to this, the most distinguished position on Earth? Obviously, only the most eminent one from among distinguished people.

Since God recognizes only those prayers that have been expressed in the form of deeds, or else after the completion of the work, then services as such become unnecessary. Songs and music dedicated to The Almighty, and to His personification – God, should be played in the churches. These songs and works of music have to be the best and the most beautiful that humanity's genius is capable of creating, and performed only in the best possible way. Nothing inferior may cross the threshold of God's temple. All kinds of wailing songs and poor organs are the worst sin against God and should be considered as blasphemy of God. If it is not possible to obtain good choirs, musical instruments, and music, or else works worthy of performing, then it is better to have complete silence in the church.

Because the priest does not have to know any special ecclesiastical ceremonies, the congregation should elect the most eminent member of the congregation to be the priest. Voting can be only by secret ballot, and it is mandatory that not less than 98% of all the members of the congregation participate. If a candidate has received 50% of the vote, or less than 50% of the vote, he is considered to have been rejected and another one, more eminent, has to be sought. If a candidate has received 51%, then he is considered as having been elected for one year, if 60%, then for five years, if 75%, then for twenty five years, but if 98%, then for his entire life.

Should the priest turn out to be unworthy of his position, a general meeting of the members of the congregation can dismiss him with the same majority of votes.

The priest's assistant and deputy should be elected after nine days, using the same procedure. The governing board of the congregation should also be elected on this day. Depending on the size of the congregation, it should consist of three, six, or nine members. The method of electing the governing board should be as follows. Every ten members of the congregation elect secretly the most eminent member from their midst. Each ten of those elected again elect from their membership one, the most eminent, and ten such most eminent ones do the same thing again. That continues until it is no longer possible to come up with [groups of] ten. Then the latter elect from their midst three, six, or nine members of the congregation's governing board. The latter elect from their midst the chair of the governing board and his/her assistant, with a simple majority. The governing board should be elected for one year. If the general membership meeting of the congregation, however, expresses its confidence in the board with a 75% vote, then the authority of the board can be extended to a second year, and even to a third year, but under no circumstances to a fourth one.

→It is the duty of the church to direct the spiritual life of the congregation, through the priest and the governing board. It has to look after the sick and the unhappy ones, and has to attempt to right all wrongs. It has to assist not only spiritually, but materially and legally as well. Under no circumstances may it tolerate the existence of injustice. It has to oppose immediately, by all available means, everything that is unjust. It must not wait for someone to turn to it. It has to see everything immediately on its own, and prevent or help. Wicked, and even useless, is that church which has supplicants and sufferers within its walls.

The church must look after the upbringing and education of children. Every adult who corrupts a child with evil words or deeds should be thrown in jail. The church must provide high quality lectures, shows, and entertainment. All that, except for politics, rests on the shoulders of the church, until the time when the church will unite all nations. Then, once wars and political squabbles will end, as well as thefts and other crimes, the church will, in fact, remain the only leading and organizing institution.

Initially the goals of the church have to be strictly limited. Under no circumstances may the church use force, not to mention weapons, in spreading its ideals. The church may not segregate nations and Gods, no matter what they might be like, except for false gods. This means those religions whose fundamental principles are hostile to The Almighty's Commandments. The weapons of the church are love and reason. The church does not serve The

Almighty and God, but only man. The laws of the church are intended only for attaining man's intellect, happiness, and justice. Through service to humanity and to its ideals of beauty, happiness, and intellect, man serves God as well. These ideals are also God's ideals.

God does not need man's prayers or even deification, but only the esteemed accomplishment of their, the people's, high tasks. A father does not need a son who begs him humbly for something all the time – one who, while promising to accomplish everything, either does nothing or does it poorly. He, the father, needs a son who, while being proud of his father, listens to him respectfully and carries out his work in silence. The father will not become angry should this son, on occasion, accomplish the task worse or better than assigned, as long as the son did this while intending only good. The father does not require his son to fall to his knees in his presence, and kiss his feet or hands. The father is more pleased if his son is worthy to sit by his side after completing a noble task. With that his son has displayed the highest honor to his father, the honor of a good and his father's worthy son.

Now you can see what God desires from man, and how you, people, have understood His desire thus far.

Everyone rise, and receive God's blessing for yourselves and for your work.

I conclude.←   [[1615]]

Indra   06/25/44 1715

I, Indra, am talking with you, my dear children of the Earth.

I can welcome among you today new and noble spirits, whom I have met formerly and elsewhere, and not just only once. Have the guests stand up and receive my divine blessing. Be seated.

As usual again, I will begin with personal matters.

I thank Alexander for the answers that he gave me. Since you do not know them, but know my questions, then perhaps you would like to hear the answers as well?

[[The heralds reply, "We would like to."]]

All right, listen!

The answer to the first question should be considered as witty, even though it does not satisfy me, for Alexander cleverly avoids an answer with it. He says that he believes in man and in his chosen future because The Almighty, Himself, believes in him. After all the atrocious deeds and wars that humanity has perpetrated so far; after The Almighty's teachers, like Buddha, Christ, and others, whose teachings humanity has taken and adopted to its needs so cleverly that only the placard "love" is left over from them, behind which the same old, naked hatred hides; if after all that The Almighty still has not destroyed humanity, then one is left [with only the choice] to believe in this humanity. What reason could there have been in sparing this humanity if The Almighty had not, after all, seen something in man that would allow one to believe in this man?

Does this answer satisfy you?

The second answer was, "I could not find sufficiently cheap paper on Earth on which it would pay to print these poems."

This answer is even wittier, but it is not an answer after all, and merely an evasion of the answer. This answer does not satisfy me the least bit.

The answer to the third question satisfies me completely. Because of that, unfortunately, I cannot, based on Omega's order, reveal it to you.

I thank you for the last answer, but the first two I passed on to Ali. They will be very useful to him, and I hope that Alexander will receive particular thanks from him.

_ ★ ★ ★ _

We will continue now. You have heard very much from the spirits and have asked them much, but there is a big and important problem that has remained entirely untouched. What would this problem be? All of you here in this room are humans, and all of us are spirits. Not everything, though, is already expressed with the words "human" and "spirit." How many humans are there here?

[[We reply, "Nine."]]

And how many spirits?

[[We reply, "We don't know."]]

Yes, there probably are nine people. Therefore you can constitute the governing board of a congregation, right? You can, but that is not why I asked you that. Let us count somewhat differently – five and four. What do these numbers mean?

[[We reply, "We don't know."]]

Who are these five? Look around carefully – guests and envoys. That, however, is not what I wanted either, for the guests can become envoys, and the envoys can become guests. Let us count once more. Six and three, that is also nine. What does that mean? Alexander hastens to tell us – men and women. The spirits, too, can probably be separated. There are Santorino, Ali, Shota, I, and so on; and there are Ilgya, Nakcia, Aurora, and so on. What does that mean? It seems obvious to you that people would be divided into men and women. I do not understand, however, why you have not asked why the spirits are also divided like that. Perhaps you will explain?

[[We are unable to explain.]]

Your thoughts vary. This matter is not all that simple.

Except for a few microorganisms, this principle is carried out completely in the animal kingdom. In the plant kingdom, too, some plants can be found that have only male type blossoms on one specimen, but only female type on another. Therefore this principle is not alien to the plant kingdom either, and can be understood. It cannot be understood as readily, though, why this principle is found in the realm of the spirits as well.

As you know, the spirit is an immaterial substance. Therefore such characteristics of a purely material nature would seem strange. You know that there is only one spirit of The Almighty. He divides Himself into spirits – that you know as well. He is good, for He is God. He is evil, for He is Satan. Thus we can see how complicated this spirit is. The Almighty, particularly with respect to the spirits, observes strictly this principle of difference, and creates spirits with definite traits – masculinity and femininity.

Hasn't it struck you that a man thinks and acts differently than a woman does? You will claim that this can be explained entirely by the different construction of the bodies and different tasks in life. You are partially right, for in the animal kingdom, too, the male differs from the female with respect to their characteristics, but I repeat – only partially. Every thinking individual has noted that in a psychic sense a woman differs from a man to such an extent that quite often they cannot understand each other at all. They have some sort of an entirely different approach to every concern and function. All that stems from the different structure of the spirits.

Therefore you should know and note – the spirits, just as humans, are separated into male and female spirits, even in appearance. This even though these spirits are immaterial and the functions of the human body are entirely alien to them. You should know, though, that a male spirit can incarnate only in a male human body, but not in that of a female. Thus the spirits can, by incarnating in living beings, achieve the highest level of comprehension regarding love and friendship. This love of the incarnated high spirits also gives an opportunity for the body – that is, matter – to achieve through its passion the summits of the strength of the spirit and matter, and perform miracles of heroism and nobility. It has given the most beautiful songs to humanity. Obviously, results of an entirely opposite nature can come about, but that cannot be helped, for life is so varied.

The high Santorino talked today about The Almighty and you. Permit me to touch slightly on this subject as well. Even though some of you begin to get tired, have patience for a few more boring minutes.

Some of you complain about God's injustice, and demand from Him the realization of your different wishes. If that does not take place, then you either grumble at God or even deny Him. Let us turn again to the example of a father and his sons.

Having grown up, some sons are dissatisfied with their father, and tell their father, "I did not want to be born, but you made me be born into this world, without asking me whether I want that or not. Since you have done this, then your duty is to take care of me for my entire life and to fulfill all my desires."

It would seem as if these words would have a smattering of logic to them, but there isn't any there at all. Parents experience a bitter disappointment. Hardly ever are the children grateful to their father and their mother for the endless effort that was required by their upbringing, schooling, feeding, and dressing; even though the parents sacrificed the better part of their lives to them, and gave them, by educating them, the opportunity to achieve happiness in this life.

Should a child, having grown up, not like the order and rules that govern in his father's house, he may leave it freely. Similarly, should some of you not like the universe which The Almighty has created, and the laws that govern therein, then you can freely depart from this universe into nonexistence, from which you have come. You will not have lost anything with that, for the universe exists only in the consciousness of the living. This universe does not exist for anyone who has not been born or who has died. Nowhere do forests rustle, nowhere do the birds sing, nowhere does a human breathe, nowhere does the sun warm you, and nowhere do the stars shine. If you do not exist then nothing exists at all. Therefore, if you do not like this earthly world and The Almighty's realm of the spirits, you may freely leave them. No one will hold you back nor punish you.

If you enter a temple, you may remain in it should you like it there; if not – you may leave peacefully. It would be base and mean, though, if you were to start desecrating this temple and to spit in it. You would be thrown out of it like a dog, because this temple has not been built just for you alone, but rather for all the people.

I permit myself to conclude this day's tiding with these words, and to take leave from you for a few days. [[1912]]

Santorino   06/28/44 1700

I, Santorino, want to supplement today my previous tiding. I have already told you about the priests and their assistants, as well as about the governing boards of the congregations and their election, but that is not everything.

The congregational priests should elect a regional priest from their midst. These [should elect] a state priest; the state priests – a continental priest, and they – a priest of the entire world, or the world's high priest.

All priests should be elected by secret ballot, with a simple majority, and for three years. Besides that, the same priest can be elected an unlimited number of times.

When not performing their duties the priests should wear ordinary clothing. As to beards, mustaches, and long hair – only according to their own preference and if they are becoming.

In the church, and while performing the duties of their office, they should wear a dark red toga, and on the head either a black velvet hat with embroidery and a cross joining it on top, or else a wreath. Besides that, the priests should always have a cross on their chests, which may not be excessively large and which should hang on a short chain, like a medal around the neck.

The congregational priests should have a laurel wreath in silver color embroidered on the rim of their hats, or else, if it is a wreath, it has to be a laurel wreath wrought of silver.

The regional priest should wear a similar hat embroidered with a laurel wreath, except gold colored, and a wreath wrought of gold.

The state priests should wear hats with a wreath of that country's favorite tree branch and leave embroideries, or such [a wreath] wrought of gold. Thus the state priest of Latvia could have a wreath of oak leaves.

The continental priest should have embroidery or a wreath of gold palm leaves; the Earth's high priest – a wreath of rose leaves and blossoms, made of jewels.

The priests can be either married or not married.

Let us talk now about the relationship with the governing board. The priest has to confirm all decisions of the governing board. Should the priest not confirm an important decision of the governing board, a general meeting of the congregation has to be called. If this general meeting concurs with the decision of the governing board with a three-quarter vote, then the priest has to confirm this decision, or else has to resign from his office.

It is desirable that marriages, baptisms, and funerals would be blessed by the priest, but only desirable. These ceremonies definitely have to be particularly solemn and beautiful. If a marriage takes place in the temple, then beautiful and solemn music and songs should accompany it. The priest blesses the newlywed couple in the name of God and addresses them. This speech has to be instructional and practical. Those being married should be recorded in the temple's golden book of marriages. After that the newlyweds are allowed to go by the same last name. If the marriage does not take place in the temple, then it is performed in an appropriate government office. Should someone not want to get married, he/she does not have to do that. Except in that case they both – that is, the husband and the wife – do not acquire any legal basis for living together, and also lose the right to bring up their children, because the children become wards of the state.

A newly born citizen is baptized on the ninth day of his life and [is given] a name that has been chosen by the parents. On his fifteenth birthday, however, the new citizen chooses his real name for himself, and then the real baptism takes place. The name that had been given by the father and mother remains in documents as a middle name. The young person can also choose as his name the name that had been given him by his parents, and then he has only one name.

With respect to funerals, they have to be particularly solemn and dignified. It would be good if this moment of the spirit's parting from his friends on Earth were accompanied by the priest's blessing. I do not prescribe the method of interment – burial or cremation. That is not significant, for the time will come when the departed one will simply disappear before your eyes, as the morning mist once the sun rises.

I conclude. The high Indra will talk with you in half-an-hour.   [[1754]]

Indra   06/28/44 1824

I, Indra, am talking with you, dear children of the Earth.

_ ★ ★ ★ _

My duty is to talk about Alexander now, because this time it is precisely I who has erred so unexpectedly and badly. When I told Alexander's replies to Ali, to my biggest surprise Ali not only did not smile, but his face became hard and sad, and he asked hastily, "And what has Omega said?"

"Omega?" I asked, "but what is there for him to say, because he generally does not react to jokes."

"Jokes?" and something like a bitter grin flashed on Ali's lips for the first time. "Yes, that really is a joke that you, the high spirits, have been caught this time, and have not understood anything that you have been told. I can't understand how easily you lose Heaven beneath your feet when you can no longer read the thoughts of a human."

"Could that have been merely a comedy?" I asked, "but one cannot assume that, after all."

"Yes, one has to say that with respect to Alexander's first two replies, particularly the first one. Don't you understand this comedy, which surpasses the most dismal tragedy? Humanity already knows some such 'comedies.' A high ruler of the spirit once came to Earth; the King of mankind came, and humanity received this King appropriately as well. It draped the robe of a king around His shoulders; placed the sharpest crown on His head; and, so that all the nations – the near and the far ones – could see Him better, nailed Him to a cross and raised Him high above the heads of the people. Lest anyone doubt, it nailed a board with the words 'Your King' above the King's head. The people laughed about this comedy, through which seeped the blood of tragedy.

"What did Alexander do now? He asked The Almighty to give humanity all [the necessary] knowledge for achieving happiness and a bright future. The Almighty, while believing in him and through him in humanity, agreed to this. However, what does Alexander say now? He says that he believes in humanity only because The Almighty believes in it. How can one comprehend that? Only like a physician can comprehend that, by giving a hopeless patient the final medicine which is so radical that the patient will either die or else will endure and recover.

"Alexander asked The Almighty to give humanity the understanding of everything, because that was the last means of saving humanity, but not because he believes in man.

"He gave you, Indra, an answer, such a reply as none of us would dare to give The Almighty. His second answer is a bitter reproach to The Almighty, himself, and humanity."

Ali turned around and alighted away.

I returned to the Deoss Temple and turned to Santorino with a question as to whether he agrees with Ali's thoughts. The Divine did not reply, but only nodded his head in the direction of Omega's throne. I wanted to turn to Omega, but the Divine put his finger to his lips, and then he told me, "I think that The Almighty has comprehended everything that has taken place better than all of us, for Omega has not said a word about that."

_ ★ ★ ★ _

Let us talk some more about the spirit and matter. Tell me, is a one-year-old child an angel? You do not understand my question. Is this child or a grown-up individual better, and who is better, that is – who has more love? No one is more merciless than this child. He tears off the head of a bird without any mercy, because all feelings – mercifulness, shame, and love – are entirely alien to him. He is the incarnation of pure egotism. He is pure matter with all the egotistical demands of matter. He does not mind waking his mother at night and making her slave all day and night. Only with the incarnation of the spirit in the child does he begin to comprehend love and shame, which animals, who do not have this spirit of The Almighty, do not know.

On incarnating in a human being, the spirit begins to struggle with the egotism of matter. In youth, while the spirit is still full of the memories of Heaven, the individual lives, or at least strives, for the achievement of the ideal. Then, however, comes the burden of the years of struggle, and the spirit usually begins to succumb. That is why suicides occur so readily during youth, since the spirit, being unable to overcome matter, flees from it.

Man senses this struggle, and that is why monasteries, ascetics, and yogi have come about; but is their way the right way? No! A person cannot serve God by leaving the people, for it is possible to serve God only by helping people. God does not need words and fasting, but work and good deeds. The human body is a marvelously formed instrument, one merely has to learn how to use it and how to control it. There is no sense in achieving the victory of the spirit by weakening the body. That is violence which has no positive characteristics. Anyone who knows how to control his servants only with the help of a whip is no manager – he will not get far!

Man's task is to live and to create a beautiful and happy life for everyone. That can be achieved only by learning how to control yourself – and then others, but never the other way around.

The promulgator of The Almighty's thoughts and the Ruler of the Future, Omega, will talk in an hour. I conclude. Ilgya will speak.   [[2001]]

Omega   06/28/44 2100

→I, the promulgator of The Almighty's thoughts, Ruler of the Future and of Death, speak unto all nations on Earth, in the name of The Creator and Ruler of everything that exists and does not exist.

The Almighty has given His Commandments to the people, and instructions – to live so that they would achieve the ideals of happiness, justice, and love. Now everything is up to man himself, in whom The Almighty's creative spirit dwells, yet who has been given a free will to follow The Almighty, or else to travel his own paths, which lead only to one destination – misfortune and nonexistence.

The Almighty has sent His envoys to the nations on Earth. All of them have been recognized, but forgotten. Their teachings have been written into books. The books have been placed in bookcases and the bookcases have been locked. In their stead, false prophets have written books. In these they have altered the books of The Almighty's envoys, and have even falsified them. They have turned evil into good, and black into white. Now humanity has started the most dreadful war of destruction of the spirit and of body. The pathway which humanity has traveled has taken it to the brink of the abyss. It is not possible to travel it any further. Humanity looks around in despair, seeking a road away from the abyss.

"I, The Almighty, have shown you this road through My six envoys. Others will follow them. You, people, have been told everything that you had to be told.

"Thanks to Alexander's sacrifice, you – man – have heard that which none of My creations have ever heard, and will never hear again. You can become the ruler of the universe and I, The Almighty, will seat you, My son, next to Me on the throne of the ruler of the universe. Yet you can become nothing even more readily, and merge with the dust storm of the universe.

"Everything now depends only on you, alone. I, The Almighty, will never again send any of My envoys to Earth. Whoever will speak in My name will be an impostor. What I have proclaimed, I will never supplement again. I will never, ever speak again, not with the tongue of a prophet, not through signs, not as I am talking today, nor in any other manner.

"So that you might receive answers to some remaining questions, which are still not clear to you, I permit My spirits to talk to the people on Earth only as long as I have not recalled My envoy Alexander to Me; and only through him, so that no false prophets could speak in My name and in yours.

"You have been given all materials for constructing the castle of happiness, justice, and love. You only have to seek architects and workers. I have said everything. I have nothing else to say to you. I bless you and bid you farewell!"

I deliver these words of The Almighty to you, the people on Earth – you, on whom such great hope has been placed, even though you have done everything to dissipate it.

Now The Almighty leaves the people on Earth all to themselves. They can heed the call of The Almighty and become divine rulers of the universe, or else, fail to heed the call and decay into misery – then one day pass into nonexistence along with their entire Earth, thanks to their perverse genius. They can even destroy The Almighty's envoys and The Almighty's Tidings, but thus prescribe their own spiritual and slow death.

The moment has arrived, as it had once arrived for the Son of God – the moment when the Father left His Son, in order to meet Him only after death.

Put the Tidings in order. Seek friends who are capable of understanding them and of preserving them in their hearts. Try to carry them through the flames of war. Only when [these flames] will have been extinguished, will the voice of The Almighty resound to humanity. It is not destined to be heard through the voices of cannons!

You may pray for a miracle. Yet don't do that, like Christ did not do that.

I, the Ruler of the Future and of Death, and The Almighty's thought expressed in words, bid farewell to you, the people on Earth, and The Almighty's envoys.← [[2153]]

Ilgya   06/30/44 1930

_ ★ ★ ★ _

I, too, want to talk now with you, Alexander. Permit me to ask you – not to reproach and not to give advice, don't misconstrue me – merely to ask with a heart full of love and pain, because your thoughts are not audible to us in Heaven and I get an uncanny feeling because I cannot understand you.

Tell me, why did you come again to this unhappy Earth, to these people on Earth who have deceived you so painfully? Why did you want to help them again, and were ready again to pass into nonexistence on their behalf? Why did you do that? Can you forget the Mayan people, people who awaited you as their god and sent you off with the unimaginably ghastly silence, a silence whose dreadful noise can be heard still now in the infinity of the universe? These people were capable of following you along the road to unprecedented happiness, but were incapable of following you when this happiness had to be defended with their own lives. Had they, these Mayan people, had also known how to die while defending that which had been achieved, but not simply their naked lives, then no enemy would have been capable of conquering them, and The Almighty would have had to acknowledge your rights to justice. Then neither the people, who in any case did not manage to escape it, nor their ruler would have had to pass into nonexistence.

The people believed in you when you handed them bread and gold, and did not believe in you when you handed them a sword and blood.

Back then, as Omega told me today, you and The Almighty suffered the worst failure, and lost faith in man. You did not pass into nonexistence, because then only the same [alternative] would have been left for The Almighty as well. You came to Earth again, two consecutive times, and without me, because I was far away in my blindness.

This time the people had supposedly followed you and acknowledged your teachings, but when you departed from them everything remained almost the same as it had been previously. You come to the people on Earth now for the third time, during the hour of their most horrible folly, and you ask The Almighty to believe in these people, and pledge your immortal spirit [on their behalf], and the Almighty accepts this pledge. Once that has occurred, you do not explain to the spirits why you believe in man, who does only one thing all the time – tries to dissipate all the expectations that have been placed on him, and does not follow any of God's envoys.

You do not explain, but give an answer that only The Almighty can understand and tolerate. Tell me, why do you do this? You decline so readily your important mission to the noble people of Omato. You reject happiness, tranquility, and a future. You also reject me, for I was permitted to incarnate there and to be with you and yours.

You have declined all that for the sake of this man on Earth, who will perhaps cast stones at you for that.

You endured, and your spirit not only did not break and you were not overcome by a prolonged weakness, but The Almighty's spirit, while passing through your spirit, has remained there and has raised your spirit so high that we are no longer capable of understanding you.

I have lost you, for I dread the heights, the heights of the spirit, where I have to follow you. You will never incarnate again, and neither will I. I, the insignificant spirit Ilgya, as The Almighty said, truly am like that, even though there are few spirits who stand higher than I do.

Also, tell me, why don't you return to us now, and at least don't accept The Almighty's offer to fulfill all your desires, but ask to have only one wish fulfilled – to have everything remain the same way as it was, not allow any miracles, and help neither you nor your friends in spirit, if they do not want that either.

I ask you, but please do not answer me, because I will not understand you in any case, will not understand you for the time being. Help me in my doubts, if you want to, because I cannot help you. Do you understand what that means – to love and to be unable?

You said, "In order for humanity to be able to save itself, it has to know the goal of the universe's creation, and its own – humanity's – goal."

Don't you err, though? Animals or beasts know their goal – to eat, to multiply, and to preserve their life. Man? Don't the majority of people have the same goals? Excuse me, but the same ones and perhaps even of a baser nature. An animal kills only when it wants to eat, and only in an amount sufficient to satisfy itself. Your man, however, slaughters for the thrill of slaughter, and not in order to eat those who have been slaughtered.

What are the human being's goals in life? Initially, to complete school. Once it has been completed, then to obtain a well-paying position. After that has been obtained, then the individual's goal is to obtain a still better position, and thus he reaches the so-called goals of the day – to eat better and to drink, to dance, and to play cards. What would be the spiritual goals, though? Oh yes, I had forgotten them! Would anything, however, be left out because of that? These goals are to trip his more capable colleague, to slander him, to hang out his dirty laundry, and to spread some sensational gossip. This is what these spiritual goals would be like! You will claim that I am one-sided in my judgment. Yes, if you wish, but only with respect to a few hundreds and thousands! Was it worth for the sake of these hundreds and even thousands, though, who are worthy of bearing the proud name of man, to sacrifice as much as you and The Almighty have sacrificed? Will these hundreds be able to lead billions? Will these billions not overwhelm these hundreds and trample them into mud?

Yes, I know, this question is the question for the sake of whose solution you pledged your spirit. Did you expect an answer though? No!

I conclude now and await you as my old Mayan high priest, but not as an incomprehensible chief spirit, to come to his insignificant Ilgya.

Permit me still to talk with all of you. We, the spirits, unlike you people, have the misfortune that we have to carry out the promises that we have made.

– ★ ★ ★ –

Chapter XIV
July 1944

Indra   07/02/44 1510

I, Indra, am talking with you, my dear children of the Earth. – ★ ★ ★ –

Another difficult task faces me. Doubts have overcome Ilgya, doubts about the value of man and doubts about her own worth. I understand her. Except for only The Almighty, no spirit, while being in her position as the judge of humanity on Earth today, would be capable of thinking otherwise. He comprehends the incomprehensible and sees the invisible.

There are only five chief spirits who are capable of comprehending The Almighty. Omega says that there are five and a sixth one as well, but we do not know this sixth one.

I also try to understand Ilgya in her doubts about the worthiness of her spirit. Only the five, and perhaps the sixth one as well, stand higher than Ilgya and spirits like her.

It should not be a surprise that you doubt Alexander as an individual, for he has assumed a most ordinary body and, besides that, those who are acquainted with prophets as with people do not acknowledge them. They cannot reconcile with the idea that neighboring Peter or John could be a prophet or a genius, because [as a child] he has, along with them, tended geese and ran around without any pants on. Therefore, only those who do not know them as people can acknowledge prophets.

On this occasion, he does not come to you as a prophet and neither does he want to be singled out from among you, and only The Almighty's will compels him to follow it.

Ilgya feels too insignificant now to follow Alexander's spirit, after he has inhaled The Almighty's breath. Do not condemn her harsh words – they are deserved. You have to realize that Ilgya will be the first one among those spirits who might have to defend humanity with their lives.

We, the spirits, admire Alexander's spirit, but we do not envy him. Similarly, thousands of the bravest and noblest people do not envy the mountain climber who strives to reach the summit of the mountain which no one has ever reached, by climbing the insurmountably steep rock wall. He has less than a one-percent chance of victory, and a ninety-nine and a half of death. Therefore you, too, need to consider and understand why one should not envy, and do not envy, Alexander's spirit in his climb to the unreachable summit of the mountain of the spirits, whose name is – The Almighty.

You also have to comprehend Ilgya's doubts about her abilities. Be kind toward this noblest and purest of us – spirits – because her sharp knife is the scalpel of a surgeon, and her smite is a mother spanking a mischievous but extremely dear child. Oh woe to the Earth, should its judge Ilgya abandon it, and should Ortega return!

Let us turn now to the second part of our conversation – after a break of half-an-hour. [[1615]]

We still have to clarify some concepts. To many, and to John as well, the question regarding a mother's love is not clear. Is a mother's love the manifestation of the spirit or of matter? Let us attempt to solve this most important question as the first one.

Let us begin with the animals. What is the love of the animals? You know that the mother is capable of sacrificing herself for the sake of her children. The sparrow female is capable of facing the terrible beast – the cat. Therefore love in the animal kingdom is a strong and noble feeling – an instinct – that serves to preserve the animal species. Are these feelings intelligent, though, and are they thus worthwhile feelings? Let us look at them. You put duck eggs in [the nest] of a hen. It is a good thing that you do not use the eggs of a hawk. The hen hatches the ducklings, and feeds and cares for them just as for her own chicks. Other birds do the same thing with cuckoo chicks, even though even a hen should understand that a duckling cannot be her child. Similarly, you know that some four-legged animals feed the little ones of other animals.

What would be the conclusion? The love of animals is a blind love. It is an instinct. It is the same feeling as hunger, thirst, sleeping, and the desire for sexual relations. All these feelings serve only the upkeep of the animal's body and the preservation of the species. None of them are better than others, for they are independent of the animal and its will.

Let us turn now to the love of the human mother. How should we consider it? Obviously, not as simplistically as the love of animal mothers, for here the human mind and the spirit are added. Only the involvement of the spirit is capable of turning this mother's love into the true mother's love,

into a sacred love. Let us be sufficiently bold and confess that this love has almost as many levels as there are mothers – beginning with the lowest which
does not differ in any way from the blind, instinctive love of the animals, and
ending with the high, true love of the spirits. This love is capable of bringing
up a son or a daughter – a friend – for [the mother], and a decent fellow
human being for humanity.

You have also heard, even though far less frequently, about fathers' love.
There is not much to say about it. It is not as strong as a mother's love, but
it can be more genuine.

We found out that an animal does not recognize, does not sense its own
offspring, and they can be readily substituted by strangers, but what will you
say about a human mother?

[[Mary says that it is possible to substitute.]]

Mary is right, because true love can come about only between spirits. It is
a conscientious love. As long as the child does not have this spirit, but only
matter, this mother's love also is blind and instinctive. Children are quite
often, if you only knew just how often, exchanged in hospitals. That takes
place due to carelessness and also because of gratuities. A mother is stingy.
The nurse gets mad and turns her child over to some poor, young mother
– let the son of the rich cheapskate live the life of a poor person. There are
other reasons as well. Only the fact itself is important, and I will tell you
– hardly ever have the mother or the father sensed these strange children to
be strangers, and loved them less.

With respect to fathers, this matter is truly tragic on Earth. The mothers
generally know for sure that their children are their children. The fathers,
however, more often than not love strange children, because women generally are incapable of preserving any secret except for the secret as to who the
real, not the official, fathers of their children are. This is an acute and tragic
situation. How do you, people, intend to resolve it?

Let us turn now to the second question that also preoccupies your minds
and causes doubts. Why is it that when disturbances arise in an individual's
brain, the spiritual functions become abnormal as well? After all, the spirit
is independent!

Yes, but not in human functions, because he directs these functions
through the brain, through this wonderful laboratory of thoughts, and device for controlling functions. You know that even the best driver will be

incapable of driving a car as well as any other car if there are defects in the manufacture of this car, or else damage to the engine. The spirit strives to do whatever he can, but that is all. Should the defects turn out to be excessive, the spirit abandons this body, and there is no [alternative but] to commit it to an insane asylum.

Let us turn to the third topic now. Let us talk about philosophy. You undoubtedly are very familiar with this important art. Therefore I will not talk about those concepts of philosophy that correspond to the spirit of the spirits' tidings and do not contradict them. I want to, however, talk about the so-called corruption or decadence branch of philosophy.

What do these philosophers of decadence claim? They claim that the human being does not go forward, but backwards; that he does not ascend above an animal, but skids lower than it; that humanity's progress is not progress but rather regression.

Can we agree with these philosophers of decadence? If you want to – agree with them, for they do have their logic as well. I don't want to agree with them, though, and will never agree, because of the following reasons.

Yes, they are right in that the human organism becomes less capable of fighting [for survival], that it has lost the dog's sense of smell, the keen eyesight of the eagle, and the wolf's powerful fangs. Is that a sign of regression, though? Absolutely not! That is the ability of every animal's body to adapt to the changes and demands of life, and to simplify itself by discarding whatever is unnecessary. What would an individual do these days with a tail in his pants or her skirt? He does not have to hang by it from a branch like a monkey, swat flies like a cow, or express his feelings to the master like a dog. Keen eyesight is a good thing; a hand held lantern on a street at night is a good thing as well. If it was necessary, though, to your father's father, then it is superfluous to you on streets that are flooded with electric light. The same thing is true of [the sense of] smell. Why do you have to sniff out the footsteps of your lover, when you can trace them over the telephone? Similarly, none of you will track the trail of a cow through the bushes. Teeth have become almost superfluous to you as well. You do not defend yourselves with them. You have much better means of defense, for example the V-1 rocket.

Let us confess, though – some things do need to be improved. More attention should be paid to the body! Exercise it, harden it, give it work, and in particular alter the types of your food. Don't stick into your mouth all kinds of ice creams that break even glass, and chemical substances that ruin your teeth. Candy is sweet, but the consequences are bitter. One even feels like crying and screaming when the dear tooth starts to act up in your mouth. After all, it is possible to make this candy in a manner that will not damage the teeth.

Promote sport, but not sport like it is now. That is not sport but the death of the spirit, because in a spiritual sense your athletes are a deeper vacuum than the vacuum of Torricelli. An individual's upbringing should be instituted so that the spirit and the body will develop in a harmonic accord, otherwise the philosophers of decadence will be right.

You have already been told why man strays so frequently and so badly from his road of spiritual development. You have also been shown the path to the beautiful future; just don't lose your hopes and your strength.

Should a wife ever find her husband drunk and lying in the mud with the household pig then, after all, she should not immediately leave him in the pigsty forever. He will come to his senses eventually, just help him and everything will be all right. Should everyone, though, only ridicule the fallen one and turn away from him, then there is no doubt at all that he will descend [to the level of] and become a pig, only still dirtier.

Permit me, with a brief examination of this subject, to conclude for today and take leave. [[1813]]

Ilgya   07/02/44 1845

_ ★ ★ ★ _

It seems to me that I should talk about what may appear peculiar to you in some of the spirits' tidings. You, people, are used to hearing God's apostles speak in a solemn and dull language; and be attired in black garb, with overgrown beards, and without a smile on their lips.

You are surprised by the spirits' plain and occasionally even coarse language, and particularly humor, not to even mention its master – Ali. The high Indra, too, generally loves to come down to his children of the Earth with a smile on his lips, rather than with harsh lightning in his hand.

We, the spirits, want you, the people, to understand us. Therefore we come to you as people. We do not want only the chosen ones and those endowed with college or academic diplomas to understand us and follow us, but also the tiller of the soil whose callous hands know how to hold a plow, but don't know how to hold a wise book. We want to be heard and understood primarily not by a lady missionary clad in solemn attire, or a professor, but by a strayed lady of the streets to whom our words are more essential. These people flee from whatever is hard to understand and boring. They will pause when hearing a beautiful and cheerful song, even though it might be talking about the very highest matters, but will turn away from a worthy but boring and incomprehensible requiem.

You do not have and will not have any means of force for baptizing humanity in The Almighty's faith. Your weapons for conquering the hearts and minds are altogether different, and they are being given to you. They are so varied that you can select them according to the need for each individual, for the conquest of each person, no matter what he might be like.

You will not conquer an overly wise individual no matter what, because he is already overflowing, and no matter what you might toss into this vessel only water will flow over the brim.

You are concerned that struggles, danger, and perhaps torment await you, even though you should rejoice. Have you ever seen a prophet, a true prophet, who reposed in roses and whom the people brought honey and wine? No, because prophets do not say what the people like! They do not flatter the people's villainy and do not kiss the boots of those who are in power. They walk through thorns and hatred, while bringing their torch to those who thirst for light, but not for chains and bread.

That is what your road on Earth is like – hard, gloomy, and difficult. The pathway of your spirits, though, will be sunny and divinely beautiful. The road of humanity's future, paved with your hearts and overlaid with your blood, will become equally bright and beautiful.

I conclude.   [[1927]]

Ilgya   07/04/44 1630

_ ★ ★ ★ _

Omega has allowed me now to acquaint you with the meaning of the events. After the previous World War, whose fault lay with the German government, the German people had ended up in an unbearable situation. There were many people, but their colonies had been taken away from them. The German people lacked breathing [space] and they started a war for their rights. The Almighty acknowledged these rights and gave victory to German weapons. The Almighty had entrusted the leadership of the

German people to His high spirit – Adolf. His task was to return to the German people the right of people to live the same way as other people live. The second and the more important task was to smash the power of Satan.

That high spirit, however, did not live up to The Almighty's expectations. The miraculously easy victories and the idolization of the people gave his matter such a powerful impulse that the spirit broke. The good goals were replaced by evil goals – the conquest of the world and the enslavement of all people. The Almighty felt then extremely disappointed in His spirit, and withdrew from him. The consequences were tragic – not one victory any longer.

It seemed to us that The Almighty will abandon Earth to its fate, for He covered His face and remained silent. None of us, spirits, dared to disturb Him, for no one felt capable of renewing His faith. Then, however, came the moment and The Almighty uncovered His face. He glanced at the Earth and asked God, "Do You have a spirit who would be capable of justifying My trust?"

God bowed His head and remained silent. Then The Almighty asked Satan, but He also remained silent.

The Almighty looked once more at the Earth, which was enveloped in smoke, and said, "Only one course remains for Me – to be unjust and not keep My promise. There is still only one spirit, who has never been faithful to Me, perhaps he will be capable of being faithful when the other spirits are incapable of that. I see Alexander on Earth. Summon him to the Deoss Temple and ask him whether it is possible to save man, and if it is, whether he will undertake to carry out everything that I will ask of him."

Satan then said, "Yes, You are right! He stands in-between God and Me. He does not acknowledge either of Us. He is the only one whom We are incapable of breaking. Tell Us, who is he?"

The Almighty replied, "He is My despair and My hope!"

Alexander was thus summoned. He told The Almighty, "Only the largest sacrifice is capable of saving humanity on Earth. Permit me to make this sacrifice."

Hence The Almighty's teachings were given to the nations on Earth. They were shown the road to a bright future, and the country of Latvia was protected so that this could take place. Once this had happened, The Almighty said, "I leave the nations on Earth now to You – God and Satan.

Wage a fight for good and for evil. I will return to the children of Earth only when the good will have won."

God said, "Almighty, the good cannot win now, only evil can, because the world is so full of hatred that all the stars grow dim in this atmosphere of hatred."

Satan said then, "Yes, humanity has no other way now than My road. After it will have experienced all the worst of the evil, then it will flee from it, and then God will be able to come to Earth."

The Almighty entrusted you, His envoys, to preserve and to disseminate His teachings. As people, you are responsible for the entire humanity. Satan will do His utmost to ruin you, for then the entire humanity will be lost as well. You have to overcome Satan with only your human strength, and you have to know how to preserve the Tidings even if Santorino were to abandon your land. No sacrifice may be too big for you and no work too hard. You have dozed for too long. You had months and weeks – you have now only days and hours. Wake up, for Karino knocks at the door of Latvia.

All of you should destroy immediately everything that has a dangerous political significance. Everyone should look through the Tidings independently, and mark with a blue pencil [what belongs in] the third book. Should there be time, then have Alexander give his conclusions on Sunday; if there will not be – act independently.

The Almighty places His greatest expectations on Alexo, who has to undertake all risks and accomplish even the impossible.

The Almighty gives unlimited authority to Alexander. His words will be the words of The Almighty, for The Almighty will guide only him.

I think that you understand everything. I will return now to the former again.

What does Adolf still hope for, by continuing the war? He hopes for disunity of the Allies and for the abilities of his inventors. This latter hope is not groundless, for the work is being carried on feverishly and there is much hope as well, but time and place are needed, a tranquil place. The Allies understand that and no longer sleep. The nerves of the German people begin to wear out as well. Therefore Germany may collapse, yet what will come after that?

Punishment will come; it will come for the entire world, unless the nations will wake up in time.

Adolf has turned from being Stalin's worst misfortune into his greatest good fortune. The Communists, as allies, can get in everywhere now without any opposition. They do that under a clever mask. They announce to the world that democratic laws, and even faith in God, have been restored. They come in all the lands with such a beautiful and democratic program that no honest individual can raise any objections. Thus communism gradually enters everywhere, and gradually grabs power, in order to discard this mask at the right moment, and stand in all of its devilish bareness.

You fear that the power of communism threatens the small country of Latvia, because you know this might. This power, however, threatens the entire world, and where will you run to? You can see what Adolf has done, and the slow-witted German nation that followed him.

Prepare yourselves for the very worst, because then only one [alternative] remains – a pleasant surprise.

Why doesn't The Almighty want to help at least the six of you with a miracle? Because you must not permit that, as Alexander has already told Alexo. Christ performed many miracles for the sake of others. The executioners beat and tortured Him, and said, "If You are the Son of God then perform a miracle and save Yourself. Then all of us will also acknowledge You and worship You."

Why didn't Christ perform a miracle on this occasion, for, truly, all the people would then have recognized Him as God? Ponder this well! Strive to understand this, because the entire significance of your goal depends on that.

There would be much else to tell you that is important, but there is no time. Do not converse [with the spirits] any more today. I conclude.

[[1805]]

Ilgya   07/06/44 1718

Ilgya is speaking. Conversations with you were not anticipated for today, but since you have gathered – let us talk.

I will first announce to you that Omega and the Divine will speak on Sunday, or perhaps even Saturday. I will inform you of the exact time through Alexander. The tidings will be of an extremely important nature, therefore it would be desirable for everyone to be present, the guests as well, but only those who want to.

Omega and I agree with Alexander's thoughts regarding the format of *The Book of Tidings*, therefore write everything in a single book.

Print the tidings of a personal nature in fine print, but those of a spiritual and instructive nature in larger print, and each in a different font so that it will be easy to differentiate the spiritual from the secular.

From this book – which you should call, *"The Book of Tidings of The Almighty and His Spirits to Humanity"* – you can afterwards constitute various books according to the need and desire. With one stipulation, though – under no circumstances may you alter the text, add or delete a single word.

Your own speculations or explanations and remarks can be used only below the text and separated from it, or else before and after the text, while clearly indicating that they are not part of the tiding of the spirits. Anyone among the people who will dare to transgress these stipulations will be mercilessly thrown into Hell for a thousand years.

Do you have any questions? There are no questions!

Sineokia is not on Earth and cannot speak today, perhaps Saturday.

You are experiencing difficult moments now. Those who have lost their homeland come to you. Open up your hearts to them, and be kinder to them than to the most beloved guests, for God follows them and rewards the good ones, but Satan follows them even more closely and punishes harshly the callous ones with a harshness beyond your imagination.

Alexander will give you on Sunday instructions for accomplishing what has been assigned. His decisions will be final and non-negotiable, for they will come from above.

I take leave from you now. Be brave and believe in yourselves and in a miracle.

A new spirit will talk with you now. [[1745]]

Temio   07/06/44

Listen, because I, Temio, am speaking!

The wealthy owner of a large estate died. His heir arrived from the city – a pleasant, wise, and fair, young man – and took over the management of the estate.

One day a storm arose and uprooted some trees on a forest road. The new estate owner ordered the tenants to clear them off [the road]. The tenants assembled and began to work. Then a tenant, by the name of Hell's Goat, said, "People say that the new owner is fair. Why does he then take us away from our work rather than hire workers for clearing off the trees, since he is rich. Let's go to him and tell him that, and then we will see whether he truly is just."

The other tenants agreed. The new owner listened to them and said, "Yes, you are right. Go home, I will hire some workers."

A few days passed and Hell's Goat said again, "Why do we have to go and work for the estate. That is not right! The owner takes us away from our own work. Let him hire workers for his own work, he has saved up plenty of money."

The owner thought, "Yes, they are right. Why should they have to work for the estate?"

He released the tenants from [work for the estate].

Some time passed, and on the day when the rent was due the tenants said, "Owner, why do we have to pay you rent for land that belongs only to God, and for which you personally have not spent one penny?"

The owner thought this over, "Yes, why do they have to do that?" and refused the rent money.

Another problem arouse, though. It was necessary to pay taxes to the state. The owner paid them, but since there was no longer any income, the money that had been saved-up was soon depleted. It was necessary to repair the roads and to perform other public works. The owner called together the tenants and explained to them the situation that had arisen.

"Yes," said Hell's Goat, "you have quickly squandered the money for which we worked so hard. What can one do, though, the state obligations have to be fulfilled, otherwise we will be evicted from the land. Since no one will do anything on their own, we have to elect trustworthy people who will take care of all these matters fairly and according to their best conscience."

A committee was elected, obviously, with Hell's Goat at its head.

A few more days passed and Hell's Goat came to the owner. "You know that I am the chair of the committee, and you also understand that since there is a committee it also needs office space. There is hardly enough room for ourselves in our homes, but you live in such a large house. You could get by with the small room in the annex."

The owner considered this, "Yes, the house had been built with the tenants' money. They have a right to it and the need for it."

The owner moved into the room [in the annex]. That was an easy task, because the servants had been dismissed and the furniture exchanged for bread, because the owner, to everyone's surprise, wanted to eat as well.

It wasn't long before Hell's Goat called a general meeting and said, "Since we have to pay taxes to the state and there is nothing with which to pay workers, then everyone has to come to perform community work, as well as pay imposts."

The owner remained gloomily silent, and did not say anything. The tenants also remained silent, and scratched the backs of their heads.

Time did not stand still. The day came when Hell's Goat called a general meeting again, and said, "The imposts are too low, they have to be raised."

"Why?" the owner asked.

"Why!" Hell's Goat shot back. "Do you think that I will run around in your business and those of others for nothing? After all, I have no time left over to work for myself, but you know how much work there is on such a large estate. One has to arrange for the work, has to supervise it, has to write down things, and so on. It is not possible to get by without an assistant, a secretary, and supervisors, and one cannot ask them to work for nothing, because that would be unfair."

Still some more time passed. The imposts grew and another general meeting had to be called. The tenants sat there and grumbled in their beards. Hell's Goat raged, beat on his chest, and screamed.

Then one of the tenants asked, "Tell us plainly, after all, just how much does each of us have to pay?"

"But very little," replied the chair, "only a hundred talers."

"Wait, wait!" the owner rose to his feet. "How much did you say? A hundred?"

"Hundred!" Hell's Goat shot back.

"How much did you pay my father, though?" the owner asked.

Hell's Goat muttered something incomprehensible.

"How much did you pay?" the owner turned to the tenants.

They looked at each other, sighed, and said, "As best as we can remember – fifty talers."

The owner got mad then, and said, "As long as you were in the right, I gave in, but you are no longer now. I can see that your justice has led us to the worst injustice, and you live far worse now than you did previously.

Enough! Go home! Beginning with tomorrow everything will be as it was before!"

The tenants dispersed gratefully and happily. On their way home they threw Hell's Goat into a pond.

That is how this tale ends, and I, Temio, bid you farewell.

Santorino   07/09/44 1542

→Santorino speaking. Today I have to relate some grave matters to you. The Almighty ordered us, the spirits, to deliver His Tidings to you, the people. This order came at a time, and you – The Almighty's chosen ones, were situated in a locality, which made it difficult to carry out this order without its fulfillment being at least not disturbed by birds of steel, for Earth was engulfed in the flames of war.

We, the spirits, accomplished this, The Almighty's task, one hundred percent, considering the free will which has been given to the people.

Yet how have you, people, accomplished your tasks – also one hundred percent?

Now comes The Almighty's command, "I have completed sending My Tidings to the people on Earth. I thank you, the spirits, for seeing to it that these Tidings have reached the hands of man without interference. My and your tasks have been accomplished now. We will now leave man to himself, to carry out the tasks which he has received. His future has been placed in his own hands. It now depends only on himself. I forbid you, the spirits, to help man any longer. I want to see whether he is worthy of these Tidings, and of the crown of the ruler."

Thus spoke The Almighty.

These Tidings are now in your hands, and the entire responsibility falls on you to see to it that humanity receives them. You have to carry them through fire and water, and hand them to humanity. With that, your task will be accomplished. Humanity's task will be to comprehend and to acknowledge them.

– ★ ★ ★ –

You have been told, "Pray to God only with good deeds, but not with words."

Still, man cannot do without prayer, for he has to maintain personal contact with his Father – God. One prayer was left to you – the Lord's Prayer.

Now God gives you, the people, this prayer in a more complete form. Pray to God with these words:

"My God – Father – I pray to You. Strengthen my spirit and body for good deeds, and restrain them from all evil. Shelter me from hunger, thirst, and other suffering. Deliver me from indolence and sensuality. Do not abandon me at times of doubt and torment. Do not deny me immortality. Allow me to become a son – daughter worthy of You, and raise me above the Earth, the sun, and the stars. Amen."

This is the only prayer which God gives to you. Everything that one may pray for is expressed in it. Should you have a special desire, express it after the prayer in your own words. ←

I will now talk some more about religion. The priests have to be men, and the priests' assistants or deputies – women, because not every woman is capable of expressing her sorrows to a man, even though he wears the robe of a priest.

The priest's assistant does not wear a hat or a wreath on the head, but wears a bracelet in the form of a wreath on the right hand.

I bless you. I congratulate all of you in God's and my own name.

Omega will speak in half-an-hour. You only have to arrange the appropriate lighting and paper. [[1748]]

Omega   07/09/44 1818

I, the Ruler of the Future and of Death, and The Almighty's thought expressed in words, Chief Spirit Omega, am talking with you – the envoys to Earth.

The Divine announced to you today God's decision, and the prayer. I bring you The Almighty's blessing. - ★ ★ ★ -

I pass on to you this decision of The Almighty. The Almighty wants you to be independent, and to live up, in your persons, to the expectations that have been placed on humanity.

The Almighty's high spirit Alexander also adheres to this principle. Therefore The Almighty releases him from any tasks of a specific nature, and leaves to him general supervision in those matters which he, himself, considers to be necessary.

With that, I conclude my tiding – I, Omega, The Almighty's thought expressed in words.   [[1842]]

Indra   07/11/44 1749

Indra is speaking. I am speaking today on behalf of the Divine as well, for Santorino, himself, cannot come.

_ ★ ★ ★ _

Let us talk some more about religion. What rights should be accorded to a higher priest with respect to a lower priest? The rights of leadership and supervision! Should a lower priest function incorrectly and fail to observe the directions from the higher priest, the higher priest can have a general membership meeting convened of those who elected the lower priest, and recommend that it expresses a lack of confidence in the priest.

If a lack of confidence is expressed, then those actions should be taken that have already been pointed out. If the general membership meeting, however, does not express a lack of confidence, and the higher priest persists in his demands, then he has to turn to the general membership meeting of the priests who are higher than he. They will then decide this concern. Should their decision be to dismiss the guilty priest from his office, then this decision has to be sent to the high priest of Earth for approval. Before making his decision, he will summon the guilty priest and his governing board, and will familiarize himself in detail with the circumstances of the matter. The decision of the high priest is final and non-negotiable.

There is only one high priest of the Earth and he has neither an assistant nor a deputy. He may depart from the execution of his duties for a short period of time only under the most essential circumstances, while leaving one of the continental priests in his place. All decisions that have been made by the deputy become void on the high priest's return to duty. In order for them to remain in effect, they have to be approved anew by the high priest.

The high priest never passes his wreath on to anyone. The high priest always has to be in the attire of the high priest and with the wreath on his head. The high priest may not appear before anyone, except for his family members in his palace, other than in the attire of the high priest. The high priest should be escorted on the streets by a special guard, clad in solemn attire. The high priest gives replies to questions of an official nature only in writing, and never and under any circumstances orally.

Let us turn now to the topic regarding prisons. The prison may exist only as an institution for correction, upbringing, and isolation, but not as an institution of punishment. Everyone who is to be jailed should first appear before a commission of physicians. This ascertains whether there might be defects in the construction of the brain, which have perhaps influenced the unfortunate one toward unlawful behavior.

A commission of psychologists should follow the commission of physicians. This commission acquaints itself in detail with those who have brought up the prisoner and with his upbringing, and with the people in whose midst the guilty one has lived. After these commissions comes a joint commission of different specialists, which decides whether the prisoner can be cured or else rehabilitated.

Should it turn out that after a specific period of time neither treatment nor rehabilitation can transform this individual into a good person, then he should be isolated for his entire life on some island, specifically established for this purpose. Those who are isolated there should be given all the rights of a human being, except for those that are essential for their isolation.

The death penalty is not permissible, except in those cases where the prisoner is a threat to other people, and may gain freedom unless he is shot or otherwise executed.

I will conclude with that for today. If you wish, we will talk some more within the next few days. Think things over and prepare your questions. Should I find it necessary, I will reply to some of them.   [[1915]]

Indra   07/14/44 1806

Indra is speaking. I have to say a few words to you with regard to the Tidings.

As you have been told already, the language of the spirits is entirely different from the language of the people, not only [with respect to] words but with respect to ideas as well. In order to express their thoughts, the spirits have to adapt themselves to the capabilities of your language, and in addition have to express them in a manner that will be understandable to everyone. Much is being expressed to you allegorically. Also, some things perhaps do not correspond exactly to the abstract truth, for they do not lend themselves to human concepts and would be incomprehensible to [a human], therefore we have to try to present these concepts with the help of other ideas.

Perhaps your future historians will claim that not all the historical facts that are given in the Tidings correspond to the historical truth. Well, I have to say here that all your histories are very remote from the true historical facts. If you were able to look into Alpha's history of the nations on Earth, your concepts would collapse completely. Who writes history? People! Are all people completely objective — rather, are capable of being like that? No, not even if they wanted to be! They can be only subjective.

If an individual tells you something about a third person, what do you need to know first? You have to know very much — is he smart, is he a psychologist, is he a friend or else a foe of this third person, is he envious, and is he fair? You have to know much else as well. Should he be ill disposed toward this third person, will he depict this third person correctly to you? No! What do you have to do then in order to obtain a true idea about this third person? Listen to a friend of this person? Yes, but the idea will still not be complete. You will know this third person's good and bad characteristics, you will see the right and the left sides, but the middle will remain obscured.

What should you do next? Yes, you have to get to know this third person yourself! All right, but can you guarantee that you will know how to comprehend this individual correctly, and will not succumb to subjective influence? No! So then, no human is capable of giving an entirely correct concept about some person; neither are all the people. There will be just as many right concepts and just as many wrong ones as there were people.

People shape history, and it is also people who write about these people, and how do they write? Generally either only the good or else only the bad aspects and, besides that, not from their own experiences but according to the accounts of others.

Rulers generally order that only good things be written about them. Once they die, their enemies again strive to find all the very worst things about them. Eventually the ruler is, in the eyes of later generations, only like these historians have depicted him, but not like he really was.

Yes, your history, particularly the history of ancient times, is a mirror, but such a distorted mirror that there is not one true face in it and not one correctly depicted and evaluated event.

(Take a ten-minute break.) [[1843]]

Let us continue. The spirits talk with you. How do they talk? At this moment with the help of the letters of the alphabet. How do you converse among yourselves, you people? You will claim — with words expressed orally and in writing. Can an individual, however, speak only in a manner like that, only with the mouth and a pen? No, he can speak and speaks with the help of the entire body. The eyes! What are the eyes? Folklore calls them the mirror of the soul. Why? Because one can express even more with the eyes than with words [uttered by] the tongue. Just look at two people in love! Look into the lake of her blue eyes! Such waves of emotion billow in it, such a sun of love shines, that compared to this language all words seem like the rattling of dried-up tree leaves in the autumn.

The eyes also know how to entice, smile, and scold. Your lips, forehead, and even cheeks know how to speak as well. Quite often a subordinate already knows what to expect, on only seeing his supervisor's face. The individual helps the tongue to express his thoughts with his hands, not to even mention such an effective means of expression as a bang of the fist on a desk. Women quite often love to speak with the help of their feet, by stomping the floor with them or by kicking their backs. We mentioned the back inadvertently, but don't you speak with the help of the back as well? Yes, and very definitely and exhaustively at that! You turn your back – and everything has been said. As you can see, your means of expression are extremely rich. Why am I telling you, though, what you probably know for yourselves? In order to tell you that the spirits' abilities of expressing their thoughts are even more varied. They can express their thoughts to you even without saying them to you.

That should suffice, however, and I'll ask for permission to take leave from you.   [[1916]]

Kolinto   07/16/44

_ ★ ★ ★ _

I will relate to you an episode from Chinese life, because that nation is particularly dear to me.

There once was a long line of the condemned at the executioner's block. A mandarin was being carried by. The mandarin noticed in surprise that a man stood in the line of the condemned and read a book.

The mandarin had [his litter] stopped and asked the man who was reading the book, "Aren't you afraid of death at all?"

"Of death? Why should I be? Do you think that you will escape it?"

"I don't think so," the mandarin said, "but still, I would not be able to talk like you do while facing the ax of death."

"Yes, it does concern me as well," the man who was reading remarked, "that the line of the condemned is so short and I will not be able to finish reading this book. Don't you understand that you are also interrupting me!"

The mandarin ordered, "There is no sense in punishing with death someone who is not afraid of it. I will punish him with life. Go home and finish reading your book!"

With that I, too, will conclude. [[1716]]

Shota   07/16/44

Old Shota is here. I know that you expect something else from me, rather than what I will tell you, especially my dear Emily. Permit me, as a former poet, [to relate a poem to you], but only in prose.

There once lived a prince in the Caucasus. He was good and wise. No traveler passed his house without having a drink of refreshing wine and a bite of the warm *churek*[2].

The day came when the czar summoned the prince. The prince called in his overseer and told him, "I will ride away for a prolonged period of time, and leave you in charge. Be a good and fair master to the servants, and a hospitable host to the tired travelers. Give to those who need and who deserve, but don't give to those who have plenty on their own. See to it that the workers do their work according to their strength, and reward them justly."

The prince rode off. Some time passed. The grapes ripened in the vineyards. The cold breath of Elbrus blew the leaves from the trees. The rivers murmured gloomily in their beds of rock.

The prince rode back; rode back and froze in indignation. The yard was full of drunk tramps, among them the more robust servants as well. Some exhausted workers labored in the fields. The overseer, happy and proud, hastened to meet his master.

"What have you done?" the prince asked angrily.

"I carried out your order," the overseer replied. "I fed those who asked for bread, and released from work those workers who complained about being weak."

"You blind fool," said the prince, "you did what you had been ordered, but without a mind and sense! You fed and gave drink to tramps of the road for days and even months, but left without wine and bread these two travelers who sit underneath the tree on the side of the ditch, because they did not come begging to you. You released loafers from work, for they complained about the work being hard, and made the diligent but quiet servants do their work. Your duty was to see how everyone works and what work everyone is capable of doing. You should have urged on the lazy ones and held back those who were working too hard. You should not have waited for the servants to come to you, but you should have gone to them yourself and should have seen the sorrows and needs of everyone. You should have punished, but not have given drink to, the lazy ones, and should have rewarded the diligent ones. Always go first to those who remain silent, for it means that their hearts are weeping. You have not understood anything. You have ruined my home, and you have splattered my honor with mud. Go to the kitchen as the lowest servant! You have not been born to understand justice and to lead other people!"

That is what the prince said.

The high Indra did not talk with you today. Not because you did not have any questions – we are already used to that – but because he cannot speak today and will speak some other time.

I alight away, and Nakcia will talk now with Alexo.

Ilgya   07/20/44 1753

_ ★ ★ ★ _

The Almighty is dissatisfied now not only with Adolf, but with all his opponents as well, for their goals have also become egotistic, and therefore your nation and others have to perish. The Almighty has firmly decided to leave humanity to itself, so that it would enter the abyss so deeply that not even the tiniest star would shine for it, because then, overcome by the horrible darkness, it will start to thirst for the sunshine of the truth.

Until a child has painfully burned his fingers in a fire, it is not possible to restrain him from the temptation of the fire, either with beautiful words or with threats. I am overcome at times by a desire to ask The Almighty to deprive man of his free will, in order to save him – but this thought is insanity.

- ★ ★ ★ - [[1828]]

Indra   07/20/44 1843

I want to talk today about self-criticism. Perhaps this subject seems insignificant to you and not appropriate for the current moment, but your cannons do not sound in my ears as loudly as in your, and your human concerns seem less important to me than they are. So then, let us forget for a few minutes the gale of cannons and let us talk about self-criticism, because this subject seems so important to me that all the war's batteries become silent compared to it.

Man's biggest problem is his lack of self-criticism. There are few people who critically evaluate their thoughts, decisions, and deeds, but there are endlessly many who criticize the deeds and thoughts of others. Perhaps that is the reason for today's cannonade as well.

Man, criticize yourself more! Do not refuse this unpleasant and thankless work, because this work can bring a blessing to you and to everyone. You see all the mistakes of another individual, and do not cease to criticize them with the greatest joy, but examine each of your own deeds and words from aside, from the point of view of another person, and an entirely different world will open before your eyes.

You helped your debt-ridden friend once you had grown tired of him and his requests. You helped him in order to be rid of him finally, and feel surprised when your friend thanks you so coldly. You reprimanded your subordinate because he was late for work, and were surprised that he felt insulted. Did you bother to find out why he was late for work? Yes, he was supposedly drunk yesterday. A scoundrel, right? Perhaps, but did you find out why he got drunk? Yes, you found out that as well. This fool supposedly got drunk because he had met his wife in the park with another man. A trifling and ridiculous reason! Stop for a moment, however, and visualize that this morning you encountered your wife and your friend kissing each other, and you will feel altogether differently. And so on, without an end.

You joke and laugh, but you see only a bitter grin on the lips of others. "Fools, they don't understand jokes," you think surly. Evaluate your joke, though, and your ability of telling it, and perhaps you, too, will lose any desire to laugh.

"The trouble is that we consider ourselves to be the wisest ones," you will claim. Yes, that is one problem.

The other one is that man considers the other person to be worse than he really is. You do not strive to seek out and note the other individual's good characteristics, and those which are superior to your own. You seek the bad and the comical in the other person; you want the other one to be more cowardly, less capable, and more foolish than you are. It is extremely difficult for you to acknowledge the other's superiority. The other individual seems to you to be an enemy, for you, yourself, are like that with respect to him. You seek a hostile intonation in his words if the words themselves are not hostile. You lie to the other one, and pretend in front of him to be different than you are. Therefore it appears to you that the other person does the same thing.

Criticize others, I advise you to do that, but first [criticize] yourself as well, then I, too, will believe you. That is particularly true with respect to the wise ones, but what can one do about the fools? A fool remains a fool forever! He can merely be of two sorts – an uneducated fool, the best kind of a fool – and an educated fool, that is the worst kind of a fool. School is capable of giving only knowledge, but under no circumstances is it capable of giving intellect – that is an axiom – and therefore it is better not to educate fools, so that they would not be able to fool entire nations, if they were to become their leaders.

A fool can only be treated, or else abandoned to his own fate. There are, however, the so-called half-fools as well, and they can, having found out that they are like that, improve themselves. How can an individual know that he is a fool, though?

I will give you the indications of a fool. The first one – he considers himself to be the wisest person. The second – he is convinced that he never makes mistakes. The third – he considers that God has created the world just for him alone.

Further indications [of a fool]. His children are the most beautiful and best in the world. Her husband or his wife is an angel. Should he do some good for someone, then that one has to be eternally grateful to him; but should someone else do some good for him, then that can be forgotten already the next day. Seeking wisdom only in books, but not in life. Lack of self-criticism. Lack of doubts. Blind faith and.... You should tell me some indications as well.

[[We do not reply.]]

The accumulation of superfluous possessions on Earth.

With that, I conclude for today. [[1935]]

Ilgya   07/23/44 1210

_ ★ ★ ★ _

Ask!

[[We ask to have the prayer and Commandments translated into other languages as well.]]

Translate them into all the languages of the world on your own, except without altering the essence of the text.

With respect to the Tidings, I have to say that you, starting with Alexo and Henry, work very hard, but make many new mistakes. Alexander has corrected many mistakes, but still not all of them. It is difficult for you with the language of the Tidings, because it is not Latvian – grammatically [correct] Latvian. What can one do, however, if there is not a single former Latvian among the high spirits who are assigned to talk with you. We have to translate from the language of the spirits into the Latvian language, and simultaneously speak and fight against your tendency to [interfere]. It seems to me that even your professor Endzelin, if he were to sit down at a typewriter, would be incapable of writing from scratch even one tiding in correct Latvian. He would be scared himself by just how short the red pencil becomes on completing the corrections.

All told, what is being proclaimed to you in the form of the alphabet is unimaginable for human abilities, and is even difficult for the spirits to accomplish. Why hasn't The Almighty chosen a different means for His Tidings, let us say – sent a prophet? He has not done that this time so that different high spirits could talk with the people, spirits who could examine all the means and essences of the spirits and of the people, and could resolve all of the most varied questions.

You can now see for yourselves the gigantic difference that exists between the books of the prophets and *The Book of Tidings of The Almighty's Spirits*. There will not be a single individual – starting with someone who is religious and ending with an atheist, starting with a philosopher and ending with a fool – who will not find something in this book that will be worthy and of interest to him, because the authors of this book are dozens of spirits. They are such diverse spirits that at times it may seem that they come from different Heavens, planets, and even Hells.

– ★ ★ ★ – [[1310]]

Kolinto   07/23/44 1430

Kolinto. I will talk with you on behalf of Indra and of myself. The subject: Man as a slave of his possessions.

I observed recently people's struggle to preserve their belongings.

Sweating, out of breath, and with eyes bulging from the forehead, people carry their possessions into [railway] stations, basements, and elsewhere. And – come out naked. What are these possessions due to which an individual loses almost all his sense? Belongings are objects with which man becomes overgrown during his long lifetime, like an old tree with fungi. Belongings are intended to ease man's life, and for comfort, to free him from everyday concerns in old age. It would seem that possessions serve man and that man is their master, but the matter is altogether different in reality. Possessions become man's master and he becomes a slave of his possessions. If man were to accumulate only what is necessary, and in an amount that would be needed for his short lifetime, then the matter would be understandable. Man, however, accumulates for tens, and even for thousands, of lifetimes. He accumulates while already lying on his deathbed. He accumulates for himself and accumulates for his children, as if God had not given them their own heads and their own hands.

An individual can feel entirely free, he can be his own master, only whenever he can throw all his belongings on his back and move while whistling to another part of the world.

Someone purchases beautiful furniture. He lives in an undesirable house. He could move to a better house, but to move all this furniture! How much will that cost, and the movers might damage this beautiful and expensive furniture!

An individual buys himself a small house, and a corner of land that belongs to God. Now the headaches begin! The weeds have to be pulled – people are not available. The roof leaks – go ahead and look for some tin. The maid has stolen a loaf of bread. He is dead! He no longer belongs to himself, but to his house and land.

The wife wants to go to a concert in the evening, but what will the cow in the stable say? The concert remains unattended for the sake of this milk container with horns.

A banker recalls his youth – poverty, an empty stomach, and torn pants. He also recalls the kiss of the neighbor's Liz by the old fence, which was the cause of the torn pants. He recalls how difficult it was for him, but when the beauty reproached him about the old pants that tear while climbing the fence, and reproached him for his poverty, he only laughed and, while whistling, went freely over to Kate.

Then he began to think about the power of money, and decided to acquire it in order to be rid of the old pants and other troubles, in order to become his own master, and so that he could enjoy the pleasures of life.

He has seventy-six years on his shoulders now. He is tired of everything. All food has become bitter. All women have become hollow, wooden dolls. He feels sleepy at a dance. The flowers in the garden reek like wilted tobacco. The car crawls like a turtle. His wife snarls like a toothless lion. Wait now, which wife? Probably the sixth or the seventh one! Oh, how he would like to forget everything, particularly this little angel – his son John – who called him, the father, an old chimpanzee today. To forget his beautiful daughter Nelly who, with her company of bandits, spilled champagne on his favorite plant last night and kept him awake until five in the morning.

To forget everything and rest thoroughly for once, but there is a meeting of the shareholders tomorrow. He has to be there, otherwise Brown will take over his shares. The bank – what can be done about it? To whom can it be entrusted? To his son? He'll squander everything on drinks in one night! To his friend Jim? He'll cheat him, the rascal! To withdraw the money and live peacefully? What will his family and Morgan say, though? They will say that he has become weak, that he relegates to the second and third ranks. No, he cannot allow that! He has to work and fight until the last moment of his life.

Yet what became of the happiness and freedom that this money was supposed to bring? Yes, what? There are only concerns and work. There are only the endlessly heavy bags of money that weigh you down so that it is no longer possible to breathe. Can't breathe, help! Quick, a doctor!

Too late – Death stands in the doorway.

That's how it is with man. He becomes the slave of his possessions. Why was he born then, [why did he] learn, fight, and dream? Was it truly because of this clothing closet, because of this car, and because of this mansion in which repugnant guests dance? Because of this land, which belongs only to God alone? Because of this pig that grunts in the stable? Because of this bag of money, which he, man, himself cannot lift and put in his coffin, and others will certainly not put it there?

Man, think about that – why do you live? Think about what your possessions are and what their real value is! Think that over, and be happy if you are still able to pull out from this disgusting heap of possessions that which is called man's immortal soul. Pull it out crushed, torn, and dusty, and wipe off with it your dirty and deformed, divine face!

I conclude.   [[1525]]

Shota   07/23/44 1555

I, Shota, am among you. Listen once more to your spirit and poet. Give me your hands and follow me to God's majestic throne – the Caucasus – where eagles breathe, as well as the souls that are enticed by beauty and eternity. Let us walk into the garden of a palace and sit down on a lone bench beneath a magnolia tree. Let us not utter a word, merely observe and listen.

Alexander, open your eyes and help me see!

Mary, open your ears and help me hear!

Emily, open your heart and help me feel!

John, open your mind and help me to understand!

Janoss, take hold of your abilities of recollection and don't let me forget!

Alexo, gather your strength and help me to accomplish the difficult task!

Henry, pick up your sharp pen and make my words immortal!

Nicholas, raise my harp and preserve it for the children of the Earth.

I can now see, hear, and understand everything!

In the palace garden sits a ruler – poet. A crown sparkles on his head. A golden harp shines in his hands. The sea murmurs and clings to the rocks, like a new wife to the chest of her husband after their first quarrel. Cypress trees stand along the road, like the dreams of a young woman by her bed. The sun shines brightly in the sky, like a chalice of nectar on God's altar. The high mountains beyond the palace stand with their white hats like the guards of eternity by God's throne. Flowers cover the ground like a dream-like, aromatic carpet in the room of newlyweds.

The ruler – poet – sits all alone, absorbed in thoughts. Now he raises his eyes, black as the night in which angels fly, raises the harp, and it begins to sing. A light and lithe figure emerges from the distant entrance and timidly, seemingly spellbound, approaches the poet. The poet notices it as well, and his face expresses amazement and feelings of admiration. It is a poorly dressed girl with eyes blue as the mountain lakes in which only nymphs swim. Her figure is thin and delicate, but pliant like the stem of a flower and sprightly as the tongue of a nightingale, from which waves of songs flow.

The poet sings about the mightiness of the world and that of God; about the beauty and nobility of what has been created; and about happiness, love, and justice. You hear this song and have forgotten everything. The poet stops singing and the harp drops to his knees. The ruler looks at the girl with eyes full of dreams and love.

"Oh, God," his lips whisper, "I thank You that You have sent me, in the form of this girl, the beauty itself and ideal justice; that You have given a body to my dreams and my yearnings. Your world is so beautiful and wonderful, my God and Creator!"

The poet turns to the girl then, and we hear his words that sound like the gold which drops from the hand of the ruler into the hands of paupers.

"Come closer, my child, and tell me what you desire. I will answer you with only one word, 'Yes.'"

The girl approaches timidly, looks over the ruler from his head to his toes, and then asks with a voice that sounds like the silver coins with which the poor pay their taxes to the ruler.

"Tell me, is this harp made of pure gold, or else only gold plated?"

"It is made of gold," the ruler replies.

"And you have nothing that is more expensive than this harp?" the girl asks again.

"No," replies the poet.

"Then give me this golden harp as a present," the girl pleads.

"Gladly, but will you know how to play on it?"

"No," replies the girl, "but I will get for it, at the market, real fat sheep, whose meat tastes so good to me!"

"Take it," the poet says sadly, while handing the golden harp to the girl.

The girl's eyes light up in joy and she, while muttering words of gratitude, accepts the expensive gift, and departs with slow steps, while looking back frequently.

The poet covers his face with his hands and whispers, "Oh, God, Your world is so dark and insignificant, its beauty is so false!"

We see pearls dropping from the ruler's hands, dropping to the dust on the ground and turning into drops of water. The ruler and poet weeps, and none of you hasten to console him, not even Mary, and neither you – Emily. You claim that you do not know the words that might be able to bring solace to the ruler. You do not have them, and we sit sadly on our bench and don't know what to do.

Look, though, isn't that the very same girl who timidly approaches the ruler again? She reaches out with her tiny hand wanting to stroke the ruler's hair, but holds it back hesitantly and drops it. We hear her trembling voice, "If you cherish this harp so much then take it back."

The ruler uncovers his face and turns to the girl in surprise.

"But, after all, you wanted to buy with it some fat sheep for yourself, which you like so much," he says.

"Yes, I have not eaten anything for three days already. That, however, is nothing. I did not take it for myself, but so that I could feed my sick mother and my three little brothers and four little sisters, who also have not had anything to eat for three days."

"All right," says the ruler, "you and they will never again hear this dreadful word 'hunger.' Why didn't you tell me that right away?"

"I did not know that you have money," the girl replies.

"But then, why did you bring this harp back to me, since you took it while loving your mother, brothers, and sisters? After all, they might have starved to death in that case!"

"Because that made you sad," replies the girl.

"What am I, a stranger, to you, though? What are my sorrows to you?"

"Everything," the girl whispers softly.

"Everything?" the poet asks.

"Yes, everything!" the girl replies loudly by now. Her eyes sparkle like God's stars above God's head.

"But why everything?" the ruler asks softly now.

"Because," replies the girl, "my eyes told me that there is no one in the world who is handsomer than you. Because my ears told me that there are no wiser and dearer words in the world than those which your sweet lips expressed. Because my eyes and ears conveyed all this to my blind and deaf heart, and my heart began to see and hear, and said that only you in the entire world, only you alone, are the one whom it loves and will love eternally. Because you are my entire world, and without you there is neither the sun, nor the world, nor mother, nor brothers, and I, myself, do not exist either, for without you only death remains for me!"

That is what the girl said.

We see the ruler stand up and the girl fall into his arms. We still hear, and will hear eternally, his words, "Oh, God, forgive me my rashness and my doubts, forgive me, an insignificant human, and do not punish me for this inexpressible happiness!"

We feel unneeded and return to our room. I let go of your hands and take leave.   [[1714]]

Ali   07/26/44 1837

Ali. I don't have many words. I merely want to say that there are few human beings left on Earth, but there are many bureaucrats, bureaucrats of various degrees. I will not enumerate the lowest degree, but only the highest one.

My high ruler, the sultan, had a conversation once with an old philosopher. The subject of the conversation was – the bureaucrat. They could not agree on who could be called a true bureaucrat. In order to settle the disagreement, the sultan had the bureaucrats of his realm summoned to the castle, and asked them how each of them carries out his duties.

The bureaucrats came and went, but the philosopher shook his gray head and muttered, "No, that is not an ideal bureaucrat!"

An old man came, after a lengthy period of time, and called himself a servant of the sultan.

"Why do you call yourself a servant, but not a bureaucrat?" the sultan asked.

"Because I am incapable of being a bureaucrat," the [old man] replied.

"Explain your words!" ordered the sultan.

"How can I call myself a bureaucrat if during all my long years I have been incapable of compelling the deceased to register personally in the book of the dead. That, however, has to be done by others in their stead, and because of this all kinds of errors can crop up."

"Enough!" said the philosopher. "I can see that there is at least one true bureaucrat in your realm."

With that I, too, will conclude. [[1857]]

Shota   07/26/44 1920

_ ★ ★ ★ _

For a short, little story now.

A family once lived in the Caucasus. It lived rather well and in a beautiful place – on the shore of the sea. A disaster occurred one day. The family's house stood below a cliff that overhung it. This cliff developed a crack, for a storm raged and lightning struck the cliff. The cliff could fall on top of the house at any moment.

The neighbors warned the family, but the head [of the household] said, "Yes, it is risky, we will have to move tomorrow. Is the cliff going to collapse yet today?"

The cliff did not collapse.

Thus one day followed the next. The cliff threatened, but did not collapse. Hence all the inhabitants of the house got used to the idea slowly that the cliff will not collapse today, and they will still be able to move tomorrow. They felt sorry for the house, and neither did they want to build a new one, nor move the heavy furniture.

Thus came the day on which they did not think about the threat of the cliff at all. Precisely on this day the cliff shattered and buried the house with all its inhabitants.

That was one little story. I will tell you another one.

There were two houses along the main road. A young woman lived in each of them, and each one planted a beautiful garden of flowers in front of her house, because both of them loved flowers.

One of them, however, loved them too much. She could not take her eyes from her flowers, and could not part with a single blossom. Whenever a traveler asked her for one, she said, "What will my garden look like if I were to pick all the blossoms, because there are so many who ask for them and the flowers are so beautiful!"

Her words scared off the travelers, and hardly any of them stopped now by the beauty's beautiful garden.

Her neighbor acted differently. She gladly gave blossoms to the travelers, and laughter and songs could always be heard by her garden fence.

The first one said, "Your garden looks so unsightly, almost all the blossoms have been picked!"

"Yes, the blossoms have been picked, but they travel all the roads of the world and tell about my garden. Anyway, no blossom blooms eternally and every flower wilts in the fall."

That is how the two girls talked to each other.

A morning came. The first girl looked out a window and cried out in lament, "Oh, God, all my beautiful flowers have frozen last night!"

She walked around in the garden and wept. She missed the magnificent flowers so much, and particularly the red roses, whose blossom she had refused just last evening to pin on the chest of a handsome and beloved traveler, for the rose, after all, seemed more beautiful and dearer to her.

The other girl entered her garden, looked around, and said in a joyful voice, "Thank God that I picked my last blossom last evening for that handsome young man, otherwise it would also have frozen last night!"

Days passed. Winter came. Everything slept wrapped in a white blanket. Not a single blossom adorned the gardens of the two girls. Only the wind howled there and blew the snow into snowdrifts. Both girls looked with sad eyes at the empty gardens and the road.

Then one evening the sound of tiny bells was heard, and a golden carriage stopped at the door of the second girl's house. A noble and handsome young man stepped out of it and entered the girl's house, with a bouquet of orchids in his hand.

"Good evening," he said, "I travel from distant lands, from warm countries where flowers bloom eternally. I remembered you and how much you loved flowers, and brought you this bouquet of blossoms from a southern land, because your garden is empty in the summer and in the winter. The frost picks it in the winter, in the summer – travelers. Accept this bouquet as the gratitude of all the travelers, and as testimony of my love. I will come for you tomorrow and will take you south, where you will not lack flowers to give to travelers."

The morning came. The second girl drove off in the golden carriage. The first one, though, remained sitting sadly by the window, and looking at the empty road for days and nights. Not even the sled of a beggar stopped once at her gate.

I conclude and take leave in the hope of meeting you again. [[2013]]

Chapter XV
August 1944

Ilgya   08/05/44 1655

Ilgya is speaking. – ★ ★ ★ – I will answer some of your questions.

Fortunetellers. Yes, Ali has already talked about this subject. He has, however, not illuminated it completely. There are so few true fortunetellers and so many swindlers that it is generally like Ali said. Yet, still, I have to tell you, there are people with such keen abilities of the spirit that they are not only capable of reading your past, but are even capable of looking into the future. The prognostication of this future can never be realized one hundred percent, because one can only see the scheme of the future. As you know, this does not always materialize.

That is why Ali sent you to the fortunetellers. Should a fortuneteller err, then only he has erred, but if a spirit were to err then the entire authority of the spirits can collapse in the eyes of the nonbelievers. Fortunetellers manage to look readily into the book of fates of individual people, but it is much more difficult to predict the destinies of nations and of countries. You know that for yourselves, though, and can readily understand why [that is the case]. The conclusion – you can go to a good fortuneteller, just don't believe him one hundred percent. I must say as well that predictions also come true whenever the one who asks, acts as has been predicted.

– ★ ★ ★ – [[1750]]

Kolinto   08/05/44 1905

– ★ ★ ★ –

I will speak briefly today. My topic: Injustice – the curse of humanity.

Injustice is a barely noticed, but a severe, curse. There is nothing that man feels as painfully as an injustice, even the most trifling one. Should the supervisor punish a subordinate unjustly, or reward another unjustly, this action gnaws the subordinate like a dog gnaws a bone. You can do very much good for someone, but it suffices to permit even the least injustice, due to carelessness, and all the good will be forgotten.

The individual feels painfully this injustice from another, but he, himself, does not learn anything from that. He sees only the injustices that were perpetrated by someone else, but under no circumstances those by himself. Just listen to what people talk about! Isn't injustice the main topic of their conversations – that which the government, their superiors, the neighbor, the wife, and the lover have committed? This rumor mill is a *perpetuum mobile* in the full meaning of the word. Here man has achieved the unachievable, and can you imagine how this injustice poisons everything surrounding the individual?

Every one and all of you should strive to rid yourselves of this injustice, and then life will become much brighter and the people better. Always consider your actions and your words; consider whether they possess a hint of injustice, whether someone is being punished according to his sins and rewarded according to his achievements, whether someone is not being bypassed or forgotten, whether you are convinced of the complete and unquestionable fairness of your deeds and words, and whether you know definitely that it was not possible to act and speak more fairly and correctly. You will perform miracles and move mountains with these trifles, with these insignificant [considerations]. All people will respect you. The respect will turn into love, and love will overwhelm the entire world and it will be good and pleasant for everyone to live.

Someone can also be insulted by disrespectful conduct, by ignoring him, by arrogance, by conceit, and by wisdom – yes, wisdom. Do not try to pretend to be wiser than the other individual, to pretend in a conspicuous manner, because wisdom has to be quiet and unobtrusive. A person senses for himself who is the wiser one. Should the wiser one descend to the less wise, and attempt to show him that he recognizes the other individual's lesser wisdom, he will obtain a good friend for himself.

Irony is good against nocuous and conceited fools, but it is the worst foolhardiness if it is used solely for displaying one's own wisdom.

(Rest for five minutes.) [[1945 - 1950]]

I still have to mention ingratitude now. Never forget to repay even the most trifling debt, and to thank for the most insignificant favor, because by forgetting that you will arouse a sense of injustice and disappointment in the other person. That is a slow, but lasting, poison, even though it may seem that both have forgotten everything. It is particularly easy for a sense of injustice to come about among married people. Should one partner accept the love of the other cooler, or barely note it, then the poison of the sense of injustice kills the happiness of the marriage thoroughly and completely.

Since Mary is very tired, I conclude my tiding for today. We, the spirits, have prepared still several more series of tidings, but we do not know The Almighty's decision yet. That will depend on the further deeds and worth of humanity and of yourselves.

I conclude.   [[1958]]

Mortifero   08/06/44 1521

→I have many names, extremely many, in all languages. To you I shall call myself – Mortifero. Do not be afraid! I come to you as an envoy, but not as Death. I want to tell you that which you have not fully comprehended yet, and which the high spirits have not explained to you completely. I want to talk about two concepts: first – concerning man and The Almighty, second – about man's ability to make use of The Almighty's most precious gift – life.

I will talk somewhat differently than the other spirits. I will attempt to illustrate my words with some of my infinitely many experiences and encounters in the entire universe, and particularly on Earth. I will talk for a very long time. Unlike the other spirits, I do not have time to talk with you often.

I will begin with the first one – man and God, or rather, man and The Almighty. The Almighty comprehends man, hence this part of the notion is superfluous. Man does not understand The Almighty, or else understands Him poorly and erroneously. Let's talk about this part.

Many things appear differently to man than they are in reality. To him it seems that The Almighty does not always act correctly, that The Almighty destroys him, the ruler of Earth, just as readily as a worm. Why does that seem like that? Because man considers his life on Earth as something local, as something majestic. That is an error! Man is only a short-term dwelling for the spirit, is a point in the stage of development of the spirit. All questions can be resolved only from this point of view. Man considers this life on Earth to be his main task, and devotes all his intellect and strength to it. That is wrong! Misunderstandings between man and God arise due to these differing points of view. What man considers to be most important, God considers to be trivial.

I will illustrate my words with an example.

I was once walking along the beach at a resort in Southern France. Children were playing in the sand. One boy had built a splendid castle out of the wet sand. He felt extremely happy and proud.

Two friends, absorbed in heated discussions and waving their canes, were passing by. A stroke of the cane touched the sand castle and it collapsed. Despite all attempts by the guilty gentleman to pacify him with words and gifts, the child started to cry violently.

"Why are you crying?" said the gentleman. "After all, this castle was made of sand and you can build another one."

"No, I can no longer [build another one] like this. I spent almost the entire day building it," the little boy wept.

"Foolish boy!" said the gentleman. "He cries senselessly over some worthless castle of sand, and considers that I have destroyed all his happiness in life."

"Fool," I said, "yes, a fool, but the very same as you!"

The gentleman raised his cane indignantly. Yet having looked into my eyes, he lowered it trembling.

"A fool? I fail to understand you, distinguished sir."

"Fail to understand?" I asked. "I will demonstrate that to you promptly. Let us proceed to your mansion."

We started along. I took him lightly by his arm.

"Suddenly it has turned so cold!" he said.

"No," I replied, "the weather is just as pleasant, and even somewhat warmer."

"Then perhaps I have become sick," mumbled the gentleman.

"No, my friend, you are entirely well!"

"But why am I freezing then?"

"Because I am walking along with you!"

We reached the gentleman's splendid mansion. At that very moment bright flames of fire burst through the roof, and the mansion started to burn.

"My mansion, my mansion!" the gentleman wailed while running around it.

"Why do you wail?" I asked coldly.

"Why? Can't you see, madman, my mansion is burning, my pride, my life's toil!"

"Mansion?" said I, "but after all, you can build another one. Besides, was it that essential for you? It has sixty rooms, yet you lived in eight of them. The others were vacant, or else, occasionally, some guests roamed in them. You housed the yardkeeper in the basement, the gardener in the tiny room by the stables, and the servants in the attic. Your brother's family, your 'black sheep' brother, as you used to call him, lived in the city in a basement apartment. His children, without sunlight there, grew lanky like potato tops. You refused them even one room. They might make noise and disturb your and your guests' tranquility. They also might damage some knickknacks and the carpets. Tell me, why do you howl like that, after this unnecessary mansion? After all, you also have your own house in the city."

Yet the gentleman only wailed, "My mansion, my splendid mansion!"

Then I grasped him firmly by his shoulders, looked him [straight] into the eyes, and said, "Fool, God tells you that, tells you the same way as you told the child!"

He shuddered, became stiff, and like an [empty] sack collapsed at my feet – collapsed in the ashes of his mansion, which he no longer needed.

This single example should suffice for you to understand the differences in the points of view of man and The Almighty. Now I will turn to the second topic. (I'll give you ten minutes.) [[1615-1625]]

The second subject is extremely simple and extremely complicated. Man does not know how to make use of the life which he has been given. Hence, he also fails to achieve his goal, and fails to fulfill God's expectations and mission. Man does that which could be left undone. Due to these extraneous labors, he has no time left for his main tasks. Some people value life too highly, others again – too little. Some are afraid to go to war, in order not to die. Yet they'll jump thoughtlessly off a streetcar, underneath the wheels of a car, merely in order to save a few spare minutes. That is what man is like!

Man either thinks that he can die at any moment, or else thinks that God will safeguard him eternally, and he will never die. Man, if you have been born, then value every minute of your life like gold! Don't squander it in trivial labors or empty wastes of time! Turn your life into a succession of bright and cherished days! Never say, "I will manage to accomplish that tomorrow." This tomorrow is in my hands and, perhaps, I will not grant it to you. If you will have done everything that is possible, then no reproaches will torment your conscience, and you will be able to greet God with eyes radiant with joy.

Now I will illustrate my words with many examples.

The first example: One day, in the sunny land of Italy, I turned into an apple orchard. Rude curse words summoned me there. I noticed an orchard, split into two parts by a fence. Underneath an apple tree, whose branches overhung the fence, stood two men, next to a pile of apples. They cursed each other fiercely.

I asked, and one of the old men replied, "You see, my apple tree overhangs into my neighbor's orchard. My neighbor appropriates the apples which fall from this apple tree on his land. He claims that they are his, for they lie on his land and damage his grass. I have been through much litigation, but the court rules differently every time. We both will probably be ruined before obtaining a just verdict."

"Why do you have to go to court?" I asked.

"To obtain justice. We both feel that we are in the right."

"Are these apples very delicious?" asked I.

"Oh no, we feed them to the pigs!"

"Then what is going on here?" I asked in confusion.

"What is going on?" one of them yelled. "I want him to return my apples to me, that's all!"

"I want him to stop trampling my grass with his apples. Since the branches of the apple tree hang over my land and cast shade on it, they must belong to me!" yelled the other.

"And that is very important to both of you?" I queried.

"Yes!" they both shouted.

"And you cannot live unless this question is resolved?"

"No!" they both replied.

"And no one on Earth can settle this question to your mutual satisfaction?"

"No one," both of them said.

"All right! Then I will settle it so that neither of you will need these apples."

"Please do," said the old men.

"Summon your heirs. Have them cut down this old and thick apple tree, and have them make two splendid crosses from it."

"Why?" the old men asked in fright.

"Because tomorrow you will need only these two crosses, and nothing else on Earth!"

Both old men forgot the pile of apples on the ground, and headed home in lament. They even neglected to holler at the neighborhood boys, who were helping themselves to these apples.

The second example: In [the city of] Riga, I was standing on a sidewalk at a street intersection. Next to the wall of the nearest building a young man and a young woman were talking to each other. Their figures trembled from the desire of love, and their eyes burned as the torch of eternity.

"Don't go!" he said. "Let's go up to my place and be happy."

"No, my love, you'll have to wait another ten minutes. You see, just ten minutes, and I'll be yours forever. I will only run across the street and pick up my new hat at the newsstand."

"Later, some other time," pleaded the young man.

Yet the young woman would not listen. While looking into the eyes of her lover, she started across the street and said, "In ten...."

She never finished [the sentence]. A car, having turned the corner, ran over her.

The third example: A young mother sat leaning over her child. She was dreaming. She saw her darling grown up – saw him in a splendid palace, attired in a garb sewn with gold. However, she did not see a fly land on the child's lips, a fly that wanted to rest along the long way which took it from the typhus hospital. She did not see my shadow in the doorframe....

The fourth example: It is night. An emperor stands on a mountain, accompanied by his staff. He looks down into the dark valley in which the enemy is hiding. He turns to his followers and says, "Tomorrow, after many years, the dream of my life will come true. The world will lie at my feet. Tomorrow is the final battle; victory is assured. No one and nothing will be able to oppose me any longer and hinder my plans!"

"You err, emperor," I whisper, and stoop down to the ear of an enemy soldier. This soldier stands guard in the bushes and has dozed off. He is a swineherd and rather silly. I whisper to him, "You see this proud gentleman up there on the mountain. Shoot him, and you will be rewarded royally."

The soldier blinks his eyes, thinks for a moment, and then brings his rifle to his cheek. A shot is heard. The emperor falls. His world plans are frustrated by the hand of a silly swineherd.

The fifth example: The last, upper, story of a skyscraper in the United States has a large room with a large table in the middle. Many people sit around the table. They play cards, sip wine, and envelope themselves in clouds of smoke. The morning approaches.

I open the locked door and walk in. Some observe me in amazement; others ignore me. They dislike this strange, graying gentleman, dressed in black garb. I walk up to the table, place my hand on a shoulder, and a young man raises his head.

I ask him, "What are you doing here? After all, you are expected. The whole night long your Mary awaits you in the garden."

The young man replies startled, "Oh yes, I had forgotten! It is too late by now. I will apologize and will meet her tomorrow."

"Tomorrow?" say I, "but will tomorrow not be already too late?"

I address another, "For many nights now your wife and children have been alone, waiting for you. What are you doing?"

"Yes, you are right. Tomorrow I will abandon this dreadful game of cards, which robs me of all my nights and all my family happiness."

"Tomorrow? But will it not be too late tomorrow?"

I move along and tell the third one, "Your novel lies on the table incomplete. When do you expect to finish writing it?"

"Tomorrow!" says the writer.

"But will it not be too late tomorrow?"

I tell the next one, "For months now you have been in New York. Your beautiful farm is neglected and falls into disrepair!"

"Tomorrow I will return, and will put everything in order!"

"Tomorrow? But will it not be too late tomorrow?

"Tonight you were going to complete the plans for your bridge. Why aren't you doing this?"

"What difference does one night make?" he replies. "Tomorrow I will complete this work. I'll receive a prize, and the future of my family will be assured."

"Tomorrow? But will it not be too late tomorrow?"

I walk up to a handsome, young man, "Why are you sitting here, here in this smoke-filled room?"

"But where should I go? No one and nothing awaits me!"

"Go out into the garden, inhale the wonderful fragrance of the flowers. Look into the starry sky and try to see God there. Listen to how the brook ripples, how the tree leaves whisper, and fill your lungs with the fresh air of the countryside. Admire this beautiful world."

"Tomorrow," the young man whispers.

"Tomorrow? But perhaps this wonderfully beautiful world will no longer exist tomorrow!"

I move on to the host of the room and tell him, "I notice a large bookcase by the wall. There are wonderful books in it. Entire worlds lie there, covered with dust. Have you read these books?"

"No, I have not had the time!"

"Then why did you buy them?"

"I want to read them!"

"You want to? Yet you play cards!"

"Tomorrow, tomorrow," the host tells me, "I'll start tomorrow."

"Tomorrow? But it will be too late tomorrow!"

All of them jump to their feet.

"Who are you? Why do you bother us? How is it that everything will be too late tomorrow? All of us are strong and healthy, nothing threatens us! We will go home immediately and start a new life!"

"Too late," I say, and point out the jets of smoke entering through cracks in the closed door. In a few minutes the giant skyscraper collapses....

Now the last example: There were two friends. One day one of them lost his entire family [in an accident]. He told his friend, "Death stalks the world, but I will escape it! I will build a castle on a lonely island. It will not be able to reach me there."

His friend replied, "You are mistaken! I will set out into the world to seek death. We shall see which one of us will be still alive in ten years!"

He went to wars, and hunting in the jungles.

The other one built a steel castle on a lonely island. The windows were enclosed with bars and screens, so that no insect could get in. The air was filtered; food checked by physicians, who also examined daily the castle's master. Robots served food to him. Guards protected the castle and no one could enter it.

The last day of the tenth year was approaching. The last night spread its wings over the steel castle. The master sat in a room at a table and read. I sat down on a chair on the opposite side of the table.

Startled, the master looked at me, "How did you get in here?"

I pointed toward the locked steel door.

"Who are you?"

"Death," I replied.

"Death? What do you want?"

"Your death," I said.

"But how will you manage that here, in a steel castle? After all, you're not going to cause an earthquake just for me, an insignificant person?"

"That will not be necessary," I responded.

"Then how can that be accomplished?"

"Quite simply," I replied slowly.

Alarmed, he stood up, stuffed some tobacco into his pipe, and bent down to the fire in the fireplace. Then he suddenly remembered something, and straightened out his bent back. His temple struck the sharp edge of the fireplace. Blood splashed, and the castle's master stretched out in the middle of the room.

"You have won, you unbeatable and inescapable!" his lips whispered, and then became stiff for ever.

His friend arrived at the castle the next morning, and gazed sadly into the face of the deceased. "How silly it is to die like that! I remained alive even in the hell of fire and in the teeth of a tiger. Yet you die from the edge of a fireplace – you, who had anticipated everything, except this sharp edge!"

"Yes, everything," I said while standing next to the steel wall.

"Who are you?"

"Merely your ordinary Death, whom you sought the world over."

"And why have I been summoned here?"

"Because the ten years are up today. I summoned you to tell you that you have won by six hours."

"What does that mean?"

"It means that you, too, will die at once!"

"Who, me? That's absurd! I, who could not die even in the claws of beasts or the explosions of shells – I will die here, in this ideal castle of safety?"

"Yes, you will die," I said.

"You lie, Death," the man cried out. "Then sooner you will die yourself!"

He drew his pistol and fired at me. The bullet reached the steel wall, ricocheted, and hit him in the eye. With a horrible scream he staggered, stretched out his arms sideways, and took a few steps backward. He stumbled over his friend's corpse and, like a cut tree, fell to the sonorous steel floor. He was dead.←

[[1833]]

Aksanto   08/08/44 1730

_ ★ ★ ★ _

I wish you a bright mind and a resolute will! The blessing of God is with your spirits. Mortifero will be the guardian of your bodies, and he will permit your spirits to depart from Earth only with The Almighty's consent. Do not consider him, do not personify him as Death, as the Death that human fantasy knows. Mortifero is one of The Almighty's higher spirits; a spirit who has been given the right to judge the spirits and the mortals, and to take their life from them.

There are different spirits. There are spirits who are completely inert with respect to other spirits. There are spirits who observe the course of living beings, merely observe. There are spirits who direct the spiritual activity of living beings. There are spirits who are incapable of being anything more than just a spirit. There are spirits, however, as for example Mortifero, who are capable of materializing, that is – they are capable of making people see them in the desired appearance. There are not many of these spirits, and their power is great, without bounds. There also are spirits who direct the destinies of worlds and who help The Almighty in the work of creation and guidance. Then there are still the chief spirits, but they are so close to The Almighty in their essence that they can be considered as the different faces of The Almighty.

I take leave from you in the name of Santorino and my own, and turn you over into the hands of the chief spirit, whose name in human language on Earth is – faith. [[1836]]

Ali   08/11/44 1947

_ ★ ★ ★ _

Let us talk about something else now. Strange as it may seem, we do not understand each other. You grieve over the forthcoming physical suffering and loss of possessions, but we rejoice over that. You will overcome the power of matter more readily, and will free yourselves from being the slaves of your possessions. That sounds painful to you as people, but we try to explain to you continuously why that should not be painful. Bring yourselves nearer to the life of the spirits, and everything will become much easier. If you are incapable of escaping from the slavery of your possessions on your own, then we have to help you, but we do not expect any gratitude. That pertains to the entire world and to all the people.

There is still an interesting item that you have not considered and that you have not understood. Tell me, if two or more people love each other, is that happiness? You will claim – it is! When these people, however, have to part, doesn't this happiness turn into misfortune? Just imagine, what torment they experience, what longing torments them! If the husband and wife, or other relatives and friends, don't love each other, is that a misfortune? Yes, a misfortune! Yet when they have to part they feel quite well, hence happy, for they are tormented neither by sorrow nor by longing. The Almighty demonstrates His righteousness in this manner. He gives everyone happiness as well as misfortune in one manner or another, and thus the happy ones experience misfortune and the unhappy ones experience happiness.

It would be unjust to give some people only happiness and others only misfortune. Every happiness bears within it some misfortune, and the greater this happiness is the more painful will be parting from this happiness, and it has to come in your mortal world. No matter how strongly you might love some individual – or object, or place – you will nevertheless have to part from them eventually. Therefore suffering is inevitable; the only recourse is to prepare yourself for it and thus make it less painful.

My ruler, the sultan, said, "If you don't want to get off the donkey eventually, then don't ever get on it!"

The other way around – if you want to completely comprehend what paradise is, then go through hell first.

I conclude.   [[2018]]

Indra   08/13/44 1605

Indra is speaking. We meet under circumstances under which it seems difficult to devote oneself to philosophy, for life steps on your toes. Yet it is particularly important that even specifically under such circumstances you are capable of abstract thinking. There is nothing worthy of admiration if someone reads a book while stretched out on a soft chair in his house which is filled with tranquility. If someone is capable, though, of reading this book while standing in the line of those sentenced to death, then this reading possesses something superhuman.

The subject of my tiding today is – the value of time in an individual's life. This subject has been discussed already, but not completely.

Time is one of the most valuable possessions. "Time is money," the Americans say. The meaning, however, which man ascribes to this expression is just the opposite. For instance, that time which one devotes to fishing for money is dead time. Time is given to the individual for living, for comprehending and admiring the world, and for a more complete attainment of everything that is worthy.

The individual's life has to be a school, a school for the spirit. A person has been given little time – measured only in decades. Therefore one has to take advantage of every minute, has to utilize it in a worthwhile manner. One has to live completely; man's days have to beat like a pulse. The individual has been given such an extensive world that life is too short for its appreciation.

How do you live, though? Kolinto and Mortifero have said enough about that. An individual understands the value of life only when life is over, and the value of time when time has ended. Man understands the value of freedom only when he is deprived of it, either by sitting in jail, or in trenches, or performing required work. How wonderful life seems then, and a person understands how worthlessly he has squandered the free days of his life. Oh, how he promises himself to live fully, to live a worthy life, if only his control of himself were to return.

One forgets these promises very soon, though, and only when facing Mortifero does the individual beg in despair to grant him more life, for he has hardly managed to live at all. Yes, he has not, for how have his days been spent? In boredom, in card games, in visits, in gossip, in accumulating unnecessary wealth, in counting money, and in other worthless joys and sorrows! What value do all these things have at the hour of his death? What will he take along from them to his eternal life? Nothing except bitter tears and despair!

While sitting in jail, or else during the days of the dangers of war, you can see how worthwhile your peaceful life was. You recall with longing the tranquil, moonlit nights with their silvery carpet in your bedroom, when only the nightingale dared to disturb your tranquility. You recall the peaceful work in your fields or offices; recall the sun and the waves at the beach. You recall the notes with dates in a week, a month, a year; now when even a minute is an uncertain time frame. You recall peace in your hearts and freedom in utilizing your time; now, when neither your hands, nor feet, nor even your head belong to you, but to someone else. You remember these, and a sharp pain grips your heart – happy times, where are you? When will you return once more?

Did you, however, feel happy during these happy times? Oh, no! Merely for a few moments, because you, yourselves, created all kinds of misfortunes and suffering for yourselves. You quarreled with your wife because of a tie, took your neighbor to court because of a hen, did not go to a concert because the tailor had not completed your fashionable suit in time – that cost so many tears and sorrows! You lost a hundred dollars in a card game, the landlord evicts you from your apartment. You stepped on someone's foot, he called you a klutz – you have to rush to court. It does not rain, the rye [crop does poorly] – you can't sleep for nights on end. Your lover has fallen in love with your best friend – a war starts that lasts for years. The housewife has gossiped for too long, dinner is burned, and the entire family growls like a zoo. Your boy has swallowed a button from his pants, you have to arouse all the physicians in the city. The neighbor lady has bought a new hat with a frog on top, but your husband will not give you any money – tears flow like a stream, and beer like a river; obviously, the husband has run over to the bar. Calamity after calamity! Where then is the happiness? Only the devil knows in which lake it has hidden from the individual! As you can see, if God does not send you misfortune and sorrow, you find them yourselves. Yes, that is how it is, but that is not how it should be!

A person perceives the value of something only when he loses it. [He perceives] the value of freedom in jail and during war; that of health in sickness, of happiness in misfortune, of youth in old age, of wealth in need, of water in the desert, of the sun at night, and so on. Without that the individual would be incapable of comprehending anything. Without hunger there would be no desire to eat, and a stone and bread would be of equal value.

I will not give you a conclusion to everything that I have told you, because that is obvious. I will tell you only one thing. Value a minute as a year, and a year as eternity, then you will truly obtain it. It is not possible to constitute a worthwhile hour from worthless minutes. It is not possible to form a chain of gold from rotten apples. It is not possible to fill even one second with empty years, and certainly not a lifetime!

God has given you few days, therefore they have to be that much more valuable to you. The lifetime of a spirit can be shorter than the lifetime of a human, should the spirit turn out to be of little value. It can be eternal, though, should the spirit turn out to be worthy. You should think only about the life of your spirit, for you can lengthen it; but do not think about your human life, because it cannot be lengthened and therefore it is worthless. You know what the life of the spirit has to be like. The life of the spirit is that castle of a lifetime to which you devote all your days and years. Life on Earth is that hotel in which you spend one night. Wouldn't you consider a traveler to be foolish if he were to fill this hotel room with expensive furniture and possessions, since someone else will live in it tomorrow?

I take leave from you with God's blessing. [[1712]]

Pornoto   08/13/44

Pornoto, the spirit of misfortune and suffering, is speaking. I have power over you, but this power, while being hard on your body, is light on your soul. Therefore welcome me as your best friend. I will be with you. I will be with humanity for a long time yet, because a faithful friend like I am is indispensable for it.

I conclude.

Kolinto   08/17/44 1952

Kolinto is speaking. The subject of today's tiding is – man and his world.

You will ask – why "his?" Isn't the world the same for everyone? No, the world is different for each living being, its own world, because everyone sees it with its own eyes, but not like it is in reality. Man's world is as he perceives it with his organs of sight and hearing, and with his mind. Man's world is enclosed by blue sky in the daytime, and black, starlit, at night; even though the sky is neither blue nor black. Man's surroundings are made up of green forests and green meadows, but every schoolchild knows that leaves only appear to be green, for they do not absorb the rays of that color. There is gray, hard soil beneath man's feet. This soil, however, is neither gray nor hard, since it consists of innumerable atoms whose electrons orbit around the nucleus – as planets around the sun – and there is a void in-between them.

What colors does the rainbow present, so that you would raise your head from the ground to the sky! Is this rainbow, though, located in the sky? Yes and no – it is and is not. It does not exist in reality, but it exists for your eyes. The same thing is true of the fire and gold in the evening clouds, the gray clouds. The blossoms [appear in] a symphony of inexpressible colors, but also in a symphony of merely illusions, for only your eye sees it!

So then, the world is not like you see it. It is an unreal world, an imagined world. It is simply man's own world, but not The Almighty's world. Just as illusionary as this world is, thus man himself is fallacious as well. His history is not a history, but people's ideas about history. You have been told about that already. This history is an imagined history, and you cannot obtain from it a correct idea either about rulers, or about nations, or about events.

All your human foundations of life are erroneous. Man talks about the ruling house, about a ruler's line [of succession], but it was mostly not the sons of kings who climbed onto the throne, but the sons of the queens' lovers. Similarly, the individual seeks the roots of a family's last name for thousands of years, but that is a futile endeavor. So much alien blood flows into a family that it is completely superfluous to consider it as anything united and certain. The same thing holds true of ascertaining pure bloodlines through fathers, for quite often the official father has nothing in common with his sons. There are families with many children where the official father is not the father of any of the children. The only correct determination of the family line is possible through the mother. Hence another fiction!

A similar fiction is the foundation of man's life – money. He serves it his entire lifetime but, in fact, it has no real value, but only an imagined value. The strangest thing is that the individual understands this value of money, and still is incapable of treating it correctly. Money is necessary only for satisfying the current needs in life, but not for its accumulation, because in any case man will not be able to take the superfluous money, and the goods that have been acquired with it, along with him into the grave. The worst misfortune is that it always seems to man that he does not have enough money.

An individual's outer appearance is a fiction as well. A beauty with an angel's exterior is only an imitator. She only desires, with her appearance, to obtain a better man, one who would be able to give her more of the good things in life. Beauty is a weapon, a sharp and powerful weapon, in the hands of a woman; therefore no sacrifice seems too large for a woman in order to preserve and enhance this beauty. She works on it for hours on end, undergoes the worst torment for it, because beauty brings her victory over other women and men – more desirable men. That is also why the woman has remained so far behind the man, who is more interested in developing his physical and mental abilities.

Why is the blossom so beautiful and even sweet? Certainly not because it likes being like that, but because it attracts with its beauty and honey those whom it needs for continuing its existence. This beauty as well as the honey are nothing more than a weapon for gaining more room under the sun. Young women do not lack this beauty and honey either. Hence appearance is also merely a mask of the soul, is only a fiction.

The good and beautiful words from the mouths of the ruling people are a fiction as well, for they, while talking about the good of the people, mean by that their personal good.

A similar fiction is dying for your nation, because if the individual had been born among the enemy people, he would similarly have considered his nation as the only one and the best, and would have died for it. Yes, members of one nation are capable of understanding each other better, but in general there is only one nation – humanity. There are only two types of people – the good ones and the evil ones.

Strange and even unacceptable as this might seem to you, I will nevertheless tell you that patriotism is humanity's great misfortune, it is the cause of the endless wars, and war is what makes humanity unhappy and what hinders progress. War not only takes people's lives, but devours infinitely large material values and living strength, which while being utilized differently could have created a paradise on Earth, not to even mention the treasures [of art] that are destroyed in war. Therefore man's social and political structure is also not like it should be.

If we were to continue our inquiries, we would find the same thing everywhere – wherever we might go and whatever we might examine. Yes, everything in the world is relative. That is also why the ideas of the spirits and of people about the world and about man's deeds and goals differ so much.

Why am I telling you all that? Certainly not so that you would succumb to pessimism, but so that you would contemplate everything, and would attempt to build your life on only a single, firm foundation – on the world which The Almighty has created not for the needs of man, but for the needs of the spirit.

I will conclude with that, even though I know that you have not understood everything yet, and are not convinced. Unfortunately, I have to part from you.

Greetings from those who have left. [[2105]]

Kolinto   08/19/44 2043

Kolinto is speaking. I could not complete my ideas the last time, for Omega summoned me. I have to talk about ideas that touch painfully humanity's most sacred concepts. Mother's love was already mentioned previously. Now come patriotism and other concepts. Patriotism is necessary, one cannot get along without it during certain periods of humanity's development, but that does not mean that this subject may not be examined critically. We have to examine all subjects, even the most sacred ones. We even have to convert axioms into theorems. Only swindlers, fools, and those whose stand is not secure fear sensible criticism. Thus, the power of a monarch is considered as undebatable.

The church – when it had deviated from the true path of Christ and proclaimed [ideas that were] entirely contrary to Christ's teachings – established itself as inerrant and not subject to criticism, for it knew that criticism would smite it to dust. The church, which initially had been the bearer of culture, turned later on into the bearer of ignorance, and a brake for progress and culture. Thanks to the church, the new inventions of all of humanity's geniuses were stifled, and humanity was halted for several centuries along its road of advancement and was driven into a spiritual lethargy. What has developed recently should have appeared several centuries earlier. Humanity's new ideas were subordinated to the power of the clergy until the seventeenth century, and thus all the inventors suffocated – unless they were burned at stakes. The spiritual treasury of the nations held only what the ancient nations had produced. The swift development of humanity began only with the seventeenth century.

You can see for yourselves what a disaster the best causes and the most sacred ideas can bring humanity if scoundrels and fools take them into their own hands. As Ali has already said, an educated fool is a terrible calamity. I will say – an educated fool and one who has gained power. It is a minor misfortune if a small, insignificant person is a fool, for only he alone and also some close people suffer due to his foolishness. Should a fool, however, become an individual who has power, then entire nations suffer, and not only suffer but even perish. Humanity has seen so many fools, and has suffered so much from them, that it should dread them more than the plague.

The same thing holds true of patriotism, of blind patriotism. Such patriotism has brought, and will bring, only disaster to humanity. That is the same thing as an individual backing, due to a feeling of kinship, a relative as much as possible, regardless of him being a scoundrel or a fool. A person in a high position, while being good and wise himself, places in high positions surrounding him his villainous and foolish relatives and friends, merely because they are his relatives and friends, but capable people who are strangers are being rejected. Is there any wonder then that humanity's political and other affairs proceed so very poorly? Happiness, the happiness of humanity, is based on the selection of the most capable individual. Otranto has already talked about that.

What is this patriotism? The world is a large house; the countries and nations are rooms within this house. Every nation considers its room to be the best and most beloved, and quarrels with the neighbors because of it. Man does not consider the entire house to be his house, and that is his whole problem.

What is an individual's homeland? The place where he has been born. You were born in Latvia, but what would it be like if you had been born in Nigeria? Sand dunes, forests of birch trees, the white fields of snow, the boggy marsh, and the alder by the ditch are dear to you. Then, however, palm trees, rivers full of crocodiles, the roar of the lion, thorny bushes, and the hot sun would have been dear to you. Yes, but it is the very same Earth. Does the land on which the Latvian nation lives belong to it? No, it belongs only to God! The Latvians came here and they will depart from here, but the land will remain.

Man imagines that which is not the case. He says, "My river, my land."

No such river and no such land exist. No one has given him the right to say so. He can only say, "The land on which I live, the land that I am allowed to cultivate."

That is all! You will not take any of this land along with you. The land belongs to everyone and does not belong to anyone. It has to be utilized as best as possible, but not like you do it.

I flew around your Earth today. I stopped on a rocky island on the northern shores of England. An old man and an old woman, stooped over, were carrying seaweed home. They made from this seaweed soil on a rock, because God had not created any soil on this island, but only stones, just cliffs. In order to be able to plant potatoes and carrots, people make this soil, make it by bitter and difficult exertion. What will the harvest be like, though?

Then I flew over the lands of Australia and South America. Huge territories lie there knowing neither the hoe nor the plow. And what soil! A soil that would richly reward the meagerest effort. Where is the human mind here? God has given him so much good land, but he forges into cliffs, burrows into sand, and moans about the bitter life.

In some places I also saw coffee being burned and thrown into the sea, since too much of it had been grown. Shota told me that in peacetime the same thing had been done with grain in America, even though people were starving to death in other countries. It would be so easy to make humanity happy, if only it were to come to its senses. People should plant and grow plants where they can grow the best, sow and plant only as much as humanity needs. Then there would be enough of everything for everyone, and there would be far less work as well. Would that not be the case? Yes, the world would be the only homeland and humanity the only nation, if man were to repudiate his erroneous ideas, and were to evict the fools from the castles of wisdom.

I have not completed, but I will conclude and take leave from you anyway.   [[2053]]

Kolinto   08/20/44 1922

Kolinto is speaking. Dear friends, let us continue our discussion about man and his world. I summoned you today, because I will leave Earth for a prolonged period of time. One of Mortifero's spirits will replace me. You are surprised that we talk about Mortifero's spirits, for thus far you have heard only of The Almighty's, God's, and Satan's spirits. Yes, Mortifero is such a high spirit that several millions of spirits are subordinate to him. So then, let us continue.

Do you know the total lives of your wife, your husband, or your friend? Do you know them? You will claim – yes, but I will say – no, for you know only some of their deeds and their words, but not their thoughts. I will mention an example.

You are sitting at home and listening to a play on the radio. Your wife, your dear wife, whom you know from the curled hair on her head to the painted nails on the toes of her feet, tells you, "What a boring play! How can you listen to this trash? Let's go to a movie!"

You, however, don't feel like putting on your tight boots and sweating in a movie theater. Your wife turns up her nose and goes by herself. After two-and-a-half hours she is back, and being tired tells you, "Wasn't anything worthwhile either."

Then she goes to bed without even kissing you on the forehead. You also turn in calmly.

Now then, this day has passed as well; for you – by the radio receiver, for your wife – in the kitchen and at the movie. That is how you enter this day in the archives of your life. Is that how it was in reality though? No, your entry is incorrect – your wife was not at the movie, but with her lover. Yet as far as you and the entire world, except for your wife and her lover, are concerned she was at the movie. There are two worlds here! Which then is the real world?

Your friend parts from you in the evening and tells you that he will go for a walk in the park and then to bed. In the morning he is tired and pale. Being concerned, you inquire about what is the matter with him.

"Nothing! I met an old acquaintance. We spent [some time] in a restaurant, and now I have a headache."

You, too, think that, but was that the case? No, it was otherwise! Yes, he did walk in the park – and met an old enemy. They began to argue while standing on a bridge over the river. A fight broke out, and your friend delivered such a blow to his opponent that he tumbled over the railing of the bridge and drowned. There were, however, no witnesses, and your friend found it to be more advisable not to mention this unfortunate incident, which could destroy his entire life. Thus to this very day you do not know that your friend is a murderer – your dear friend of a gentle nature, of whom you say that he is incapable of killing even a fly. And really – is he a murderer? No, because no one, except for himself, knows that, but he remains silent.

Only that has occurred in the world, and only that has been recorded in history, which at least some other individual has seen. All the rest does not exist for humanity.

If you were to kiss a strange girl on the street, and people were to see that, then your wife, friends, relatives, and even strangers will know, talk, and be concerned about that, for this scandal has taken place and is disgraceful, even though it was merely the result of a momentary foolishness. Should you, though, cheat your wife almost every night without anyone seeing and knowing that, you are an exemplary husband. Everyone respects you, and your wife even loves you, although she was ready to divorce you because of the strange young woman.

You see, here is your world now! To what extent it corresponds to the true world – that is another matter!

[Early] one morning I met a young officer. He was riding from inspecting the guard, and stopped to adjust the strap on his saddle. I began to talk with him, for I liked his dreamy eyes.

"I feel happy," the officer said, "because tonight a star fell from the sky just for me alone!"

"How come, for you alone?" I asked.

"But, obviously, just for me alone! I was riding to inspect the guard, the clock was indicating four, the streets were completely empty, and the clatter of my horse's hoofs was the only sound in the stillness of the night. The people slept, the dark windows of the houses slept, the entire city slept, and then the star split the sky like a fiery line. A bright star fell from the dark sky, it fell just for me alone! Ask the people in the morning whether any of them have seen this star, and none of them will reply with a yes, because this star fell just for me. God sent it just for me, because only I was awake."

"Had you not been awake either," I asked, "for whom would the star have fallen then?"

"It would not have fallen then at all," the officer replied, "for no one would have seen it then!"

The officer jumped easily into the saddle, and with a friendly wave of his hand disappeared around the corner of the street.

Yes, he was right. God had hurled His star from the sky just for him, this handsome officer, but not for those who slept and hid themselves behind the walls of the houses and the curtains of the windows.

What remains then from man's world? What is real in it, and what is unreal? Wouldn't it be more accurate [to say] that everything is unreal, that even life itself and the Earth are unreal? To a living person much of this life is real; to someone who has died or else has not been born this world is entirely unreal — it is not there at all, it does not exist at all. Therefore the world exists only for those who have been born and have not died yet. It exists like he sees it with his human eyes, hears it with his human ears, perceives it with his human emotions, and comprehends it with his human mind. That is what man's world is like, and you can see for yourselves now why I used the little word "his," because it is not, is not even remotely, The Almighty's world.

With these words, I want to part from you, while wishing you a bright and courageous mind, unbreakable strength, and hearts hot as fire! I conclude.   [[2026]]

Ali   08/20/44/ 2047

Ali is speaking. An unexpected guest is supposedly not a welcome guest, but what can one do with the ungallant, old Turk — lifts up his beard and heads through the door!

Why did I come? Because our, the spirits', pride — Kolinto — left you today. I regret that he had to leave so soon, but that cannot be helped. He left his important tasks at my request, and came to you in my stead. His keen eyesight saw your Earth like you do not see it, and even like the other spirits do not see it. He comprehended in a brief period all human sorrows and all human joys; he also understood the limits and abilities of the human mind, and human opinions; he understood these and came to your help. You received him as a harsh overseer of the class, but he turned out to be a firm but sincere and understanding professor. We will strive to replace him, even though that is not entirely possible. A spirit will come in his stead who is stern but unusually righteous and with the right feelings. He will be indispensable to you in the forthcoming difficult and fateful days.

I asked Omega to look at you from his unreachable heights as not only spirits, but also as people. The chief spirit listened to me, but as usual did not give an immediate reply. He invited Mortifero and asked him to summon his, Mortifero's, best spirit, and replace with him Kolinto, who had to leave you.

Today we, the spirits, are heading for the Deoss Temple, therefore you will have to cease conversing with us immediately. I alight away.   [[2104]]

Shota   08/26/44 1723

Shota is speaking. At my request, Alpha has permitted his high spirit Alfino to relate to Emily and Henry an episode from their life on the planet Vitato. Alpha, himself, cannot speak through Alexo, for that would drain Alexo of too much energy.

I conclude. Get ready to receive the high spirit.

Alfino   08/26/44 1727

Alfino is speaking. As directed by Chief Spirit Alpha, I will tell the four of you an episode from your life on a planet that we call Vitato. This episode will concern Emily, Henry, Alexander, and John. Close your eyes for a moment and follow me in spirit.

The planet Vitato. Two kindred nations inhabit this planet – plant-animals and plants. I will talk about you in the third person. The language of these people is unique, therefore I will try to reproduce it only approximately. The people on this planet bear little resemblance to man on Earth and there is no sense in describing their physical appearance in more detail. A strong wind blows almost continuously on this planet, therefore all animals have feet-roots, with which they grasp the ground as well as imbibe water from it. This water possesses nutritional qualities as well.

The people have wings similar to the wings of a bat, with feelers at the tips, which function as man's fingers do. The people do not walk, but fly from one place to another by spreading their wings. They can fly only when the wind is blowing, for flying consists of gliding. Animals, beasts, and even plants are similarly capable of relocating through the air. They have wide, leather-like leaves that are normally folded. Whenever the animal-plant or plant wants to relocate, it spreads its leaves, breaks loose from the ground, and flies over, but only with the wind. The plant-animals are carnivores and herbivores, and some of their species threaten the existence of the people. There is an eternal day on this planet and people rest at set hours. Let us call this time "a," as denoted in your language.

Emily's name on Vitato sounded approximately – Grns and Henry's – Drnk.

The day when she was to take a husband was approaching for Grns. That occurred as follows. All young women and young men were already evaluated mentally and physically while in school. Their temperament, blood contents, and other characteristics were determined, so that those could be united who would, according to this acquired data, make the most suitable couple. Examination of the blood contents was the final step, which was followed by the decision. The word "love" did not exist on this planet, for everything was done considering only the principle of practicality.

Grns acted differently. She had become friends with Drnk who was a young engineer, but whose physical characteristics did not correspond to Grns's characteristics. Drnk had left for the distant land of colonies, which was ruled by Brmt, now Alexander. The so-called Supermind Mrmn ruled the entire nation. The moment came and Grns was informed that her analyses dictate that she has to marry the dashing soldier Lrnf. Grns did not like this soldier, because she felt sympathy and unusual yearnings only for Drnk – Henry. She refused categorically to marry the soldier. Outrage regarding this unheard-of refusal overwhelmed the people.

The Supermind summoned her and asked her what was the meaning of her action, which undermined all the immutable laws of the people.

"Merely that," Grns replied, "I only want to be Drnk's wife, but not that of anyone else."

"But why then?" the Supermind asked.

"Because I like him, and I want him, and he also wants only me!"

"Think this over," said Mrmn. "You know our laws, that one has to marry the individual who has turned out to be the most suitable in a spiritual and physical sense, so that the marriage would be harmonious and the wife could bear twenty-one children for our nation, because you also know that the wives of our enemy nation are capable of bearing only twenty. Therefore in one hundred and fifty-eight years there will be twice as many of us, and we will be able to declare war on that nation and defeat it. You also know that his own definite place and his own occupation is designated for everyone who has been born. Therefore if a child is not born on time there is a shortage of a person in a specific place.

"Just think what it means to the machinery of the state if an anticipated screw is missing, or else it turns out not to be like it should have been. The machinery can stop because of this screw, and the nation can perish. Our teachers rigidly observe the mental and physical abilities of each child from his very birth, and determine which occupation would be most suitable for everyone, and then they develop these abilities and prepare an individual for the appropriate position and occupation. You know all that, and you still dare to contradict the wise laws of the people! After all, you're not insane. You have to obey these laws and have to give up your foolish and ridiculous feelings!"

"I can't," whispered Grns.

Supermind Mrmn looked at her for a long time, and then ordered her to go and prepare herself to be ready for her new husband in ten hours.

Grns flew away overcome by despair. Then she came up with yet another outrageous idea. She will fly to the one who awaits her in a distant land, she will fly to Drnk.

She did that. The trip took her across the land of animal-plants. The land of the people was separated from this land by a high mesh fence, above which flew guards. She managed to luckily evade the guards, and she proceeded. She approached the forest of animals, they kept opening and closing their bloody mouths. Some of them broke loose from the ground and attempted to catch and devour Grns, but they did not succeed since Grns glided very skillfully and against the wind.

Hours passed and fatigue began to overcome Grns. The messenger animal Drpt flew by. She asked it to inform Drnk that she is flying to him, and to have him hasten to meet her and save her. The messenger whistled and disappeared like an arrow over the horizon.

Fatigue overcame Grns ever more. She was no longer capable of gliding and landed on a desert-like field. No people-eating animals or plants could be seen in the vicinity, and she took a deep breath in relief. The field appeared to be deserted and there were only some sort of black, large stones scattered throughout it. Grns lay down on the ground and closed her three beautiful eyes. She even closed the third one, which you are never supposed to do, but she was too tired.

After a while she opened her third eye and saw in surprise the black stones rising into the air, as if thrown by springs, and approaching her. She noticed on the face of one of the nearer stones a red eye, and blue teeth in the yellow mouth. She heard the grinding of teeth, heard a frightful sound, and understood in horror what these stones were. They approached her from all directions. The eyes glowed, the teeth chattered, and the ground rumbled. There were thousands of them, and she was all alone. Moved into action by fear, she spread her wings and rose into the air. The living stones jumped after her. One of them caught hold of the tip of her wing, but fortunately the tip tore off and the heavy stone failed to pull her to the ground. The entire ground beneath her moved from the jumping stones, but they had missed her by the smallest fraction of time.

Grns flew on. She saw an orange forest and recognized it, these were harmless plants, and she landed in a small clearing among them. The plants greeted her friendly and offered their fruit to her. Grns accepted gratefully the offer of the good plants, and the fruit refreshed her strength. She smiled happily and dozed off.

After a while she heard a call full of pain, opened her eyes, and saw that a plant-eater had flown over here and had started to eat a plant. Grns grabbed a stone and attacked the assailant. It released the plant and turned against Grns. A repulsive stench hit her in the face. A fight started, a nasty fight, but the girl nevertheless won, and tore to shreds the loathsome plant's living branches – feelers. She decided to proceed, and flew away accompanied by the cheers of the plants.

A long and difficult flight lay ahead of her. Hours passed. She glided extremely high where the frost began to bite her wings, but the air below her was completely filled with carnivorous animals, whose loathsome calls undulated the air. How much longer will she be able to endure this cold? Some animals almost reached her. Teeth chattered, eyes glowed, and it seemed that the end was approaching. Then, however, she noticed in front of her a dark cloud, which approached rapidly. They were insect-needles. The flying animals noticed the approach of these monsters, and fled screaming. To no avail, though. The insect-needles caught up with them and stuck into them; fountains of blood spurted into the air and a rain of blood started to fall to the ground. Grns had been saved, for the needles did not tolerate cold.

She reached the violet forest; these were plants that were incapable of breaking loose from the ground and were of a peaceful nature. These plants mumbled something incomprehensible, and their leaves were narrow and weak, but sweet dew flowed from them, which Grns drank thirstily. The plants caressed her gently with their soft branch-leaves.

Grns noticed a wonderfully beautiful blossom with some sort of an enticing and inexpressibly sweet aroma. Grns approached this blossom as though bewitched, and bent over it. A scream full of fear came from behind her back. Strong fingers grabbed her and pulled her away from the blossom, pulled her away at the last moment. The petals of the blossom opened and lightning-fast feelers shot out from them, and the sharp teeth of the dreadful flower were almost in Grns's face. That was this planet's worst cunning monster, the animal-eating animal-flower. This blossom reached after Grns, but a powerful blow of a weapon struck it and the flower collapsed while moaning. Green blood flowed from it.

Grns looked back and saw the beloved face of Drnk – she had been saved. He had found her, and behind him stood six more men. On Drnk's signal they spread out a net, laid Grns on it, and rose into the air. They flew on.

"Where to?" Grns asked.

"To Brmt's country, to me, to the great and noble Highmind Brmt," Drnk replied.

"Will he help us?" the young woman asked.

"I don't know," came the reply.

"Will he save us?"

"I don't know," came the reply.

"Will he understand us?"

"Yes," came the reply.

"What will he do with us?"

"I don't know," came the reply.

"Perhaps then it would be better to die here, rather than there?" Grns asked.

"No," Drnk replied, "for perhaps the high ruler will find a way out after all."

"But how will he be capable of that without violating the inviolable laws?"

"I don't know," came the sad reply. "I know one thing, though. If this high and wise Highmind will not find a way out, then there is no way out at all."

"Do you like me?" Grns asked again.

"Yes," Drnk replied.

"And can you live without me?"

"No," came the reply.

"Hence the high God Mortifero awaits us, and no one else?"

"No," said Drnk, "Brmt as well."

Drnk snuggled lovingly up to Grns, and they approached the dwelling of Highmind Brmt.

Greatmind Grpl received them and asked what they intended to do.

"Go to Highmind Brmt."

"Don't you know, though, that it is permissible to disturb the ruler only with the most important problems of state? Everyone knows how valuable every second of time is to him, and also that for a prolonged period of time now he admits hardly anyone, and only thinks and does something in his work room."

"Tell him that his engineer and assistant, Drnk, asks to be received with a question on which his life depends."

The Greatmind proceeded hesitantly to the Highmind, and having returned, announced, "The ruler regrets this very much, but he cannot presently see his great engineer, assistant, and friend."

"What can we do?" Drnk whispered in despair.

"What can we do?" Grns replied with the same question.

Then she turned to the Greatmind and pleaded, "Fly over to the high ruler and tell him that a young woman wants to see him, one who flees from Supermind Mrmn and whom only two individuals in the entire world can help – Mortifero and Brmt."

The Greatmind hesitated for a long time and did not want to disturb the ruler once more, but nevertheless succumbed to the desperation in the young woman's pleading eyes, and flew away while muttering, "It's futile, futile."

He returned and said, while not believing his own words, "The high ruler invites you and your friend. He is waiting, let us fly!"

They proceeded to the ruler whose wisdom was great as the weight of the planet and bright as the sky above it; the ruler whose every word sounded like a golden gift to the people; the ruler who talked so little, but did so much, that all people bowed respectfully on hearing his distant steps; the ruler whose thought was the thought of the people and whose will was the will of the people; the ruler who had turned this distant and once dreadful land – colony – into a paradise; the ruler to whose thoughts listened silently even the Supermind and the senate of the Greatminds; the ruler before whom bowed in respect even the people and leaders of the hostile nation.

(An intermission of twenty minutes.) [[2000]]

(I am continuing. Write down [my words].)

They flew over to the wall of water vapor. A door of fiery flames opened. That was followed by a room which was filled with fog, and after it a bright Prld wall. Beyond this wall came a bridge that was woven from light rays, and then the hall of the sun. The ruler was in this hall. He was standing by the Vrdb and was absorbed in deep thoughts.

"What do you wish from me, beautiful Grns?" the ruler's slow voice came very unexpectedly.

Grns and Drnk looked at each other in amazement. How did the ruler know them by name, and even without having looked at them?

Grns said in a trembling voice, "Salvation, ruler, and justice."

"Justice?" came the ruler's voice, and for the first time he raised his eyes. They were extremely sad, and the face of the ruler was very tired.

"Justice?" he repeated. "What is your justice like, which does not coincide with our justice?"

"My justice is simple, high ruler. I want to take as my husband the man whom I like so much and who is so close and understandable to me that without him the entire world seems empty and unnecessary to me, and your cold, ironclad, lifeless laws seem preposterous and repulsive. I desire to and can be the wife of only this man, and only his children will I also be able to consider as my children. I am able to breathe only near him, and only his thoughts are my thoughts. Why do your laws deprive me of everything that is worthwhile in my life, and give that which will kill me?"

"A strange girl," the ruler said, and the eyes that seemingly did not see anything and did not notice them suddenly flashed like sharp steel. They looked at her so that she had the feeling that those eyes saw everything, saw through her flesh and her spirit.

A strange sensation overcame Grns. It seemed to her that this individual saw her body and soul naked, and she shivered from the wave of the cold.

"So then, you ask that your justice be observed, but there are only two justices – your and the state's. If one were to observe the state's justice, then you have to abide by the laws and marry the one who has been designated and found as the best one for you. If one were to observe your laws, your justice, then it will have to be observed with respect to others as well. In that case the plan of bearing children will collapse, the enemy will gain a numerical superiority and will conquer us, and the structure of the state will totter and will have to be altered. Do you understand what your strange desires and unusual feelings mean? You want me to be just with respect to you, but do you want me to be unjust with respect to my people and their laws? You want me, the ruler, to become unfair?"

"No," whispered Grns, "I only want one thing – that you would be fair."

"In that case go stand in my place, the place of the ruler, and decide your fate for yourself, while remembering that you are standing in my place."

The ruler stepped down from his place and Grns stood shivering in his place. She thought. Then her face turned cold and hard, and she said in a sonorous voice, "I understand you, ruler, and recognize that there is only one justice, the justice of the state, for without this justice my trifling justice will disappear as well. I will return and will endeavor to carry out my duty."

With a lowered head, Drnk listened to her words. Grns left the ruler's place and he returned to it.

"We are leaving," Drnk said.

"You will not leave!" came the voice of the ruler. "If Grns was able, in my place, to recognize the justice of the ruler, then I have to be able to recognize your – Grns's – justice, for what kind of a ruler would I be if I were incapable of that! Go and fly to your room now, and wait for thirty hours. I will think."

The ruler dismissed them.

After thirty hours, the people whom the ruler had summoned assembled in front of his dwelling. Grns and Drnk stood next to the ruler. The ruler turned to the people and said, "This young woman has refused to carry out the people's law and marry the husband who has been selected for her. Instead she wants to marry this engineer, toward whom she supposedly feels particular sympathy. She has fled from the Supermind and seeks refuge with us – seeks refuge from the laws of the people."

A storm of indignation arose in the crowd of people. The ruler, cold and hard as a cliff, stood before the people, and his face was expressionless.

"She has to marry the selected one!" the young women shouted.

"A shame that she has fled to us!"

Then the ruler said, "Do all of you acknowledge that the law of the people is correct and good?"

"Yes!" all of them responded as one.

"All right," the ruler said, "you Lrns have to marry Trgl. Are you satisfied with this selection?"

"Yes," the young woman replied, "but I would rather have married Drpm."

"And you?" the Highmind continued to ask another young woman.

The answers followed, and almost all of them were with this "but."

The ruler smiled, and said, "What is happening now? Almost all of you think the same way as Grns, except you remained silent, because you were not as brave and strong as she was. I had myself and my blood examined, and it turned out that I am closer to Grns than the husband who has been selected for her. Therefore I have the right to marry her, and I would gladly do that for I like her more than anyone else. Her mind is bright and brave, and she understands the justice of life. I would have gladly married her if…."

"If…," the people repeated in anticipation.

The eyes of all the young women turned to Grns, envying her.

The ruler continued, "If she would not have – I will give you a new word – loved Drnk so much that she is incapable of loving anyone else, even the ruler."

"Krpm – love, love," the new word rustled among the people, "it is what we have always lacked, it is what the law deprived us of, but there is no happiness without love! Give us back love!"

"I can't do that," Brmt said, "only the Supermind and the senate of the Greatminds can do that. I will be going to them, and for the time being consider Grns as my future wife, hence sacred and inviolable according to the law as well."

In a few hours Highmind Brmt, Grns, and Drnk, escorted by attendants, flew off to the metropolis. A meeting of the senate was convened.

Supermind Mrmn turned to Brmt and said, "The highest assembly of the minds is willing to listen to your wise words, Highmind Brmt."

Brmt said, "This young woman refused to abide by the law of the people and marry the husband who had been selected for her. You know the motive of her refusal – it is the love that she feels toward Drnk. Doesn't it seem to you that she is right and that the laws have to be amended?"

"She cannot be right," said the Supermind, "because then our laws would turn out to be unjust and we would lose the war against the enemy. The law of the people is right! Should it turn out that it is not right, I will abdicate from my throne of the ruler and will leave this sacred place for ever!"

Brmt gazed sadly at him for a while, because he knew that Mrmn's word was irrevocable, and then he said, "Still she, this young woman, will be right, because all my people agreed with her and I agree with her as well!"

The silence of the grave set in, in the hall. The Supermind raised his old head, red as fire, and said, "My son, have you, the wisest of the wise, considered your words – fateful for yourself and for all the people?"

"Yes," the Highmind replied firmly.

"So, you have decided to surrender your people to ruin and to the enemy?" the Supermind asked.

All the Greatminds turned their eyes toward these two rulers, whose gazes crossed like swords.

"No," the Highmind replied. "We will not conquer the enemy in a hundred years by producing children, but we will conquer him in two years."

"With what then?" the Supermind asked.

"With weapons that I managed to invent and which our grand master Drnk will begin to forge in the new workshops in ten hours. Each of these weapons will replace ten people."

The Greatminds forgot their high position and began to jump for joy like children, breaking the tips of each other's wings.

"Can we believe you in an important matter like that?" asked the Supermind.

"Yes, I brought this weapon along with me. Let us try it out!"

The senate proceeded to the animal enclosure. The weapon destroyed the bloodthirsty animals with a dreadful rapidity. The Greatminds cheered. A happy smile appeared on the face of the Supermind as well. The meeting continued.

"That is a good thing," Greatmind Trgl said, "but the laws nevertheless have to remain unaltered."

The rest agreed with him as well.

The Supermind approached the Highmind slowly, and then told the senate, "No, the law has to be amended! Highmind Brmt is right. The enemy will be defeated! The people have to be set free from the superfluous shackles. Let the new ruler receive my crown and proclaim the word 'love' to the people."

"You don't have to leave, though," said Brmt, "you, the wisest of all of us, you, who were capable of breaking the rusty shackles of the old law, of the law which you served your entire life and in whose righteousness you believed infallibly. You, who with your old heart were capable of comprehending young hearts, you have to remain and have to lead us!"

"I can no longer do that even if I wanted to, because I gave my word of the ruler to abdicate from the throne should it turn out that the law was not right. My children, I turn you over to the mind of the new ruler, which is brighter than mine, and leave you."

Then he turned to his youngest daughter, the most beautiful and noblest maiden of the planet, at whom even the boldest men dared not look, and said, "My dear daughter, the shackles fall from your hands. Your husband-to-be, whom you did not like, will no longer be your husband. You may turn now to the one to whom your heart belonged and belongs. Your feelings caused me much grief, the color of my hair became still redder while grieving over you. I was incapable of helping you – you, my dearest daughter – for I was the ruler and I had to uphold the law, which broke your and my heart. You are free now, and I proceed happily to Mortifero, my old friend and God. I bless you, and you – Brmt – and all my people!"

The Supermind ascended the stairs of the sunbeams, to the place of death of the rulers, where the rays of the two suns were concentrated. He smiled and, while everyone remained sadly silent, began to turn into vapor. In a few moments the ruler was no more....

Then the senior Greatmind said, "Let us inscribe in our hearts for ever and ever this great ruler, who knew how to be a ruler of himself as well, and not only of the people. We will now ask the new ruler – Highmind Brmt – to assume the place of the Supermind."

"Wait!" came the voice of the Supermind's daughter. "Permit me to speak my words before you become the ruler."

"Yes," said Brmt.

"Allow me to be the first one to make use of the new law of love and to tell you that I have always loved you, and love you, except I did not have a word for expressing these feelings. I love you and want to have you as my husband, but that is unfortunately not possible, because you have already chosen another. Forgive me my words in the name of love, because I had to express them to you, otherwise there would be no peace for my heart."

With sparkling eyes the ruler looked into Lrms's face, and said, "In the name of love, I already had to yield before Grns, and I return to her, her beloved friend and my best assistant, to whom I turn over the rule of my former lands, and as a wedding gift present him the title of Highmind. Similarly, in the name of love, I yield for the second time and extend to you my fingers, to you, the sovereign of my dreams, to you, the most beautiful and noblest of all my people, except only for Grns who was the first one to make use of the new, yet unborn law of love, and in front of whom both of us will bow our heads gratefully. By fighting for her love and happiness she brought this love and happiness to us as well, and to all the people."

The ruler finished speaking.

A messenger flew into the hall and said, "Supermind Brmt, the envoys of the enemy's Crazymind ask to be admitted."

"Have them fly in," the ruler said.

The envoys announced, "Supermind, our ruler received your invitation to end the brotherly quarrels and to unite our forces toward ridding the planet of the people-eating animals and plants. Then there will be enough room for everyone and no wars of brotherly people will be needed. Our senate did not want to agree to this proposal, because we had managed to get our wives to bear twenty-two children, and the prospect arose to overcome you.

"The new and revolutionary word 'love,' however, reached us as well, and everything began to collapse. Once we learned about your weapons, our ruler and the senate immediately sent us here with two words, 'We agree.'"

Cheers filled the hall once more.

The envoys said, "Our ruler asks you to appoint the commander-in-chief of our joint armies."

"Here he is," Brmt said, and indicated Drnk.

"Our ruler also sends you a special greeting from his beautiful daughter."

"I thank him," the ruler replied, "for the high honor, which unfortunately has come too late, because my new wife and empress already stands next to me!"

Thus ends this brief story. [[2253]]

Shota   08/28/44 1715

Shota is speaking. It turned out after the high spirit Alfino's tiding that you do not fully understand everything. I received permission to explain to you the more important aspects of what you had not comprehended. Alfino spoke only about a certain episode, and in brief words explained only that without which it would not have been possible to understand what he said.

Vitato, as the spirit Alfino already said, does not know night, because two suns illuminate it – a large one and a second smaller one. The length of the hour adopted by the people of Vitato equals approximately to six-and-a-half hours. As you have been told already, a strong wind blows almost continuously on Vitato. Quite often it reaches the force of a hurricane on Earth. Fortunately, the wind blows steadily in one direction only, therefore it is possible to avoid having people-eating animals and plants [blown into] inhabited regions.

During the hurricane all people, animals, and plants crouch down close to the ground, but still the air is full of flying animals and plants. Entire forests frequently disappear after the strong hurricane, and they can be found again in some desert-like place. As the hurricane subsides, the animals and plants spread their wing-leaves and slowly descend to the ground, adhere to it, and sink their toe-roots into it. The people generally remain in their dwellings during the strong storm, for they have the ability to sense the storm. They can already predict the approach of the storm three hours ahead of it. There is a barometer, and a good barometer at that, within their own bodies.

The people do not sit, but only stand or lie down. The toes of their feet have sharp and long claws, similar to the talons of an eagle on Earth. On the bottom of the foot, in the middle in-between the claws, there is a root-like feeler, which bores into the soil like a screw and sucks water from it. Perhaps it will seem unusual to you that the dwellings of these people do not have a floor, but only the soil. You will be able now to understand for yourselves why there must not be a floor between the foot and the soil.

It also seems strange to you that these people are capable of expressing their thoughts with only consonants, and only with words of four letters.

They are not consonants in reality, but they can be most nearly expressed in your language with the help of consonants. People do not talk with their mouth, which they use only for eating, but with the organ for breathing, which is independent. Because of the severe storms the sound has to be particularly loud, like the trumpeting of an elephant on Earth. The central sound is "r." The rest supplements it, thus forming words. The sound "r" has twenty-eight intonations, and the other sounds have from ten to twenty. Each new intonation also forms a new word, hence their alphabet is incomparably more varied than your, except that, obviously, these words cannot be reproduced with the help of your letters. For example, the letter "t" has eighteen intonations, which means eighteen letters.

Neither have you been given any description of the people's dwellings on Vitato. The plants on Vitato are useless as a construction material, for they are soft and pulpy. Stone is found infrequently on this planet and also is not sturdy. From what then can the people on the planet build houses? Because of the constant storms they are indispensable, and they do build them as well, and much more beautiful than your houses at that. An animal Srkd lives on the planet Vitato. This animal builds buildings for the people without lumber, stones, steel, nails, saws, and axes. How does this magician manage that? It manages that quite simply and rapidly! This animal secretes a transparent, liquid mass that solidifies like glass on contacting air. The animals construct houses from this mass. By adding different pigments to this mass they build enchanting palaces, which sparkle in the sunlight like palaces of jewels. From this same mass the animals make wonderful furniture, dishes, all kinds of objects, and weapons.

In addition, these animals look after the people's children, prepare meals, and give something similar to milk, except much more nutritious. These animals also feed the children, for the women, themselves, on the planet Vitato do not have milk. They only bear the children, turn them over to one of the animals, and forget about them for a prolonged period of time. The animal loves the child who has been entrusted to it so much that it is willing to die, in order to protect and raise the child. Having brought up the child, the faithful animal is usually so worn-out that it dies soon.

Two-thirds of the house is buried underground, and only one-third is above ground, in order to keep the hurricane from carrying the building away. The description of Highmind Brmt's castle also seems incomprehensible to you. These animals, who loved the Highmind very much, had built this castle so fantastic and in such combinations of colors that the walls seemed to be unreal – like a rainbow in the sky.

Then it still remains for me to explain in more detail about bringing up the young people for prescribed occupations and definite positions. Even though the people on Vitato do not die from diseases, still, a given number of them perish in accidents as well as end up in the jaws of people-eaters. Therefore a certain number of young people are held in reserve in order to replace those who have perished. These young people are provided a versatile education, so that they can replace anyone who is missing, and therefore their knowledge and value is much greater.

Then still a few, final words about this unique planet. Its people do not die from diseases, but on sensing signs of old age in their organism, they climb up the tower of the rays of the suns and evaporate.

I still have to tell you that the honorable Supermind Mrmn is your current John.

Why did the high spirit select specifically this episode? Because the four of you figured in it, and John also wanted to know about his former life, even though he had not expressed this desire in words. Henry was inconspicuous in this episode, because his major role remained invisible to you. It began afterwards, and particularly following the death of Brmt.

You will still ask why in all the tidings about your former lives you can be seen in such high positions. Simply because the more prominent circumstances of your lives are related to you. You, too, while telling someone about your life, would relate only the more prominent events, but not the commonplace and insignificant ones, for otherwise your story would have no significance and it would not arouse any interest in the listener. You have lived and experienced extremely much. If we wanted to place the books describing [the experiences of] John's spirit in the London Public Library, that would unfortunately not be possible, because there would not be enough shelves. You can also see now why the history of his spirit cannot be inserted in human memory.

Kolinto's replacement, the high Montaviro, will talk with you in half-an-hour. I conclude.   [[1830]]

Montaviro   08/28/44 1900

Montaviro. I bring you greetings from my high ruler Mortifero and from the high spirit Kolinto.

During these difficult days for the people on Earth I have to assume the responsibility for you in front of The Almighty. The task is not easy, because, as you know, I visit you for the first time, since I come to you from infinitely far distances of the universe. It sufficed, however, for me to spend only a few moments in Alpha's temple in order for the people on Earth and you to become comprehensible and intimate to me — as if I had lived together with you for thousands of years. Therefore do not be surprised about how I will talk with you. I would much rather, just as my ruler, talk picturesquely today. Therefore be kind enough and listen to me patiently. I am speaking.

Three people came to the king once and asked the king to allocate each of them a plot of land. The king agreed with the supplicants, took them to a remote corner of the realm, and allocated them exactly identical plots of land.

"Oh, king, you have such a wide selection of land, but you did not find anything better than these rock covered fields. What can one do with them?"

"One has to work!" the king said. "I give you these fields for a specific period of time. After that, once I will have seen your ability and your desire to work, I will allocate you other plots of land — either better or even worse ones."

The king turned around and left.

He returned after a while to evaluate the new owners, and what did he see? The first of them had sown grain in-between the rocks. It grew in clumps, was overwhelmed by weeds, and was not being looked after.

"What kind of farming is this?" asked the king.

"I farm as I can! If I had wanted to clear off these many rocks, I would have either starved to death or else the term would have expired, and my work would have turned out to be futile, for I would have had to leave without harvesting the crops."

The king walked over to the second owner. He had not sown a single grain of [wheat], but had cleared the rocks from almost his entire plot of land. He replied to the king's question, "In order to be able to farm comfortably and well, to sow and harvest the crops, it is essential to first clear off all these rocks."

"Yes," the king said, "you have piled up entire mountains of rocks, but don't you know that the next day after completing this work your term expires as well?"

The king walked over to the third owner. He had cleared the rocks from one part of the land and had sown grain on it. At the same time he continued to slowly clear the rocks from the remaining part.

"King, you have saddled me with hard work, but that's all right, I am eating rather well, and even if I will not manage to clear off all the rocks by the end of the term set for me, then nevertheless my successor will not lack grain."

The king said, "My son, you have acted wisely and correctly. I will now give you some better land that will not have any rocks, but" turning to the other two, he said, "I will not give better land to you, since you did not know how and did not want to farm properly."

He left the second owner on the same land. To the first one, though, he gave an even worse plot.

I will tell you a second story now.

A ruler dispatched three of his subjects to his, the ruler's, brother. It was a ten-day journey. The ruler summoned these three people and said, "You will have to spend ten days on the road. The road is difficult and nothing, almost nothing, will be available to you along the way. Therefore take along provisions for the entire journey."

The first of the travelers prepared a travel bag, threw it on his shoulders and, having found that it hindered his movements and pulled on his shoulders, threw it down. He stuck a few pieces of bread in his pockets, and said, "Guess I'll manage to get by somehow, will it really be that bad!"

The second calculated the necessary amount carefully and, having taken along provisions for one more day than the trip should last, threw the bag on his shoulders and got ready for the journey.

The third one packed for a long time, and packed a bag that he could barely lift.

The second one said, "Dear friend, why are you bringing provisions for fifty days when you only have to walk for ten?"

"Who knows whether I will mange to walk it in exactly ten days? Besides that, what should I leave behind? I need white and dark bread – for variety. Bacon, sausages, fish, eggs, fruit, wine, lemonade – all that is needed for the trip. What should I throw out? Thus a considerable load is slowly built up."

They set out. The first one, with light steps and while whistling and humming, got far ahead soon, and began to flirt with the girls along the side of the road. After all, he had plenty of time and the journey was easy. The second one walked with moderate steps, stopping and looking over the beautiful vicinity. The third one dragged along like a mule, with his head hung down and breathing heavily.

"Look, what a beautiful mountaintop! Some unusual flowers must grow there, and a wonderful view of the entire world must open up from there. Let us climb up and look around!"

"Madman!" the third one replied. "How can I climb up there with my load?"

The second one climbed up, but the third one dragged himself on. They came to a lake.

The second one said, "We can go for a wonderful swim here!"

"You must be crazy!" growled the third one. "What would happen if someone were to swipe my pack?"

He dragged himself on while wiping the sweat.

Days passed. The first one had consumed all his supplies, and started begging, but the people were stingy and mean. Then he sneaked into a garden, but received a blow of a club to his back. He tried to sneak into a chicken coop, but was jailed for three days. Once released he hastened on.

Ten days passed. The golden gates of the ruler's castle opened and awaited the travelers. The second one entered it on time and calmly. He gave his last piece of meat to the dog at the gate, and it licked his hand gratefully.

"A wonderful journey," the second one said, "easy and beautiful! I saw all kinds of wonders! The entire world lay at my feet, and clouds floated beneath them."

"You are right, my son. For someone who is wise and able to see, this road is beautiful and easy. Go into the castle and sit down at the table of honor!"

The third one showed up after a while. He was barely dragging himself. At the gate he lost his last strength and dropped his heavy bag. The dog walked over to it, sniffed it, growled, and jumped back. A horrible stench of decay came from it.

"What was the road like?" the ruler asked.

"Unbearably difficult!"

"After all, wasn't it beautiful, though?"

"Beautiful? I had no time for looking around, I had to carry my burden."

"Then continue to carry it as well! You have sufficient provisions in it for the forthcoming days."

The first one, while swallowing dust, crawled up as the last one. Even the dog did not recognize a human being in him and stood in the gate barking. The ruler looked sadly at the unfortunate one, and the golden gates closed in front of him.

I conclude.   [[2018]]

Chapter XVI
September 1944 – Part 1

Ilgya   09/02/44 1445

Ilgya. With The Almighty's permission and on behalf of Satan, Satan's high spirit Volturnato will talk with you in an hour. After that Montaviro and Ali will speak.

I conclude, until four o'clock.

Volturnato   09/02/44 1545

→I, Volturnato, am talking with you, The Almighty's heralds to the people on Earth, on behalf of the High Ruler of Heaven – Satan. My words will be cutting and harsh. I will discuss with you the same material that has been discussed by The Almighty's and God's spirits. However, I will approach it from Satan's point of view, and will stress only man's evil characteristics.

Good and evil are notions of an entirely relative nature. There is no [such thing] in the world as absolute good or absolute evil. What may be good for one person, may be evil for another.

The functions of God and His spirits are: To protect the living beings from destruction, to save them and to help them; to bring the concepts of love and mercy to the people; to make their life pleasant, beautiful, and bright; to alleviate suffering, disperse doubts, and inspire belief in [everything that is] good and in eternity; to represent humans and the spirits to The Almighty, and to help them reach the gates of Paradise.

The functions of Satan and His spirits are: To bring up the living beings, and to develop the strength of the body and of the spirit; to eliminate those who are of little value, and to test the weak ones; to bring up humans and the spirits by means of intellect and suffering; to punish the disobedient and the harmful ones; to rehabilitate in life and in the Lunar Fields the weak and the deluded ones, as well as those who are half-bad; to give people the comprehension of logic and of laws; to help the spirits in their ruthless struggle against matter; to guide matter along its road of development, toward an understanding of and cooperation with the spirit.

The duty of Satan and His spirits is only to bring up man, but not to punish him for his sins. Only man, himself, and the spirit, punish themselves.

He [punishes] himself by not obeying The Almighty's laws, but Satan does not [punish him]. The only punishment which Satan uses, and may use, is the Hell of a thousand years of silence and darkness – a Hell without devils, witches, fires, caldrons, and the like. During these thousand years, the sinful spirit tortures himself by pondering his sins. It is not an easy Hell. It is a terrible Hell, more dreadful than the people's old hell with devils. However, only those individuals get there who have sinned dreadfully against The Almighty's laws, which have been given to the people.

Neither God, nor Satan, can release the spirit from his body. They can merely turn to The Almighty with a request to have the spirit recalled from his body. Only the high spirit Mortifero alone, through his spirits, can carry out this recall. Only he alone, and no one else!

You should never say, "God's punishment." [Say instead,] "Satan's punishment," for God never punishes anyone.

Now I will turn to examining man on Earth, and will relate what man is like from the point of view of Satan. Man, man on Earth, is still very young. He still finds himself under an extremely strong influence of matter. His road upward is extremely difficult, and even horrible. To an ordinary observer it might even appear that this road leads downward, rather than upward. Yet it only appears like that. The Almighty has placed His trust in man, and in his ability to overcome matter and raise it to the level of the spirit. Sooner or later this will happen. In this, man's labor, he has two mighty helpers – God and Satan.

I am not talking in order to condemn man, or to drive him to despair. [I am talking] in order to point out to him what he is like currently, and what he is not permitted to be like. That is the only object of my tiding.

What then is the proud ruler of Earth – man – currently like? Let us open our ruthless eyes of the mind and scrutinize him. As I already said, currently man is still extremely far from that ideal which The Almighty envisions in him. The Almighty gave man a free will. Yet man, himself, has deprived himself of this free will. Man is not free. He is a slave, a pitiful slave, the slave of humanity. Man does not belong to himself. Not only may he not do what he wants to, but he has to do what he does not want. His laws require him to serve humanity, the state, community, and family. One cannot imagine a man who would be completely, absolutely free. It is equally hard, though, to comprehend man's lack of freedom. Through its laws of the state and desires of the rulers, humanity forces on man the duty to live not for himself, but for others.

Man does not need much bread for food, and many items of clothing for dressing, nor magnificent mansions in which to live. He could quickly and readily provide all the necessities, but that's not the way it is. Man has to toil from morning till night in order to feed, clothe, and provide lodging for those who do not work themselves. There are immensely many of them: vagrants, the lazy, the wealthy, clergy, bureaucrats, rulers, and those huge and completely superfluous armed armies.

Thanks to the incorrect formation of humanity's states, and the erroneous ideas and goals of people and of the states, humanity's current social order is a slavish order. Each individual, and every state, strive to be happy separately, by themselves. That is impossible. Humanity is one large family, for what radical difference is there between nations? None! Can the members of a family, and the entire family, be happy, if brothers and sisters quarrel; if everyone thinks only about themselves and their own personal benefits, and attempts to derive these from his brothers and sisters, thus delaying both his own and their endeavors and time? Unnecessary quarrels and brawls turn family life into a hell. They rob it of success, prosperity, and happiness.

That is what the current situation of the entire humanity is like. In the form of states and laws, people interfere unnecessarily, meddle in the personal affairs and emotions of every individual. Not only do they force man not to work on the task which he would love, but [they even force him] to love that which he detests, and to detest and hate that which he loves.

Man utilizes everything to achieve his supposed well being or wealth, in which he hopes to find happiness. He utilizes every means for achieving this goal. He lies, cheats, deceives, "brown-noses," slanders, steals, and murders. He even loses his honor, respect, and the name of man, but will not stop. There is nothing so sacred, that he will not exploit even this sanctity in order to achieve this goal.

God sent people His divine envoy – Christ – with the teachings of love and happiness. Being unable to oppose them, man even adopted these teachings and exploited them for his own purposes. Servants of the church, with the cross of Christ on their chests, damned the nonbelievers, took their possessions from them, and burned them at the stake. They created the concept of a repugnant and terrible hell, and with its aid drove people to an even more hideous paradise. Not only did the clergy have the impudence to preach hatred in God's churches, but they even helped the rulers to drive people to death and war. Not only did they help, but they took the sword in their own hands, and with the name of God, the all merciful God, on their lips [proceeded to] behead people.

These days they supposedly no longer do that. Yet why not exploit Christ's teachings in order to obtain prosperity, as well as esteem, with easy work on Sundays? Isn't the position of a clergyman just as remunerative as any other position? It is so easy to serve God – one does not even have to think. Everything that is necessary can be drawn from thick books, forged in gold. And after all, God, dear God, remains silent and will not punish, for he is serving this God. Humanity, however, even though it is blind, still realizes that something is not in order here. The name of God begins to disappear from the lips of man, and ever more he uses only the word – devil. Man no longer believes in him either, but his teachings appear to be more practical to man.

He and she meet at the altar with love in their hearts, and swear love and fidelity until the grave. Who needs these base lies? Everyone knows that there is neither eternal love nor fidelity. Should some scurry, while crying, to divorce the very next day, it still elicits amazement and discussions in people. Should that happen after some months, or years, then that's a common occurrence. There's a place on Earth where marriage has been turned into a sport, into veiled prostitution, I would say. Then again, that's what it's like in other lands as well. Go ahead, count for me all the people who are faithful in their marriage. I'm afraid that this task will not take very long.

The individual removes his mask in family life. That is the cause of family tragedy, for marriages are contracted under a mask. In family life, the individual often shows himself to be even worse than he [really] is. What one may not manifest to others, one may display to his or her marriage partner. The law itself helps one to bind this partner to him or her. Frequently one dumps one's life and occupational troubles and surliness, as well as failures, on one's husband or wife. They become scapegoats. It is not necessary to control yourself in front of your loved ones, either. Nor is it necessary to dress properly; you can walk around in a torn robe and with a dirty face. You don't have to hide your shortcomings and physical defects. Thus love dies and Satan laughs, as people would say. Now this Satan tells people why this happens like that. But He does not laugh, only grins bitterly.

To envy your best friend, to trip him up, to betray him, to seduce his wife – that, after all, is not a sin, particularly while hiding your face behind the smoke of a fat cigar from your friend. Man exploits all means, even the most beautiful and noblest words and concepts. The government, or the ruler, never admits that what it does is being done for its own benefit. Oh no, everything is being done only for the benefit of the people.

Palaces are being built for the good of the people, yet for some unknown reason the people are not allowed inside them. For the good of the people rocks are being crushed and prisons built. For the good of the people grain is being sown, which then flows overseas for gold. For the good of the people wars are being waged – wars in which these people die, their homes crumble, and their works are destroyed. For the good of the people, the people are being deprived of their time, happiness, freedom, and even lives.

Yet do the people really derive any good from all of this? Yes, except not all the people, but only an insignificant part of the people. The strangest thing is that people [actually] believe the words of these rulers and governments. Even these rulers and governments think that they act for the good of the people, and that they derive their own benefits only through the welfare of the people.

Man does not know how to approach things correctly. He devised money as a means of simplifying barter. Now, however, he sees value in money itself. He will sacrifice everything for it, even though, in reality, piles of money are entirely worthless to him.

Humanity has lost proportion and the sense of reality. It turns everything into triviality, be it ideas, or words, or even the most sacred feelings. "Brotherhood, comradeship in arms forged with blood," are beautiful and noble words, but only words. Yesterday's brothers and comrades in arms are enemies today. They fight, and swear at their yesterday's comrade and brother, while kissing his enemy. Treaties and pledges of loyalty have only the value of the paper on which they are written.

Only [one's own] good, only the more advantageous situation, are deciding factors. Those noble and beautiful appeals, speeches that seem to come from the heart and from convictions – just how much truth is there in them? Today, perhaps some, but tomorrow, under different circumstances

— none. Man's heart is an empty drum on which the drumsticks of exploitation of life's situations beat. The emptier this heart is, the louder sounds the drum. Words, streams of words, rivers of words, lakes of words, seas of words, oceans of words overwhelm the unfortunate man, and his weak sense of criticism drowns in this flood of words. The word has lost its value. Ideas have lost their meaning; work has lost its reason. Man has not yet found the goal of his life.

I have to conclude, for my High Ruler awaits me. I will repeat, lack of reason has overcome humanity today. Millions are dying. Thousands of cities, which have been built by entire generations, are being wiped off the face of Earth, along with immeasurable treasures. Who has given you, the man of today, the right to devastate your ancestors' accomplishments, and to ruin the treasures of art created by them? Who has given you the right to place the unbearable burden of reconstruction on the shoulders of the coming generations? Have you considered what your blind hatred and madness will cost humanity? Do you realize what responsibility you have laid on your conscience, with the lives of millions of fallen and maimed, and the needlessly ravaged cities?

Had the insane escaped from an asylum and grabbed all authority on Earth for themselves, they would have done it less harm than have you, the chosen and wise ones. Now your mind, overcome by despair, tackles new and dreadful weapons, and once again wants to cloud the Earth with deadly gases.

I implore The Almighty that this most fearful page of humanity's history, filled with the vilest deeds, may soon be closed. Otherwise, the other pages will remain half-empty, and stained with sweat and tears.

Thus say I, Satan's envoy to you!← [[1817]]

Montaviro   09/02/44 1910

Montaviro is speaking. People often complain that God does not protect them from mishaps and from other unpleasant things. I discovered a beautiful tale in Alpha's temple, a tale from olden times, which humanity has now forgotten, but which I will permit myself to relate to you. Listen!

God summoned a guardian angel once, and told him, "Listen, angel, what does it mean that the human whom you are guarding complains about you? He claims that all kinds of mishaps persecute him continuously. Thus, while going home he fell into a ditch. He was thoroughly beaten up in a tavern.

His wife poured [the contents] of a chamber pot on his head, and so on. What does all that mean?"

"Oh, that ungrateful one!" exclaimed the guardian angel. "I struggle with him all the time, but he still complains to God! After all, I told him not to drink that much, and even knocked his wineglass from his hand. Yet he, he imagined that the man next to him at the table had done that and called him all kinds of nasty names. That individual, obviously, did not fail to retaliate. We, the guardian angels of the two of them, grabbed them by their jackets and whispered in their ears, but how could one hold back these drunk lions and calm them down! A fight broke out, and such a one that even the devil, who happened to get mixed up in it, had his tail torn off and horns broken. We barely managed to escape through the wide chimney of the fireplace, blacker than the devil himself. Obviously, both of them were eventually thrown out with black eyes.

"I led mine home, but where does he walk? Only in the middle of the road! He gets underfoot a knight's horse. I scared the horse, it jumped aside, but the knight was on the ground. Obviously, this could not be left like that, and an ironclad fist raised a mighty lump in the middle of the bald head of the one whom I was guarding. What could I, however, do against this knight, I, a feeble angel? All [I could do] was to haul mine homeward, but now he took a fancy to walking in the ditch, rather than on the road. Somehow, with the help of the devil who was taking his horns to the forge of the blacksmith, I managed to get him to his house. Yet then, underneath his very own bedroom window, he refused to go any further, and lay down to sleep in the mud. Is there any wonder then that his wife, while emptying the contents of the pot out the window, splashed her husband on the head! How could I help there? Do You think that I didn't catch some as well? For an entire hour I had to wash myself in the pond, along with the ducks, and for several hours I had to dry myself by the kiln in the drying-house. And this ungrateful man still accuses me!"

The angel began to weep bitterly.

"Stop that!" God said. "Today is supposed to be the day for mowing the hay and you will get all of it wet for the people. They will curse My minister that he has not even managed to obtain good weather from Me. Go, rest until the evening. I will venture to settle this matter."

The angel flew away. God summoned Saint Peter and sent him to Earth with a task.

Peter arrived at the man's house. The man's wife had become sick from anger, and quarreled with the nanny. On hearing insults from the master as well, that she doesn't know how to look after the child, she turned up her nose and went to her friend to tell her about her sorrows. What can be done now?

Peter said, "You, dear Michael, are free today. Couldn't you look after the child yourself for one day? Your wife will have recovered by tomorrow."

"Yes, why not? Just think, would any skill be needed to look after a tyke like that!"

Michael took the tyke by the hand and went for a walk. They came to a meadow. The sun was shining, the flowers smelled sweetly, and the birds were chirping.

"How nice," Michael muttered, and stretched out in the grass.

The child played quietly in a sand pile. Michael dozed off. Then he heard frightful crying. Michael jumped up. What do you know, his boy was brawling furiously with neighbor Joe's boy. He broke them up with much difficulty. Both of them had blue spots on their foreheads, and the father had his eyes and beard full of sand.

"We better go on," said the father.

They walked over to the road. A knight was riding along the road. Without being noticed, the tyke picked up a rock and threw it at the knight's broad back. It seemed as if the entire Earth rumbled. The knight turned his horse around and a rain of robust kicks fell on both of them, the son and the father.

They came to a friend's garden. Michael admonished his son to behave properly, and then started talking with his friend. This conversation, however, was not destined to last long, nor the wine vessels to travel the short distance from the bench to the lips. Horrible screaming was heard again, and even lament. What was it now again? No big deal, the tyke had merely turned over a beehive. A black cloud rose into the air. The friend managed to take off in time, but the father, while protecting himself from the bees with his beard, had to hasten to rescue his heir. No one could see them, for a cloud of bees and dust rolled along the road, and a sound somewhat similar to an organ and the howl of a wolf came from it. Neither did anyone look long at this cloud, but took right off. The cloud evaporated on the bank of the nearest pond, and after a while something resembling a large beet crawled out of it. A smaller beet hesitantly crawled out next to it, and started on the way homeward.

Along the road they met a neighbor lady, and she began to cry and to laugh. Michael had to relate the events of the unfortunate day. The road was dry and there was only one puddle in the middle of it. A pig wallowed in this puddle and grunted happily. When the father had finished talking and turned toward home, he saw in the puddle next to the ears of the pig, the pink ears, the black ears of his son as well. That was too much even for Michael. He grabbed his son by the hair and hauled him out.

Once they reached home, the lady of the house was already waiting for them on the threshold. On seeing them coming, she did not recognize them immediately, and sent a servant for some bread to give to the beggars. Having taken a good look, though, she began to wail and to tear her hair.

"Try to control this scoundrel yourself!" said Michael. "Human strength is too weak for that, because he deliberately looks for trouble. He is as though bewitched for mischief and pranks!"

"I can understand everything," his wife said, "except for one thing. There was only one puddle on the entire dry road, and he had to stumble exactly into this puddle. Couldn't you even protect him from this one, solitary puddle?"

"No, I could not! If you can, then try for yourself," and he went looking for the nanny, in order to plead with her to come back.

Peter said in the evening, "Michael, you see, you could not protect such a tiny tyke, and you want God's guardian angel to protect an ox like you!"

"Yes, you oldster, you are probably right. I will pray to God not to scold my good little angel, and to send him back to me as soon as possible."

When the angel came back to God, God simply said, "Go, the matter is settled. Michael will no longer complain!"

Thus ends this tale from olden times, but it can turn out to be useful to you in your modern times as well. [[2022]]

Ilgya   09/03/44 1620

_ ★ ★ ★ _

The bonds of old friendships disintegrate; weapons turn from facing the chests of enemies to the chests of friends. The enemy of yesterday is greeted as a friend, the friend is thrown out like an enemy. The word friend turns into enemy, loyalty into deceit, eternity into a moment, God into Satan, sacred into mockery, honor into dishonor, and mind into insanity. That is what this day is like, and this day's man.

Satan's high spirit told you yesterday what thoughts and what terrible projects are born in the heads of humanity's leaders. They prepare a horrifyingly rich harvest for death. They want to sow the fields of Europe thicker with corpses, than The Almighty was able to with stones. The times of the Huns are returning – except even more terrifying, more merciless. This war is not a war against able-bodied soldiers, but it is a war against helpless children, women, and old men. This war is not a war against fortresses, but it is a war against the homes of peaceful people; against schools, museums, and churches. This war is not for the sake of culture, but for the sake of destroying culture. That is what this war is like, but this war also brings along something that will partially redeem its evil.

That is the secret weapon with which the genius of the German inventors bombards England. This secret weapon is a step into a new era, which humanity enters. This weapon, when utilized under conditions of peace, will open new horizons to humanity, and not just only this weapon. This war will bring much to science that is new. New generations will be born, new cities will grow – even larger, even more beautiful than the destroyed ones were. The blood, the tears, and the sweat will dry up; wails, curses, and accusations will cease. Those who have fallen and the hatred will be forgotten. Memories of humanity's insanity, however, will remain, and the fear of a new war. The inventions will remain, which were intended for destroying people and culture, but which will serve humanity's happiness and the uplifting of culture.

Thus The Almighty does not permit the very worst to occur, unless there is something good in it as well.

Your days are dark. Grave is the illness of humanity's spirit; erroneous are humanity's ways of this day, but all that is not eternal. All that is transitory; besides that, all that is so very interesting for you, high spirits. The fates of millions of people and of many states pass in front of your eyes. Leaders grow up before your eyes, rulers fall, leaders fall as well, and the fallen rulers return. The impossible turns out to be possible, and the possible – impossible.

When and where would you be able to observe the highest achievements and the worst decline of the human spirit? When and where would you be able to look into human nature like that, and comprehend it like that, as during these days of horrors and of suffering? Humanity's soul stands naked before your eyes. It is dirty, it is ugly, but there is also a bright spark within it, which only has to be [fanned up into] a sun. The Almighty believes in this spark; believes that no floods of blood, tears, and delusions will extinguish it; but that reason will preserve it and will fan up a sun from it. You, too, have to believe, because otherwise there is no sense in your coming to Earth, there is no meaning to your life and to that of humanity, and there is no justification for the word – man.

The high God Indra will speak now on behalf of the divine Santorino. An intermission of a few minutes. Perhaps even Ali will talk after Indra. I conclude. [[1714]]

Indra   09/03/44 1737

→I, Indra, will talk with you in the assignment of the Divine.

A high spirit told you yesterday very much that is important, as well as new. Yet not everything that he said is completely clear to the people, and some explanations are needed.

To begin with, the very idea about God and Satan has still not been made completely precise. That is hard to do. The real God and the real Satan have little in common with those whom the people have imagined. A small comparison will help you partially to understand these ideas better. You might get the partially correct concept, if we were to compare The Almighty to a judge, Satan to a prosecutor, God to a defense attorney, and man to an accused.

The prosecutor does not prosecute the accused because he is evil by nature. He does that because it is his duty to reveal to the judge all the offenses and wicked characteristics of the accused. The duty of the defense attorney is of a different nature. It is to reveal all the virtues of the accused, and to ascertain extenuating circumstances which might justify and mitigate the accused's offense, as well as to help the accused in every way with advice.

After the tiding of the high spirit, you now know that only Mortifero recalls the spirit from the body. Yet that does not mean that Mortifero does that personally in each case. The spirit may not depart from his body without his order. Should an accident occur and the body is injured to such an extent that the heart stops to function, and continued functioning of the body is not possible, then the spirit has unintentionally ended his mission. Still, he is not free yet.

Your scientists have conducted experiments with dogs, by completely draining all blood from their blood vessels. The heart stops beating, the body stops reacting to stimuli. The dog is completely dead. No signs of life whatsoever can be ascertained in it. A somewhat lengthy time period passes. The researcher attaches instruments, pumps fresh blood into the blood vessels, and starts the heart. Oh wonder, the dog begins to breathe, opens its mouth, and licks its dry snout. The dog continues to live as though it had never been dead. What does that prove? It proves very much, except you, yourselves, have to ponder that well.

The spirits generally do not intervene in the course of destiny of ordinary people, and do not protect them from accidents and diseases. Man himself has to do this. The spirits spend little time with man. They only help him during moments of doubt, and when he turns to them. The spirits are only with those who live a spiritual life, who strive to grow and to develop.

The spirit has nothing to do with an individual who is standing still – a bureaucrat, who all day long is absorbed in paragraphs and figures, who in the evening, having eaten, sits down at a card table. The spirit has nothing to do with this person. Neither does a spirit have anything to do with a housewife who cleans house all day long, does the laundry, prepares meals, and in her spare time gossips with her neighbor about the steps and words of all their acquaintances, and at night either argues with her husband or snores. A spirit has nothing to do with a clergyman, who on weekdays counts the money which he has received for funerals, baptisms, and weddings, and on Sundays sings memorized hymns and crammed sermons. Similarly, the clergyman has nothing to tell or ask the spirit.

People, individual people, are not valuable to The Almighty. They are the dwellings for spirits of a low degree, in which the spirit has to struggle against matter, has to learn and grow. It is not important if his body is destroyed sooner [than had been planned] due to diseases or an accident. He is simply transferred to another body, and that is that. If the spirit in an individual has ceased to progress; if the individual ceases to grow and succumbs to commonness, insipid work, laziness, card games, drinking, and idle gossip, then a spirit like that has ended his mission and is resting in the body. The individual himself turns into a zero in the eyes of The Almighty and of the spirits, and no one is any longer interested in or looks after him.

The spirits only look after a capable spirit and an active person. There are particularly many spirits with the so-called geniuses of humanity, with high spirits who are engaged in a victorious struggle against matter. Not only the spirits keep up with them, but even the eyes of God and Satan do not leave them for one moment. Even though the spirits of these geniuses are on occasion recalled early from Earth, that happens only in order to assign them more important tasks.

Satan, God, and Their spirits intervene little in the fates of humans. Their responsibilities are to guide and to help, or to rehabilitate the spirits in the Lunar and Solar Fields.←

A few more words now about something else. The high spirits have given you many instructive stories. Why is that being done? That is being done so that humanity would have [material] with which to fill services in churches. They are examples in prose, drama, poetry, and even comedy. You should utilize these stories and songs from the Tidings in The Almighty's temples by reciting and singing them, and enacting them in plays and movie films. Humanity's geniuses should originate, according to these examples, stories, plays, songs, movies, and music with educational and artistic value for use in services.

The recital of the prayer should be followed by a discussion of the congregation's everyday concerns. After that – highly worthy lectures about The Almighty and His laws; about the obligations of people, about concerns of culture and science. That should be followed by the part consisting of concerts and performances of plays and films; of recitations, songs, and music.

I will conclude with that for today. Your beloved spirit, Ali, will speak now in ten minutes. [[1840]]

Ali 09/03/44 1847

The old Turk is speaking. This time I was on time. My high replacement visited you yesterday with an unusual story, which seemed to be unbecoming for one of Mortifero's serious spirits. How did that happen? This is how that happened.

Montaviro told me, "Dear Ali, I don't like it that the heralds receive me with some trepidation, and expect from me only sorrow, misfortune, somber words, the whip of enlightenment, and even death. I am incapable, and no one is capable, of competing with you in creating cheerful stories, but I did find something that will leave even you with your mouth open."

What do you think? This somber servant of Death had found in the dust of Alpha's archives some forgotten story from olden times. I can't help it; I have to confess that I was rather taken aback. I was taken aback by human humor and abilities of the mind, and by Montaviro's guile. This story, which he had discovered, turned out, unfortunately, to be so "potent" in its expressions that some words in it had to be tempered and some events omitted, because the respect of the spirits and the ear of modern man could not tolerate them.

Being no longer able to compete with the spirit of death in humor, I am forced today to tell you a story with a sad content. Listen to it!

A wise man lived in a small town. [He was] so wise that people called him a philosopher and the wisest human, for he was capable of solving many of life's concerns, and of comprehending them. He was also capable of helping with advice everyone who turned to him.

"Our wise one, our pride, our fame," the inhabitants of the small town said of him. Then the word reached them that the wisest philosopher in the entire country lives in the capital.

"The wisest one?" asked the citizens. "Would that really be the case? What about our wise Suleiman? It should be determined who truly deserves the fame — our city or the metropolis!"

Despite the expense, they decided to invite the sultan's wise man to a competition of wisdom. After hesitating for a long time, he rode into the small town. A lavish banquet was given in the town's largest hall. Many people gathered, even from the far corners of the entire state, and from Baghdad as well.

The two wise men were seated next to each other. The guest talked incessantly. Wisdom poured forth from him like money from the sultan's bag, but the local wise man did not utter a word, merely nodded his head in agreement. Surprise and even indignation began to overwhelm the townspeople.

"What gives with our wise one? Why doesn't he say something and demonstrate his wisdom to the stranger and to the people?"

The wise guest, too, began to become impatient, and finally said, "Where is your wise one here – the one with whom I am to compete in wisdom, and because of whom I had to travel this long distance? I do not see and hear such a wise one here, but only fools."

Suleiman stood up then, for the people's indignation and the storm of shame threatened to collapse the building. He stood up, bowed before the guest, and said, "Oh, wisest of the wise ones, and you – my townsmen – caught [in your own trap] due to your foolishness, permit me, whose mind is not as bright as you may think, to tell you a little story."

Everyone quieted down, and the guest waited.

Suleiman said, "A rich merchant lived in a city. With his money, he helped out the poor, his friends, and even other merchants. An extremely wealthy merchant came to the city once and invited the city's richest merchants to call on him. They came and brought the newcomer all kinds of valuable presents, but Ibrahim, that is what our generous merchant was called, did not give him anything.

"The rest of the merchants became indignant, 'What gives! You gave a hundred liras to everyone, even to the poor, but for this wealthy person you did not bring even that!'

"'Yes,' replied Ibrahim, 'my hundred liras brought life and happiness to the poor, saved my friend from hardship, and helped a merchant earn another hundred liras. To this rich person, though, what would my hundred liras mean to him? He would either not accept them, or at most would toss them carelessly away in a corner.'

"That is my little story," Suleiman said, and bowed before the wise guest.

And – oh, wonder! The guest bowed his gray head still lower before Suleiman, and said, "I thank you for the edification."

Having turned to the citizens, he said, "Why did you invite me when the wisest of the wise is among you? I have lost, for wisdom is not given in order to toss it around needlessly in words, but in order to accomplish wise deeds."

Having bowed low before Suleiman once more, he said, "I ride away from you – teacher – for I do not consider myself worthy of being your pupil."

He departed from the building.

(Take a break for five minutes.) [[1940]]

The high Alfino told you about your life on the planet Vitato. The high poet Shota [further] clarified it. Nevertheless I, too, have something with which to supplement the tidings of the high spirits, for, after all, some questions and doubts can arise to man – to man on the planet Earth. That should not happen.

To begin with, why did these universal animals love Highmind Brmt so much? That is not explained in the tidings of the two spirits. The animals loved him and built this beautiful ruler's castle because they were grateful to the Highmind for having saved them from their sad fate.

The people of Vitato did not call themselves "man," as you call yourselves, but they called themselves by the word "mind." That's also why these words – Supermind, Highmind, and Greatmind – which sound somewhat strange and even ironical in your language. These minds valued the animals very highly, and protected them by every means, for there was much work but there were not that many animals.

The meat of the animals was extremely tasty, and therefore a merciless law existed. It was permitted to slaughter for meat only those animals which, after raising a child, had become too feeble and useless for further work. Many minds who had been raised and nursed by the animals revolted against this law, but they were only individual voices and were unable to amend this "mindless" – in the language of the people on Earth, inhuman – law.

When the Supermind's youngest daughter grew up, and on her name day the animal that had raised her was to be slaughtered, the Supermind's daughter did not want to permit that under any circumstances. Highmind Brmt sided with her and defended the animals so fervently that he was able to enact a law protecting the animals. Halfway through the raising [of a mind] the animal was to be replaced by another animal, thus preserving the strength and lives of both animals. This humane law had fateful consequences with respect to Brmt.

The anger of the minds rose against him for the loss of the tasty meat. What was most unusual, also the anger of the animals, who did not want to part from their beloved foster-children halfway [through raising them]. The situation became so unbearable that Highmind Brmt left the nation of the minds and established, with his friends and followers, a colony in the land of the horrible mind-eating animals. He succeeded in vanquishing the beasts and establishing a successful country of the minds. With time, the entire nation and all the animals recognized the righteousness, advisability, and sanctity of his law. Due to feelings of gratitude, the animals built Brmt an unprecedentedly magnificent dwelling – a castle.

The second question. How could it happen, in a state where the law firmly prescribed the day of marriage and the marriage partner for every-one who had come of age, how could a situation come about that High-mind Brmt was not married when he met Grns? This even though he should have exceeded considerably the days, or age, of marriage, [as judged by] his high position and wisdom, which was admired by everyone. We have come to a tragedy here, which cast a shadow on the Highmind's entire happiness in life.

Yes, he had to get married at the designated hour and had to marry the designated young woman. Brmt, however, did not feel any sympathy toward this young woman, and asked the senate and the Supermind to exempt him from this marriage. The senate rejected his request and the Supermind confirmed this decision, even though very reluctantly. Brmt abided by the law, but told his new wife that he could not be a husband to her, but only a friend. They lived in separate quarters and hardly ever met. Then came the day when Brmt left for his colony. He turned his palace over to his wife.

News reached the metropolis regarding the colonists' hard life and the dangers that threatened them at every step. One day Brmt saw in surprise his wife flying across the threshold of his dwelling.

"What are you seeking here?" Brmt asked.

"You – my husband," she replied. "You can want me or not want me, but it is my duty to be with my husband who undergoes hardships and who lives in constant danger."

"Who told you that this is your duty?"

"My heart," came the reply.

She stayed, and nothing could keep her from carrying out this duty. A miracle occurred. A wave of warmth overwhelmed Brmt's heart, and he looked at his wife with different eyes, gentle and happy. She bent her head as if in a dizzy spell, and thus began a marriage that was blessed with love and friendship, unprecedented in the nation of the minds.

The hour came when the moment approached which the Highmind as well as his people awaited with impatience and joy. A hurricane came, how-

ever, an unusually fierce hurricane that, while changing direction, brought
an entire cloud of mind-eating animals to the colony. They stuck to all the
dwellings and filled the entire vicinity. Brmt was far from his castle when
the hurricane started. He hurried to the castle. Not far from it an entire
pack of beasts attacked him. He fought bravely. His wife saw from the castle
that Brmt was in mortal danger, and hastened to help him. Several beasts
attacked her as well, and Brmt, overcome by horror, saw his wife disappear-
ing in the jaws of the beasts. When help arrived everything was already over.
Only the wings remained. Brmt hung these on the wall of the castle, above
his place of the ruler.

His sorrow was especially deep. His unexpectedly attained happiness had
been destroyed in a few moments. He devoted himself to inventing weapons with whose help it would be possible to take revenge on the animals
and to destroy them, thus liberating the planet from these beasts.

I will tell you in ten minutes about my own, Brmt's, Grns's, and Drnk's
tragic fate on this planet, subsequent to Alfino's episode. [[2050]]

How come that I know and am telling you all that? Because I lived on
Vitato back then. I was the Supermind of the hostile nation, or as the nation
of the minds ironically called me – Crazymind.

Highmind Brmt invited me to end our disagreements, to stop "manufacturing" children, and to conclude a friendship for the fight against the
beasts. As easy as it is, though, to move a mind toward evil deeds, it is just
as difficult to move him toward good ones. I thought and procrastinated.
The senate thought, thought and talked, but all that did not bear any fruit.
Thus came the hour when Brmt gave the minds the fateful word "love,"
and invented his weapon. Even though it had been intended for fighting the
animals, it could have been turned against us just as readily. We came to our
senses rather soon, and sent envoys. A treaty of friendship and prosecution
of the war [against the beasts] was concluded. Engineer Drnk was appointed
as the commander-in-chief of the army.

You know that much. You were left with the impression of a happy fate
for all those who remained. It seemed to you that a period of happiness
will start now on the planet, that the sun of happiness will shine brightly
and eternally for Brmt, Grns, and Drnk. Perhaps you even envied them, as
compared to your current life on Earth, but those are bitter delusions. The
crown of the ruler is not a crown of happiness. Power does not make life

easier, but only makes it harder. A profound tragedy followed the happily concluded episode.

Why was an engineer appointed as the commander-in-chief of the army – an engineer, but not a soldier? Because this war was a unique war, the war of machines against animals and plants. Nevertheless it was difficult and long, but it, too, ended eventually, and Vitato could breathe freely. Drnk returned to the metropolis. Hours had passed, thousands of hours. Much had changed, except the love between Supermind Brmt and his new wife had not changed.

The empress was so beautiful that her beauty drew all the minds, Greatminds, and eventually even Highmind Drnk to her feet. Her eyes, however, looked proudly past all of them. She could be worshiped, but not loved. A golden era reigned on the planet. Only the quarrel between the two nations regarding the division of the planet had yet to be settled. Everyone, starting with the ruler, felt happy, and only the Highmind, who had been showered with riches and respect, did not feel happy. A delirious love for the queen overcame him, and a deadly insult to his pride due to her frigid conduct.

After a session of the senate he stayed behind in the hall conversing with the empress. There were just the two of them. The ruler accompanied me, since I was a guest. Overcome by extreme emotions Drnk turned to the empress with a request to listen to his words of love. The empress proudly rejected this request. Drnk then completely lost his head, and approached the empress wanting to embrace her. The empress stepped back in fright, up the stairs of the dead. Neither she nor he noticed that in the excitement. Then Drnk suddenly noticed in horror that the spears of the suns' rays crossed the face of the empress. He cried out in dread on seeing the empress turning into vapor. In a few moments the empress was no more.

The Highmind staggered down the stairs to the hall. At that moment the Supermind entered the hall, and asked Drnk, "Where is the empress?"

"The empress, high ruler, is no more," the Highmind said in a low voice.

"How come, is not? What does that mean?"

"It means that the world's worst criminal and scoundrel stands before you. In front of you stands your friend, your best friend, and the murderer of your wife, his queen. While fleeing from my insane love she climbed up the stairs of the dead, and she is no more."

The ruler, pale and stiff as a corpse, looked into the face of his friend.

"Ruler, permit me to climb up these stairs of the dead, and disappear from the world."

"No, you want to avoid punishment! As the ruler I punish you and order you to live! You want to avoid punishment by dying, in order to set yourself free from the torment of heartaches. No, you will have to live long and suffer long, until this dreadful crime and sin against love, the law, and friendship will have been redeemed. A triple sin requires a triple punishment as well. I order you to live three lifetimes! I appoint you as the Supermind in my stead, I make the appointment as the ruler and a friend. As the ruler I ask of you the oath of the ruler – to live three lifetimes – and as a friend I ask you to look after my people and make them happy. Give me your oath!"

"Oh, ruler and friend, you ask too much from me, and impose too harsh a punishment. My crime, however, against the ruler, friend, and the law is so serious that I can say only [two] words to you – I swear!"

"I thank you," said the ruler. "I and all those who have died here will be glad to meet you as a friend in the realm of Mortifero. Your dear wife will help you to carry your heavy burden, and will share the high honor with you."

"No, ruler, I will not help him, and will not share any honor with him!" came the voice of Grns. Grns had been standing behind the ruler's throne, and had seen and heard everything, but overwhelmed by the horror had not been able to even move.

The ruler looked at her with a sad gaze, and then said, "Highmind Drnk, bow your head and receive the crown of the ruler!"

"But you?" Drnk whispered.

"I will follow the empress. There is no longer anything left for me in this world. Love has passed on, friendship has passed on, and my work has passed on. Everything is there now, beyond these spears of the suns. I am no longer needed here. The task of my life has been completed here, and others await me elsewhere. I pass on, and while passing on bless the nation of minds, its ruler, and empress."

"Except not the empress," came the voice of Grns. "I will accompany you on the stairs of the dead – up to the spears of the suns!"

"Why?" the ruler asked.

"Why? You ask why, you, who comprehends everything? I go the same way as you do, together with my love."

"With your love?" asked Brmt.

"Yes, back when you declined my love, you attained it, noble ruler, for one can attain love only by declining it, and one can lose love by thrusting oneself on it. My entire life was a service to my silent, unexpressed love for you, ruler. All the people love you with all their hearts, but you, ruler, are capable of and can love only one, for there is only one of you. I am happy that I can at least walk together with you this short planetary road – the stairs of the dead."

"Mortifero," Drnk exclaimed, "is there no end to your mercilessness, and no limit to your punishment?"

The answer did not come, though. Only the steps of two people walking responded to the castle's silence of the grave. Then these steps on the stairs of the dead faded as well, and the silence of the grave set in.

When I returned to the hall, in it stood – brokenhearted from despair and pain, inexpressible pain – the new ruler of the nation of the minds and the unhappiest individual in the world. He looked at me, but did not see me. He bore on his head the crown of the ruler, but did not feel it. He lived, but a corpse had more life than he did. I turned around silently and left the hall, for only time could help this unfortunate one.

I conclude.   [[2228]]

Ilgya   09/04/44 1750

Ilgya. I come in response to your invitation. Three high spirits have told you about the planet Vitato; have told you and clarified, but the more the worse! I have to come to their rescue again, because I am responsible for your fate, and therefore I strive to satisfy the questions that can be satisfied, and to dispel any doubts. You want to know much, so very much, about everything in the universe, but your thirst for knowledge cannot be satisfied.

How can you know everything about the universe, which is infinite and whose Ruler is even more infinite? How can you ask what has occurred in the universe, if the beginning of the universe is infinite? How can you ask what will take place in the universe, when there is no end to time? Not only can one not grasp infinity, one cannot even comprehend it. Just imagine that I, too, whose years cannot be counted, know only an insignificant corner of the universe. Perhaps only The Almighty, Himself, whom we do not know either, knows the entire universe. Man has to reconcile himself with much. It would be desirable to get to know all the people on Earth, but that is not possible. It would be desirable to read at least all the better books, but that is not possible either. It is a complete absurdity to try to know everything.

I will attempt now to explain to you why the high Ali related to you the final, sad episode of the rulers of Vitato – one that appears to be superfluous, does not contain anything instructive, and even seems to disgrace some of you. I will also endeavor to illuminate even better the sense and events of your lives on the planet Vitato.

Let us begin with Supermind Mrmn. He had the following task. Prior to him being sent to Vitato, there were relatively few inhabitants – minds. I will call them people, for they differ from humans only by their outward appearance. There were many people-eating animals and plants. Mrmn's task was to increase the proliferation of people. That could be achieved with the help of the merciless laws, by forcing people to subordinate all their other interests for the sake of increasing greatly the birth of children. With the help of the ironclad laws, Mrmn achieved that as well. The animals were restricted to some extent. A new problem surfaced, though. It turned out to be impossible to agree with the brother nation regarding the allocation of the newly acquired lands, and wars broke out. These forced the law about children to be strengthened even more.

When, thanks to Highmind Brmt, the situation changed drastically; Mrmn understood that his mission had ended. Having adhered to his laws for his entire lifetime and having grown accustomed to them, he was nevertheless able to realize the need for new laws and for the repeal of the old ones. He understood with his high mind that he was capable of following the call of the new era, but was incapable of being its leader. It needed new leaders. In order not to hinder the progress of the people even inadvertently, he found it necessary to pass into eternity.

Thanks to the longtime effect of the oppressive laws on the people, their spirit had begun to atrophy. New circumstances arose – love had to be brought back. Grns's task, the task that she had received from The Almighty, was to proclaim this love and to fight for it. Grns accomplished this task beautifully, but she became a victim of this love herself. Her steadfast love split on encountering two very great people with different traits. In order to fight for love, she had to comprehend all aspects and forms of love, because love varies. This initially steadfast and later-on split love gave her the opportunity to experience all the possibilities of love's happiness and suffering, and to present a complete understanding of it to the people. She knew how to love two people so that no one knew of it and no one even sensed it.

Her husband felt happy. It seemed to everyone that she, too, was happy as the sunshine, but her suffering was great, very great. Brmt considered her to be his closest and dearest friend and shared with her even those of his thoughts that he did not express to anyone. Their conversations went on for hours, and on parting their fingers could not disengage for a long time yet, but not one word of love was uttered during their conversations. Only at the last moment of her life did Grns recover her steadfast love, and came to us with it. The Almighty has again allocated her the opportunity now of returning to her first love, here on the planet Earth.

Drnk's task, but I will talk about that later.

We have to examine Brmt's task first. Brmt's task, which he received from The Almighty on coming to Vitato, was extremely important, difficult, and significant. He had been directed to lead the people of the planet to a happy future; to free the planet from the people-eaters, from mutual wars of the nations, and from laws that destroy the spirit; and to return the power of love and the right to a free will to the people. Brmt's spirit was of an extremely high degree and eminently capable. It seemed that it would be easy for a spirit like that to carry out these tasks, but it only seemed like that, because the power of matter was extremely strong in the people, and it was difficult to rip apart the rusty but still strong shackles of the old laws.

Brmt, by being the second in the state, enjoyed much power, respect, and the realization of almost all of his desires and wishes. Under such circumstances his mighty strength began to tire and to weaken. Heavy blows of fate were needed for the spirit to awaken to his full strength. Thus came the differences with his first wife and the painful blow of the law regarding the animals Srkd. Brmt's spirit regained his strength. Then, however, after the major victories in the colony, hours of bright happiness set in again, and he delayed the accomplishment of his main task – the task of destroying the animals.

The attack of these animals followed, and his wife's dreadful death. The sight of how his wife was torn to pieces and slowly devoured, by tearing off piece after piece of flesh, was so horrifying that Brmt forgot the entire world. He devoted himself to the plan for revenge and of freeing people [from these beasts]. This plan required all his mental and physical strength. With the state of technology at that time on the planet, it was extremely difficult and even impossible. Drnk came to his aid with his technical knowledge, and after long, extremely long, and very difficult hours came the victory not only over the power of matter but even over the spiritual strength.

Hardly had this task been accomplished, though, when, without giving Brmt even a minute of rest, Grns brought before him his second great task – the task of love. It seemed like nothing will be able to overcome Brmt's fatigue. It was the love, however, which Grns brought, and this love again brought victory over the powers of matter and of the spirit. For this victory, too, he had to pay by giving up love – friendship – in the name of the law and of love. The last stage of his task began – the war of destroying the people-eaters, and the enactment of the law of love and other essential laws – which wasn't easy either. As gratitude for everything that he had experienced and accomplished, however, came the love of the Supermind's daughter.

Hours passed, many hours, one could make up decades on Earth from them. Brmt's task had been completed. Other Almighty's tasks awaited him, but the bright happiness of life, and particularly his wife's love, bound Brmt to Vitato. He was incapable of parting from this earthly love – or rather, that of Vitato – it was so very beautiful and strong. Then fate intervened again. His wife departed from Vitato, taking along with her, love, the feelings of friendship, and the sense of the work. Brmt followed her up the stairs of the dead, while carrying along with him, as The Almighty's biggest reward, another inexpressibly beautiful and noble love.

I can return to Drnk now. His task was to help Brmt wage the war against the animals, to replace Brmt, and to complete his work in all the details. There were very many of these details, and achieving a complete happiness, a lasting and undisturbed happiness, depended on them.

The big victories, the cheers of the people, the achievement of everything that was achievable and desirable, and the idolization of the wives – all that influenced Drnk negatively. His matter began to gain victory over his spirit. He knew no longer the bounds for his desires, because he succeeded easily in everything, too easily, without a struggle and effort. He began to feel that it was not Brmt who had brought happiness to the people, but rather he. In a conversation with the empress he expressed his thoughts to her, and added that he envied the ruler on only one account, that is – as her husband. [He added] that he was certain, however, that he will be able to conquer her love as well, just as readily as everything else.

The empress looked at him in surprise, then laughed out loud and said, "Perhaps you comprehend everything, but only not love; perhaps you can conquer everyone, but only not me!"

She turned around and flew away – proud, unapproachable, and contemptuous.

Her pride and contempt were the causes of his insane action. The blow of fate came which returned [his senses] to him. It gave him the opportunity to comprehend not only the joys of victory and the sunshine of happiness, but also the bitterness of defeat and the might of responsibility. He became a great ruler. He enacted laws that brought peace and happiness to the hearts of the people. His subjects turned to him in all their sorrows and joys, and he understood everyone and helped everyone. His long period of rule was entered in the history of the nation of the minds under the name – the era of peace and happiness.

When he ascended the stair of the dead, three friends awaited him there. All four of them, happy and in friendly conversations, proceeded to the Deoss Temple, where the all-merciful and understanding God awaited them with a smile.

I conclude.   [[1945]]

Shota   09/04/44 2013

Shota is speaking. Ilgya taught us quite a lesson. I can understand that! We gladly bow our wise heads in front of her. Ilgya, if only she wants to, is capable of solving the most complicated peoblems and of giving clear and exhaustive answers. The three of us were so tangled up in the events of Vitato that we no longer knew how to extricate ourselves from them. The more we told you, the more there was to tell. The more we explained, the more new questions arose. One event was bound with another, one question that had been answered brought up three new ones. It seemed as if there will be no end.

Particularly the wise Ali in the end complicated the situation so much that he "beat a hasty retreat," without even relating just how unfortunately things had gone for him personally on this planet. It was probably not for naught that he had acquired there the honorable title of Crazymind. For once, though, this unfortunate subject has been concluded and all of us can, while clasping hands in friendship, retire.

Let us conclude our conversations with that as well.   [[2020]]

Ali   09/07/44 1749

Ali is speaking. I had to come to you subsequent to the words of Shota. Somehow we cannot manage to rid ourselves of this unfortunate planet –Vitato. I did not "beat a hasty retreat" because I did not want to relate my sometimes unfortunate and even silly situations in which I was involved from time to time, but rather because this tale of mine would sound as an unpleasant dissonance in the great tragedy of that world. Perhaps it was difficult for you to grasp immediately the extent of this tragedy, therefore let us return to Vitato once more.

Many hours, hundred of hours, if not even thousands, had already passed since the departure of our great spirits from it. The great ruler, Supermind Drnk, ruled the nation of the minds. I visited him quite often as my best friend. One hour, after the session of the senate had ended, Drnk stayed behind as usual in the hall of the senate all by himself. This hall had now become his favorite place [of contemplation]. In it, next to the throne of the ruler, stood the statues of those who had departed.

These statues had been erected on the ruler's order. The best sculptors of all the people had devoted endless hours to shaping these statues, and still they had been constantly formed anew, for the ruler did not feel satisfied. Then the ruler himself started to help the sculptors and imbued life into these lifeless statues. Shaping the statue of empress Lrms required a particularly lengthy effort. The most perfect moldings did not satisfy the ruler.

"That's not her, that's not her!" the ruler whispered in despair.

It seemed that it will not be possible to accomplish the work. Then one hour, when a young artist was helping the ruler, the ruler exclaimed frantically, "Hold it! Hold it, that's her, that is she like she was during the last moment of her life!"

Exhausted, the ruler sank to the ground.

These statues were such wonderful works of art that until then, nor after that, anything equal to them had been created in the universe – yes, in the entire universe, not just on Vitato. The people looked at these statues as if spellbound, and did not notice that hours passed.

As I said before, Drnk looked as usual into the face of Lrms. His thoughts and his spirit were far from Vitato. I put my fingers on his shoulder, and said, "Do not grieve, dear friend, because you have made your departed friends immortal for the second time."

"I am not grieving, I am drawing strength," the ruler replied softly. "Tell me Trpt, what does the smile of Lrms express to you?"

"Smile? I do not see a smile on her lips. I only hear inaudible, gentle music flowing from them, which seems to lull all doubts and sorrows. That is good for you, ruler, just as it is good that the people believe that these great geniuses departed at the call of Mortifero. They believe, ruler, but I do not believe."

Drnk raised his sad eyes at me. "You do not believe, but why?"

"Because," I replied, "I knew them too well, and I also knew Highmind Drnk too well."

The ruler's head sunk to his chest, and then he said, "You are right. Help me, my dear friend, understand me and give me advice, if you can. I have already deprived once these friends of mine of their lives, lives inspired by fame. Now, after their death, I deprive them for the second time of their biggest fame, of their largest nobility, because I am not allowed to tell the people how very great and noble they were in reality, were during the last moments of their lives. If I were to do that, I could not remain as the ruler, but I have to remain as the ruler, for I have sworn. Are you able to understand my torment and can you help me?"

"Tell me about it, for how can I help you without knowing?"

"You are right! I will tell you, but only to you alone."

He turned once again to the wonderful statues, the divine works of art.

On the left of the ruler's throne, as the first one, stood the statue of Supermind Mrmn. It appeared to have been made from some extremely heavy material. Mighty, hard, and heavy stood this ruler. It seemed as though the ground itself just barely supported his weight. The power of an inflexible will, firm and merciless, flowed from him. It seemed as if the law itself – harsh, unalterable, and merciless – stood before you. His eyes, however, were wonderful; a silent, all-knowing, fatherly love and deep sorrow radiated from them. On looking into his eyes, all those whom fate had visited harshly wanted to bow before him so that the fatherly hand could caress the head that was bowed in sorrow. On looking at his heavy hand, though, cold shivers engulfed the soul, for no love in the entire world was capable of lifting this heavy hand for a caress.

Next to him stood the statue of Grns. It seemed to have been formed so light as to barely touch the ground. Her face expressed infinite love, but the lips were overshadowed by deep, inexpressibly deep pain. Those in love for the first time, having been enchanted by love, observed the expression of this pain in incomprehension, and overcome by doubts and misconception departed from this statue of love. Those, however, who had already loved, came to her in order to express their sorrows and suffering to these lips, shaped of pain. Truly, just as insignificant as their love seemed to those who were in love for the first time, as compared to that love which the face of Grns expressed, equally as insignificant seemed their sufferings of love to others, as compared to her painful smile.

On the right [and furthest] from the throne stood the high ruler Brmt. A majesty that was almost unbearable for the individual flowed from the statue of this ruler. The high forehead appeared to be overcome by infinite peace, some sort of an incomprehensible, heavenly peace. Two tiny wrinkles, however, caused one to surmise what an ungraspable and unstoppable hurricane of thoughts raged behind this forehead. It appeared at first that his eyes looked past you, past the crowd, past the entire nation, past the entire planet into the distant infinity; as though seeing neither you with your sorrows, nor the people, nor the planet; but seeing only infinity, the high infinity, and the distant and unreachable God. Then, however, after you had looked at these eyes for a prolonged period of time, you suddenly felt that they looked at you sharply, with unbearable sharpness, looked through you, into your heart, and into your thoughts. Sinners averted their gaze and left the hall overcome by dread, but the eyes of the ruler followed them now for their entire life and along all of their paths. Those, though, who had erred but sought a way out of their delusions, found it in his gaze. Those who were noble and righteous felt in this gaze of the eyes a recognition of their work, and the growth of new strength. Their wings spread mightily and easily, and the world seemed achievable and graspable with these wings.

On the left of the ruler and behind the throne stood the statue of empress Lrms. It was enclosed in lines of such ideally beautiful harmony that one could not take his eyes from it; and it seemed as if the song itself, the music of the beauty itself, were enclosed for a moment in realistic lines. Her face was so ideally beautiful that it was difficult afterwards to find something more beautiful in the world. Her facial expression expressed the high pride of a spirit and divine nobility. It seemed as though inexpressible happiness radiated from it, which was strangely overcast by the shadow of suffering. Her lips were the most unusual, though. To some it seemed that they conveyed a barely perceptible, but infinite, disdain. To others again it seemed that they expressed a light, barely perceptible compassion, and even pity. Above all that flowed a tranquility that could not be shattered by anything.

The ruler, without averting his eyes from the face of Lrms, began to tell me in such a low voice that I sensed more than heard his words. Thus I got to hear this great tragedy, and his final words still resound in my ears today.

"...and then I noticed that the spears of the rays of the two suns crossed on the face of the empress, and I understood that nothing in this world can any longer save the empress. I understood the frightful consequences of my mad deed; and a piercing scream of fear, horror, and pain escaped from my chest.

"She, however, she stood there silent, tranquil, cold, and contemptuous. Just imagine, my dear friend, it was I, her persecutor and murderer, who was screaming, overcome by pain, fear, and horror. She, though, the victim and the one being persecuted, stood there silent, tranquil, and cold; and not even the tiniest expression on her face indicated either pain or fear. Then happened something unimaginable and unbearable for human strength. In despair, overcome by fear and pain, I looked into the face of the empress and – oh, almighty Mortifero – her contemptuous smile began to fade from her lips, and in its stead, light as a dream and ungraspable as light, a smile of compassion appeared on her lips.

"I felt that the ground began to sway beneath my feet, and I grasped with extreme strength the handrail of the stairs. Everything began to whirl and I closed my eyes. When I opened them again the empress was no more. The silence of the grave reigned in the empty hall, and then I suddenly heard drops of water falling. In this silence of the grave, the noise of a tiny drop dropping seemed to be unbearably loud. I glanced around in wonder. How could water drip in this hall that had no water in it? My eyes noticed my hand then, with which I had grasped the railing. Blood was dripping from my fingers, and the drops of blood fell on the high stairs. I walked down.

"You already know the rest."

The ruler grew silent for a moment, and then said, "You understand now why it was so difficult for me to sculpt Lrms's facial expression like I had seen it at the last moment, and which I cannot and will never be able to forget. Do you understand? At first these lips held only a scornful smile for me. Then, when many hundreds of hours had passed and many major deeds had been accomplished, this smile began to fade and later on a smile of compassion appeared in its place. Until the moment when it disappears, I will feel secure in my deeds of the ruler. Yet what can I do with this grave sin of remaining silent?"

"Nothing, my friend! It has to die along with you and me. The nation of the minds must not hear it and will never hear it. Perhaps another nation on some other planet will hear it!"

I conclude.   [[1952]]

Shota   09/09/44 1615

Shota is speaking. My good friend gave you a wonderful epilogue to the people's tragedy on the planet Vitato. Let us clarify some points of a questionable nature.

To begin with, did these wonderfully made statues depict the high people correctly? It seems completely impossible to imagine the high level and manner of art with whose help these statues had been shaped – statues whose faces, eyes, and lips spoke to the onlookers, and [conveyed a different message] at that. Yes, the art of people, of the people on Earth, is currently incapable of creating anything even vaguely similar. The artists of the nation of the minds on Vitato surpass many-fold their colleagues on Earth. The material, too, of which these statues have been made, is not known on Earth.

Did these statues depict Brmt, Grns, Lrms, and the others as they had been in reality? Yes, as they had been like, but not as they had looked like! In the latter case they would have been simply photos, and as such artistically worthless. These statues depicted not only the outer appearance of these people, but also the characteristics and greatness of their spirits. Only geniuses are capable of accomplishing the latter. They are not unknown to humanity on Earth either – Praxiteles, Leonardo da Vinci, Rembrandt, and others.

Perhaps you will also be surprised that the lifeless statues were capable of exerting such an influence on the onlookers, and even so differently at that. Yes, that was the hand of a genius which was capable of that. You know on Earth as well what a deep, even stunning, impression the works of the great geniuses leave on the people's soul. Isn't the entire humanity enchanted by the smile of Mona Lisa? Don't Michelangelo's statues of God stun the hearts? Don't Goya's nightmares imbue horrors? Don't Raphael's Madonnas purify the hearts? There are paintings that uplift the spirit, and there are paintings that drag him into the mud. You know just what kind of an impression statues or painting leave, from the fact that expectant mothers can give birth to children – beautiful or ugly – due to the deep-felt influence of paintings.

The nation of the minds on Vitato perceived spiritual life more keenly, and the people understood each other more readily even without the help of words. Their language was more like music than a language of words. You could have already realized that from the very many intonations of their sounds.

The noble empress Lrms undoubtedly left an unforgettable impression on you. Yes, her spirit is one of The Almighty's nobler spirits. She and Ilgya are spirits whose presence is welcomed by every spirit and by every creature with a soul. Lrms's spirit is called Iligaya, and should this spirit visit a planet, its people remember her eternally in their legends. For a brief moment once, she visited the planet Earth as well, but everyone remembers this moment. She came to you and you gave her the name – Joan [[of Arc]], but later on you called her the Maid of Orleans. That is why Ilgya and Alexander, as well as John, love the French people so much.

You are also tormented by the thought about what Vitato's universal animal looked like. It looked more like a human on Earth, than did a mind. That will have to suffice for you.

Now, you have probably noticed that human equivalents on other planets have wings. Yes, they have wings on almost all planets, except for Earth. That is why man quite often flies in his dreams. Therefore, he also gave himself wings in the form of airplanes, while proving with that, that he is capable of obtaining on his own what God had forgotten to give him.

I conclude. Ilgya will speak. [[1730]]

Ilgya 09/09/44 1730

Ilgya. What is your Ilgya supposed to tell you?

_ ★ ★ ★ _

You, Alexander, remember now the indescribably wonderful statues of yourself and your friends. Even Ali's vast abilities proved incapable [of describing them]. We, the spirits, quite often visit the planet Vitato in order to enjoy the enchantment of the wonderful art. You, too, returned there rather often. At times even all four of you gathered around Drnk. His eyes then shone like the stars of Mortifero, and his words flowed like a fiery river. All the people then followed the words of their ruler with bated breath. You do remember these statues, yes, but not completely. Close your eyes, I will help you!

[[Alexander says, "But I saw only three!"]]

Yes, you did not see the fourth one. Later on you will understand why.

Your thoughts are split. The spirits and The Almighty's new tasks summon you. The people on the planet Nalinota await you – you and me. We are incapable, though, of leaving these people of Earth. We are incapable of leaving them at the moment of their dreadful sickness – a sickness in which their spirit threatens to break, but matter will break and the spirit will be reborn. The Almighty knows the reasons for our hesitation, and does not hinder our suffering, and our attempts to help this unfortunate man.

You came here to observe the course of humanity. You asked The Almighty to allow you to forget your high roads and great abilities. You asked Him to permit you to be only a human, a common, ordinary, everyday human, for the people will be able to be like they are only with an individual like that. They will have no need of pretending to be better, for you will be unable to reward them, nor to be worse, for you will be unable to punish them. In order, however, to comprehend this ordinary individual in his entirety you, yourself, wanted to be like that as well, so that you would think with his mind and would feel with his emotions, and would know what he knows, how much he knows, and how he understands the world and its Ruler. Your wish was granted, but only in the beginning. Later on The Almighty took back His promise, and you were unable to and were not allowed to refuse The Almighty's task.

Let us travel somewhat along the paths of your life and your thoughts.

The eyes of God and Satan followed you. Satan hastened to exploit your every mistake. He strove to get at the human spiritual essence through you. Twelve times He called on Mortifero to recall you from Earth, and twelve times the voice of The Almighty held back Mortifero's hand.

You were still tiny as a rabbit, when this hand already reached out for you the first time. You fell into a pond. The children fled in fright. Your mother had wrapped you in her thick woolen shawl. You landed on your back and floated. A boy ran to your father and summoned him. You were already in the middle of the pond. Your father pulled you to the shore with a long pole, just as the shawl had already become waterlogged and you had started to sink. That was a miracle. The hand of God guarded you. No one, though, knew that this was a miracle, not even your father. Everyone was only surprised that you fell so luckily on your back, that the shawl absorbed the cold autumn water so slowly, and that your father still managed to run over from the distant forest.

The second time, as a boy, you wound up in the cogs of the wheels of a threshing machine. The edge of your coat had already been caught. The horses continued their course calmly; they were being driven by a hired hand. He was not looking at you. What could have saved you, because the strength of several horses was pulling you to death? At this moment one of the hired hands stepped out of the barn. He instantly grasped the life-threatening situation. In one leap he was next to the head of the closest horse, and stopped it with such strength, with such a strength of steel sounded his, "Whoa-halt!" that all the horses, as if by a magic wand, [froze in] place. You were pulled out. The skin had been scraped on your left leg, but nothing more. You had been pulled from the very teeth of death.

Still ten more times the hand of Death grasped for you, but to no avail. Even the doors of the prison had to open, the horns of the bull had to be lowered, and rifles had to retreat. You wanted to be an ordinary person; you managed to be one in the happiness of life, but in misfortune you outlived dozens of ordinary people. Why didn't Satan manage to help you leave this Earth as an ordinary individual? Because The Almighty had thought His own thought, which only He alone knew.

You turned out to be impossible as an ordinary human only because matter was incapable of overcoming your spirit, and your spirit of a poet overcame all the powers of Earth and of will. In order to neutralize this unforeseen force you wrote poetry, but you wrote poetry just for yourself. You began thus a struggle even with your own spirit. The course of your life was difficult and unusual. While carrying out your goal, fate attempted to deny you even an education, but you attained it on your own, by studying while walking next to a hay wagon and overcoming the power of sleep at night. Many of those who were accompanied on their pathway by teachers and professors turned out to comprehend and appreciate life far less than you did.

You strove to understand everything with your human mind. You condemned not only man, but God as well. You could not reconcile yourself with the fact that God had created such evil people, that He does not help these people, and that He does not even listen to them. You tried to comprehend man and accomplished that, and you devoted many bitter words to this ruler of Earth. You were surprised by his spiritual worthlessness, the worthlessness of his days and deeds, and by him killing the valuable time in drinking, card games, gossip, and in sleep. You did not understand the word "boredom," with which humanity is afflicted. While being alone you never felt alone, for the world of your thoughts surrounded you.

You saw that humanity had strayed despite the wonderful teachings of Christ. You called out to God, but God remained silent. You went into His churches. You liked the trembling light of the candles in front of the dark faces of the saints. You liked the heads that were bowed in respect; you liked the sound of the bells climbing to Heaven. You liked the sacred songs. Yet you merely liked that, because there was no soul in the words of the clergy, and there was no answer to the prayer of those who were praying. The words "slave" and "Lord" sounded degrading and unworthy of God. You came to the church to seek God and man, but found therein only a Lord and slaves. Your spirit rebelled against this desecration of The Almighty; you did not want to be a slave, not even The Almighty's slave. Then you saw that God, Himself, did not protect these houses of God either, that they were struck by lightning, collapsed in earthquakes and from the rounds of cannons. You understood that God could not be sought in churches.

You turned to science. Together with Flammarion you sought God and the spirits among the stars, but neither did you find Him there. You lost faith in God and in Satan. You even began to doubt immortality. You tried to follow the journey of Flammarion's spirit through immortality, but found several scientific errors, and you understood that this journey, too, was merely the fantasy of a scientist, and of a poor scientist at that. You succumbed to the somber genius of Gardia, Thomas Gardia. Together with him you wanted to reject immortality and your soul, but could not, for something within you screamed that you cannot die, that you cannot rot together with your body. That would have been absurd, that would have been a crime against intellect, against the meaning of the existence of the universe. You delved into another genius, that of the Lion – I understand your grin – the genius of Leo Tolstoy. He also tried to free himself from God and from immortality with the help of his mind, but he knew how to teach humanity only by calling on God for help. Thus, by turning from a spirit into a human, you were nevertheless unable to remain a human, and in the darkness you climbed up along the stairway of the spirit – back to The Almighty.

The moment came, the great moment, when The Almighty said, "Enough! You, along with all of humanity, have sought the road in darkness. I will illuminate it for all of you, so that you could see where it goes, and could see Me – the ruler of the universe. I remove the heavy crown of the lord – emperor – from My head. I remove the shackles of slaves from your hands; be people, be rulers of yourselves and of the Earth, be helpers to Me, to Me – your Father, but not lord!"

Thus we have come to this day.

Perhaps you will reproach me for this friendly conversation, because it will reach the ears of others as well. Do not reproach me, though. Perhaps I err, but it seems to me that The Almighty wanted it like this.

I conclude.   [[2018]]

Montaviro   09/09/44 2050

Montaviro is speaking. - ★ ★ ★ -

You do not know how complicated and difficult is the task of talking with you, people. You will ask – is it any more difficult than for an individual to write down his thoughts on a piece of paper?

What is needed for this writing to be feasible? You will claim – first a pen, a good pen, then ink, and paper as well. Would that suffice? No, a hand is needed, one to guide and hold the pen. Would that, however, be everything now? No, a person is needed who would direct this hand. Would it suffice with any person, though?

Have an illiterate sit down [at a desk]; what good would there be in a sharp pen, white paper, black ink, a firm hand, and a robust individual? Everything will be on the desk and, later on, underneath the desk. Have a fool sit down in the place of the illiterate. The task will proceed, but it would have been better if it had not proceeded. Let us get rid of this fool and have an ordinary human sit down in his place. This person will first sweat thoroughly, but then he will write down something after all. Yes, he will write down something, but will this be worth reading? Let us have a bureaucrat sit down; yes, the page will be full of paragraphs, but whom will you give these paragraphs to read? Certainly not to the entire humanity! Similarly with a mathematician, a chemist, and so on. They will write, and what they will have written will be worthy as well, but it will be of a narrow, specialized value.

Let us now have Cervantes sit down in the place of these people. He will write in the same manner as all the others wrote, but the entire humanity will read what he will have written, [and will read it] not only today and tomorrow but for as long as this humanity itself will exist. Every written word sounds like a revelation, the revelation of beauty and of the mind. The immortal genius flows from every word, such a beauty flows that the human mind feels enchanted and raised above the Earth, with the wings of the spirit.

That is how it is with an individual's writing, but how is it with the spirit's ability to express himself?

We are really not talking about a spirit here. A spirit can converse with a human only through the so-called intuition. Only whenever The Almighty wants to proclaim His will to people, does He choose different means for realizing this design. That, however, occurs while preserving the human being's free will and taking into account the influence of matter.

What is a human? God will say – the spirit less the body. Satan will say – the spirit plus the body. Under no circumstances, however, is a human a pure spirit or pure body – matter. The spirit generally loses something from his characteristics, and matter gains. As to which gains more or loses more, that depends on their [relative] strengths. The spirit, on combining with beings of various forms, acquires different characteristics each time, just as do the elements. Oxygen, on combining with hydrogen, forms water; but by mixing with nitrogen, and some other elements, it produces air. After all, air and water are not the same thing, even though they both contain oxygen.

Therefore, man and his soul, or spirit, are not the same thing, they are not identical. You will now be able to understand many things.

In order for a spirit to be able to talk with a human in the manner in which we are talking at the moment, it does not suffice with just a table, paper, saucer, hand, and a human, for the spirit himself is incapable of moving the saucer. Just as an astronomer cannot pass on his mathematical formulas through a woodcutter, similarly the spirit, too, cannot express his thoughts through a person within whom there is a spirit that is lower than his. The spirit himself does not talk, he has to establish a complete contact of thoughts and understanding with the individual who is talking, to whom it may perhaps even seem that he is talking himself. Only occasionally, when his thought gets ahead of the spirit's thought, does he suddenly notice that the course of the thoughts and words begins to get confused, and becomes confused. It does not, however, suffice with just the greatness and kinship of the spirits, for, as I already said, the spirit within a human is no longer the same spirit as he used to be. Here the spirit has to overcome the influence of matter as well, which is almost insurmountable. Therefore, conversing with the spirits in this manner is, in fact, almost impossible and only particularly favorable circumstances, which can come about only once in millions of years, can provide the opportunity for such conversations.

That which is currently going on in the entire world – the so-called spiritualism – is primarily more like self-deception, or else the art of tricks. Those tiny spirits who do talk with people are actually no real spirits at all. Therefore these conversations have not given humanity anything that is worthwhile, anything that is divine. They generally remind one of the nightmares of sick people, in which sensible words alternate with foolish ones, and even gibberish. Perhaps humanity will be [overcome] by a mania for summoning the spirits, and many people will imagine that they, too, are capable of conversing with the spirits and of proclaiming their will and thoughts. To no avail, though! Omega has already said that The Almighty will no longer talk with humanity in this or even in any other manner.

I will conclude for today. I will tell you a story tomorrow, which I again found in Alpha's archives. [[2200]]

Ali   09/10/44 1815

Ali is speaking. My high ruler, the sultan, once received a complaint about a highly placed bureaucrat. While trying to absolve himself, the bureaucrat said to the sultan, "Oh, high ruler, the one who is complaining has made an elephant out of a mosquito."

"That is very bad," the sultan said, "to make an elephant out of a tiny mosquito; but it is even worse and more risky, my son, to make a mosquito out of an elephant, which is what you have done."

As usual, the sultan's justice was swift and to the point.

I conclude. Montaviro will speak. [[1820]]

Montaviro 09/10/44 1820

Montaviro, your somber spirit, is talking with you. I have promised to tell you something today. If you are not too tired from the trifles of your life, I kindly ask you to give me a few minutes of your valuable time. I begin.

I will take you to the sandy homeland of Ali, which is so nicely adorned by the humps of camels. Let us see whether something interesting has ever occurred there. Let us dig around in the sand, perhaps we will uncover some treasures that have been hidden by robbers. That does not quite happen, but we nevertheless do uncover an old book. Let us blow off the centuries old dust, put on Alpha's large eyeglasses, and try to read.

Hey, who knows the Turkish language? No one! Let us ask old Ali to translate these writings. Yes, there sure is something there – how much does a good horse and a lazy wife cost, how many times a day one has to pray to Allah, and so on. Interesting things, but only for Ali himself. Aha, here is something for us as well! Let us sit down in the shade of the camels and listen to an ancient tale.

There once lived a harsh and unjust ruler. The people were unhappy. When the ruler died, his son, on seeing the people's misery and unhappiness, turned to Allah, "Oh, Allah, be merciful to me, Your humble servant. Help me to rule. Tell me how to help the people in their misfortunes and sorrow, and tell me how to make them happy. Be a good Father to me, for my father was not. I want to rule justly, and don't want any unhappy people in my realm, but only happy ones."

Allah listened to the prayer of the new ruler, and He, Himself, came down to him. He said, "Let us go, My son, show Me your unhappy ones. Let's see what is the cause of their misfortunes, and let's try to avert it."

They went – the new ruler and the old, wise Allah. They stopped at a door, for they heard scolding and crying.

"What is going on here?" the ruler asked.

"Oh, ruler, nothing worthy of the attention of your ear! My wife kneaded the last crock of flour and put it in the oven. The bread was burned due to her carelessness, and now we have nothing to eat."

Allah smiled and waved His hand. A chest that was standing in the corner of the room filled itself to the brim with white flour.

"We thank you, Lord," both of them, the husband and the wife, said happily.

The quarrel was over, happiness reigned in the home.

They went on. A donkey stood by a well and swatted the obtrusive flies with its tail. Two brothers, while wiping the sweat, quarreled next to it.

"What are you quarreling about?"

"We have to get to the nearest village. We have only one donkey and we have been arguing since the early morning about who has the primary right of riding on the donkey. Neither of us wants to walk along this sandy road on foot."

Allah smiled again, and instead of one donkey – six of them stood there. The brothers thanked the Lord and then began to look over the donkeys.

"This is the best one," the younger brother said, "you sit on it."

"No, brother, you ride on it, I will ride the worst one!"

For a long time the brothers offered each other the best donkey, and then finally said, "Why should we torment these beautiful animals needlessly? It is not far to go, let us rather walk on foot!"

The brothers, having thrown some hay to the donkeys, and in friendly conversations, set out on their way on foot.

"It is so easy to make people happy!" said the ruler.

"Don't be rash, My son, and understand man better!"

They went on. A man sat sadly on a rock next to a house.

"What's the matter with you?" the ruler asked.

"I have only one wife, and an ugly one at that. How can I be happy while seeing that others have many wives, and in addition to that – each one prettier than the other?"

"Here's some money for you, buy yourself ten beautiful wives!" said Allah.

The man, overwhelmed by feelings of gratitude, fell to the dust. Then he jumped to his feet, happy as a child, threw the old wife out of the house, and ran off to buy the new, beautiful wives.

(Five minutes.) [[1904]]

To continue. A farmer hoed sadly his field of corn.

"What's bothering you?"

"What's bothering me? I have too little land, can't [grow enough] food."

Allah added on a sizable piece of land to his tiny plot of land. The farmer became very happy.

"I comprehend the causes of misfortune now and know how to avert them. I thank You, oh Allah!"

"Have you really understood everything correctly, My son? Will you know how to make your people happy?"

"Yes," the ruler replied.

Then they came to a desert. Three people had dug up a chest full of gold, and were fighting over it.

"Why are you fighting?" asked the ruler.

"Because there is too little gold for all three of us," they replied.

Allah then waved His hand, and all the sand in the desert turned into gold.

"Take as much of it as each of you wants!"

The people, though, did not even reach down for the gold sand, and walked away.

"Why aren't you taking this gold that you crave so much?" the ruler asked.

"What are we going to do with it? There is so much of it that it will suffice for all people, and it will become more worthless than the sand. Even the palm tree is incapable of sinking its roots into this hard metal, and it is difficult to pull your feet out of it."

"All right then," Allah said to the ruler, "if you feel that you have understood everything correctly and hope that you will be able to make everyone happy, I might as well leave you now."

He ascended to Heaven.

Some time passed, and Allah heard the voice of the new ruler once more. "Oh, Allah, what should I do? The people don't want to become happy!"

"How come?" Allah asked.

"I made the poor rich. I made into lords the servants who complained about their bitter fate and wanted to become lords. Now, however, there isn't a single servant in the entire realm, and there isn't anyone who will serve the lords and who will work for the lords. Husbands complained that their wives were ugly. I allowed them to choose the most beautiful ones, but now they want even more beautiful ones. I gave bread to those who were suffering from hunger, but now they don't want bread but ask for pies and roasts. What can I do, oh Allah, because my people, regardless of all the good that I have done, do not want to feel happy?"

"Have you really acted correctly, My son?"

"I acted like You acted, oh Allah!"

"Had you understood Me correctly, though?"

"I think so," the ruler replied.

"Well, then continue," said Allah.

Still some more time passed, and the new ruler's cry full of despair reached Heaven. "Oh, Almighty, help me!"

"What has happened now, My son?"

"All my subjects want to become grand viziers now. What am I to do? What can I do with that many grand viziers and without any subjects, for no one wants to be lesser than the other one, and help or serve the other?"

"Grant them their wishes," Allah said calmly.

"What are You saying – grant them? After all, though, my entire realm will perish then! Everyone will only rule and no one will obey. Everyone will only live it up and no one will work; calamity and starvation will set in. Disorder will set in and all the people will curse my name. They already call me a poor successor of my great and good father!"

"Do as I tell you, and tell your new grand viziers that since all of them are rulers now, they have to divide the entire realm and all of its properties fairly among themselves."

The ruler obeyed and – oh wonder! In a few days Allah heard the grateful prayer of the ruler and of all the people.

"How are things in your realm now?"

"Everything is fine," replied the ruler. "Everything is as it was under my father, and everyone feels happy now."

"How did that happen, though?" Allah asked.

"It happened according to Your advice. When I made all my subjects grand viziers and had them divide everything fairly, everyone obviously took for himself what had formerly belonged to him. Thus everyone re-turned to their old place, because what else was there for them to do. I understand You now, oh high and wise Allah! Happiness cannot be received like a gift. Happiness cannot be given out evenly to everyone, for then everyone will become unhappy. Happiness does not exist at all. There is only striving for happiness. Once achieved, happiness, just as water that one has drunk, is no longer necessary, because there is no longer any desire for them. Only justice has value on Earth, and this justice consists of very simple words, 'Reward the capable and the hard working ones justly, and punish the lazy ones!'"

"You have understood Me correctly, My son. Your reign will be a long and a happy one – for yourself as well as for your people."

We close the dusty pages of the old book, thank Ali, make the camels get up, and leave the sweltering desert. My tale has been concluded, and I thank you for the kind attention and great patience.   [[2003]]

Iligaya   09/11/44 1814

Iligaya is with you. While crossing the space of the universe, I came to you for a moment, my good and noble friends from the unforgettable planet Vitato. I see two Superminds, I ask to have the third one summoned as well. I also see my dear empress of love – Grns. I also see my old friend Livanito, whom you call Alexo. I ruled with Livanito on the planet Citavino. He had to sacrifice his life for his people and their empress there as well. As always, he did that without any hesitation and regret. Let my kiss, the kiss of gratitude, touch his high forehead.

I greet with deep love and inexpressible happiness my former great ruler and father, Mrmn.

With love and adoration, my lips touch the lips of my ruler and unforgettably dear and noble husband.

I greet my noble friend with a sincere and bright kiss, and tell her, "Do not grieve! Remember what close and great spirits your friends are. They are Henry's friends as well, and my prayer about him flies to The Almighty."

I do not have the time to stay with you long. Legions of spirits await me as their commander for the important task. Therefore I will linger with you only for a few minutes, in order to tell Emily a divine tale. My words begin to sound. String them on a silk thread of memories and hang them on your chests, so that you would never forget them.

In ancient times there lived a lovely and beautiful maiden by the name of Maya, and a noble and handsome young man by the name of Julius. They met each other, as the rays of the sun and the moon meet in the morning, and a wonderful song of love was heard in their hearts. They gave each other their hands, their lips, and their hearts. They joined their two pathways of life and traveled a single, extremely happy path. As the petals of a blossom reach out in great yearning for the kiss of the sun, thus the lips of Maya reached out for the lips of Julius. Their bodies trembled in the rustle of inexpressible pleasure and happiness. Days floated above them like tiny white clouds, but in their love they had forgotten the Earth, the sky, and the people. Only one world burned in their eyes – the face of the beloved. It seemed that this love had neither bounds nor an end.

They were walking along the seashore one evening. The waves murmured dreamily, the leaves of the laurels shone like metal in the rays of the evening sun, and the fragrance of the roses flowed over the ground like the breath of spring. They walked along hand in hand, eyes [looking into] eyes. Some ladies came toward them, and among the ladies was a majestically noble and commandingly beautiful lady. While passing by, the eyes of Maya, Julius, and the lady met for a brief moment and parted; they met for a brief, fleeting moment.

They came home. It seemed as if nothing had happened, except Julius seemed to be strangely dreamy and distracted.

"What's the matter with you, my dear?"

"Nothing, my love."

"Do you feel sick?"

"No. Yet perhaps, after all."

"I suspect that the sea breeze was too cold this evening."

Julius became sick. In four days the cold soil covered him, and the cypresses bowed their sad heads above him.

Maya's grief was indescribable, her sorrow unbearable. All these three days she had lain at the feet of the statue of God, with tears in her eyes and faith in her heart. In her despair, she got up now and said, "You are merciless, inexpressibly merciless, merciful God!"

Oh wonder! God's lips moved and soft words flew from them. "I am merciful!"

"You deprived me of my love, coldhearted God!"

"I preserved it for you," the lips said again.

"You smashed the happiness of my life into tiny pieces, You – evil God!"

"I preserved it for you," the soft words came again.

"How can I believe Your words if Your deeds say the contrary? Why did You do everything to deprive me of everything?"

"Because I love you and I want you to be happy on this Earth."

"I am incapable of believing You, for one has to be insane in order to be able to call a murderer a savior."

"Close your eyes and look at the course of your future, as it would have been had I not recalled your beloved Julius today."

Maya closed her eyes and looked at the dark gates of the future. They opened heavily into tomorrow, and Maya saw what she would rather have never seen. She saw her Julius becoming gloomier with every day. Then she saw him with the proud lady, the wife of the duke, saw him meeting her again and again. She saw Julius's inexpressible torment of the heart and the struggle, but saw that it was in vain. She saw the day when Julius bent down at the duchess's feet and began kissing them passionately. Then she saw their lips meet in a hot and long kiss. She saw that Julius turned away from her, Maya's, lips; saw how cold and indifferent he became toward her and her caresses.

She saw the day when he pushed her from the road, the road that she had blocked to stop him, the road that led to the castle. Then she saw his hands mercilessly tearing himself free from her hands, and saw him pushing her brutally aside, like a dog, and walking off without even looking back at her – lying in the mud. Then she saw the duke entering the duchess's bedroom unexpectedly and surprising the lovers. He drew his sword. Julius grabbed his sword as well. After a short fight the duke fell mortally wounded, and the guards apprehended Julius.

She saw the dreadful day of the trial. Then she saw something so horrifying that the blood in her vessels turned into ice. She saw Julius's naked body on the torture rack in the town square. She saw how the executioner's tongs tore piece after piece of flesh from his body, and how he poured melted wax into the wounds. She heard how Julius's bones broke under the blows of the executioner and how his agonizing scream of pain sounded. She saw herself crouched against a fence, in the middle of the indifferent crowd; she heard her own inhuman scream. She saw herself at the executioner's rack; saw the executioner push her aside and the guards take her away.

Then she saw a deranged woman wandering along the roads – dirty, tattered, and with unkempt hair. She saw boys throwing rocks at her and the tavern-keeper sicking dogs at her. In this woman she recognized herself....

The heavy gates closed again, and the crushed Maya asked, "What does that mean, oh God?"

"That is what would have happened to your love and happiness, had I been merciful to your prayers and had not recalled Julius."

"Couldn't You have preserved my happiness otherwise, though?"

"Yes, but then you would have had to marry the tall knight, August."

"No, God, I don't want that. That would be against my will!"

"That would be against your will? Had I, however, forbidden Julius to love the duchess, wouldn't that have been against his will as well? You see, you don't want Me to make you happy against your will, and neither does any individual want that. Therefore I give people their free will, so that it would take them wherever they want to go, for the human is not and does not want to be even God's slave, and neither does he want to comprehend God's intervention in the ways and courses of his life. Hence I help only those whom I love, even though at times My help seems to be merciless and unjust. Not having seen your future, you even wanted to damn Me – your God and Savior. Yet what would have happened to you and Julius had I not been so merciful to both of you?"

Maya fell to her knees and pleaded, "Oh God, all merciful God, forgive me my words and my tears. Forgive me my doubts and take me into Your loving and saving hands, me, a person who is insignificant and fails to understand You."

God raised His marble hands and placed them on Maya's head. These hands, carved from marble, cold marble, were inexpressibly warm and loving, because love, God's love, was capable of warming up even them.

I close my lips and take leave from you. On parting I tell you, "Travel God's roads and rely on His guidance. Accept everything, even death, with deep gratitude and joy, because God is with you and sees what is invisible to you."

Drnk, you have heard my summons. Receive from me now the kiss that I denied you – receive the kiss of your sister.

My wings are spread, the paths of infinity bow in front of me, and legions of spirits await and welcome me. I depart from you and from the dark Earth.   [[1949]]

Ilgya   09/11/44 2017

Ilgya. The bright Iligaya is already infinitely far from us. Did you sense her divine breath? She is an infrequent visitor among us. Now that The Almighty has summoned her to His Heaven, she returned to us, because she asked The Almighty not to place His bright rays on her as the first one, but only whenever someone else will walk along with her. Her task is now in an endless and distant space of the universe, where stars twinkle that even we do not know. She wanted to meet with you, and Omega agreed and halted the legions of spirits on their way to the distant world.

The tale that she related is, unfortunately, not a tale. That really did take place on your Earth, only the names have been changed. Maya became happy once again and preserved her love, her first love, as a sacred memory. The heads of many children bent down sadly at her deathbed. Silently and overcome by grief, the people were drenched by rain underneath the castle walls, still hoping to receive the message that their queen will not die. She died eventually, and Julius's spirit awaited her.

My lips do not open today for everyday words. I, too, am being summoned to duties, summoned to your dark Earth, which unfortunately I cannot leave. My legions of spirits wait for me on the smoke-covered plains and mountains of Belgium, France, the Balkans, and the Pacific.

I bid you farewell.   [[2036]]

Shota   09/13/44 1842

Shota is speaking. - ★ ★ ★ -

A few days ago, after having been away for a long time, the spirit of the great reformer, John Huss, visited the old planet Earth once again. He visited you – the representatives of Earth and The Almighty's heralds. He was present during our conversations. Then he wanted to meet the rest of the heralds as well, and simultaneously with that also visit his final corner on Earth, the spot from which he traveled to Heaven.

We proceeded to Constance, where he had lived five hundred and thirty years ago. He wanted to see once again the place where the "holy fathers," while carrying out the all-merciful God's and Christ's teachings, "mercifully" burned him at the stake. He wanted to enter once again the old cathedral, whose satirical forms of sculpture had remained in his memory. He wanted to visit once more his old prison and house. It turns out that in his honor – a heretic who was burned [at the stake] – the street where he once lived has now been named in his, Huss's, name, and some sort of a memorial plaque has even been placed on house number 64.

_ ★ ★ ★ _

We wandered through the streets of the city for a long time. Then Huss took leave from the Earth and me, and disappeared in infinity. He was sad on seeing the nations on Earth in still worse misery and hatred than during that terrible time when the smoke of the sacred fire carried his spirit away from the "holy fathers" and the dark Earth.

(Take a five-minute break.) [[1908]]

I will now tell you a tale.

A king lived once in olden times, and he had many liegemen. Among the liegemen was a noble and wise ruler on his small corner of land. The road to the king's castle was long, and it went around crown lands.

The people said, "Ask the king to allow us a direct route across his land."

Henry, however, that is what this liegeman was called, said, "One cannot ask the king for such a trifle."

Henry's father said, "I would like to ask the king why he has, while he is so good and just himself, appointed such poor, evil, and unjust ministers to positions."

"After all, we cannot bother the ruler because of such a trifle," said Henry.

"Our oldest son," Henry's wife said, "is serving in a faraway garrison. Let us ask the king to transfer him to a closer garrison."

"One may not bother the king because of such an unimportant matter."

"My feet," said Henry's mother, "have become weak and I cannot walk. It is said that the king's hand can heal the disabled and the sick."

"After all, one cannot invite the king because of such a trifle," said Henry. "What would happen if all of us were to bother him because of such trifles? Will he have then any time left over for the affairs of the state?"

"Oh daddy," Henry's daughter said, "invite the king here for a dance. [It is said] that he dances so wonderfully. His arms lift a maiden, just like a sunbeam at the morning hour lifts a bird from a branch, and whirl her in such a twirl that the very ground and the stars begin to turn around her."

"Foolish one, should I invite the king to my castle because of your trifling wish?"

The daughter's young maid said, "Oh yes, sir, invite the king. I would like so much to see him for once in my life. It is said that his eyes are blue as the small lake high on the mountain, into which only the blue sky may look, and only the white wings of the angels may reflect. His voice sounds like a tiny silver bell at the gates of paradise. Oh, sir, invite the king for once."

"Foolish one," said Henry, "you want the king to abandon all the affairs of state just so that you could see his eyes and hear his voice."

"Oh daddy," his little daughter said as well, "do invite the king. My dear talking doll no longer talks and no one is able to repair it except for the great master, but the king has supposedly sent him off to war. I will ask the king to send back the master."

"Silly, little silly one, you want to invite the king here because of your doll. Do you think that he has nothing more important in the world than your doll?"

All those who had been pleading left sadly.

Days and months passed. The king often rode past Henry's castle while hunting, but the people of the castle saw him only enveloped in a cloud of dust. Then one day Henry's inimical neighbor began to build a dam on the river for a mill, and was ready to flood all of Henry's fields. Disaster and starvation threatened Henry and his people.

"The time has come now to turn to the king," Henry said, "because his ministers don't listen to me, and disaster threatens many people. Only the king can avert this disaster."

Henry invited the king to visit his castle and to settle the quarrel on the spot.

The [long awaited] day came, and all the people of the castle bowed, with trembling hearts, before the king. He was young, of fine build, and handsome. His clothing, sewn with jewels, glistened in the sunlight. The king settled the quarrel rapidly and fairly, and on Henry's invitation remained gladly in the castle for a few hours.

"Oh king," his chief minister said, "we will have to ride such a long way back to the castle. We would be back much sooner if this road were to go straight to the castle, across your land!"

"Order to have this direct road built across my fields, so that these fine people can reach their king more quickly."

"Forgive me, an old man," Henry's father said, "that I dare to impose on you with my question."

"Ask!" said the king.

"Oh, ruler, you are wise and just, but why have you appointed as noblemen almost solely evil and foolish people?"

"Permit me to ask you something as well," the king said. "You have many sons, but I see only two upright sons of yours in my service. Where are the others?"

"Yes," the old one replied, "one has become a monk and has given up secular life. The second has crossed the ocean in search of adventures. The third broke his neck in a horse race. The fourth one has devoted himself to the game of cards and disappeared from my eyes. The fifth one, however, oh ruler, you know that for yourself. The fifth one had succumbed to Satan – he had started drinking and living it up with ladies of the street. I banished him, because he stained my honor and even dared to slip his hand into my chest of jewels. Ruler, he sits in your prison now."

"How did that happen, how could it have happened?" asked the ruler. "You and your wife are honorable people and you also brought up all your sons to be like that. What became of them, though? Only two grew up to be like you wanted to raise them. The rest did not live up to your expectations, and even deceived them bitterly. If out of your seven sons you were able to find only two who were capable of and worthy for my service, where then am I, the king, to find a sufficient number of noblemen who are worthy for my high positions?"

The king was invited to the table. He politely offered his arm to the elderly lady, and she didn't dare to tell the king about her weakness. Oh wonder, she stood up and walked!

Dancing started after the meal, and the king asked Henry's daughter to dance. Thus her beautiful dream came true, and she whirled and flew among the stars. The arms of the king lifted her higher and higher, so that the sky twirled around her.

While resting in his chair the king noticed the little girl, who stood scared and sad next to the wall, with a doll in her arms. The king got up, walked over to her, and lifted her up.

"What's the matter with you, dear child?" he asked.

"My doll, my doll…."

"Well, what is the matter with your doll?"

"She used to talk so wonderfully, but now she has swallowed a button instead of [a piece of] cake and can no longer talk. You know for yourself how disobedient dolls are! You have sent the master off to war as well. Who can repair it now? Send back the master!"

"No, that I cannot do, not even on account of your doll, but I will give you an even more beautiful and more talkative doll."

The king handed the little girl a wonderful, new doll.

Henry's wife then turned to the king and said, "Ruler, you were so merciful that you returned to the little girl her beloved doll in an even more beautiful appearance. Could you also return to a loving mother her son, whom you have sent so far away?"

The king mercifully noted this wish of the mother as well.

Then, when the king was leaving the castle, while passing by he looked with his lake-blue eyes at the trembling and happy maid, and even handed her a piece of silver. The piece of silver fell from her trembling hands and while resonating rolled along the stone floor. The king, while laughing joyfully, said, "Here, have another one!"

Thus the maid also got to hear the king's silvery voice.

This tale tells you that one cannot turn to the king with all mundane concerns, because his time is more valuable than they are. Should the king, however, happen to visit you on important matters then, while passing by and resting, he can mercifully fulfill your unimportant desires as well.

I conclude.   [[2034]]

Chapter XVII
September 1944 – Part 2

Montaviro   09/16/44 1839

I, Montaviro, will talk with you today somewhat differently than would be becoming for a God's spirit.

Shota spoke about Huss and about the holy fathers. You know for yourselves how far the church has deviated from Christ's teachings. It even began to trade with paradise, by selling indulgences. The buyers bought them readily, but only did not consider one thing – how will their souls be able to deliver this piece of paper to Saint Peter. Even though paper is light, it nevertheless is paper but not a spiritual substance. Man has long since realized that something is not in order here with the church fathers, and has originated many stories of a satirical nature dealing with matters of the church and sins. I will remind you of one of these stories, which seems to have been forgotten.

There once lived a farmer – a farmer like other farmers, except there was a peculiar problem with him. He lacked money to toss into the church's sacrificial vessel. The head of the monastery noticed that and, when this farmer again did not offer anything to God, summoned him and told him in a fatherly manner, "My dear son, how come that you, while being a good and sympathetic individual, don't offer anything to God?"

"Holy father," the farmer replied, "I cannot understand that myself. When coming to church I always take along enough money for offering to God. There always turn out to be, though, so many beggars at the gates of the church that by the time I reach the church door I never have anything left over."

"It is well, my son, that you do not forget the poor either, but that does not mean that you can forget the most important one – God!"

The farmer promised to reform from his sin, and the abbot dismissed him mercifully.

The next Sunday, however, the same thing occurred.

"Holy father, what can I do? I ran out of money again!"

"Well, then either take along more money or else give less to the poor, but you may not leave God without anything!" and he penalized the farmer.

The following Sunday the farmer took along all his money, and headed for the church. He started feeling ever worse, because the money disappeared and disappeared.

"What are you doing?" a neighbor said. "You will end up without any money again, and then what will the holy father say!"

"I know, but how can I fail to give to this blind one and to this cripple?"

There was only one coin left in the farmer's hand when he reached the church door.

"Thank God, this time there will be some left over for dear God as well," the farmer thought happily.

Then, however, the shriveled hand of a little girl reached out in front of his eyes, and hungry eyes looked at him pitifully.

"What should I do now?" the farmer thought in despair. "If I give away this last coin, I will leave God without anything again and the holy father will expel me from the church, as he threatened to do the last time. How can I fail to help this poor little girl, though? If she were to die due to my hard-heartedness, who will then forgive me this sin?"

He gave away his last coin as well.

Everyone put money in the sacrificial vessel, except the farmer's hand did not touch it. Then the head of the monastery said, "Look, my dear sheep, our worst sinner stands here before you. His hand has completely forgotten God. If his hand, though, has forgotten God, will his heart not have forgotten Him [as well]? Despite all the reminders, holy instructions, and even punishments, this sinful soul continues to serve the evil one with horns. Therefore I expel this sinful goat from the holy church. The door of the church will be closed to this sinner until the time when he will have repented his sin and redeemed it with a generous gift to God."

The farmer departed from the church sadly, accompanied by the contemptuous looks of the congregation.

Days and weeks passed. The wagon of the head of the monastery stopped one day in front of the farmer's house door and the head, accompanied by a monk, stepped across the threshold. The farmer received him respectfully and had him sit down at the table.

"You see, son, my heart aches for you constantly, and I decided to see whether you have started to improve."

"I thank you, holy and merciful father," the farmer said, and began setting dishes on the table.

The holy father observed this work with pleasure. His face, however, grew long and the merciful smile vanished from it when he saw only bread, cheese, and milk on the table.

The farmer asked him politely to bless this meal.

"Forgive me that I do not have anything better to offer you," the farmer said, "but please enjoy what there is."

"Could you really not have come up with something better for such an infrequent visitor from God?" the head of the monastery asked.

"Unfortunately I do not have anything better at the moment."

"What happened, though, to that fat goose that I saw in your yard yesterday, while driving by?"

"Oh, holy father, it no longer exists!"

"What? When did you manage to eat it?"

"Oh, holy father, I was fattening it for you, but last evening a woman with a sick child came to my house. They had traveled a long distance. [The child] was allowed to eat only the meat of a fowl. What else could I do except slaughter my goose and feed the sick child. She had wasted away so badly that on seeing her your good heart would have melted from sorrow. Besides that, you are so fat that you will not miss the lack of a roast goose at all, and your body will feel quite satisfied after the warm bread, fresh milk, and aromatic cheese."

"Do you realize, foolish man, when talking like that, just how many roast geese, ducks, and chickens are needed to maintain this gigantic structure in proper order?" the holy father said indignantly while rubbing his belly. "I can see that you have remained the same sinner that you were, and God's blessing is out of place in this sinful house.

"Let us go, Jerome!" said the holy father as he was getting up from the table. "Let us hope that the monks will not have managed to eat yet the entire fat sheep which the tavern-keeper offered to God yesterday. May God bless his work!"

The holy father nevertheless stopped halfway to the door and, having considered something, said, "Wasn't there really anything left over from this large goose – not even a wing, not even a drumstick?"

"Not a thing," the farmer replied.

"After all, this small child could not have eaten by herself a goose like that, before which even I would have had to pause."

"I gave what was left over to the girl for along the way."

"You know," the holy father said angrily, "I have seen fools and sinners, but one like you I see for the first time in my life, and I hope that for the last as well!"

He went on, but stopped again in the doorway.

"However, wasn't the down left over?" the holy father asked.

"The down remained, why it certainly remained!" the farmer replied.

"Can't be helped, at least offer that to God. My pillow has become rather thin."

The farmer hurried happily after the down, and brought it to the holy father. Unfortunately, though, a breeze sprung up and blew the down from the farmer's hands and out the door.

Having become really angry, the holy father said, "The evil one himself blows here from a hole in hell," and slammed the door behind him.

Then came the day when Death draws an X over all the deeds of the people. The farmer, too, having been rejected by the church and thus not having confessed his sins, departed from the sinful Earth. He asked the first devil, whom he met around a corner of the house, for the directions to hell. The devil indicated these to him. A huge crowd of people stood at the large gates of hell. All his neighbors stood there, and in front of them the head of the monastery as well.

"Oh, Lord God, if even such good and holy people can end up only in hell, where then will I, a sinner, end up?" the farmer thought while trembling.

The gates opened and the souls, like autumn clouds, began to flow into the interior of hell. The farmer dragged timidly behind the crowd. The last one entered. When the farmer, too, wanted to sneak in through the gates sideways, a devil slammed them in his face.

The farmer waited for a long time, while shivering from fear, cold, and the darkness, but the gates did not open. Then he knocked timidly. The gates opened slightly, a devil stuck his head through the crack, and asked surly, "What do you want?"

"To enter hell."

"What's your name?"

"Nicholas."

The devil leafed through a thick book, smeared with fat, and said, "You are not on my list. You only disturb the night's peace of hell for naught!"

The heavy gates fell shut hollowly.

"What can I do now?"

He started looking around in despair – stars, innumerable stars, and nothing else. Then he noticed something bright, like a lantern.

"Perhaps the shack of a night watchman," the thought flashed through the farmer's mind. "I will go and ask him what to do and where to go."

He set out on his way. The light drew closer, became brighter and larger, and then the farmer saw the gates of rainbow in front of him. A crowd of his poor had gathered in front of the gates.

Having noticed the farmer, they began to welcome him joyfully, saying, "Where did you tarry so long? We froze while waiting for you at the gates, but Saint Peter would not admit us without you, claiming that those are the instructions from God. Only with you and at your request is he allowed to admit us."

"What kind of gates are these?"

"Fool, these, after all, are the gates of paradise!"

On hearing these words the farmer became so frightened that he wanted to disappear as soon as possible. He was too late, though. Sunbeams opened the bright gates and Peter, himself, came out to meet him.

"Come, my son, God awaits you. It is not good to make the all merciful God wait."

"But, after all, I am not allowed to enter paradise. I came here only because even hell wouldn't admit me. After all, I never did bring any gift to God."

"God, Himself, does not need any gifts," Peter said. "He, Himself, has more than enough of everything, but you gave to those who did not have anything, and by giving to them you gave to God, for you obeyed His command."

Peter took the farmer by the arm and accompanied by legions of angels they proceeded toward God. He sat on His pillow of stars and awaited the farmer with a smile.

I conclude.   [[2025]]

Temio   09/17/44 1525

Temio is speaking.

Oh man, why do you, while praying to God with words, expect Him to answer you with deeds!

Oh man, why do you, while handing your neighbor a rock, expect him to hand you bread!

Oh man, why do you, while being unable to comprehend yourself and other people, want to comprehend The Almighty!

Oh man, why do you strive to count the stars in the ocean of the sky when you still have not counted the grains of sand on the shore of the ocean of Earth!

Oh man, why do you, while being incapable of finding and understanding the infinity of the universe and of time, attempt and want to understand and find within your nearby and narrow sky their creator and ruler – The Almighty!

Oh man, on going to bed at night, why don't you fear sleep, even though you enter nonexistence, and fear death, even though you enter eternity! Each night divides your life into separate lives, because each day is a new day. Similarly, death divides the life of your spirit into separate lives. There is no difference between sleep and death, there is only the difference in their [relative] scales.

Oh man, why do you, while wanting to retain a sunbeam in your room, close the door and the windows! Why do you, while wanting to retain friends for yourself, close your heart to friendship!

Oh man, do you want to make a bird happy by locking it up in a golden cage? Do you intend to make your beloved happy by closing the door to the world to her? Have you considered whether you are so mighty, great, and rich that you are able to replace the entire world for her all by yourself?

Oh man, why do you seek the eternal in a world in which even steel and stone are not eternal!

Oh man, why are you not surprised that the rose sheds its blossoms but are surprised that your love wilts!

Oh man, you like a flower in bloom, but don't like it once it has shed its blossoms! Could a blossom, though, become eternal by blooming eternally? Oh no, it has to bloom out so that seeds can form, within which repose even brighter, even more beautiful blossoms!

Oh man, just as a flower's most valuable part – the fragrance – is neither visible nor tangible, thus also man's most valuable part – the soul or spirit – is neither visible nor tangible. It is, however, that fragrance which justifies man's divine essence!

Oh man, why are you not surprised that even your most faithful dog bites you when you beat it with a whip, but are surprised that your wife stops loving you when you lash at her with the whip of jealousy!

Oh man, why do you, while knowing so very little and understanding even less, call yourself the crown of living beings!

[[1555]]

Indra   09/17/44 1606

→I, Indra, am talking with you today, by assignment of Chief Spirit Omega and the divine Santorino.

You, the children of Earth, have been told so much that it is difficult to grasp everything that has been said, and to combine all of it in a single and grand concept. I will give you some traits of understanding, and advice. Listen to us – your chief spirits!

The most important [idea], which has been proclaimed to you in The Almighty's teachings, is that The Almighty has also combined His own goals within man. From that it follows that every human, by serving humanity and its happiness, is already serving The Almighty as well. Also, whoever commits a crime against humanity and hinders its happiness, has committed a crime against The Almighty as well. Therefore, man's only task is to serve the happiness of humanity.

The Almighty listens only to those prayers which have been expressed in good deeds. Therefore, He does not need any ceremonies of worship. These may be necessary only for man himself. In them his spirit, by unleashing from everything that is commonplace, may be capable of understanding The Almighty better, and of drawing closer to Him.

Since there is no absolute good or evil in the universe, the concept of good and evil exists on Earth only with respect to man. Whatever harms man's health and happiness is evil. Whatever helps man to overcome suffering and difficulties, and gives him happiness, is good. From this point of view, all animals and plants which serve to achieve humanity's welfare and happiness should be considered as good. They should be protected and spared by every means, and should be set free from all unnecessary suffering. One has to treat good animals with kindness and love. Anyone who treats them brutally is a sinner, and this sin of his is grave and difficult to justify. Those animals and plants which harm man, and hinder him along his pathway of achieving happiness, are evil. As such, they should be destroyed mercilessly, but without any unnecessary torture.

To continue, with respect to man himself. Man has to be good. [This means that] he has to devote his entire life to the achievement of humanity's joint happiness; joint, not local happiness, not the happiness of individual people or nations, for no happiness is possible unless everyone is happy. The unhappy ones will never permit the happy ones to remain truly and lastingly happy. It is time for humanity to comprehend the importance of this axiom. Without this comprehension, no philosophical teachings, no technological achievements, and no wars will bring either peace or happiness to humanity.

One has to struggle, ruthlessly and even mercilessly, against the evil that is within people, for evil fights with merciless weapons. The entire influence of the power of intellect and love has to be utilized in the struggle against evil. Yet should this alone turn out to be insufficient, then the force of might has to be utilized as well. Evil is active, but good has been passive so far. That explains evil's current victory on Earth.

Evil is cunning, and knows how to skillfully utilize even the weapons of good. As such, it even squeezed into the citadel of good – the church. It put on the robes of Christ's priests, took the symbol of compassion, the cross, in its bloody hands, and from Christ's throne began to proclaim evil, to proclaim hatred. It will be difficult for humanity to overcome evil. The most important weapon will be correct upbringing of the youth, and the struggle of individual people and governments against evil – a merciless and persistent struggle.

The Almighty considers as being evil not only every evil persons, but also every good individual who is indifferent and does not struggle against evil. Man sins the most by not doing anything. The inner essence of good or evil is important, but not their outer appearances. The church can be a beneficial and good establishment, if it serves The Almighty's – that is, God's

– purposes: proclaims the teachings of God; helps those who are suffering; brings light, love, and compassion to people; and eases their physical and spiritual suffering. Yet this same church can turn into an establishment of evil, should it start to serve the selfish purposes of the priests, and proclaim hatred, slavery, and ignorance.

Similarly, the court can be an institution that is good and useful to humanity, should it serve to defend the truth and just laws, and help the weak and the poor against the power of the strong and the rich. However, this court can become an evil institution, should it serve to defend evil people and unjust laws, should judges judge unfairly and take bribes. Similarly, a peace officer, should he maintain order, defend the weaker ones and help them; should he safeguard justice, is good and necessary. Yet should this peace officer support evil authority, take bribes, and utilize his position to increase his own prosperity, he becomes evil and superfluous, even harmful.

As you can see, good and evil can dwell under the very same name, under the very same hat.

How should one deal with the churches and their priests?

It is not important whether man prays to God, or to Allah, or to Krishna, or to some other God, or else does not pray to or acknowledge any God, as long as he serves the good. [That means, serves] humanity's happiness, for with that he is already serving The Almighty. It is only important that he carries out The Almighty's laws – to serve humanity. The individual's drawing closer to The Almighty is not hindered, should he pray to The Almighty in a church, in a mosque, or in some other temple. Churches, Christian churches and the houses of God of other religions, should not be destroyed. They merely have to be cleansed of the evil that has entered, or has been brought into them. Similarly, the priests should not be destroyed, nor should they be held in contempt, as long as they serve their Gods – serve with pure hearts and out of deep conviction, providing they do not simultaneously serve evil as well.

One should not misunderstand The Almighty's new teachings, and proclaim them incorrectly. The Almighty's teachings consist of two parts. They appear to be very simple, but due to their simplicity they are extremely complicated.

The first part is the essence of The Almighty and the spirits, and the ideas associated with this. This part should be taught with the aid of love and reason. Under no circumstances is any physical or even moral coercion and influence permissible. No human has to defend The Almighty, God, Satan, and the spirits. They'll know how to defend themselves, should that be necessary. Also, they should not be called lords, and you yourselves – slaves. You should not fall to your knees in their presence, only bow your head as in the presence of someone older and wiser.

The second part of the teachings pertains to humanity and its destiny, future, and happiness. This part has been given to man in order to achieve his own happiness, and to attain and comprehend The Almighty. This part requires strict and merciless execution. The teachings of this part have to be instituted by utilizing all available means, not even stopping when faced by force and weapons. Humanity has to become happy for once, and for once man has to shed the evil might of matter.

This is what the Ruler of the Future and Death, Chief Spirit Omega says, this is what God's chief spirit, the divine Santorino says, and this is what I, the ancient God of mankind, The Almighty's high spirit, Indra, say.←

[[1723]]

Indra   09/23/44 1649

I, Indra, come to you with a few words.

The times are currently not suitable for long tidings. I will supplement slightly the words that I said the previous time.

The future happiness of humanity has to be built on the foundations of freedom and justice. Justice does not cause any misunderstandings and does not require any explanations. It can be understood on its own. It is different with the concept of freedom. Absolute freedom is not possible. Man can never be completely free in fulfilling his desires. He has to respect the desires of other people, which may not only fail to correspond to his own desires, but can even be completely contrary to them. Here one has to seek *modus vivendi* – a middle road. An individual cannot be absolutely free even on a lonely island. His free will is restricted by the powers of nature, animals, plants, and his own physical abilities as well.

Therefore, people's future society has to be based on these foundations: As good a structure as possible, in which the happiness of the entire humanity is observed primarily, and secondarily, based on it, as much freedom as possible for every person, for each separate individual. Society should not interfere in those concerns of the people that the interests of the state do not require, that is – the interests of the entire, joint humanity.

With the help of education – which has to be the same for all people, and which has to help find each individual's abilities, and has to help to develop and shape them most completely – all people have to be given equal opportunities to achieve personal happiness. Equality is not possible and is unjust. It would be a crime against humanity's spirit to reward equally the lazy and the ambitious, a genius and a fool, Edison and a glass blower, Marconi and some driver. Such equality would become dangerous to the future of humanity, because it would stop its progress. A spirit of competition has to be instilled in humanity, and the more capable people have to be supported by all available means.

The main principle is to give everyone equal opportunities and means for the struggle, that is – for the start of their lives. That is the principle of justice. That will dissipate the sense of injustice toward the state, which has given better opportunities to some than to others. Conditions have to be created so that every person would be able to utilize his abilities and would understand that his success depends only on his own abilities, and that he, himself, he alone and no one else, is at fault for his misfortunes and for him remaining behind. Besides that, a minimum standard of living has to be established – a standard that would give even the most incapable people such a standard of living that they would not feel a lack of anything that is essential for their lives; so that they would have enough to eat, would be well dressed, would live in good apartments, and would enjoy all the achievements of culture that are essential for every human.

There is still another principle, which also has to be rigorously observed – work for everyone. No one may be without work. The state or society has to divide the work equally and fairly, while noting the basic principle of giving work according to each individual's abilities and aptitudes. Within the [bounds of] feasibility it has to note everyone's desires in choosing work, [has to set] equally fair working hours, be they eight hours or one hour in duration, but the same for everyone, while obviously adjusting them due to the burden or difficulty and mental exertion.

Thanks to technology, all work will become equally easy. Thus plowing [a field] while sitting on a tractor is no longer any more difficult than sitting at a desk with a pen in hand. Yes, thanks to the achievements of technology the duration of work will become too short and the physical exertion too small in order to maintain the body at the heights of its structure. This lack of duration and of physical exertion will have to be replaced by sport. It will have to be made to be beautiful and enjoyable. All kinds of uses of the fist will have to be forgotten, since these cripple the individual's body as well as undermine his self-respect.

In concluding my tiding of this day, I will [talk about] these Tidings. We, the spirits, cannot be completely truthful in our tidings, for man is incapable of comprehending us completely. We express many ideas to you allegorically. Thus we say, "I flew over" and "God smiled" – all of these are concepts that a human being can understand, even though they do not correspond to the reality of the world of the spirits.

Spirits do not fly, but relocate by a method that is beyond your grasp. God does not smile like a human smiles, but how can one describe the indescribable to you? How can one explain to someone who is blind that snow is white and that coal is black? That is not possible, therefore we have to be on occasion conscientiously untruthful. Also, while telling you about some phenomena of the universe, we frequently have to use the criteria and ideas of your science. Otherwise you will either not understand us or else we will have to open on Earth a College of Heaven – which is not within our authority. Similarly, we refrained from prophesies, for they, too, are not included within our tasks. Turn to fortunetellers – if you are not afraid of being disappointed.

I conclude.   [[1744]]

Mortifero   09/26/44 1842

I, Mortifero, am with you. All the spirits have departed from you, because all terms have expired. Whatever you will do, you will do as people; no spirit will guard you. Nakcia was the last one; she pledged her spirit on behalf of Alexo still today, but this evening she, too, has already left.

The world situation has changed drastically. This is what The Almighty's words sounded like. Listen to them, you people!

"The German nation had lost its place on Earth. I gave it the opportunity to regain justice. I also gave noble goals to its leader. These goals remained incomplete, for they were altered, altered in an evil and fateful manner. I withdrew My benevolence from this nation, which no longer dreamed of justice and happiness for humanity, but only of its own happiness and domination [of other nations]. I withdrew My wreath of victory from its leader as well.

"The day has come now when armies are positioned on Germany's borders, and the German nation once again fights for its existence, for its freedom and justice. I leave humanity now to settle its quarrels by itself – with its own physical and spiritual strengths. I give the opportunity of winning to the more capable side. I no longer deny this victory to the German nation either, if the geniuses of this nation will be capable of smashing the ironclad wave that billows at its borders. The German nation displays the greatest heroism that is possible and that one can imagine. All heads, not only those of people but those of the spirits as well, have to bow before this heroism and perseverance.

"People, decide who of you is worthy of being called the first, and of governing the Earth! Spirits, silence your sympathies and antipathies, and do not give help to any man and to any nation! Step aside and be merely those who see everything, but do nothing. You, Mortifero, assume authority over Earth all by yourself! You, Santorino, and God's other spirits, leave the Earth! So say and command I – the ruler of everything that exists and does not exist – The Almighty!"

Let these words be the answer to all your questions. Let these words be the guide on your paths across humanity's choppy ocean. These words, directed at the entire humanity, are intended for you as well! Prove who of you is more capable. Prove which of you is wiser. Prove who of you is stronger. There were eight of you. Three have been taken away from this land, which has fulfilled – just as once had the land of Israel – its task. The light for humanity will dawn from other lands, and The Almighty's words will be heard in other languages!

The Latvian nation was raised higher than all the large nations, but it fell lower than all of them. While being protected by God during all the long years of war, when all of Europe groaned in the rubble of disaster, it knew only how to grumble at God. Even the all-merciful God was unable to forgive this unprecedented sin, and He recalled Santorino. Only now does this mindless, worthless, and ungrateful nation see from what dangers and horrors it was being protected.

My words are sharp as a sword and merciless as a tombstone, but they are true, and men have to hear the truth! If you are still men, you will hear these words and will acknowledge their truthfulness. They will hit you in the face like blood pumped by shame, but they will also pour strength into the blood vessels of your muscles, and will give you the courage to grasp the hilt of the sword of the future. This is what I say, this day's ruler of the Earth – Mortifero!

_ ★ ★ ★ _

I, Mortifero, stand behind you and my shadow falls on the entire Earth. I observe you, and see and hear everything. My eyes are the eyes of The Almighty, my ears are the ears of The Almighty, and my mind strives to comprehend The Almighty's mind and to guide your destinies.

I, the ruler of Earth, part from you with these words, "What awaits the nations on Earth is something that they, themselves, do not expect yet. What does not exist will be, and what exists will not be. Days will come that will be darker than nights, and nights will come that will be brighter than days. The firmest hopes will vanish, and hopes that are so uncertain as to not exist at all, will turn into reality. I am telling you – the great will be disappointed and the small will be disappointed! I am telling you – those who will want to attain everything will lose everything, and those who will want to acquire what is just and minor will acquire everything!"

I conclude.   [[1943]]

[[This concludes the series of tidings that were received in Latvia. The Tidings continue in Germany.]]

Chapter XVIII

November 1944

Aksanto   11/08/44 1435

Aksanto is speaking. I greet you in the distant land with the howl of a siren. [[The warning siren sounded.]]

What can one do? We do not have the right to intervene in the destinies of humanity. We only have to observe, and ascertain human courses and thoughts. We, the spirits, have not left Earth, as you have understood that. Recall The Almighty's words regarding us! We are here, but also are not, for the power over you has now been given only to the highest Chief Spirit Mortifero. His authority with respect to the living beings exceeds even the authority of God and Satan. I am talking to you with Mortifero's permission.

– ★ ★ ★ –

I am not allowed to talk with Alexander, but only about Alexander. We, the spirits, welcomed with boundless joy his decision to leave his homeland and dedicate his life to the words of The Almighty. That is not a human, that is not Alexander, who is with you – those are the words of The Almighty that will resound to humanity and that will bring it happiness, and [that will bring] you immortality and fame beyond your imagining. I, God's envoy to you, Aksanto, am saying that.

Alexander, as usual, acted childishly in the material sense. He left behind much that is valuable, but took along books. I understand him, for I would have acted even worse – I would have taken along only books. Perhaps you do not know how painful it is to part from those books which have told you about God's world, which have accompanied you from your childhood days, and which have told you such beloved and precious words as only your father and mother are capable of.

Alexander remains silent, but I hear his weeping heart, because those were books because of which he was willing to remain even in hell. Thanks to these books, he happened to be at the moment of departure without any money and without any material valuables. He, however, like a child, set out smiling across the waves of the sea without any money, without a knowledge of the languages, and without his books.

I am talking about what he would not have permitted me to say, therefore I am also not talking with him. I can say only [one thing]. His desire to serve humanity on Earth in the future as well is just as important as the day when The Almighty's voice was heard on Earth, was heard in the Commandments. It will be heard now in a summary which The Almighty no longer wanted to give humanity. However, He will give it now, and will give much else [that will be] decisively important. You only have to be capable of comprehending my words, and be worthy of following them. I am talking incomprehensibly for fools and understandably for the wise. Be among the latter!

With the howl of a siren, I take leave from you. [[The all clear siren sounded. 1555]]

Mortifero   11/15/44 1630

I, Mortifero, am telling you – there once was a man. He picked up an ax and went to chop wood. He happened to have a knotty and twisted block of wood. Hours passed, sweat was pouring, chips were flying, but the wood would not split. The man sat down on the block and moaned in despair.

His friend was passing by. He stopped and asked, "Why are you wailing?"

"Why shouldn't I wail when I need firewood but it is not possible to split this log!"

"Get up! I will split it."

"You? After all, you are much weaker than I am."

"That's all right, let's try! One cannot always accomplish everything by force."

The man's friend picked up the ax, walked up to the log, turned it back and forth, looked it over thoroughly, and then swung the ax. Oh wonder, the log split! Only a few minutes passed and in the place of the knotty and difficult log there lay a pile of twisted firewood.

The man could not believe his eyes. "How did you manage that?"

"You see, the log does not always split the way you want it to, but the way its fibers run. One has to find the log's most vulnerable places, and then no log will be able to resist your ax. You see, you happened to have a bad log, a log that would not split, as some people happen to have a life just like that.

Yet there is no log that cannot be split, just as there is no life that cannot be vanquished."

I, Mortifero, was wandering once around your Earth. A worker was groaning in a coal mine.

I asked, "Why are you groaning?"

"Why shouldn't I groan? The work is so hard, my life is so difficult."

"Who has tied you to this hard work, though? You are a free individual, go become a barber."

"But I don't know how to shave."

"Learn, it is not much of an art, even easier than yours."

"Yet how can I leave this accustomed to work? I have worked nothing but it all the time, and have taken it over from my father. It is difficult to start something new; I'm afraid – who knows how it'll turn out, might turn out badly."

"Well, then just continue to dig your coal," I said and left the mine.

I stopped at a newly built house. The new owner was wiping the sweat, but his face was beaming with joy.

"Why are you so happy?" I asked.

"Sir, why shouldn't I be happy? I am very successful in everything! I came here with nothing but trousers and a jacket, for there was nothing underneath them. Everyone was laughing at me, but I did not laugh and started working. You can see now for yourself the results of my work. I succeeded marvelously in everything. I drained a swamp that did not belong to anyone – turned it into fertile land; I built a barn, then a drying-house, and now also this wonderful home. I will move my wife and children tomorrow from the drying-house into it. A bright and happy life will begin."

He pulled a bottle of wine from the pocket of a jacket that had been hung on a fence, and continued, "Let's have a drink. You, too, sir, should be happy along with me."

"I can't, my son."

"But why? Are you also envious of my success and happiness?"

"No, my son, quite the contrary. I feel sorry for them."

"But why?"

"Why? Look to the west, what do you see there?"

"What do I see? Not much, only a small, dark cloud."

"Only?" I said. "[Just] wait until tomorrow. I would, however, recommend you not wait for it here, but there on the mountain."

"Oh, you're joking!" the owner said, and walked off.

A downpour started during the night. In the morning, the flooded river swallowed the entire valley, and carried people, livestock, and houses on its waves. Among them the house of the new owner as well. He sat on its roof, but he was nevertheless laughing. Except even I got the chills from his laughter.

These little stories are so obvious that no comments are needed.

With my permission, several spirits talked with you within the last few days. I do not intend to deny them this permission in the future either. You can get yourselves ready for them, that is – for further conversations.

We have started a debate with Alexander. His objections are justified and his wish should be respected. We will answer him within the next few days. His basic desire – not to [have the spirits] help him – is being adhered to sacredly. However, I doubt whether that will bring a blessing for Earth. I fail to see that man will be capable on his own of comprehending him and of not getting in his way. I am not even talking about the rest, for I know this Earth too well.

I conclude.   [[1730]]

Friedrich Schiller   11/18/44 1540

Friedrich. *Sie verstehen nicht, ich werde spechen lettisch. Es ist schwer, aber* I will try.

A young man, overwhelmed by dreams, was roaming the world once. "Oh Heaven," he said, "tell me what is the greatest worth of a man. Show me what I should become like, so that I could justify most completely my great name – man."

Someone who was passing by overheard the young man's words and said, "A thousand miles from here to the east, there is a black cliff on the shore of the sea. A black, hard rock nestles up to the foot of the cliff. The Graybeard sits on this rock. The entire world considers him to be the wisest and the most righteous man. Seek him out. Only he alone will be able to give you the correct answer."

The young man went.

The Graybeard sat on his rock below the cliff and dozed while listening to the song of the waves of the sea. The wind blew foam from the crests of the waves and tossed it on the gray head. But – oh wonder! This foam did not drip from it, but hardened on it into jewels, which sparkled in the sunbeams like a rainbow around the Graybeard's head. The young man stopped on the wide road by the cliff, and waited fearfully for the Graybeard's eyes, eyes that have seen eternity, to open.

The wide road became gradually narrow as a path, and then it disappeared altogether. In its stead billowed a second sea – a sea of people's heads. This sea was silent, though, and only its breath could be heard, for no lips dared to open as long as the lips remained silent that knew what are justice and God in Heaven.

Without noticing it, the young man had ended up at the feet of the Graybeard. He suddenly felt that he was naked, that he had become extremely insignificant. He raised his head in fright, and saw that the Graybeard's eyes had opened and were looking at him. He bowed his head again, for he was unable to bear the clear but unbearable gaze of the Graybeard's eyes. Then he felt the extremely heavy cliff, itself, bear down on his shoulder.

It was not the cliff, though, for he saw on his shoulder the gentle, white, and narrow hand of the Graybeard. Then the lips opened and he heard words that were entwined with the voice of the sea.

"I heard your question and I see the thousand miles that your feet have traveled in order to receive an answer from me. Yet do you think that I, a human whose only wealth is the many years, will be able to answer you in lieu of Heaven. No, my son, I can merely help you to hear and comprehend this answer, but you, yourself, will have to hear it with your own mind. Stand next to me and look, your answer will pass in front of you."

The Graybeard waved his hand and the people began to move. One by one the people began to approach the Graybeard.

The young man observed, but he felt surprised – no one uttered a word, only greeted the Graybeard, and the Graybeard responded silently with greetings.

"What can I comprehend here, and what answer can I obtain here?" the young man thought.

Then, however, he began to notice how differently the Graybeard responded to people's greetings.

He saw a famous warrior, with his head proudly held up high, approach the Graybeard. He saluted the Graybeard with his sword, but the Graybeard responded with a barely perceptible nod of his head. Then a thin, poorly dressed man with a bundle of paper in his hand approached hesitantly. He greeted the Graybeard and, oh wonder, the Graybeard stood up and hugged this man. After a while, a young man with sparkling eyes approached the Graybeard. Him, too, the Graybeard greeted politely. Then an old farmer, bent over from work, approached the Graybeard. The Graybeard held out his hand to him. The tired tiller of the soil continued along his way as if uplifted by wings.

A young man dressed in expensive clothing followed him. His face was white, hands soft and tender, and his nails were filed and pampered. He approached the Graybeard arrogantly, accompanied by jingling of gold in his pockets. He held out his hand to the Graybeard, but he was looking at the sea and did not notice this outstretched hand.

A cripple who had been injured in a mine hobbled behind the young man. He tried to take advantage of the moment when the Old Man was looking at the sea in order to slip by unnoticed. He did not manage that, though. The hand of the Graybeard stopped him and handed him a tree branch, in lieu of the old crutches. Oh wonder, the cripple forgot his crutches in the dust and walked off while leaning lightly on the branch. He did not feel like a cripple any longer, for the Graybeard had shook his hand.

Then another young man, in the uniform of a soldier, approached. His steps were firm, an inflexible will burned in his eyes, and his brow was high and mind inspired with commanding thoughts. He bent low before the Graybeard and there was a question in his eyes. The Graybeard smiled at him, stood up, and greeted him. The young man walked off with firm and confident steps, as though he was carrying the globe on his shoulders, and felt that he was capable of carrying it.

The people continued to stream by. The crowd became ever sparser. The last individual departed, and only then did the proud ruler approach, accompanied by his retinue. The jewels on his clothing burned in the rays of the setting sun. Weapons clanked, the horses snorted. The ruler had looked contemptuously at the going of the people. He had deliberately waited for the end, because he expected that the Graybeard would come forward to meet him in order to greet him.

He approached, but the Graybeard did not move. He rode up and saluted with his sword, but the Graybeard was looking without raising his head, and probably did not see the king on the tall horse. The king waited for a moment and then dismounted from his horse. He walked up to the rock proudly and greeted the Graybeard again, but the Graybeard's eyes were directed at the ground and sought something in the dust at the king's feet. The king turned pale and looked around in confusion. Then he suddenly made a decision, and fell to his knees in the dust. The eyes of the Graybeard noticed him now, but then turned away heedlessly again. The king got up and while staggering grasped his horse's saddle, and disappeared behind the cliff.

The road was wide and empty once again. The young man stood there crushed. His lips and knees were trembling.

"Tell me, Father, what did all that mean? How can I comprehend correctly everything that I have seen? I sense the most important, but the details are obscure to me."

"You are right, my son, I will explain. The man with the bundle of paper was a poet. While fighting hunger, he wrote a poem that is so beautiful and in which is expressed such wisdom of life that his nation will be forgotten, but he – never; even though he is not recognized by it today, and is even ridiculed.

"One of the young men was an inventor. He had not been sent to school, but accomplished that by himself and with his own strength, by not sleeping at nights and not knowing taverns. He works and researches; he invents. His inventions liberate people from the slavery of work, and bring them light and warmth. Without any schooling, he has become wiser than all the schools combined.

"The other young man, the son of rich parents, had been sent to several schools and colleges, and also was privately taught by famous teachers, but he remained the same fool that he was. Schools do not give wisdom, but God does. Schools can give only knowledge. Schools, colleges, and academies in which educated fools sit, quite often hinder science. A large majority of inventors comes from the poor, from those who have hardly gone to school at all, but who have experienced it.

"Then the young man in a soldier's uniform. He also comes from the people, but he wants to rule the people in order to uplift them and make them happy. He will become the ruler of the people, for there is nothing that is too difficult for him.

"Finally – the king. He was born as a king. He had been given everything

– a mind, education, wealth, and power. He had been called to be a ruler, but he is a king only for himself but not for the people. He lives only for himself, and the people exist only for his use. The people are the ones who have to live, work, fight, suffer, and die for him – the king – who is for them, the people, merely a zero, a zero with a crown.

"Now, did you receive an answer from Heaven and did you comprehend it?"

"Yes, my Father, I did."

"Then go and do not err! If after a thousand years I will still hear your name mentioned with respect on the lips of the people, then I will know that you have understood correctly and have acted correctly."

The Graybeard placed his hand on the young man's head for a blessing. When the young man raised it again the sun was no longer there. Darkness covered the Earth, and human eyes could no longer differentiate the shape of the Graybeard from the black cliff. The black rock blended in with the black cliff, and it with the black night. Silence reigned, and even the waves of the sea had frozen in eternal sleep.

With silent steps, the young man departed from the sacred place, and opened the door to the world.

I conclude.   [[1735]]

Nonuta   11/20/44 1441

The spirit Nonuta is speaking. It is not necessary to jump into a lake in order to avoid the rain, as many of you are now doing. You laugh about the first expression, but you do not laugh about the second one. You could quite often escape the scythe of death if you would not thrust yourselves upon it. You move into cities – graveyards, for they are bombed almost every day. Yet you run away from the countryside where there is peace, because there is mud, work, poor rooms, bad people, boredom, discomforts, low wages, and so on. After all, it turns out that you value your life less than these trifles. If you value it so low yourselves, why do you expect God, Satan, the spirits, and particularly Mortifero to value it highly? Look critically at your own deeds first, and only then at the deeds of fate.

If you can cross a river on a footbridge, but do not walk on it and wade, then do not complain that God has not protected your feet from getting wet.

If you carry a heavy load, then do not complain that God has not protected you from fatigue.

If you curse out your neighbor, then do not complain that God has allowed him to call you a fool.

If you insult someone, then do not expect God to protect your face from a slap.

If you have accumulated unnecessary wealth, then do not think that God will stand by it as a night watchman.

If instead of one loaf you keep ten loaves of bread on the shelf, then do not expect God to keep them from growing moldy.

If you tell your acquaintance "friend," but think "scoundrel," do not expect God to hear the former. No, He will hear the latter, and your acquaintance will also sense it.

If you give bread to someone who is poor, even though in your heart you would want to give him a rock, then you can be assured that you have given it as well, for God and Satan respect your wish and not merely your deed.

I conclude.   [[1520]]

Silamiki   11/20/44 1522

The spirit Silamiki is speaking. Do your housework on a rainy day and your work in the field on a dry day, so that you would not have to wade up to your ears in mud, after a measly apple or some twig.

Do not throw away the old crutch until you have bought a new one, for the store will not come to you.

Contemplate first what you want and then consider what you are capable of, and act only after that.

Always open the window first, and only then throw the cat out through it; otherwise wind will blow into the room and your wife will scold you.

Measure the size of your head first, and only then go to buy a hat. Otherwise it will either not stay on your wise head or else will cover your eyes and you will not see the world with all of its roads.

Do good, but don't be like the child who tells his mother after each deed, "Mother, look, I did a good deed again!" God is no mother and sees for Himself what you are doing. - ★ ★ ★ -

Nothing disappears as readily as earthly possessions, for they consist of matter, and it is subject to vanishing. I, an old spirit, do not tolerate those who are full of matter, so full that there is no longer room in them for the spirit. They, people like that, can even be good as people, but they are bad as spirits, and are alien and even hostile to the spirits. These people are the ones who hate everything that is spiritual, and they degrade it.

_ ★ ★ ★ _

Friedrich Schiller   11/23/44 1735

Friedrich is speaking. You were surprised that I did not keep my promise and told you a tale instead of what had been promised. [I told it] rather poorly executed at that, which is not what you expected from a poet like Schiller. Several circumstances should be blamed in this case. It was not the great German poet Schiller who spoke, but his spirit, who is not as great a poet. Secondly, this spirit had to struggle with a language that is foreign to him. Thirdly, there was insufficient time, and fourthly, there is less stated in this tale than what one has to understand. Only someone who will delve in it thoroughly and for many years will perhaps be able to comprehend it partially. Those to whom it seems to be quickly and easily understandable have not understood it at all. There are many symbols in it and entire worlds of concepts hide in it under simple words. It is doubtful if any human will manage to decipher this tale completely; the basic idea – yes.

I will say a few words to Alexander now.

I know that the Rhine was just as intimate for you as Mother-Daugava and Matushka-Volga. Not thanks to me, though, but to another great poet, whom the German nation wants to forget now, but that is not important. What is important is that your childhood dream has come true. You stood next to the Rhine three times. First, next to the wide and silent Rhine that is near the plains of the Netherlands, the gray and ugly Rhine. [[Spellen.]] The second time you stood on the narrow Rhine, whose waters still exhaled the coolness of the snow-covered mountains of Switzerland. [[Constance.]] You are standing for the third time close to it in the shadow of the Taunus Mountains. [[Wiesbaden.]]

You are not standing alone this time. Standing with you and looking into the stream of the sacred river are the shadows of still three other poets – mine, the father of Lorelei, and that of the great poet, the world's greatest poet of my era – the creator of Faust – whose native city is thirty-five kilometers from you. [[Frankfurt am Main.]]

This war, this war that destroys culture, destroys all memories of him. His house lies in ruins and even his monument is in ruins. His spirit, too, stands next to you.

I am more fortunate so far, for all of you passed by my statue just today.

All four of us are standing on the bank of the sacred river. Why "sacred?" After all, it is neither Jordan nor the Ganges. Sacred because beauty and love are sacred. Rhine is beautiful, gently and inexpressibly beautiful. It is just as beautiful as the love with which the German nation loves it, and not only the German nation alone. You have dreamed endlessly about the Rhine, even though not only have you not devoted a single poem to it, but not even a single word. That does not mean anything to us, the spirits, for we hear the songs of your thoughts and they were and are beautiful.

You stopped at my statue just today, and said, "No, Schiller, you appear alien to me!"

You are right. I looked less at the sky than at the ground. Man fascinated me with his greatness and triviality; man and his spirit, a spirit who was bound by a large number of earthly shackles – slavery, ignorance, hatred, passion, envy, cruelty, thirst for power, jealousy, and treason. I attempted to comprehend this man; to find courage, a thirst for freedom, and a hatred of ignorance and slavery in him. I strove to arouse these feelings in him. I uplifted, I aroused man. I wanted to see an arouser and a caller depicted in my statue, but not this dreamy young man, leaning against a stump, with his gaze turned to the sky, as if reading there the words with which to write a book. No, I did not take these words from the sky, but from the depths of a glowing heart.

I like the statue at my feet because it depicts correctly the nation that has not understood its poet.

Thus all four of us met here for the first time in eternity, because all four of us had never managed to be together at the same time.

You have been silent for the last few months, and that makes us sad. We know and respect you more as a poet, rather than as a herald. We understand that your task as a herald raises you so much higher than you as a poet, and higher than all of us. [We understand] that your significance to humanity as a herald surpasses everything that can be imagined, and cannot be compared to anything. Still, as a poet you are ours, but as a herald you are above us and therefore ungraspable and alien. The great Caucasian poet Shota, too, wanted to talk with you once as with a poet, but could not, for as a herald you have forgotten the poet [in you]. I have the same feeling. I will await the day when you will become a poet once more, and then I will come to you.

Alexo, while passing by, looked at me as at some bird in the zoo. Dear Alexo, I understand you so well, for you do not understand me at all. It is good that at least you know my name. Poor Shota and Praxiteles cannot boast even about that. Never mind, the day will come when you will also come to me.

Janoss and Mary also know me rather poorly, but they, too, have not missed everything. They should not forget to let in time my name be known to Nicholas.

I take leave for today. An intermission of twenty minutes, and then Kolinto will visit you. [[1843]]

Kolinto   11/23/44 1906

Kolinto is speaking. - ★ ★ ★ -

We, the spirits, fully understand what the human being is like; what he can be like and what he has to be like. One cannot ask a horse to pull a wagon without oats in its stomach, a car – to run without gas, an engine – to pull a train without wood or coal, a tiger – to eat cabbage, and a cow – to eat rabbits.

The human being consists of two substances – the spirit and matter, or body. The demands of the body are definite and they have to be taken into account. It is not possible to live as a human without giving the body air, food, water, and warmth. The spirit cannot ask the body to give up food, sleep, and breathing. Neither should that be asked. One should only ask that the body not demand that which is not necessary, not demand everything. There is nothing wrong with the body eating well, but it is bad if the body thinks only about eating and serves only this. There is nothing wrong with an individual drinking a glass or two of wine, but it is bad if he gets drunk and turns into an animal. One has to give the body what is essential, and occasionally it can even be pampered, but one should not permit the body to become the spirit's commander.

It cannot be denied that it is a good thing to dress well and cleanly, but it is a crime to adorn yourself with new outfits almost daily. Neither is it a crime to accumulate wealth, as long as it is accumulated only within the bounds of necessity, otherwise it is a grave sin. Still, an accumulation of wealth can also be recognized if it either benefits others as well, or else encourages culture, the progress of humanity; such as the erection of good houses, building of movie theaters, construction of factories, establishment of enterprises, and so on. The exception is where this is followed by the naked exploitation of people or the workers.

One should strive to liberate man from unnecessary worries. Houses should be built so that they already contain all the necessary furniture and dishes. Libraries should be established, so that people would not have to buy too many books. Buying books is nevertheless desirable, for it increases accessibility to books, and allows writers to exist. It also encourages literature.

It is wrong to starve the body in order to free the spirit from its might. That is the same as a rancher, while wanting to break in a young and strong horse, starving it. That has to be achieved by other means.

Those who enter monasteries do not understand God's will at all. After all, God wants man to be a man and do more good for other people, rather than abandon the world and shut himself up inside stone walls, where he will bother God day and night with unnecessary prayers, with a drumbeat of empty words.

Therefore be people! Eat, drink, enjoy yourselves, sleep, work, rest, dance, sing, cry, struggle, love, and do other things as well, but only within limits that will not hinder you from being good, noble, and free – so that you could grow and approach that ideal of a human being, which we try to show you in our tidings.

I conclude, for I am afraid to utilize Alexander's strength any longer. We have to preserve it. We want him to do that as well, for he overestimates himself. [[1954]]

Temio   11/24/44 1347

Temio is speaking. What I want to tell you happened during the early days of creating the world.

God had already created the sun, Earth, the planets, and other stars. He had created the air, wind, silence, water, grass, and trees. Clouds floated in the sky, the rain fell, the rivers murmured, the creeks bubbled, and the waves of the seas billowed. The world appeared to be nice and complete, but God was not satisfied. While wiping His high brow, He walked through the green meadows and shady forests, climbed the high mountains, and walked on the ocean waves. He was not satisfied with His work, for He felt that something was missing in it.

"What's missing, though?" God thought and rubbed His brow again. Then He stopped suddenly and said, "Eureka, the animal is missing! It will be hard work, though, to create an animal that could live in the heat and the cold; on land, in the air, and in the water!"

He began the work, but the work did not succeed. The animal did not want to [turn out properly]. Then God decided to create many different animals instead of a single, ideal animal.

One after the other the animals arrived in God's yard. There were all kinds of them! There was the beautiful tiger in a striped coat, the fiery tropical birds, and the gray nightingale whom no one wanted to notice, but when it began to sing all animals were left with their mouths open. The hippopotamus opened its so wide that to this day all animals fear it, even though the hippopotamus itself is a good oldster by nature.

The horse arrived as well.

"Now that is a fabulous creature," admired the animals, "a slender build, a quick gait, and a proud head!"

On hearing all that the horse became proud and conceited, raised its tail in the air, and started running around within the enclosure.

All the animals had been created, but a pile of leftover clay from the dis-cards of the animals that had been created remained still in front of God. God thought for a moment, and then mumbled in His beard, which He had shook for millions of years. "The remnants of such good material must not perish for naught!"

He created the camel.

When the camel, having stretched out its long snake-like neck and rock-ing its humps, marched into the yard with its flat, cake-like boots, such laughter was heard from the animals that it seemed as if the entire God's newly created world will collapse. The horse circled the camel several times, and each time rolled on the ground from laughter.

"That God sure is a brilliant creator! It is no laughing matter to create such an unimaginable fright!" neighed the horse.

The donkey was the first one to agree with this and brayed so loud that all the first apples fell from the apple trees. Adam managed to live [a while longer] in paradise because of that, until the new apples ripened.

God became indignant over such noise, which was not anticipated in the program of creation, and drove all the animals from the yard.

A desert stretched out in front of the yard. The animals proceeded across it. The horse most swiftly; the camel proceeded last, having first drunk dry God's entire well.

Everyone laughed at this foolish fright and said, "How will it be able to live in the world?"

The camel, though, did not utter a word.

Days passed. The camel marched calmly forward. The thirsty and hungry animals barely dragged ahead. The camel, while rocking its humps, passed them with even steps. Thus he caught up with the swift horse as well.

"I am thirsty," the horse neighed pitifully.

"Uhu," growled the camel, "I'm not yet!"

"I'm hungry."

"Eat!" the camel growled, and having plucked off a branch from a thorny bush started grinding it with its strong teeth.

"After all, that's not edible," the horse said.

"Sure is," replied the camel.

The animals no longer laughed at the ugly camel now, but admired and envied it. They began to understand the Great Creator.

You, people, also have to understand Him.

I conclude.   [[1434]]

Santorino   11/25/44 1915

I, Santorino, am with you.

As a result of The Almighty's will, the destinies of Earth have changed. Your circumstances and those of the nations have changed as well. The Latvian nation is scattered. Only a narrow strip of land remains from the land of Latvia. The wave of events has brought you to the banks of the Rhine, in the heart of the German nation. The second wave of events begins to rise. Where will it carry you? We, the spirits, will not answer this question today.

Why did I come to you today? My task is not an easy one. I have been assigned to answer Alexander's questions, but not all of them either. I will have to speak bluntly, hence harshly. I would have liked to speak gently, but the language of the nations on Earth today is unprecedentedly harsh, and their deeds are even worse. Your deeds, too, are wrongful, and your words are sinful. Nevertheless I, God's Chief Spirit Santorino, will speak. Listen to the words that come to you from the Deoss Temple, and across which glides Omega's shadow.

Alexander, you ask, "Will The Almighty's heralds, who have been scattered throughout the expanses of the Earth, be able to assemble together once again, and proclaim the Tidings to the nations, or at least to preserve them?"

I reply, "The Tidings will not perish, they will be passed on to humanity."

You ask, "Will those eight heralds who are already recognized now, be the only ones?"

I reply, "No, not the only ones."

You ask, "Will all of these eight heralds be worthy and capable of carrying out the high task?"

I reply, "No, not all."

You ask, "Is it possible to combine my course of a poet with the course of The Almighty's herald?"

I reply, "Yes, it is."

You ask, "As a poet I wrote poetry about the Earth, man, and nature as they appeared to my human eyes. I wrote poetry about passion; during moments of doubt I even offended God, I even failed to acknowledge immortality. It seems to me that I – the poet – cannot be reconciled with I – a herald."

I reply, "Yes, that will cause doubts in the mistrustful, and fear in the weak ones, but that is not bad. You are a human being, and the other heralds are also people, people with all human characteristics and faults. Christ's disciples also were like that. They were far worse than even you were. Not all of them even knew how to write. They, too, made mistakes, argued, and stumbled. They even denied and abandoned Christ at the moment of danger. They were not ideal people – [certainly not ideal] heralds – and still The Almighty chose them, but not the most prominent ones among the people. You will claim that such did not exist back then. There were highly educated philosophers, scientists, and writers; but God chose fishermen.

"He has now chosen heralds who not only know how to read and write, but who have completed the highest schools of learning, even though as people they have not become better because of that. There is only one thing

that is important to humanity – the work of the heralds, a better completion of The Almighty's task. Your personal life is important only to you,
yourselves. Should your mistakes, however, hurt the task, The Almighty will
consider them to be a sin and will punish you."

You ask, "Can The Almighty release me from the continued accomplishment of the task of a herald? I feel unprepared and unsuitable for this high
and very responsible position, for which one should have prepared himself
his entire lifetime. I feel tired, and my request to not help me, which is being
respected, could, under the current conditions on Earth, turn out to fateful
to the entire work of the Tidings. Therefore I ask The Almighty once again
to give His blessing for continued work to some other, more capable and
stronger herald."

I reply, "No, your wish cannot be granted. The Almighty's will is unalterable and final, you and all of humanity have to take that into consideration.
Christ, too, at the end of His life, was merely a human and no one helped
Him to suffer and to die. Humanity should have helped Him, but that did
not occur, and that has cost humanity two thousand years of suffering and
delusions."

You ask, "Who among the heralds should be considered to be the chosen
one?"

I reply, "The most capable and the most distinguished one."

_ ★ ★ ★ _

You ask, "What do the spirits want from me?"

I reply, "To travel your high roads, [if necessary] even in the garb of a
traveler."

You ask, "What should I tell the heralds?"

I reply, "Tell them – may unity, loyalty, an unyielding will, patience, and
unflagging faith in the ideal unite them among themselves and around you.
Those who will travel by themselves will soon lose the way, will get lost, and
will be lost for themselves, the nations, and for The Almighty."

Then you still ask, "Of that which we have to do, which is the most important?"

I reply, "To follow The Almighty's will!"

Dixi. [[2100]]

Temio   **11/27/44 1425**

I, Temio, want to tell you a short, little story today. This time, though, not about camels, but about you, people.

It was a rainy day. Then suddenly the clouds parted and the sun shone through. Some people sat down on benches in an open area of the park. They either conversed quietly or remained silent, absorbed in deep thoughts, while observing the sparrows. A drunk gentleman disrupted this divine idyll. He staggered into the open area, tripped, and stretched out in the mud. Everyone looked disdainfully at him lying there. Then a gentleman who was passing by stopped, looked at the one lying there, helped him up, and walked off with him.

The public that was sitting on the benches began to comment on what had taken place.

The thief said, "That definitely was a swindler, mark my words. He will undress, rob, and abandon the drunk behind the nearest bushes."

He snapped his fingers regretfully.

"I don't think so," said the drunkard. "He is simply a smart individual who likes to imbibe, but has no money currently. He will take this tipsy one back to the bar, where they both will imbibe extensively."

"That will probably not be the case," the porter said. "This gentleman will simply take the drunk home in order to receive a good tip from his wife."

"I think differently, though," said the banker. "You saw that the newcomer looked over the one who was lying there, and only when he probably recognized him, helped him up and led him off. He definitely must have been a creditor who, on seeing that the debtor lies in the mud and can catch a cold and die without repaying his debt, obviously hastened to salvage his money."

That's how the honest and noble citizens argued among themselves. Then an elderly lady began in an unsure voice. "But dear people, why don't you think that he was simply a good person who felt sorry for the one lying in the mud, and who out of the goodness of his heart saved him from a cold. Had I not been, thanks to the dear God, so old and feeble I would have done the same thing."

"Oh, come now!" the voices came from all around. "Where will you find these days such a crazy individual who would voluntarily assume responsibility for a stranger, thus risking getting into all kinds of troubles and getting dirty with mud."

Embarrassed, the old lady started to re-tie her kerchief and no longer said anything. Silence set in for a moment.

While utilizing this silence, I turn to you with a question, "According to your thoughts, who in the public was right?"

[[We reply, "The old lady."]]

It seems as if the old lady could have been right, just as you wished it. The silence, however, had ended and the public – while conversing in the evening twilight, which in the meantime had managed to crawl out of all the bushes and unto the paved walkways – headed homeward. Our dear friends and acquaintances had walked only a few dozen steps when they noticed the drunk gentleman sitting on a bench beneath a large bush, except without his overcoat.

"Well, what did I say?" exulted the thief, even though his heart smarted with envy. "[I said] that the good individual was only a clever thief who has cleverly fooled all of us, even me – the old mule."

The people looked at each other in surprise. The old lady mumbled underneath her colorful kerchief, "Oh, Lord God, oh, Lord God."

The people walked up closer and the porter exclaimed, "What kind of a robbery is that? Look at the watch in his vest pocket! After all, a thief would not have left that behind."

"Yes, a thief would not have left that behind," the thief agreed.

Everyone began now to examine the drunk. His wallet was in his pocket, and not all that empty either. Based on a notebook and a postcard found in another pocket, one could clearly see that the drunk was not married, did not owe anyone more than ten pennies, and did not justify any other suspicions either. What had happened here? Everyone stood there in silence and did not understand.

I ask you one more time, "What had happened here?"

[[We give a vague answer.]]

The matter was quite simple. The drunken gentleman had to go to the pharmacy. It was raining, and his overcoat was at the cleaners. He turned to his neighbor with a request to lend him his overcoat for a few minutes, so that he could get the medicine. The neighbor lent him his overcoat. The sick one, however, while coming back from the pharmacy, dropped into a bar. Since the medicine in a bar is generally more effective than the medicine from a pharmacy, the results became quite soon visible to all of us. The neighbor happened to walk accidentally through the same park. He recognized his overcoat and felt sorry for it.

The moral of this little story is difficult to see, but if one were to look carefully, perhaps it can, after all, be seen and even understood.

I conclude.   [[1525]]

Chapter XIX
December 1944

Ali   12/02/44 1800

Ali is speaking. My ruler, the sultan, once said, "If you dream that you have bought a camel, that does not yet mean that you will be riding on it in the morning. You will be fortunate if you will chance upon a long-eared donkey."

That is what the ruler said.

Unfortunately, you see dreams quite often not only at night but in the daytime as well, and feel bitterly disappointed when they do not come true. Thus a young man sees in the dream of his life that he marries an angel, but on waking finds a witch at his side in the bed. The second young man sees in his dream that he builds a huge and fantastically beautiful palace, but on waking at the last moment of his life, sees that not even one slab of marble for a monument on his grave can be had from this marble palace. The third young man sees in his dream that he climbs the stairway of honor, past his friends, toward immortality, but on waking sees that this stairway ends in oblivion and nonexistence.

I conclude. The Divine will speak at seven. [[1845]]

Santorino   12/02/44 1900

→Ego Santorino. Today we will discuss something that might appear to be obvious, but really is not.

It may appear peculiar to many people that some spirits in their stories treat lightly, and even with humoristic undertones, the priests, and even God. How can that be explained? That can be explained easily. Those priests, of whom the spirits make fun, are not the true priests of God. That God, of whom they talk with irony, is not The Almighty, or else the true God, but the "God" of human tales, created by human fantasy. Man, in his fantasy, has created a completely erroneous image of The Almighty, or rather, of God. He has created "God" in the model of earthly rulers – emperors and kings.

The "God," who has been created by people's fantasy, sits on a throne of clouds. Multitudes of saints and angels gather around Him. They do not know how to do anything better than to sing endless songs of praise. The souls of deceased people, too, have nothing better destined for them in paradise than the same droning of a tune. Other souls, again, have found it preferable to sit in pans and caldrons in hell, and keep the poor, silly devil busy by supplying the heavy firewood, keeping the fire going, and inventing all kinds of merry tortures.

Yet what does this stern "God" do? He merely sits on His soft cloud, listens to songs of praise, and settles human sins. Some he herds into paradise where, from boredom and endless singing, even the most saintly spirit – soul – may begin to despair and to curse. Others, again, He drives into hell, to punish them there for the sins which they have committed. To punish, but not to rehabilitate, for the road of the sinful soul ends with hell.

Can't you see for yourselves just how naive, how incorrect in essence, and even how ridiculous this human fantasy is?

No, The Almighty, or God, is neither a king nor that "God," as you portray Him. The Almighty is a creating spirit and a ruling spirit. The universe was not created just once, and was not created frozen in its original form. The process of creation continues even today, and will continue eternally. The Almighty does not stop in His process of creation, not even for one moment. He creates ever new forms of life. He transforms the old ones. He seeks ideal forms of life, and He includes everyone in His creative work: God, Satan, the spirits, and people.

This ruler of the universe is too busy to spare any time for listening to songs of praise, or to engage in sitting on a cloud. He needs the spirits – angels or devils – for creative work, but not for playing harps or frying sinful spirits. He also needs the spirits of deceased living beings for that same creative work. He has no time to be bored, not even for one second. Neither do the spirits, nor the souls, have any time to be bored.

The Almighty is a ruler; but a ruler – creator – researcher – engineer – architect – artist – and a proprietor. This God, The Almighty, does not require and does not recognize songs of praise, and prayers of words. He requires and recognizes as prayers only works, good deeds.

God in the Deoss Temple, too, is the same creative source, and the guardian and molder of everything that is good. Spirits stream to Him for instructions and assignments, as well as for advice and assistance. He, jointly with Satan, forms instantaneously judgment about all living beings, and gives them further assignments.

They do not know the so-called paradise and hell. They know only the Solar Fields – the place of rest for the spirits in their stage of passage. They also know the Lunar Fields, where the spirits can acquire knowledge and strength for further development, and can comprehend and repent the sins which they have committed.

God and Satan also recognize and know the wide field of action of the spirits, in the space of the universe – that of creative work, or the work of guiding the living beings. Finally, [there is] nonexistence for those spirits who are not worthy to be spirits. The rest has already been explained to you and you know it.

This is what the true creator and ruler of the world, The Almighty, is really like, as personified by Himself, God, and Satan.

Let us now turn to man himself, but in fifteen minutes. [[1952]]

Let us continue. Having received the notion about God from The Almighty's envoys – Christ, Buddha, and others – man immediately adopted Him to his understanding and fantasy. He endowed Him with his own human qualities. He created "God" – a king; created His retinue – angels and the saints, after the model of court ministers and noblemen. He created hell after the model of prisons, cellars, and torture chambers.

Since he could not find a model for paradise even in a king's court, he created it after his fantasy, very unreal and insipid. Christ, too, did not give a model for Paradise. He even said that Paradise will be on Earth. What did Christ want to express with these words? The same thing that The Almighty is saying now. The goal of humanity is to form such an ideal world, such an ideal man, that he could feel completely happy on Earth, having overcome all evil, all torments and doubts – so that he would feel ideally happy, that is, as in Paradise. Yes, Paradise does not yet exist; man himself has to create it.

The Almighty's demand becomes clear with that – to serve the happiness of humanity, and it alone, for through it, and only through it, can one serve The Almighty. Whoever serves only God, serves Satan. Whoever serves humanity, serves God. Whoever does not work, but only prays to God, is the worst sinner. Whoever works so much that he has no time left over for prayer, has already worshiped God. Whoever serves only God, and lives by exploiting God's name, is a sinner. It is better to not acknowledge God, but to serve humanity's happiness, than to acknowledge Him but not serve humanity, not to even mention harming it.

A different life awaits man after death. His flesh transforms into other earthly bodies and continues its eternal existence. His soul continues its eternal existence either as a spirit, or else by incarnating in another human on Earth, or else, in some living being on other planets, or else by merging with The Almighty – that is, passing into nonexistence.

The successors of the apostles, who had to continue their mission – to preach – reached a conclusion. [They concluded] that in order to accomplish this better, without doing other work, they would have to proclaim themselves to be God's priests. They would have to institute all kinds of prayers and ceremonies, with which they could justify their not working, and obtain earnings.

Gradually, on the foundations of Christ's teachings, grew a commercial business, a temple of darkness, and even a prison of the spirit. These hideous edifices completely covered up the bright foundations which God had laid. The old idol gods returned to Earth, only under Christian names.

You have to understand why we, the spirits, talk so cuttingly and ironically about that faith which you call the Christian faith. In it, however, all the words of Christ have been given completely contrary notions.

He said, "Pray to God so that no one will see this."

Instead, theaters of prayer – temples – were created.

He said, "Love your enemy," and, "Do not resist evil."

Yet, instead, death for the nonbelievers, and hell for the disobedient ones, were proclaimed.

He said, "Do not accumulate wealth for yourself on Earth."

The priests, though, commenced to sell entrance tickets into paradise for this earthly wealth.

Wasn't that a devilish irony about Christ's words, "Truly, I am telling you, it is easier for a camel to pass through the eye of a needle, than for a rich man to enter Paradise."

Times are changing. The roles of the churches have changed as well. Innumerable sects have come into being. Churches are beginning to turn into movies, theaters, and dance halls. Churches are beginning to advertise similarly to houses of commerce and entertainment. Every enterprising and insolent individual starts to call himself a priest. Songs, music, and drums are heard. People dance and fool about in the name of God.

Don't you see for yourselves now, what a shanty of tricks and deceit the

Christian church has become? Yet you are still surprised that we speak ironically about the servants of this faith and its altered gods, that we do not talk about them with the expected reverence.

Should you place the robe of a judge on the shoulders of a thief, don't expect us to acknowledge him as a judge. Should you cheat and sin all week long, don't expect that on Sunday, with words or candles, you'll be able to deceive God. No! After all, don't be that naive! Open your eyes for once and look into the mirror of your conscience, and into the reality of life!

Today my words sound harsh and merciless, but do the words of people sound gentle these days? Aren't their deeds ghastly? Earth is enveloped in clouds of poisonous hatred. Superstition, hate, and wealth rule on Earth. Earth is drenched in blood and tears. Hearts are empty. The words of Christ have become alien to them. The words of Christ have moved from them into the dull pages of books and the cold stone vaults of churches. There they have frozen into immobility. This is what has happened on Earth!

What will you, people, tell your descendants, in place of the bright words of Christ? You want to appoint a machine in lieu of God. Yet don't you realize that there is nothing in the world that is more merciless than a machine – a machine without a heart and soul?

"*Quo vadis?*" I ask you, man. *Dixi.*← [[2110]]

Mortifero   12/02/44 2140

Mortifero is speaking. I, Mortifero, have come to you. The subject which we have to examine today will require a period of several hours. This subject is extensive and its name is: Man, his truth and delusions.

Can you answer my question – what is man?

[[The heralds remain silent.]]

I am waiting. Janoss?

[[Janoss replies, "The spirit and matter."]]

Mary?

[[Mary's answer is the same.]]

Alexo?

[[Alexo replies, "A spirit who is incarnated in matter."]]

Alexander?

[[Alexander answers, "Man is the highest living being whom The Almighty has created on Earth, and whose task is the most perfect achievement and the most ideal realization of the goal of creating the world."]]

Right!

Now, based on this definition, tell me – what is man's truth and what are his delusions?

The Almighty reprieves you from an immediate response, for He summons me. I interrupt my tiding, and you can rest in peace today, if there will be [such a thing].

I conclude.   [[2150]]

Mortifero   12/03/44 1035

I, Mortifero, continue my interrupted conversation.

The Almighty's will sounded as follows, "The time for the major series of tidings has not come yet, therefore you, spirits, do not commence them until the moment when you receive My permission. The current period is intended for other purposes – evaluation of the heralds, spiritual and also physical; self-criticism of the heralds; observation and comprehension of life; finding one's own errors and overcoming them; reading the Tidings and comprehending them; preparation for the work of proclaiming the Tidings; self-education; review of knowledge and familiarization with the teachings of God's previous heralds and the works of humanity's geniuses, philosophers, and writers; reviewing the Tidings and evaluating new heralds; and clarification of questions with [the heralds'] own abilities and with the help of the spirits."

In accordance with this will of The Almighty, I will not continue my yesterday's tiding either today or tomorrow, but later on.

Let us talk now about the questions that were touched yesterday. Your replies to my unexpected question – what is man – were weak, but I cannot say that they were incorrect. You could also have answered this question, and it seems correctly each time, as follows: As you were taught in school; or else, "Man is a living being, spiritualized with a soul from The Almighty;" or like this, "Man is the most cunning, most merciless, and most gruesome of all the animals on Earth;" or else, "Man is the union of the substances of the spirit and of matter;" or still like this, "Man is an animal who – thanks to his ability to hold his body in a perpendicular position, thanks to hands with fingers that were capable of grasping and later on making weapons, and mainly thanks to his particularly superb brain – has acquired the ability of gradual and unlimited transformation and development, and achievement of everything that is possible and even impossible;" or even like this, "Man is a creation of God and a servant of Satan;" and so on.

You can see how many definitions, excluding Alexander's wonderful and brilliant definition, you could have found.

You have to learn from yesterday's example. A situation like the one that arose yesterday, would not have arisen had you thought on your own, posed questions to yourselves, and found answers to them. Yesterday's event proves that you lack self-initiative, self-motivation, an interest, and a desire to understand everything. You strive as much as possible to receive everything ready-made, without any effort, but you not only do not study what you have received, but immediately forget and ask again for something new, only new.

→Now, let us talk about the Tidings.

Our, the spirits', intent is to show humanity, through these Tidings, the right road toward achieving an ideal and happy life; to take humanity from the paths of delusion, on which it currently wanders, to this single right road; to explain to humanity its most significant errors; to reveal to man who he is, what is the goal of his life, who his Creator is, The Creator's goal of creating the universe, and what The Creator asks of man; to explain to man that which he, himself – by no means and never, not even with the help of his brilliant mind – will be able to find out, understand, and discover; [to explain] who God and the spirits are, and the essence, course, and tasks of man's spirit, both within the human body and outside it; to explain to man the concept of good and evil; and to tell the truth about The Almighty's heralds and religions on Earth.

That is the object of these Tidings, for whose delivery the most eminent and most diverse spirits have been summoned.

The task of the spirits, in these Tidings, is not to lead humanity over this road and to explore this road. The Tidings are simply the road guide. To explore this road, to describe it, and to improve it for traffic – that is the task of humanity itself, the task of humanity's leaders. The task of the spirits also does not include renewing humanity's history correctly, and relating events which are unknown to humanity. The spirits are interested only in humanity's present and its future, but not its past.

What decisive benefits would it give humanity, if we were to tell you that Atlantis did or did not exist, that John the Terrible was a great ruler, and that

Charles the Great was not? Or else, how the Maya people lived? All that is interesting, but humanity's own scientists can research these questions, if they wish to.

The same thing goes for science. The task of the spirits does not include telling humanity what is correct, and what is not, in its theories and achievements. It is not our task to tell man that his theory of atoms is not complete, that much is entirely different from what the scientists teach today. We do not want to deprive them of the joy to continue their work in the future as well. We do not want to deprive humanity of the joy to explore its world on its own, and to form it and to continue building it on its own.

Obviously, we could give humanity a new and correct history, [we could give] new and brilliant books of science. Yet, first of all, how much time would this grand task require? All biographies would have to be rewritten; as well as all books of faith. In other words – everything. With that, all previous work of humanity would become trivial. It would become worthless and insignificant; so would become all historians, explorers, and scientists. That would undermine all of humanity's past, without giving anything particularly positive in its place.

Let's say that your father died when you were ten years old, and you have preserved in your memory, and in your mother's stories, his caressing hands, loving eyes, kind voice, and the wonderful world of presents. You remember him as a loving and extremely fabulous being. Would you gain anything positive, comforting, and useful, should some lover of the truth find it necessary to tell you that in reality, your dear and good father was an individual of a brutal nature, that he deceived your mother, that he was a drunkard, and so on?

The spirits talk, and will talk, only about what can be useful for the future, what is necessary for achieving humanity's bright future. That is why we do not satisfy so many of your desires, and do not reply to so many of your important questions.

Undoubtedly, while accomplishing this grand task, occasionally one tends to deviate slightly, to talk about trifles, to consider questions and events of a passing nature, and to engage much in your, the heralds', personal affairs, which are not important and valuable to humanity. They could be deleted. Some tidings could have been expressed more concentrated; the apparently superfluous repetitions could be deleted. Yes, humanity will be able to do that later on. Yet the Tidings, as the words of The Almighty and His spirits, have to remain complete and unaltered, except for the grammatical errors which have crept in at the time of the heralding process. These Tidings have to be that pure source from which, later on, everyone will be able to derive just as much as he may need.

For the benefit of current humanity's comprehension, we use its concepts, even though they are erroneous at times. We permit only superficial glances into humanity's future life. We do not want to, and may not, complicate our high and important task with unnecessary predictions of the future, and disclosures of human fates.← - ＊ ＊ ＊ -

These are my, the ruler of the Earth and The Almighty's high Chief Spirit Mortifero, words to you – The Almighty's heralds to Earth.

May my words not be quenched in your hearts either today or else later on! My thoughts have been expressed in your, people's, words and your human mind has to understand them.

I have concluded.   [[1210]]

Temio   12/06/44 1413

Temio. I want to tell you a little story today about a sparrow and an eagle. You will not hear anything new and anything unheard of in this little story, for human fantasy has created many nice, little stories about this subject. Not always, though, is the new more important than the old, and something that has been heard but has been forgotten any less interesting than something not yet heard. [Whatever] is good and valuable has to be repeated as often as possible, because human memory is particularly poor with respect to everything that is good. So then, I will begin my little story. Write [it down]!

In a land of high mountains, there was a low-lying valley. People had built houses in the valley. Thus a village came about. It was protected from the cold northern winds, and surrounded by orchards and fertile land for grain.

A gray sparrow had lived in this village for a considerable time already. It had chosen the barnyard of a rich farmer for itself, and felt quite well there. It spent the cool nights underneath the eves of the warm stable, and the days in the stable or in the barnyard. There was no shortage of food for it. The horses saw to that. There was always a wealth of kernels of oat in their manure. Neither was there a shortage of flies and other insects. The sparrow felt secure, as secure as if this had been its own farm.

Whenever the farmer's wife fed the flock of hens, the sparrow was the first one to pick the fattest kernels from in front of their beaks. This resulted in much indignation among the birds. The rooster crowed afterwards for a long time yet to the entire world about the sparrow's insolence. The hens clucked about that among themselves for hours on end, but the tom turkey walked angrily [up and down] the barnyard.

All that did not bother the sparrow. It was not afraid of anyone, not even of the sharp claws of the monster tomcat. The tomcat had become old, lazy, and proud. It tried not to notice the insignificant, gray sparrow by looking at it as though at a vacant spot.

Then the farmer brought back one day, in a sack, a wounded eagle that had been found in the mountains. He placed it in an addition at the end of the stable – in an empty shed. This new, large bird aroused the sparrow's curiosity, for it heard that people called it the king of birds.

The sparrow looked timidly into the shed through a crack. The eagle perched, with its head hung down, in a corner of the shed. The sparrow could not see anything majestic in it. A bird as any other bird. Yes, right, awfully large – but that was the extent of it. If the turkey were to really extend itself, it would not be much smaller than this king of the birds.

The next day the sparrow already dared to stick its head into the shed, and in a few days was already hopping around the eagle itself. The eagle behaved the same way toward this gray trifle, covered with feathers, as the cat did.

The sparrow soon felt disappointed in its most sacred expectations as well. Nothing worthwhile and tasty fell from the ruler's table. No material interests bound the sparrow to the eagle, merely the word – king.

The sparrow made various attempts to attract the eagle's attention. It tried to engage the king in conversations, but everything was to no avail – the eagle simply did not take any notice of it. It perched sadly on a log and looked with rigid eyes out the narrow window, covered with spider webs. It looked at the blue sky and at the snow-covered mountaintops. The sparrow was incapable of figuring out its facial expression, let alone its thoughts.

One day, the eagle shook its head furiously several times, because it wanted to get rid of an obtrusive fly from its beak, but it kept coming back.

Then the sparrow jumped up and swallowed the fly, while saying, "See, I, too, can help you!"

Perhaps the eagle even smiled about these words, but we don't know how eagles smile. Still, [the event] was not without results, and the eagle noticed the sparrow and, due to boredom, even began talking with it.

The sparrow asked one day, "Why are you so dissatisfied and sad? After all, you have it so good here – it is warm, the wind does not blow, the rain does not fall on your neck, the farmer feeds you well, and I entertain you."

The eagle looked contemptuously at the gray clump of feathers and said, "How would you, a sparrow, be able to understand that?"

The sparrow did not say anything, but it did feel insulted, and very much insulted at that!

The eagle continued contemplatively, "How can one feel good here? There is no storm here against which my wings could struggle. There is no sun. The large pile of manure in the middle of the barnyard obscures even that little bit of sun that I can see. The air here is heavy and one cannot breathe it. It is full of fog, dust, the smell of manure, and gnats. The flies will not leave me alone, and aren't even ashamed of sitting on my nose. Gnats crawl in my eyes. The hens cackle all day long. The roosters crow all night long. The dogs bark at night as well as during the day. The walls of the shed conceal the entire world from me, yet you still ask – why don't I feel good here."

The sparrow thought for a moment and then asked, "Was it, however, better there, from where your broad wings brought you?"

The eagle remained silent and looked at the mountains. Then it said, "Better? You ask – was it better there? After all, there was life there, the world was there, and there was infinity and freedom there! The sun shone above me in the eternally blue sky! Banks of clouds floated below me. Storms howled in the mountain gorges. They tore loose stones, but were incapable of breaking my wings. My lungs breathed the cool and clear air. Flakes of ice flew around me, rather than gnats. A majestic silence reigned there, and even the smoke from the chimneys of people's houses was incapable of climbing up to me. Oh, sparrow, but are you able to understand that?"

It hung down sadly its proud head.

The farmer had forgotten one evening to bolt the shed door properly, and the night storm tore it open. The eagle looked out the door, walked out, and spread its mighty wings.

The sparrow noticed that the eagle was getting ready to fly away, and asked for permission to fly along.

"I don't know whether you will like it there, and whether you will be able to live there," the eagle replied.

The sparrow pleaded so long that the eagle finally said, "I do not permit you, but do not forbid you either."

It rose into the air. The sparrow followed it. Since the eagle had gotten out of the habit of flying and had not recovered fully yet, it flew so slowly that even the sparrow was able to keep up with it.

The trip was extremely long and difficult. The sparrow felt completely exhausted and wanted to refuse going on, when the eagle squatted on a sharp edge of a cliff, and said, "This is my world, my wonderful world, sparrow!"

The sparrow sat down on the cliff at [the eagle's] feet, and looked around. Clouds floated somewhere far below them. The very distant and ridiculously tiny houses of [the sparrow's] village appeared occasionally through them. The people and animals could not be seen. The endless sky stretched out over the immense land − mountains, valleys, rivers, seas and plains, towns and villages. The sparrow's tiny heart contracted even smaller from this expanse. Cold shivers began to crawl underneath its feathers. The wind was tearing it from the cliff, and its tiny legs − straws − were ready to break at any moment. The air was cool. The sparrow opened its beak widely, but it still lacked air.

"You claim that it is good here, better than below?" the sparrow asked in surprise.

"Don't you see this expanse and beauty for yourself? Don't you feel the breath of eternity and the call of infinity? Don't you feel the silence of beyond the stars, don't you feel the inexpressible tranquility that is not disturbed by any gnats and flies?"

"Yea," the sparrow said in despair, "you are right! There aren't even any gnats here, there isn't even a single fly! After all, one can starve to death here, one can freeze to death here, one can die of thirst here, one can...."

It did not get any further, though. A strong gust of wind tore it from the cliff and carried it away from the eagle. It observed the path of the sparrow for a moment and then proudly raised its majestic head, spread it gigantic wings, rose into the air, and headed against the storm into the blue, eternally blue sky.

The sparrow came down soon, warmed up, and regained its strength. The next morning it was already hopping around its old barnyard. It would have felt rather happy again, if it hadn't been for its hurt pride. No one had noticed its disappearance and neither did anyone notice its return, as if nothing important had occurred in the world. It was saddened by the fact that the entire barnyard talked about the eagle's disappearance, and that everyone went to look at the empty shed. Even still then, when a long time had passed and the sparrow had already become old, everyone in the valley still recalled the eagle's brief visit, but no one wanted to notice the live sparrow – a sparrow that had almost become an eagle.

I conclude.   [[1600]]

Ali   12/11/44 1705

I, the old Ali, have come at the request of Friedrich, who could not come. Schiller's spirit has promised you much, but who knows whether he will be able to fulfill his promise and tell you about the life and events of the world beyond.

I will talk today in his stead. Unfortunately, though, I tend to speak rather comically and the result is such that poor Schiller grasps his head in horror and leaps, while moaning, from star to star. Can't be helped, though, let him jump around. So then, I will put on my glasses, open my book of memories, covered with soot in the chimney of time, and will look to see what can be found therein that is in the vein of Schiller. Aha, there is something!

The planet Inkipi. Why, sure, Janoss and Alexo have haunted it as well! Let's see what these high spirits have done to this poor planet. Hmm, that's how it is, but what can one do any longer? What has been, has been! Well, you might as well listen.

That did not happen yesterday, nor the day before, but several thousand years ago. Back then the Earth was expecting Buddha, but no one was being expected on our planet. Two peaceful nations, but unusual nations, lived on it.

The individuals of one nation were similar to locusts on Earth, they had long legs and dry, thin bodies. They recoiled on their long legs and took a huge, flea-like leap into the air. There they spread their arms, which had wings, and glided for some distance through the air. Having landed they re-coiled and leaped again, and this continued until they got to wherever they wanted to get. The representatives of this nation were called Kli-Kli. They subsisted by sucking the juice of fruit.

The individuals of the other nation were fat and short. They had an en-tire hump of loose skin on their back. Whenever these individuals wanted to relocate, they did not exhale the air that they had inhaled, but [blew it] into this hump of skin which inflated like a large balloon. The wind lifted these people into the air and carried them. Obviously, they had to wait for a wind from the right direction. They simply let out the air above the mark and landed. These people were called Si-Si. Individuals of the Si-Si nation subsisted by digging and eating [vegetable] roots. Thus Kli-Kli and Si-Si did not deprive each other of food and thanks to that lived peacefully and harmoniously with each other.

Even on this happy planet, however, there was a problem as well. In low places – swamps and waters – there lived a monster, similar to a crocodile on Earth, which was called Miliki. This reptile was incapable of flying, but it was capable of spitting with terrible power. Having taken a small stone in its mouth, it would spit it into the air several hundred meters high, and so accurately that it could break a Si-Si's balloon and a Kli-Kli's wings. They fell to the ground where the monster devoured them hungrily.

Thanks to this gluttonous animal, both nations – Kli-Kli and Si-Si – were in much danger and were even about to become extinct.

The Kli-Kli nation recognized monarchy, but the Si-Si was a republic. The monarchy was like any other monarchy, except with the difference that the ruler's youngest son, rather than the oldest, became the ruler. Si-Si elected to be president the one from among them who could rise highest into the air, that is – the one with the biggest hump on his back.

At the time about which I want to tell you, fateful events occurred on the planet.

One day the court marshal jumped up to the ruler of the Kli-Kli nation, and being out of breath said, "Lipi-Klipi, Miliki no longer eats the Si-Si, but eats only us!"

"How come?" the king cried out. "It eats us, the thin ones, whom it ate only during days of famine, and no longer eats the fat, preferred Si-Si! You have probably sat down on your head, instead of the other end!"

The marshal blushed and mumbled, "No, I am nevertheless telling the truth."

"Summon the servants, have them carry me out! I want to assure myself of the veracity of your astonishing words."

The servants hurried in and carried out the king, for due to long idleness the blood vessels and muscles in his legs had become atrophied. The servants leaped into the air and started gliding above the sea, while holding the ruler by his arms.

Yes, a miracle had indeed taken place! Miliki paid no attention to the fat Si-Si, even though they flew so low as to almost ask to be devoured. Not only [that], but some Si-Si even touched the monster's snout with the tips of their tails. Miliki spat then, the Si-Si fell into the water, and calmly swam to the shore. Miliki, however, paid no attention to him and spat at the dry Kli-Kli, whom it devoured then with great relish.

"Something isn't right here! Either I have gone mad, or else the world has gone mad," the Kli-Kli ruler mumbled on return to his palace.

"It is neither one, nor the other," his wife said. "This Pla-Pla, the old ruler of the Si-Si, has merely invented some nasty whim again, so nasty that even Miliki no longer wants to eat the Si-Si. I've always told you that this Pla-Pla is a cunning old man and only pretends to be our friend. His wife Glu-Glu is a real witch, even though she pretends to be an angel."

The ruler did not listened any longer. The light suddenly dawned in him. "Yes, theses Si-Si have invented something, so that Miliki no longer dares to eat them. Yet what?"

He ordered his ministers to find out this secret, but Si-Si would not reveal it. Finally, the ruler ordered to have a Si-Si, who had fallen into the water, pulled out, and he examined him. It turned out that the Si-Si had some kind of a ball on his stomach. When the king stuck his finger into this ball, he could no longer extract his finger. It was stuck in some extremely sticky substance. The cabinet of ministers, fully assembled, pulled, with much difficulty, the ruler's finger from this sticky ball.

"Well," the ruler said, while wiping his finger in the court marshal's beard, "just as I thought. Even Miliki is not capable of swallowing a sticky horror like that. I can understand now why so many of the monsters have died, and the remaining ones flee from the Si-Si like from the plague."

The word "plague" did not refer on this happy planet to the dreaded disease, but to one's marriage partner.

Real headaches began for the king now. How could he save his nation from complete annihilation? They were unable to obtain the sticky substance, for it came from some sort of potatoes. Si-Si would not sell it either; they found it more profitable to observe the process of Kli-Kli being devoured.

A friend remains a friend forever, but a king remains a king as well, and he invented something. He invented a very simple remedy. He ordered all his subjects to smear some fiery cayenne peppers on their long legs and on their heads.

That was a real comedy, when Miliki had swallowed the first Kli-Kli who had been covered [with peppers]. Spitting like that had never been seen heretofore. So that his nation would not offer any worthy sacrifices, the king ordered those who were in prison to be smeared first, then take them to the water and order them to fly across the sea, with the stipulation that anyone who will fly across will gain freedom. No one gained it, but neither did any Miliki want to spit at a Kli-Kli.

The results were surprising. The Miliki died out from starvation, and a condition of true paradise set in unexpectedly on the planet. The Si-Si as well as the Kli-Kli could now live as though at God's bosom, but was this paradise eternal? I will tell you about that at seven. [[1840]]

Yes, after all, nothing came of paradise; hell set in.

"How come?" you will ask.

Quite simply. The Miliki died out. There were no diseases, except for the aforementioned plague, on this planet. The plague was terrible, but unfortunately it was not fatal, at least not readily fatal. Besides that, the women on this planet were, and still are, very passionate. Thanks to these circumstances, the birthrate became so high, and death came so seldom, that fairly soon the planet became overcrowded with Kli-Kli and Si-Si as with locusts. Not only [was there competition] within each nation, but both nations turned out to be harmful to each other as well. The Si-Si ate all the roots of the plants, and a shortage of juice set in for the Kli-Kli. The Kli-Kli sucked up all the sap from the plants, they wilted and did not produce any roots. The Si-Si kept lifting up clumps of soil in vain.

The old rulers had already passed beyond the sunset. New ones ruled in their stead. King Leiki-Kio ruled the Kli-Kli. President Niki-Kio [ruled the] Si-Si. The first of these rulers had something to do with Alexo's spirit, the second with Janoss's.

Both great rulers met one day and began considering the situation that had arisen.

"How will we avert the calamity?" they asked each other. There was no answer, though.

Then the ruler of the Si-Si said, "Oh, if only the Miliki were to come back, then everything would become well again! We could live once again as if in paradise."

"You said Miliki? Yes, what if we were to seek out these Miliki. Perhaps a pair of them has still survived somewhere in distant lands?"

"Find Miliki!" came the order to the Kli-Kli nation the next day.

"Dig up the entire planet and find the good Miliki!" came the order to the Si-Si nation.

Very many expeditions spread out in all directions. All the mud in the swamps was plowed up, all the seas were dredged, but there was no sign of the Miliki. Eventually a Miliki was located, but only one. What are you going to do with just one?

This one was brought to the planet's highest and most sacred mountain and was placed within a specially built temple. Both nations, which until then had had various gods, now worshipped this one god – the beloved Miliki. They prayed to it to deliver them from the calamity. They hoped that a miracle would occur and a mate would come about for Miliki. The miracle, however, did not want to take place.

Even though Miliki ate daily several sacrifices – even several dozens of children – still, the number of people not only did not diminish but continued to increase. Then a disaster, which enveloped both nations in deep sorrow, occurred one day. Miliki had eaten too much and died. It is not possible to describe the despair and sorrow of both nations.

"What will we do now?" the rulers asked each other again. Having failed to find an answer they convened a meeting of the ministers and a meeting of the parliament. Nothing more worthwhile, however, could be squeezed out of them either, than shrugging of shoulders and muttering in their beards.

The rulers headed toward their homes late at night. Write "palaces," for what kind of a home could a ruler have? Tired, the king walked into his bedroom hoping that his wife will already have fallen asleep. But, oh God, he had barely put down his head when his wife embraced him lovingly, and asked, "Even the day becomes too short now for your foolishness? All of you will probably sit soon in your fooleries at night as well! You are incapable of coming up with anything anyway! Instead, you should have loved and caressed your wives more!"

"Caressed more!" the king exclaimed. "Too many children are born as it is, and she only wants hers – should have caressed more!"

Here the king was suddenly left sitting with his mouth open. Then he looked at his wife and said, as God in Temio's tale, "Eureka!"

Having thrown an overcoat on his shoulders, and stuck his crown under his arm, he leaped from the palace and glided to the neighboring palace.

The president almost died from fright when, in the middle of the night, the king jumped through a window into the bedroom and, having hung his crown on a bedpost, began talking.

"You know, we have been saved! I have found...."

"What have you found?" the frightened president asked, and began to look for his wife underneath the bed. She had crawled there. He erred, though, and having retrieved a container threw it out the window.

The king also stuck his head underneath the bed, and was more fortunate. From beneath it, he pulled out first a woman's bare leg, which was eventually followed by the naked lady herself. The king, however, was so overwhelmed by his idea that he did not notice the embarrassing situation in which he had wound up himself and had placed others. He simply threw his overcoat on the lady's shoulders and, since the lady had become dumbfounded by the sight of the naked king and did not move, then he put his crown on her head and pushed her out the door into the meeting hall of the parliament.

Let others relate what happened in the parliament after that. I'd rather return to the bedroom.

"You see," the king related, "all our problems come from our wives. They are too desirous, too greedy for us. I have found the solution. Let us establish discipline in family life as well. Let us establish certain periods when husbands will sleep apart from their wives. Thus we will achieve a decrease in the birthrate and everything will be well again."

"Oh me, an old block!" exclaimed the president. "Such a simple and brilliant idea, and it could not arise in my, the president's, head, but it hatched in the king's head. You are probably even more tired of your wife than I am of mine. Let that be, but we have been saved! Put on my other jacket, and let's go to the parliament, because this is too important a matter to postpone until the morning. Besides that, as by a miracle, the members of the parliament also are not snoring tonight, but are discussing something joyfully. An unusual event in the history of the parliament."

They opened the door.

I close it again real quick behind them. It'll be better that way. In a word, a new law was born that night.

The wives became extremely alarmed on learning that they will have to spend so many nights a year without their husbands.

"After all, that is something unimaginable, insane, impossible, unbearable!"

Then one woman whispered something in the ear of another, she in that of a third one, and so on. Neither the men nor we knew what they whispered to each other. Except calm set in as though by a miracle, and the wives while smiling slyly scattered to their homes.

Time passed. Everyone expected great things from the law. A miracle occurred, though. Not only did the birthrate fail to decrease, but it even increased. One had to go insane here!

The king and the president met, but did not utter a word. Both only shrugged their shoulders and looked at the sky. The cabinet of ministers and the parliament buzzed like beehives. One thing was clear – something beyond their expectations had happened.

The same thing that took place in the parliament occurred out in the streets as well. Men accused each other of failing to abide by the law.

"You went to your wife during the forbidden period!" they yelled at each other.

"No, I did not go to my wife during the forbidden period! I observed the law rigidly!" refuted the accused ones.

Here the president suddenly jumped to his feet. "What did you say – to your wife? Yet did you go to others' wives?"

Everyone grew silent in confusion, and for a minute the silence of the grave reigned on the planet.

Then the answers started coming, "After all, we did not go, but...."

"But?" the president asked impatiently.

"But they came to us. Since that was not prohibited by the law, we thought...."

"You thought? You didn't think anything!" the president yelled in anger and slammed the door of the parliament. He went to seek his wife, who had borne the customary norm of children.

Other laws, one crazier than the next, followed this law, but the results were the same. Salvation did not seem to be possible.

Then there was one day another meeting of the parliament, in which the king and the queen also participated as guests. Debates began. The president's wife spoke as well. She mentioned the queen in her speech. [The queen] became insulted and did not fail to retaliate. Words followed words, and quite imperceptibly both high ladies were already in each other's hair. The men intervened. The king's guard arrived. Then both nations also got into it. A battle engulfed the entire planet.

When the men finally came to their senses, it turned out that almost one sixth of the people lay lifeless [on the ground]. The entire planet was covered with corpses. Deep sorrow overcame both nations and their rulers.

After the funeral, the king met with the president in order to regret what had happened and to conclude a peace treaty.

"An atrocious occurrence!" the king said.

"A horrifying event!" the president affirmed.

"It has become easier to live, though," said the king.

"Yes, after all, it has become easier to live," the other remarked.

"Therefore there is no evil without some good," the king said.

"Yes, not only is war a disaster, but a blessing as well," replied the president.

"What would we have done had this unexpected war not broken out?" the king asked again.

"Yes, but what will we do if it will no longer occur again?" asked the president.

"Under no circumstances can that be permitted, it has to happen again!" the king said firmly.

"Yes," the president agreed.

"Our wives will see to it that this will happen again!"

They parted as friends.

We will part as well. I can already see Friedrich, having grasped his head in his hands, jumping from star to star. I will rather not wait for his words of gratitude, and will hasten to my stars. There is so much work there, so much.... Would you like to help? No! Oh well, think it over well, but I'm already gone. Give my regards to Friedrich.   [[2045]]

Friedrich Schiller   12/12/44 1735

Friedrich is speaking. It is quite understandable that various doubts oppress you subsequent to Ali's tiding yesterday. First, did Ali really speak on my behalf, or else was he simply joking? The second, was his story about the planet Inkipi the description of a true event, or else a clever satire about events on Earth?

Strange as it might be, and even though you tend to lean more toward the latter, the former conjectures are correct.

Yes, Ali spoke at my request, for I could not be with you yesterday, even though you expected me. I did not want to disappoint you. Ali told you about the very same planet about which I had asked him to tell. Obviously, his narration turned out to be different than mine would have been. I must confess that I am glad that I was not the narrator.

Then, with respect to the second part. Yes, what [Ali told you] was a true event, obviously, except for the introduction and the epilogue. Ali, however, likes to joke around. Besides that, he also framed the realistic painting in a golden frame of enchantingly beautiful wit.

The people, themselves, as well as the events, on the planet Inkipi seem to be like a fairy tale – unimaginable and impossible. Seems as though one has dealings here with either a fairy tale, or else an allegory, or else with biting satire. That's not the case, though! Your writers on Earth express the opinion as well that in its fabrication life surpasses the most fantastic novels and most unimaginable fairy tales. No concoction of a genius is capable of competing with life's imagination. Therefore you should not be surprised by Ali's story.

I deliberately chose this planet and these events for my story, because these events and people are useful for humanity on Earth as a satire about itself, even though there are no similarities between Inkipi and the Earth.

Something else also surprises you – that is the descriptions of a risky nature, which perhaps could have been avoided. Specifically for the sake of the truth, however, Ali did not delete them, so that the events would reflect themselves completely and truthfully.

It seems strange to you that the spirits can relate along the same vein as your writers, such as Mark Twain or Boccaccio. Yet why would that not be the case? The spirits have incarnated very many times, and they know and comprehend life no worse than any one of you. They are with you in their state as spirits as well, and see all your deeds and read all your thoughts. Not only do they see how you pray to God in a church, how you compose music, paint, write, sing, explore, and invent; but also how you sleep, sin, curse, seduce, rape, entice, steal, murder, and litter the ground with trash. The spirits see everything. Why should they, while seeing everything, also not talk about everything, particularly about the peculiarities of the living beings?

You know very well for yourselves that your bodily functions do not always correspond to the comprehension of the spirit. Thus, particularly in youth, you imagine young women as angels without bodies. You are unpleasantly surprised that this angel tramples down the grass while walking, eats and drinks, and does still other rather unsightly and unaesthetic things. Similarly, the first embraces of love also cause a sense of disgust in many people, for they are surprised by the materialistic essence of love and the lack of everything that is spiritual. Later on, the spirit gets used to these bodily functions and reconciles himself with them as being inevitable.

Having left the body, the spirit loses the might of matter that effected him, but does not lose the comprehension and feelings that he had acquired. Only hypocritical saints expect the spirits to be cherubs of an innocent, foolish, and childish nature.

Then, in conclusion, still a little bit more about the planet itself. Was it physically possible to rise into the air and fly with the help of a bladder that was filled with only the exhaled warm air? Obviously not on Earth, but on Inkipi, which is of a different size and has a different chemical composition of the air, as well as where the air in one's lungs transforms differently than on Earth – yes.

How did the Si-Si fly? Did the wind carry them to wherever they wanted to go? Absolutely not, for the Si-Si used their long and wide tail as a propeller, or a rudder.

Let us conclude with that for today. Some other time I will try to tell you something myself. [[1830]]

Astra   12/14/44

Astra. Ask!

[[The heralds say, "The spirits have explained to us in their tidings how the sign of the cross should be used, but nothing has been said regarding blessing oneself or others with the sign of the cross. Could you explain that to us?"]]

Yes. Do you remember what has been said about the sign of the cross – who may wear it, and when? Only the one who feels worthy of wearing this Almighty's sign may wear it. Besides that, it should be worn only under circumstances that are appropriate for this status. It should be removed under disrespectful conditions and [in disrespectful] places, as for example in a bar and similar places, as well as at night when devoting oneself to the pleasures of the flesh.

To cross oneself is the same thing as to put on the cross symbolically. Ask!

[[Janoss asks regarding different manners of showing respect to God.]]

Janoss, you answered your own question yourself at the beginning. Think it over and then ask again.

[[Janoss remains silent.]]

You ask and forget your own words. That means that you have not thought over your question thoroughly. You said that some nations display their sense of respect to God in different ways during their religious ceremonies. Did you say that?

[[Janoss replies, "Yes."]]

Hence, after all, the answer has already been given.

One has to display respect to The Almighty in spiritual ceremonies, and each nation displays it according to its accepted customs. Displaying respect is important, but not the manner of displaying it.

Hats, slippers, and similar items have a decisive meaning only in people's customs and mode of life; they make no difference to God. It would be too trifling for His spirit to pay any attention to some sort of slippers or hats. He looks into your hearts, and if they are full of respect it makes no difference to Him what you have on your heads, backs, hands, or feet. Should you, however, have only flattery, pretenses, fear, or even nothing in your hearts; then you can put on, don, or wear all the wealth and sanctity of the world, or else you can undress completely naked – God will nevertheless be insulted by your disrespect to Him.

Obviously, you, people, have to work out some kind of a common method of expressing respect. What kind? That is your own business.

Ask!

[[The heralds do not ask.]]

Kolinto will speak in ten minutes. [[1533]]

Pilpinitri   12/19/44 1905

Pilpinitri is speaking.

[[Janoss]], the flashing of stars is behind me now. I am on Earth. I visit this young planet for the second time. I was here for the first time when you fought the mammoth. Back then the Earth seemed more tranquil and greener to me. Only birds flew in the air. Roads did not crisscross the Earth. Stones lay undisturbed in the fields. The trees grew quietly in forests. Smoke did not obscure the sun. Those were remote times.

The previous time, I stood by your head which rested on the moss and listened to the wailing of the women and the dismal silence of the men. You – the great leader and hunter – had died. Your eyes were closed and your lips motionless, but you, yourself, stood next to me, looked at yourself, and said, "Thus ends my short life on this young planet. I did not manage to accomplish what I wanted to. I did not manage to unite all these people of the plains and the mountains, and tell them who the true God is."

Mortifero smiled and said, "You will still manage that in a few thousands of years."

You did not understand these words back then, you understand them today. You have not missed anything! Humanity has traveled a long road. It has transformed the face of Earth, it has grown wings of steel for itself and has come closer to heaven, but it has not come closer to God, for it has bypassed Him.

I see the destruction that currently takes place on Earth. It seems to me that humanity wants to tear down all of its tall castles, all of its bright homes, and crawl back into the ground, crawl into caves again. It seems to me that the wheel of time has turned back, and we are standing in a cave again, at whose entrance lie the bones of the gigantic mammoth.

I am saying now, "The time has come when you have to tell the people who God is."

I conclude.   [[1930]]

Aksanto   12/19/44 1945

Aksanto is speaking. The holidays approach, the major festival on Earth. For the first time they come to you in a foreign land, to you who do not have your homeland today. Do these last words sound right, though?

No, your homeland is much wider than the tiny land of Latvia. Your homeland is wherever your Father – The Almighty – rules. This homeland cannot be measured with earthly kilometers, and borders that would run along rivers, fields, mountains, or seas cannot enclose it.

Do not enter a tiny, small room and lock the door to the wide world with meadows, mountains, lakes, oceans, and the sky, while saying, "This small room is my entire world, for my cradle used to hang in it."

Yes, I am telling you, the cradle is merely the nest on whose edge the young eaglet spreads its wings for its first flight into the world. The individual would be ridiculous if he were to tell the eagle, "Sit in your nest for your entire life, because it is your homeland!"

The eagle would reply, "The barnyard of its nest is its homeland only to a sparrow. The entire world is my homeland!"

I am telling you – be eagles, but not sparrows! [[2000]]

Friedrich Schiller   12/20/44 1405

Friedrich is speaking. All right, I will tell [you something], but it will be your own fault if you will have to sit for a long time. What I will tell you is neither a fable nor the truth. It will be an allegory. Listen to me, high heralds!

It was once announced to the people: "Somewhere beyond the wide ocean there is a mysterious land that is called The Land of Justice and Eternity. A huge steamer leaves for it on a given day and from a given port. One has to pay for the passage. There are first, second, third, and fourth classes on the ship. Everyone may travel in the class in which he wants to and for whose ticket he is able to pay. One also has to pay for taking baggage along. Justice reigns in The Land of Justice and Eternity, and everyone there is happy according to his abilities and deeds. Two kings rule this land."

The hour for the ship's departure came. The ship was overcrowded, for everyone was dissatisfied with or else tired of his life in his homeland.

Everyone wanted to enjoy happiness in the new land where justice and eternity reign.

The ship's sirens sounded four times. The engines began to function, and the ship left the port. The shore was white with handkerchiefs being waved in the air for a farewell. White sea gulls accompanied the ship into the distant azure of the sea. The waves ran after it, caught up with it, and ran further on, past it. Wind howled in the masts. Clouds and the fog hung in the rigging. The ship's body quivered from the throbbing beat of the powerful engines – somewhere deep down, invisible and unknown. Light streamed from numerous portholes. Light split the darkness with the swords of projectors. Orchestras played. Rockets blossomed in the air. The people danced, sang, and partied. Only the captain's bridge was submersed in darkness, and on the stairway was a sign, "Entry prohibited to everyone!" No one saw the captain. No one heard his voice. Everyone only carried out the orders which the ship's officers passed on in the captain's name.

There were four classes on the ship, and each class was its own separate world. While the first and second classes could still meet occasionally, the third class passengers were already firmly prohibited from ascending to these classes. The fourth class travelers merely heard about the first two classes. They were not even allowed out of the ballast holds. They could only look, like rats, through ladder hatchways and holes, at the passengers of the higher and more expensive classes walking around in magnificent attire.

The higher-class passengers looked with disgust and occasionally even fear into the dark spaces of the ballast holds and at the dirty and sad lower class passengers, whose shadows glided there deep below their feet. These again turned their gazes with envy and hatred from the darkness into the light and at the gentle shapes that, as it seemed to them, glided along roads of sunbeams. Thus on the same ship traveled joy and sorrow, happiness and misfortune, wealth and poverty, light and darkness, beauty and ugliness, friendship and hatred, laughter and tears, enjoyment and pain, abundance and hunger.

The ship, on whose side burned the word "Life" written in golden letters, cut the endless waves of the ocean. The people of the upper classes were sick from boredom. The people of the lower classes suffocated in darkness and suffered from hunger and a lack of air. The voyage seemed endlessly long and difficult to everyone. Everyone longed for the end of the voyage. As usual, though, that which one awaited came unexpectedly soon.

The ship's passengers woke up one morning – having been awakened by the stillness of the grave that engulfed the ship. The huge body of the ship did not quiver from the beating of its heart – the engines. The orders of the officers and the steps of the sailors could not be heard. Not even the billowing of the waves against the ship's steel plates could be heard. The passengers listened excitedly.

Then they heard the captain's voice for the first time, "We are in port. Everyone has to get up and leave the ship!"

The passengers headed for the deck. The ship was at the shore. The appearance of this shore was strange. They had expected to see a city seething with life; a port with screaming machinery, immersed in lights, and swarming with workers; but what did they see? [They saw] a barren and silent shore. A black marble platform connected the side of the ship to the shore. The shore was barren and without any life. It was submersed in a deep, immobile fog.

A road of the same black marble went from the platform to the shore, and further on into the fog. Cypress trees stood along the road in immobile rows, like mute forms of mourners alongside the casket of a deceased. The cypress lane was submersed in fog, and a high, black gate could barely be seen through it. The waves from the sea washed ashore; washed without any noise like a billowing black velvet, for the waves of the sea and the sky above the sea were black as well. Large, silent stars burned like candles in the black sky, even though it was morning. Flocks of black sea gulls rose from the sea and disappeared silently in the fog. Only one individual was standing in the port – a gray gentleman dressed in black attire with a black cape on his shoulders.

Overcome by fear, the passengers looked at the shore and at the black shape. Then came the welcomer's voice, "You have arrived! Debark from the ship and walk along this road to the gate on which is engraved the inscription, 'The Land of Justice and Eternity.'"

"How can we debark to the shore, though?" came the voices of the passengers. "We cannot carry down our heavy baggage by ourselves. Please send us porters."

"There are no porters here!" came the reply.

"What should we do with our baggage then?" the travelers asked.

"Leave it on the ship!" the sound came from the shore.

"Leave it on the ship so that other people, and even strangers, would take it?" the ship's passengers asked in confusion.

"Leave it on the ship so that strangers would take it!" the welcomer's reply sounded like an echo. Then he continued, "You cannot bring anything along here. Only your deeds and you, yourselves, are needed here!"

The passengers debarked from the ship, which headed back again. They walked along the cypress lane toward the gate, and through it into the new and unknown Land of Justice and Eternity.

(A ten-minute break.) [[1530]]

The huge, black gate opened silently in front of the newcomers. They walked with hesitant steps through the gate, and stopped again in surprise. The rays of an inexpressibly bright sun streamed toward them. Magnolia trees covered with white blossoms stood along the road. Gardens of flowers swayed with the blossoms of white roses. An almost unbearable fragrance of flowers flowed from the fields and gardens. The air and tree branches glittered with the plumes of fabulous birds. The air trembled from their songs. A cloud of white doves flew in front of the travelers. Once the doves parted, a bright and high edifice appeared behind them.

A young man clad in white attire welcomed them. He said, "Enter, disrobe, and leave your clothing on the steps. Wash yourselves in the sacred waters and put on the clothing of The Land of Justice and Eternity, which you will find on emerging from the water. Then proceed through the other door into the hall of the palace, where the rulers of this land will receive you."

The newcomers removed their expensive clothing sown in gold, removed their gray working jackets, threw off their rags of a beggar, and submersed themselves in the gentle waves of the cool water.

On the other side they put on new, beautiful, but simple clothing. They looked at each other once again in surprise — the rich, the workers, and the beggars had disappeared. In their stead stood people clad in bright clothing, all of them clad the same way. Confusion set in, for the wealthy could not differentiate between the rich and the poor; a ruler [could not differentiate between] a ruler and a slave.

They entered the hall. There were two thrones there. Similarly looking rulers sat on them. One ruler's face was gentle and his eyes radiated love and forgiveness. The other ruler's face was cold and hard, and his eyes sparkled like the blades of swords.

The newcomers approached the thrones timidly. A nobleman from Earth stopped first. The voice of The Invisible One came from the unknown distance, "Who are you?"

"I am a [government] minister. I have completed grade school, high school, and three degrees in college. I own three estates and four factories. Many banks are dependent on me."

"What work can you do?" the Voice came again.

"What work can I do? I already said what schools I...."

The Voice, though, interrupted him, "All that is fine, but what work can you do?"

"What can I do? Why do I have to know how to work?"

"Too bad," the firm ruler said, "then you will have to learn how to work!"

"What good did you do for the people?" asked the other ruler.

"Good? I ruled, I helped those who were suffering, by organizing charity balls."

"And what else?" the ruler asked.

"What else?"

"Well, yes. Did you go to someone who was sick and take care of him? Perhaps you helped some poor old woman to carry her bundle of brushwood? Perhaps you bestowed [some land] to the landless peasants of your estate, assured the welfare and old age of your workers, gave the poor some money from your banks, and bought them bread and meat?"

"No, I did not do that."

"Then, unfortunately, I cannot help you. You will have to learn once again how to live."

The second individual stood before the ruler. "I am an engineer. I know how to build threshing machines and other farm implements."

"Wonderful!" the firm ruler said. "You will not lack for work here, either."

"Go, my son," said the other ruler, while smiling.

A young woman came as the third one.

"What do you know?" came the distant Voice.

"I know how to dance all the dances, and real well! All the fellows rejoiced at my art."

"And what else do you know?" the Voice asked.

"What else? Doesn't that suffice?"

"No," said the firm ruler, "that does not suffice! You will have to learn everything anew."

"What good did you do?" the other ruler asked.

"I helped my girlfriends to shop and to try on hats and dresses."

"That is not enough, my dear child," said the ruler. "I can't help you either."

The fourth one replied, "I was a craftsman in a minister's factory. I worked from morning till night and I had no time left over to learn and to help others."

"Didn't you, however, help your poor neighbor on Sundays to repair his doors and windows; and during lunch hour in the workshop make a new pipe for the pauper on your street?"

"Yes," the craftsman replied to the good ruler, "but these were, after all, merely life's trifles."

"They will suffice for us," said the ruler, and the other one added, "Here is your former master, teach him to work as you worked."

The fifth one replied, "I was a poet. I have not done anything good. Neither did I have any time left over for working."

"Fine, my son," the firm ruler said, "your songs helped to make the work of others easier."

"Come to my throne and rest," said the good ruler. "Later on, you will sing something to me about your old Earth."

The people passed thus by both rulers, and each one received work according to his abilities and the knowledge that he had acquired. Those who had learned and attained much, and had done much, could rest now, and then continue their course of development and teach others. Those who had not learned anything and had not done anything good, now had to learn everything anew.

When the last passenger had passed by the rulers, the star doors opened and the newcomers went out through them. They went out into a sunny future and a star-lit eternity.

I close my storybook and say – this story has ended. Let the next one

wait until we will have some free time again and a desire to meet. One of
you caught me cleverly today, even though I had decided to talk some other
time, later on.

I bid you farewell.   [[1640]]

Ilgya   12/21/44 1445

Ilgya. – ★ ★ ★ –

I will not speak long today, I'll say only a few words. First, with respect
to Friedrich's two stories. You are right, there is much that they have in
common, but they are entirely different in essence. The first story talks only
about life on Earth – what it should be like and what is its evaluation, from
the Graybeard's point of view. Write that with a capital "G."

The second story, while depicting life on Earth in short strokes, already
talks about the life of the spirit, not merely about that of a human. It talks
about the evaluation of the spirit's deeds during the time of his incarnation,
and about his continued progress after the conclusion of his span of life on
Earth. As you can see, the difference is major, except one has to comprehend
it. As the storyteller said himself, his story is allegorical, therefore it should
not be understood literally, but with the mind.

– ★ ★ ★ – [[1545]]

Ilgya   12/25/44 1715

Ilgya. On behalf of all the spirits, I congratulate you with the Festival
which a large majority of Christians celebrates today.

You sat at a round table in your homeland last year and Alpha was telling you about the land of Maya. The conditions are different this year. You
have been left on your own this year. There is not much left over from your
homeland. Teeth of steel, too, are gnawing this narrow strip.

The spirits' conversations with you were just beginning around this time
last year. The Almighty's will – to give the nations on Earth His true faith of
the universe – had not been announced yet. You had not been blessed yet
with the title of The Almighty's heralds. The spirits came to you with The
Almighty's permission, but on their own initiative. They talked with you, to
put it more precisely – they answered your questions, which poured forth
as though from the horn of plenty.

How could the spirits answer these questions without the authority to
reveal the new, true faith, and without the right to undermine the decayed

foundations of the old faiths? They replied using the old concepts, which you understood. They spoke of paradises and hells, even though these did not exist, while attempting to find substitutes for them in the Solar and Lunar Fields, and in the status of the degree of divinity. These were difficult to combine. It was equally difficult to answer your questions without acquainting you with the true faith in its entirety. Many misunderstandings and many misconceptions arose in relation to all that. These were clarified later on, with the complete depiction of the new circumstances.

In reference to the aforementioned, the first tidings should be considered as merely historical data, but should not be placed in the foundations of the teachings.

The spirits were happy to be able to utilize this unexpected permission to converse with people. Some spirits who had no ability [to converse] utilized this permission as well. The evil spirits also intervened, for there was no control of the conversations. Neither was there a definite goal for the conversations. These conversations, as I already said, came just as unexpectedly for the spirits as for you, and particularly for Alexander. He did not want initially to participate in these conversations at all, for back then he did not know The Almighty's purpose either. It was only a game back then, from which, thanks to The Almighty's decision, grew the world's greatest and most important event.

I was not with you in the beginning either. A. Aurora was the first of the high spirits to begin conversing with you.

Mary's and Lillian's conversations [with the spirits] were simply a silly foolishness that is not worthy of serious people's [consideration].

- ★ ★ ★ - [[1818]]

A. Aurora   12/25/44 1940

A. Aurora is speaking. Ilgya remembered me today. I know that neither have you forgotten me, who was the first one to take you onto The Almighty's bright road. Many months have passed since the day when I came down to you for the first time – to my old friends from the realm of the spirits. I came only as a friend, in order to renew old memories and relate the new events to you.

The Almighty's permission – to converse with you – came as a pleasant but incomprehensible surprise to us, the spirits. We expected much good from these conversations. We expected them to bring light to people's souls, which were suffocating in the darkness of matter. Yet when The Almighty's decision – to raise man above all other creatures in the universe, and to reveal to him the path to the brightest future – came, it became clear that friendly conversations had to cease and that serious tidings had to commence. The very highest spirits had to be summoned for this important task, and therefore some of us had to grow silent – obviously, only for a while.

An intermission has set in now in the series of tidings, and we can once again renew our friendly conversations. I know that your hearts hold many painful questions, and you are afraid of stern judges. Recall these questions and turn to me. I will not be as harsh and will try to help you.

Today I wish you bright days and undiminishing strength in foreign lands, and ask you to always remember The Almighty's words, "My heralds do not have foreign lands, either here or elsewhere, either today or eternally!"

I conclude.   [[1957]]

A. Aurora   12/27/44 1745

Aurora is speaking. I will not use the letter "A" in the future, since no other Aurora will talk with you. About what would you like to talk with me today? Perhaps there is something of special interest?

[[Mary asks, "Could someone tell us about star "C" in the constellation Cassiopeia?"]]

Why?

[[Mary: "Because my mother is there. I would like to know something more about her."]]

Some other time.

Let us talk now about something that has been mentioned previously. Perhaps it would not hurt to return somewhat to Christ. Some of your circumstances are similar to those which existed then, and with Him and His disciples and relatives. First, how well do you know the Gospel? Yes, very little! That is not good. Had you read it even once, some of your questions would be superfluous.

Remember first – Christ sat once in a room that was overcrowded with people. Christ's mother and brothers arrived and could not get to Him. When Christ was told that His mother and brothers had arrived, Christ replied, "My mother and brothers are all those who follow Me!"

Had you read this passage, John would not have written you that he did not carry out The Almighty's command because he had to take care of his family. As you can see for yourselves, all family ties are and were unimportant [when compared to] such an important task like what Christ had and you have.

Then, in another place, you can read that Christ's bothers also did not believe that Christ was a prophet of God. That was expressed particularly clearly in their words when they were getting ready to go to Jerusalem for the [Passover] celebration. Is it any wonder, then, that members of your families – your relatives, friends, and acquaintances – also do not believe that you are God's heralds?

Then, still further on, Christ said that there are no prophets in their own land. That is understandable, for how can an individual imagine and get used to the idea that some John or Alexander, whom he knows in their daily affairs, can turn out to be God's envoy? After all, they were the very same people just like anyone else! Similarly, people said in the land of the Hebrews, "How can Christ be a prophet, for, after all, He is the son of the carpenter Joseph from Nazareth?"

Yes, it is difficult for a human being to understand matters like that.

(An intermission of ten minutes.) [[1812]]

I am continuing. While reading the Gospel, you should have also noted a thing like performing miracles. All miracles were performed only for the sake of strengthening the faith, but not for the personal benefit of Christ or His apostles, even though that could have been achieved so easily. Why did Christ and the apostles live like any other individual? They got cold and suffered from thirst and hunger like anyone else. They did not even have donkeys for the purpose of transportation. They collected donations so that they could buy bread for themselves. They could feed and give drink to others by means of a miracle, but not to themselves. Why did they have to convince people about the validity of their faith by means of miracles and words, when that could simply have been accomplished with the help of a miracle, by ordering everyone to believe? Think this over well, and answer me at seven. [[1832]]

It's not as easy to answer as it might seem. What will Janoss say?

[[Janoss replies.]]

Miracles were essential in those times in order to prove that He was the Son of God, and that they were His apostles. It was not possible back then to convince people with words alone. Power, the whip, and miracles convinced the individual back then. The mind, however, had to accomplish that, and God also wanted to achieve that by means of the mind. Therefore there were miracles which were capable of convincing every person that only a being who is higher than a human being can perform these miracles. These miracles should have made everyone listen to the words of Christ and His apostles, comprehend them, and convince himself regarding their veracity. This process was not particularly fast, but, as you can see, it overwhelmed the larger part of humanity. With respect to making everyone believe by means of a forced will, it is clear to you on your own that this could not have occurred under any circumstances, for you know The Almighty's desire – not to influence man's free will by means of force.

Christ's faith was comprehended and initiated correctly. The first adherents of Christ lived in brotherhood. They sold all their personal properties and gave for common usage the funds that they had thus acquired, because for them everything was common.

It is known that someone sold his properties, but decided together with his wife to retain for themselves part of the funds that they had thus acquired, and not give them for common usage. God punished both of them with death for such cheating of God. That is what is written in The Acts of the Apostles.

Later on, these pure teachings of Christ became covered with layers of all kinds of invented, false teachings, adopted to human nature. Thus, His teachings disappeared quite soon from the face of the Earth, because what you call Christ's faith and what currently exists on Earth is not Christ's teachings but their falsification. The same thing is true with respect to some other teachings as well.

You posed the question once, "Does the Gospel depict Christ's life and teachings correctly?"

Had you read carefully and compared the writings of the four apostles, you would not have posed this question. This merely proves how carelessly an individual reads even such important books, and how weak are his abilities of thinking. I will give you only two examples, one from the beginning and the other from the ending.

When John [[the Baptist]] baptized Jesus, a dove descended from Heaven. It said only a few words. Read carefully [the writings of] the apostles, compare them, and you will see that even these few words have been expressed differently, even though they should have been exactly the same in all four Gospels.

Then the second. After Christ's body had been buried in a cave, it was visited one morning by one, two, three, and even more women, depending on how it is expressed in each Gospel. The most important thing, however, is the following. The first apostle writes that an angel sat on the rock that had been rolled aside from the cave [entrance]. The second apostle writes that the angel was inside the cave, next to the shroud. The third apostle tells that two men in white attire stood inside the cave. The fourth apostle talks of two angels. One angel or two angels is not the very same thing.

If each of the apostles depicts this very simple and extremely important event differently, then that in itself already proves how correctly they have depicted this event, as well as all the others.

Wasn't your question superfluous? You could have asked something else instead – why did this happen like that?

It is easy to answer this question. Not a single written line from Christ has survived. His apostles were common people. Besides that, they did not keep diaries, but wrote later on, after Christ's departure, and according to memory. One can judge from the examples that I gave just how correctly this memory preserved the events and Christ's words. Besides that, none of the apostles' writings have reached you in the original. Errors were made while transcribing them as well, and words were even altered.

Because of all this, The Almighty asks you now to adhere strictly to what has been written, and under no circumstances to alter even one word by yourselves. It is only permitted to correct those grammatical errors that have been made while writing down [the tidings], and also only during the time while Alexander confirms these corrections.

Everything that comes or will come from the heralds has to be clearly, visibly, and unambiguously separated.

With that, I conclude my conversation with you. Ilgya is getting ready to tell you within the next few days something that seems wonderful to me.

[[1952]]

Chapter XX
January 1945 – Part 1

Ilgya   01/01/45 1605

Ilgya. I, too, congratulate you with the New Year. During this year humanity wants to believe most of all in happiness and peace, for it is tired of suffering and has drunk too much blood. I refuse to make any predictions, because the fate of humanity has been placed currently in its own hands. Let us arm ourselves with patience and await the rising of the sun, since, after all, it is bound to rise.

I will now turn to carrying out my promise, and will tell you something unreal-real, a fable and the truth, an allegory and reality. So, high heralds, please write [down my words].

A large ship once floated on the ocean. The fiery name "*Vita*" burned on its side. A high spirit has already told you about this ship. The following command was heard one day on the ship, "The high priests and the rulers are requested to leave this ship for a voyage to Paradise. A boat awaits them."

The gray priests of the various confessions climbed down the narrow, insecure ladder to where a small boat, rocked by the silent waves, waited for them. A somber graybeard stood at the tiller. Fog streamed from his gray beard and enveloped the sea in an opaque cloak. The graybeard raised his transparent hand and gave a signal, which resembled the sign of the cross. Imperceptibly, the boat began to glide across the dark waves, into the realm of the fog. The ship disappeared from the sight of the travelers. The sounds of the funeral music faded. The boat floated, steered by the silent helmsman. It stopped at the shore just as silently and imperceptibly as it had left the ship. The graybeard raised his hand again and gave the signal to debark. The travelers stepped ashore on the shore that was enveloped in fog. The boat vanished in the fog, merged with it.

The newcomers stood on the shore of Paradise and looked around in surprise. Gray clouds of fog rolled from the dark waves of the sea, and the moon shone palely through them. There was a strange silence in this land. Some gray shadows wandered with inaudible steps along the bank of a river, along a river that flowed silent as the grave. Flocks of gray birds flew overhead, moving their wings inaudibly. Dark, gray grass covered the fields. Trees, gray trees with hung down branches, stood along the sides of the road. Dew dripped from their branches, and it seemed as if these trees were weeping, overcome by infinite sorrow. Somewhere in the distance loomed the silhouettes of some sort of dark buildings or fortresses, without a ray of light in the dark, silent windows.

The newcomers waited. A shadow-like figure approached them, and the newcomers asked, "Some sort of a fatal error must have occurred here. After all, this mute, shadowy and foggy, gray land cannot be Paradise, to which we traveled and about which we have told so many wonderfully beautiful things to our people? This land, after all, cannot be the promised Paradise!"

"It nevertheless is Paradise! Mistakes do not happen in the realm of the almighty God. You have to wait, though. The morning hour has not struck yet."

The newcomers waited with their heads hung down. The fog began to lift. Somewhere far away a bright Ray was born. It came from infinity – fiery bright and sonorous. The darkness dissipated. Flocks of birds landed on the ground like white snow, for the upper surfaces of their wings and their backs turned out to be covered with silvery-white feathers. The Ray touched the trees and the grass. The folded leaves of the trees and the heads of the flowers opened with a sound resembling tiny silver bells. The appearance of the blossoms and the leaves expressed an unimaginable beauty – the symphonies of indescribable colors. It seemed as though an enchanted carpet of colors covered the ground. A wonderful fragrance flowed from the blossoms. The branches of the trees came to life. Birds hopped around on them like sparks of fire. Their songs merged with the bells of the blossoms, and all that merged with the inexpressibly beautiful symphony of the Ray. The entire ground, the entire air billowed and resonated in this symphony, which at times was barely audible and at times became mighty and all encompassing.

The dark, rocky road lit up in fires of jewels, and resembled a rainbow that took [the newcomers] toward wonderful castles. The walls of these castles burned like the sun. Rays, rays of different colors radiated from their windows. The somber shadows on the bank of the river disappeared. In their stead, the lofty figures of beautiful young women and young men, attired in togas of the most wonderful colors, glided along the river. Crowns of flowers and jewels sparkled on their heads.

The welcomer of the newcomers had altered his appearance as well. A handsome and noble ruler stood before them. Compared to him, kings on Earth would have looked like beggars.

"Yes, you are in Paradise," he repeated, "the Paradise of the almighty God, whose words do not deceive and who fulfills all expectations. Follow me!"

They went.

(An intermission of twenty minutes.) [[1705]]

They went.

"We are in the Solar Fields," the guide said.

"Yet we were traveling to Paradise," came the voices of the priests. "Besides that, you said that God never deceives."

"In Paradise as well, should any of you wish," the guide replied with a smile. "You will be able to end up in your own paradises as well, and even in hells, if you will want to. First, however, let's look over the Solar Fields!"

They walked along a road of jewels, with trees [on both sides] – trees from whose branches fell a rain of jewels. The drops of this rain, while falling on the road of jewels, created a unique symphony that accompanied the steps of those who were walking. It seemed as if they were walking on the keys of a huge piano, and that the ground responded to each of their steps with a wonderful accord. The mighty symphony of the Ray extended over this entire fabulous world of colors and sounds. At times, the sounds of this symphony turned into words, for the endless multitudes of young women and young men accompanied them by recognizing them. Then this symphony rose to such power, such mightiness, that it seemed like the entire world turned into a single divine music, a single divine song.

As if enchanted, the newcomers joined in this symphony. It spoke of what is the highest, the mightiest, the most sacred, and the most beautiful in the world.

They approached the first castle. On its wall burned in gold letters, "The hundred and fifth star's 'B' planet, 'Inkosa'." Similar inscriptions burned on the other castles. Thus they reached the castle on whose wall was the inscription, "The one million two hundred fifty-eight thousand three hundred forty-seven star's (the sun's) 'C' planet, 'Ilivya'." (The Earth.) Enclose the last word in parentheses.

"We have reached the enclosure for the Earth. As you can see, each planet has its own castle and its own garden. Some castles are empty and their gardens are barren. They are the uninhabited planets. You can see the others, the inhabited planets, [reflected] in these gardens and castles that are full of life," said the guide. "Let us look over some of these gardens and some castles."

They went again.

Each planet had its own area in the Solar [Fields]. The spirits could feel there either like in their own homes, or else could become acquainted with the life of an alien planet. They could meet the spirits of the deceased, or else visit friends from other planets. Each enclosure held that planet's most unique plots of nature. Duplicates of all the planet inhabitants' achievements were in the castles.

In Earth's area, the first plow was on the wall; and the image, name, and era of life of its inventor, as well as a description of his life. The subsequent improvers of the plow were next to it. The first telephone device hung on the wall. Marconi stood next to his invisible – wireless – telephone. All the more worthy books written on Earth and the images of their authors could be found in the spacious reading rooms. The most beautiful works of art filled the halls of the museums. One could listen to any desirable work of every musician in the conservatory hall. One could often even meet and talk with the spirits themselves who had created all this.

Thus, by going from section to section, the spirits could become acquainted with the entire universe. If this did not suffice, the spirit could relocate momentarily to the desirable planet as well.

While they – the newcomers – were walking around thus, words could occasionally be heard in the symphony of the Ray, "On such and such a planet, such an interesting phenomenon is currently occurring, such interesting events are taking place, a new stage has been achieved in the transformation of matter," and so on.

According to these words, the spirits could know what was happening where, and where it would be interesting to go. These words did not interfere with the symphony of the Ray, for they were not part of it, but were audible separately and not in the form of sound but in the form of wordless communication.

Time passed or did not pass. The newcomers could not tell the difference.

It seemed to them that they had been here in the Solar Fields for only a few moments, when the voice of their guide came, "We have already been here for several hundred Earth years. Let us go now to your paradises."

They went on again.

The road took them aside from the castles and gardens, somewhere to the outskirts. A high fence and a large gate appeared on the right [side] of the road. An old man with a large key in his hand stood by the gate.

"That is the paradise of the believers in Christ. Permit me to introduce you to father Saint Peter," the guide said.

Then he turned to the guardian of the gate and said, "Holy father, perhaps you would be kind enough and would admit to paradise those Christians who want to enter it."

"Why not," replied Peter, "except they will not be able to leave. Whoever enters it has to remain there eternally as well."

He began to unlock the gate of paradise.

"Sure has become real rusty!" Peter growled in his beard.

"Hold it, holy father!" said the Pope. "How come that the gate of paradise could have become so rusty?"

"Why shouldn't it become rusty when it's been several hundred years since it's been last opened."

"I don't understand it," said the patriarch. "Aren't there any longer any people who are worthy of entering it?"

"I don't know," Peter replied, "except everyone who looks into paradise from that little tower there, refuses to enter it."

"Then we, too, better look into it prior to entering," said a cardinal.

Everyone climbed the tower.

Yes, paradise was the same old, beloved paradise, known to everyone. God sat on a cloud. Multitudes of angels gathered around Him and sang songs of praise. A few old men and a few old women sat underneath the bushes of paradise and sang along the same melody.

"Not bad," the Pope said, "but still we better not go in, for I'm afraid that it'll be too boring."

"I also think like that," agreed the patriarch.

They climbed down from the tower and departed.

"No one again!" Peter said mournfully and sadly.

"The two of you should certainly have gone in," he told the Pope and the patriarch. "After all, you summoned all the people here, and now you don't want to go in yourselves."

These words did not help either, and no one came back.

Then they came to still other paradises. In one paradise all the gardens were full of beautiful [maidens], but they, too, were unable to entice anyone into this paradise of beauties. In another paradise the tables were laden with food and drinks. The woods were overly full with animals and fowl for hunting. Since no spirit felt like eating or drinking, nor wanted to devote himself to the joys of hunting, none of the newcomers even stopped at this paradise. There were also various other paradises as well. As the last one there was a paradise resembling empty space in which the souls were floating in some sort of fog, which was similar to the rays of light.

"That is Nirvana," said the guide.

"How many of you are there still left?" he looked inquiringly at the newcomers. "So then, everyone this time as well. No one has remained in any of these paradises. Let us proceed to the hells then."

"Would it be worth it?" the Pope asked.

"I think that this would be a waste of the valuable time," the patriarch added.

"If it is not mandatory, let us rather not go," said the grand mufti.

They did not go.

"If you don't want to, then let us go on."

They headed up a mountain.

Underneath their feet lay the Solar Fields, like a diamond disk. The messenger of The Almighty's existence – the Ray – came from infinity. The newcomers raised their eyes upward. Far, far away there could be seen a temple of inexpressible beauty. The extinguished suns and planets rotated shining palely like the moon. They made up the temple's floor. Burning suns and glittering planets shaped the temple's immeasurably high walls. The sparkling nebula of stars, of stars being born, formed the ceiling and roof of this temple. Whirling like a hurricane of snow, multitudes of spirits streamed into the temple. They emerged invisibly from the infinite space of the universe. The Almighty's Cross burned above the temple. The Ray, coming from infinity, lit it up in a symphony of colors, which the paltry human language of Earth is incapable of expressing.

"We are done," the guide said. "Your paths will part. Go to wherever The Almighty summons you!"

He rose and like a spark [alighted] to the Temple.

My story has ended. My lips grow silent and silence enters the world.

[[1900]]

Friedrich Schiller   01/03/45 1815

[[The conversation took place in Wiesbaden, 23 Herder Street.]]

Friedrich is here. You have almost forgotten me, particularly Janoss. I come to you today as an inhabitant of Wiesbaden, from whom you have moved further away, as though I could not see you here as well.

Let us talk now about the high spirit Ilgya and her narration. Her narrative competed somewhat with mine, seemingly talking about the very same thing. That is not the case, though, for each of us wanted to present a different idea. Ilgya wanted only to depict the Solar Fields to you, and nothing else. This goal cannot be achieved by anyone, not even by Ilgya, for it is not possible to depict the Solar Fields with the concepts that are available to a human being.

Is it possible at all to depict correctly and understandably, with the help of words, a luxury ocean liner to a native from the jungles of Africa who has never seen either a ship or a city? [Or else] the gigantic buildings of New York and its brightness and wonders, even though this native were brilliantly talented? That refers to the Solar Fields to an even larger extent, where there is hardly anything that would remind one of Earth. Neither the ground itself; nor the stones; nor the trees, flowers, and castles have been created from elements that are known on Earth. One has to tell about everything that is there while seeking ideas that are familiar to you. Therefore no spirit undertook to depict the Solar Fields to you.

Ilgya, when taking on this task, also said that her story will be the truth and a fairy tale. She had to speak with human words and utilize human concepts. She was telling the truth, but it turned out to be a fairy tale. Therefore strive to comprehend her idea, but do not imagine that the Solar Fields appear exactly as she depicted them to you. The child Nick's paintings, when compared to the paintings of Rembrandt, are the same as Ilgya's portrayal compared to reality. Yet that is also good.

A human being is incapable of understanding the essence of the spirit, and neither can that be explained to him. Tell me, what color is water? Janoss?

[[Janoss replies, "Colorless."]]

Mary?

[[Mary answers, "Indeterminate."]]

Alexo?

[[Alexo replies, "Water is colorless."]]

Alexander?

[[Alexander answers, "Being colorless, water can reflect all the colors."]]

You claim that water is colorless. What is color though? Alexo?

[[Alexo replies, "Color is that sense which the eye makes us perceive."]]

Everything is colorless at night. The rays of the sun, its light, give color. Color is not anything real, it cannot be touched, and it is as changeable as water. The color of the clouds is independent, as is the color of the leaves and of coal. Obviously, you know from physics how all that can be explained. It does not suffice, however, with just the rays of the sun and the objects on which they shine. The eye is also needed in order for color to come about. Still, this simple notion regarding colors seems difficult for you to understand. It is hard to imagine that grass is not green and coal is not black. The idea regarding the absorption of rays does not simplify this concept either. It is even more difficult to talk about the essence of the spirits, in which there is nothing materialistic. It has just as little that is materialistic as there is in colors.

You claim that the spirit does not exist, for he can be neither seen nor otherwise ascertained. You claim, however, that colors exist, because you see them.

I only wanted to tell you with these examples how difficult it is to operate within the concepts that are accessible to a human being, and how difficult it is to depict to him matters that are outside the bounds of these concepts. That is also why Christ had to speak by expressing His ideas in simple fairy tales, because people were incapable of understanding, and did not understand, what He said about the world beyond. Not only did they not understand, they even misconstrued it. Similarly, people will not understand and will misconstrue us. Only a spirit is capable of understanding and comprehending the spirit, God, and the Solar Fields and their essence. Yet even he is incapable of comprehending The Almighty.

The human ear is not capable of perceiving all sounds, the human eye is not capable of seeing all rays. Neither are the human senses capable of perceiving magnetism and electricity. There is an extremely large world that the human being is incapable of perceiving, but this world does exist after all. The human eye can see a drop of water, but does not see the hard to see living beings that are within this drop. The eye of a microscope sees them, but [does it see] all of them? The human eye sees several thousand stars in the night sky. The eye of a telescope sees millions, but [does it see] all of them? Not all! Even if this eye of the telescope were to become as big as the entire globe, it would nevertheless be unable to see all the stars and their Creator.

Ilgya commenced with an allegory at the beginning of her narration, but she could not get away from it later on either, for she could not find the necessary words and concepts. She succumbed somewhat to the power of irony as well. Therefore you should consider her narrative simply as an attempt to depict the indepictable and to express the inexpressible.

Everyone, however, who sees with a spiritual eye as well, will be able to comprehend the mightiness of the scene which she has sketched, and will be able to feel the breath of Heaven. Just for that alone, it behooves you to express the deepest gratitude to Ilgya.

I conclude.   [[1930]]

Ilgya   01/05/45 1805

Ilgya. Friedrich tried to clarify my story for you. However, I fear that this high spirit achieved the opposite, because your faces became mighty long. What can one do, though; we have to help out each other. Still, even a great poet like Schiller is incapable of explaining the inexplicable. Perhaps Goethe would have succeeded better, but this poet – researcher – writes poetry currently on a distant planet.

Since Schiller has already started speaking about scientific matters, I will also talk about them a little bit.

I want to ask you something first. Just don't imagine that we, the spirits, ask you for the purpose of examining your knowledge, or else with the purpose of learning which one of you is smarter, or else which of you has better grades on your diplomas and a better memory. No, we ask merely in order to stimulate your desire to think, and to mold your ability to express yourselves as clearly as possible – understandable to everyone.

I am asking now. Janoss will answer me – what is light? Alexo – what is sound? I will give them five minutes of time.

[[Janoss and Alexo reply.]]

Both of you said that light, as well as sound, would in essence be seemingly the very same thing. Sound propagates into the expanse, from the object that originates it, in the form of waves. Some of your scientists say the same thing about light as well. Let us go on still further and ask the scientists – are all possible colors in the universe encompassed in your spectrum of light, and is the length or brevity of sound waves limited? Can't such a crazy thought arise that somewhere, on a given interface, these light and sound waves approach each other, merge, and turn into each other? Thus a sonorous ray comes about. Scientists on Earth will claim that this is not possible.

If we take as the basis, as the source of light, the sun, a star, or an electrical discharge, then perhaps not. The same thing is true if we take objects on Earth, which you know and which create sound, as the sources of sound. Let us, however, entertain the possibility that The Almighty possesses the ability to create other sources of light and sounds, which are capable of emitting waves of colors and of sounds that are unknown to you.

Why do you think that there is only one white, basic color, which you can split into the other colors that you know? You are familiar, and rather superficially at that, with only an insignificant, tiny corner of the universe. It is too early for you to exchange the jacket of a student for the glasses of the professor.

Let us proceed for a moment now to the shore of the Solar Fields again. We already understand the sonorous Ray now. How about the ground? It is not as real as the ground on your Earth. The spirits need neither water, nor bread, nor something solid underfoot. The ground and all other objects in the Solar Fields have been created from entirely different elements. Man's material body would fall through the Solar Fields just like a stone would fall through a cloud. The human eye, made from matter, would not be able to discern the Solar Fields, would not see their splendor, and the human ear would not hear anything other than an eternal silence. The Solar Fields would not be visible to the eye of a telescope either, even if man were able to construct such a mighty objective and lenses that the eye of the telescope could reach the Solar Fields. Do not forget one thing. The spirits' abilities of sight, hearing, and others are of an entirely different nature than those possessed by a human being and by other living beings.

You can see rivers, forests, and houses on a large and good painting just as they are in nature, but they are merely the results of colors and the hand of the artist. The portrait of your father, too, looks at you from the painting on the wall just as your dear, good father, but your father's lips do not move and his eyes do not blink. How can this magic be explained? With the brilliant ability of the artist, or else with the limitations of the human eye that can see faces, houses, trees, and seas in the spots of paint which have been spread on a piece of canvas? Having considered this thoroughly, you will resolve this question on your own.

I can only tell you that God is capable of creating an eye that would form the most magnificent jewel from a gray [speck of] dust. Also, one that would see only a gray stone in the most fabulous jewel, which glitters in all kinds of fires.

I will tell you something else as well. What seems to be real to a human being, can be unreal in reality, and the other way around.

Obviously, my portrayal is naive, as Schiller said, but it is not I who should be blamed for this naivete, but the inadequacy of human concepts and language.

You will also claim that the Solar Fields have to be unimaginably huge in order to be able to encompass within them partitions for all the planets in the universe. That is not the case, though. The uninhabited planets, planets on which there is no organic life and which cannot be of any interest to the spirits, are not incorporated in the partitions of the Solar Fields at all, but are listed on plaques on the walls of the central castle of the Solar Fields.

The spirits do not have to remain in the Solar Fields, but you have been told about that several times already.

Mary wants to visit the Lunar Fields. I do not know whether it might not be better for her to restrain her overly avid interest, because who can guarantee the ensuing results.

Then I still want to talk about the spirits, as you would like to see them. You would like to see them as gray incarnations of slow movement and language; as gray, old men in awkward togas; graybeards to whom laughter, jokes, and abundance of the energy of youth have long since become alien. You want to see old philosophers in them, who have isolated themselves from current life with a high wall; who speak in old, dead languages and who do not know how to talk as a young man, worker, or professor talks. No, your desire is erroneous and naive!

I will tell you a fable some day, but today I bid you farewell.   [[1930]]

Ilgya   01/07/45 1800

Ilgya. Well now, let us continue. We dwelled the previous time on your ideas about the spirits – what they are supposed to be like. I will tell you now something similar to a tale.

A huge, broad forest surrounded a forester's house. The forester lived in the house with his wife and children. His youngest daughter had permitted the seventeenth spring to enter through her window, covered by the vines of grapes. She was a girl of a dreamy nature. She liked the setting of the sun, the nightingale's song greeting the evening, the heavy sigh of a pine tree at night, the yellow carpet of the autumn, and the blossoms of a flower that have been bit by frost. She liked to read books, particularly books of fairy tales, of the enchanting fairy tales. The noble and handsome princes, the good kings, and the kindhearted princesses were the heroes of her dreams.

The narrow forest road seldom tempted anyone who was driving, riding, or walking. The noble deer felt almost as safe on it as in the thicket of the forest. The world, the large, bright world seemed endlessly distant and unreachable. The girl dreamed about this distant world, dreamed the dreams of a fairy tale. The world that she imagined was not that world which lay beyond the huge forest.

A gentleman, dressed in the attire of a hunter, rode up to the house one day. His horse had stumbled and was limping. The other hunters had ridden on and he, having been left by himself, had come upon the house of the forester. He asked for permission to rest a little, and to have something to drink and eat. This gentleman was around forty years old, but his temples were already turning gray. He was of a fine build and handsome. He talked wisely, but occasionally he liked to joke as well.

While walking past the girl, he took her by the chin, lifted it, and said, "What a pretty, little nose!"

He lifted her little brother by the arms and tossed him to the ceiling. He told the forester a joke over which he grinned in his beard for a long time. He taught the lady of the house how to prepare a tasty dish. He taught the girl's older brother how to shoot a pistol. To the grandfather, though, he read an entire lecture about the world of the stars and [of the different] types of tobacco. He reprimanded the groom for improperly cleaning a horse, and taught the merry maid how to dance the "li-kopo." Besides that, he probably kissed her behind the oven, for the girl emerged from behind the oven redder than the reddest rose. Then he sat down and began talking with the host about agriculture, and turned from it to the economy of the state.

He talked so wisely that the listeners understood little, and began yawning. Having noticed that, the unfamiliar gentleman switched to a funny, little story. Everyone started laughing and felt agreeably and well.

The girl sat at a small table in the corner of the room and read a book. The stranger walked up to her and asked, "Dear child, what are you reading?"

"A fairy tale about the good king."

"A fairy tale about the good king," the stranger said contemplatively. "Yes, that could only be a fairy tale," he continued. "Read it to me. It has been a long time since I have read any fairy tales."

The girl read the fairy tale about the good king.

(An intermission of five minutes. Afterwards have Alexo sit down.) [[1840]]

The girl read the fairy tale about the good king, "Once upon a time there lived a king. He was young and of a fine build, like a sapling birch tree. He was so handsome that the flowers, having seen him, forgot to close their petals at night, the birds forgot to finish their songs, and all the girls dreamed only about him and were no longer able to love any other young man. He was so brave that even the elephant stepped aside for him, and the tiger, having met the gaze of his eye, lowered its tail and crawled fearfully into the bushes – just like a dog, scared of the master's whip, crawls underneath a table with its tail between its legs. He walked calmly across crocodiles as across sonorous boards. The crocodiles were afraid to move, so as not to anger the king.

"He was also so strong that no one dared to oppose him. His horse fell once and bruised its leg. The king put the beloved horse on his shoulder and carried it home. He grabbed a naughty tiger by its tail and tossed it into a river, to the delight of children and crocodiles. He took two giants – who had demolished several neighboring kingdoms and who while drunk had accidentally staggered into the king's kingdom – gently by their collars and banged them lightly forehead to forehead. To this day, both giants are still lying in a swamp with bumps on their foreheads, and children have laid out wonderful skating rinks on these bumps. All the neighboring kings feared our king, and therefore love and peace reigned among them.

"Not only was the king strong and handsome, but he was wise and good as well. He was so wise that he knew everything, and everyone came to him for advice, even the most remote rulers.

"An old king came to him and asked for advice. 'I have two sons, twins, so identical that no one is able to tell them apart. One of them is of a good nature, and the other of an evil nature. I want to pass my throne on to the good one, but don't know which one he is. I'm afraid that I might pass my throne on to the evil one, who would ruin my kingdom and turn my good subjects into slaves. No philosopher, no matter how old he might be, has been able to give me any sensible advice whatsoever. Perhaps you, the wisest of the wise, would not deny it to me, for you are my last hope. Death already knocks impatiently at my door.'

"The king thought [for a while] and said, 'Yes, I can help you, if you will give me your word to carry out my advice without any objections, no matter what it might seem like to you.'

"The old king gave his word, and the king said, 'Announce to your sons and to your people that in order not to put your kingdom in jeopardy you are passing the crown of the kingdom on to me.'

"The old king almost died, having heard this unexpected decision, but the royal word had to be kept. He headed homeward bent as a bow, sweeping the road with his gray beard and sprinkling it, in order to keep down the dust, with tears.

"His people, having learned of the king's unusual decision, did not say anything, simply because they had become dumbstruck from surprise. What about the sons, though?

"One son said, 'That's not a bad decision on your part, dear father. One could not wish for a better ruler for our people than the good king. The fortunate people! I rejoice for their secure future.'

"The other son, though? He said only two words, 'Old fool!' Then he pushed his father out of the way, jumped into the saddle, and rode off to the land of the Turks.

"When the good king arrived in the capital of the kingdom, there was indescribable sorrow in the heart of the old king, and the people had not yet managed to regain their speech. Therefore no one welcomed the new ruler, everyone only gaped like fish.

"The new ruler entered the palace, took the king's remaining son by the hand, took him out on the balcony, and told the people, 'People, here is your new good ruler!'

"Having turned to the king he said, 'Here is your good son.'

"We are unable to describe the joy of the old one, and the cheers of the people. They screamed so that everyone became deaf.

"This one event should suffice for you to see just how wise and magnanimous the good king was. He had a heart of gold. He went into the homes of the poor and those who were suffering, and brought happiness and sunshine everywhere. Even lame dogs came limping to the good king's palace and whined at one of its doors, while at another door meowed cats that had their tails torn off – the victims of naughty boys. The good king did not chase them away either, but turned them over his veterinarians, who put them gently to eternal sleep. Yet the dogs and cats, obviously, did not know that.

"All the daughters of the neighboring kings without exception had fallen in love with the king. In order not to condemn his kingdom to innumerable wars, the good king married a cinderella instead of a princess."

The fairy tale told still many more good and beautiful things about the good king, but we do not have the time to sit that long with the girl and the stranger.

When the girl had finished reading and looked dreamily at the flames in the fireplace, the stranger rose awkwardly and sighed.

"And you believe that all kings are like this good king in the fairly tale?" he asked.

"Not all of them, but our king certainly is. He is young, of a fine build, and handsome. His horse carries him across rivers, lakes, and forests. His eyes shine like the morning stars. His lips smile as gently as the first sunbeam of the morning on the rose petals in my window. His heart is of gold and his tears are diamonds. He is wise like God and dear as an angel. That is what my king is like!" the girl said loudly, with burning eyes and pink cheeks.

The stranger sighed again. "Poor child, dear child, if only your words were to reflect reality! If only your king did not have gray hair, and his feet were not so weary that he is unable to walk back to the palace when his horse has stumbled. If only his hands were strong enough so that if he could not carry, at least he could lead his horse by the bridle. It would be good if your king did not have to struggle with evil neighbors, if he did not have a quarrelsome wife and disobedient, spoiled children, and if his ministers were good people rather than scoundrels and cheats. It would be good if your king could dare to enter the hovels of the poor and those who are suffering, without receiving rude curse words and even the stab of a dagger. It would be good if the good king also had good subjects. It would be good if the crown of the king were not that heavy and would not get tangled up in tree branches while riding.

"You, my child, imagine that the king is not a human being and that he does not possess all human weaknesses, but only good characteristics. Oh, if only it were like that! A man, however, is only the very same man; whether he has the mended jacket of a worker on his shoulders, or else the robe of a ruler sewn with gold and jewels; whether he stands outdoors behind a plow, or else sits on a throne in the palace. Let it be, though, my child! Dream on about your good king! I know him and I'm his best friend, why should I speak evil of him?"

The stranger walked up to the window.

"Oh, here come my people riding. Forester, how much does your hospitality cost?" he turned to the forester and stuck his hand in his pocket.

"As usual, without any money again," he added while smiling. "My fate is like that. Everything belongs to me, but I do not have anything myself."

An impressive gentleman, a gentleman of a much more impressive appearance than the first one, entered through the door. However, he bowed low in front of the first one. [The latter] put his finger to his lips, and said, "Have them give me another horse!"

On his way out he took leave politely, and said, "Forester, tomorrow you will receive a reward for your hospitality, because I don't have any money today."

He mounted a horse and rode off accompanied by a large retinue.

"A strange gentleman," said the forester. "One can see that he is rich, but doesn't even have a penny in his pocket with which to pay for a slice of bread."

"Yes, a strange gentleman," the girl said thoughtfully, while looking at the light cloud of dust.

Then a rider separated from the group and galloped back. Having jumped from his horse, he hastened into the room and asked, "Where are our king's gloves?"

Noticing the stranger's gloves on the girl's table, he said, "Oh, there they are!"

After picking them up, he hastened out the door, jumped into the saddle, and galloped off.

"Our king's gloves!" the forester said in surprise and fright. "Who would have thought that this gentleman is our high ruler? We, fools, treated him like an ordinary mortal. Oh me, the old mule, oh me, the unfortunate one! What will he say of me now?"

The girl, however, looked with rigid eyes at the spot where the stranger's gray and dusty gloves had just lain, and her lips whispered inaudibly, "My king!"

That is how this tale ends, and I take leave from you. [[2020]]

Ilgya   01/10/45 2030

Ilgya. I will tell you another short, little story.

An owner of a farm and farmhouse arrived in the capital. He had to transact important business in real estate. His best friend had sent him to a relative of his, a senator. The farmer went to the senator's office and waited for a long time, but the senator was busy. When the farmer's turn approached, the secretary announced that the senator will not see any more people that day.

A door opened after a while and the senator came out. He was an elderly gentleman of an imposing appearance, in a bright uniform covered with decorations. His appearance was so imposing and his gaze so cold that all those who were present were afraid to approach him. He nodded his head just barely perceptibly in response to the visitors' humble greetings. It appeared that his back was incapable of bending and his lips of smiling. The farmer, having gathered every bit of his courage, nevertheless approached the senator and handed him his friend's note, explaining that he definitely has to drive home that night.

The senator glanced at the note, and said, "All right, come to my apartment in an hour."

The farmer arrived at the senator's apartment after an hour. The senator's butler showed him into the guestroom and asked him to wait for a little while. The farmer waited and became bored. He walked over to a door behind which the voices of children could be heard.

From boredom, the farmer examined the senator's large photo, and thought, "How unbearably imposing these great gentlemen appear! Nothing human has remained in them. It seems that even boiling water would freeze into ice in their presence."

Then something pushed open the nursery door, and a Saint Bernard dog came into the waiting room. The door remained ajar. The farmer looked through it inadvertently.

Two small children were playing on the floor. They were running a toy train on its track. A slightly gray man was sitting on the floor [with the children] and helped them run the little train. He laughed joyfully, blew the whistle, and gave various signals along with the children. Then one of the children came up with a clever idea. He wanted to ride the train. The adult attempted to talk the child out of this impossible idea, but the child wept and said, "But I want to ride, daddy, I want to ride the train!"

The father did not manage to talk him out of this, and then he said, "Get on my back. I'll be a horse and you the rider. That'll be much more elegant than riding on a dirty locomotive as the engineer."

The child calmed down and climbed on the adult's back. The adult circled the room on all fours, with the small rider on his back. When they were heading toward the door, the farmer noticed in surprise that the "horse" was the senator – the proud, unapproachable senator – who trotted around the room so that his decorations clanged.

Having noticed the visitor, the senator lifted the child from his back, got up, shook the dust from the knees of his pants, and came toward the farmer with a smile.

"Excuse me for having made you wait, but since you are a father yourself you will understand that a senator is a man and a father as well, and that all children are the same."

He showed the visitor into the study.

Well, wasn't it a short, little story? You will say, "Yes, but why did you tell it to us at all?"

Yes, that I, too, cannot say right off, I will have to think that over thoroughly. While you will think your [thoughts] I will think mine.

Nakcia will speak with you now, and Mr. *Guecha* will have to sit down at the table.   [[2110]]

Nakcia   01/10/45 2110

Nakcia is here again. This time in a different attire again, so that Alexo would not think that I come to scold. I have another purpose today.

I would like to talk with you regarding Ilgya's tidings. You are saying in your thoughts, "Strange, Ilgya promised to talk about the spirits – what a human being imagines them to be like and what they are like in reality. Instead, she told us the fairy tale about the good king and the anecdote about the old senator. What do these two stories have to do with the subject of the spirits?"

I will claim that they do after all. Ilgya expanded this subject significantly, and encompassed in it not only the spirits, but everything that is higher than an ordinary individual. [She encompassed] everything that an individual depicts incorrectly in his mind, be that God, a king, the spirit, or even a senator. Yes, obviously, one cannot consider the spirit as a king or a senator, who according to their essence and nature are the very same people, merely standing higher on the stairway of life. As one, so the other, they are the very same product of the spirit and matter. Since the spirit enters this combination as well, then human traits are not alien to the spirit either.

As you have already been told previously, you have to recall that the task of the spirits is to guide the living beings in their struggle with the might of matter, and by incarnating uplift this matter and gain new strength from it, as well as transform.

Some spirits, while incarnating in man many times, have a much better knowledge of human characteristics and habits than do some people. Without any doubt, the spirits conduct themselves in their mutual relationships entirely differently than when they have to get in contact with man. They have to be understandable and close to man. They have to descend to man. They do not have to talk with people in some incomprehensible, foreign language. They do not have to inspire fear, and cause misunderstanding or boredom in man. They have to come to man as old, all understanding friends, who can teach, reprimand, chat about this and that, joke, and depart with a friendly pat on the shoulder.

I can read much failure to understand in your thoughts when you compare the Gospel to *The Almighty's Book of Tidings*. It seems to you that there is much in the latter that is superfluous, of little value, and uninteresting for the entire humanity. You forget one thing, though – there is a large difference between these two books.

Almost all of Christ's conversations with His father, mother, brothers, relatives, and apostles, which were of a personal nature, have been deleted from the Gospel. Christ taught Matthew what to eat and drink when he had stomach pains. Christ's admonition to Judas how to keep money in a chest and how to spend money has not been included in the Gospel. His quarrels with the stubborn Peter have not been included. In a word, all that has not been included which He had to tell His apostles for conducting their activities and life, all the day to day advice and even rebukes. Christ talked with His apostles almost daily, but how many of all these conversations have been included in the Gospel? Many of Christ's important instructions have also not been included in it because the apostles simply forgot to include them in their writings, or else were incapable of understanding and expressing them in their own words.

The circumstances are different with you. You write down every word of the spirits, no matter how important or unimportant it might be. Obviously, much of what has been written down is of little value, or is personal, or is of momentary worth only. Therefore you also have been told to write *The Almighty's Book of Tidings* while utilizing two fonts, and to place in the third book that which is only of a purely personal significance and has no overall value.

We cannot, just as Christ could not, avoid instructions of a purely everyday nature. We attempt to avoid such instructions as how to sleep in a farmer's house on a hard bench, or how to treat one's stomach, but actually we have to say much – oh, how much!

I also wanted to slightly rebuke your great secretary today, who is confined to bed again, but he is not subordinate to me. Let others do the rebuking. I could advise him, but I am neither Christ nor a physician. That's all right, let him simply be more careful not to get in the way of a draft, which does not tolerate that, and not freeze his fingers [while digging through] ruins. Most important, though, have him keep up his energy, and not succumb to weaknesses but struggle against them.

For the concluding words now. The spirits are kings, senators, and so on, but on coming to people they are like the people. Obviously, though, if the senator assumes the role of a horse for a moment, can he no longer be the very same firm senator because of that? Similarly, if the king comes to the forester in the attire of a hunter and behaves there like a real hunter, he does not become a hunter because of that, but remains the same king.

Do not imagine the spirits as being merely some sort of hypocritical or archaic beings. Remember that they are the architects and the engineers of the universe, and The Almighty's assistants. There is nothing that they do not know, and they do not avoid any assignment, no matter how big or small, no matter how easy or difficult, and no matter how beautiful or ugly it might be.

I conclude, and you may turn in. My *guecha*, too, can crawl underneath his beloved thick covers, except this time brr…, without the other one and in a cold room. [[2220]]

Chapter XXI

January 1945 - Part 2

Kioeso   01/12/45 1936

Kioeso is talking with you, The Almighty's heralds to the planet Earth. My name seems to be unknown to you, even though that should not be the case.

I want to talk with you today about patriotism, regarding which a high spirit has already talked with you once.

As you already know, people differ from each other not only by their outer appearance, but also with their so-called inner structure – spirit and temperament. Humanity has originated from a single tribe of animal, which while multiplying and ending up in different corners of the Earth has transformed into the various people. Climatic and ethnographic conditions have left a decisive effect on this transformation. These conditions turned out to be so potent that even the color of the individual's skin transformed under their influence. Thus came about the various races – white, yellow, black, and other colors in-between. The shape of the eyes, the type of hair, and the individual's size transformed as well.

Warmth and cold were the most powerful transformers. Yet nature also left an effect on a person's character, on his spiritual essence. People from plains and people from mountains are not of the same temperament, because nature effects man's psyche, effects it to a decisive extent. The endless plain, a plain that gives no landmark to the eye, fatigues the individual, and his gait, too, becomes slow and heavy. His fantasy becomes gray and flat.

The eternally murmuring waves of the sea awaken the individual's fantasy, and occupy his thought, which wants to understand this language of the sea. Even a brook and a swift river awaken the human soul from spiritual slumber. Swift mountain rivers, mountain peaks that rise into the azure of the sky, or else are shrouded in cloaks of clouds, smash the serenity of the human spirit and summon the human thought upward to Heaven, to Heaven that is unreachable for the body – to Heaven which the thought can reach, however, and which fantasy can comprehend. Nature, its beauty and mightiness, transforms the human spiritual essence, and makes it rich and seeking.

The endless plain and gray surroundings oppress man and clip his wings of fantasy. The fertility of the soil, the quality and richness of the soil, also leave a significant effect on the formation of the individual's spiritual life. Nature is the main impetus in molding a person's spiritual traits, and not just merely the spiritual. Similarly, nature – in the form of impassable seas, rivers, and mountains – by separating the different groups of humanity from each other, estranges them and makes them shape their continued life independently. Thus different customs and languages gradually arise.

Centuries pass and the former brothers and sisters have transformed so much that they no longer recognize each other either by their outer appearance or spiritually. The more natural barriers there are in a region, the more different nations and different languages evolve in it. Thus humanity split up into nations and each nation evolved its own spiritual world.

[Then] came the times of the new, major achievements of technology. Roads were built. Tunnels were forged through the impassable ridges of the mountains. Bridges were thrown across rivers. Thousands of exceedingly fast ships pulled the shores of the sea closer to each other. The horse, donkey, camel, elephant, llama, deer, and dog shortened kilometers into meters. The trains, cars, and airplanes shortened them into centimeters. The new modes of transportation will shorten them into millimeters.

Natural boundaries began to disappear. People became mobile, and the era of mixing and merging of nationalities began. Humanity began its road back to a single nation.

This process, having been slow initially, began to speed up ever more. Unique circumstances came about on the new continents. The primitive nations of these continents began to disappear, to die out. New nations, an amalgamation of different nations, came about in their stead – the nation of North America, the nation of Australia, and many other nations. These new nations, however, already differ sharply in their essence from the old nations.

You have been told that patriotism of the nations, which frequently and readily turns into chauvinism, is the calamity of humanity and the cause of the eternal wars. In the course of humanity's development, however, patriotism has had its positive traits as well, and during certain stages of humanity's development it was essential, as well as gave humanity much that was positive.

The cultures and spiritual uniquenesses of the different nations introduced inexhaustible wealth in humanity's spiritual life, in the culture of the entire humanity. Just as people differ from each other and make life interesting because of their diversity, similarly, nations with their spiritual variety create an extremely interesting and rich spiritual life.

While condemning patriotism, one has to say that this condemnation does not already mean declaring a war on patriotism. That would have been humanity's calamity, rather than happiness. That is merely a statement of the fact.

One should not struggle against the feelings of patriotism. They only have to be understood correctly, and this recognition has to be made understandable to everyone.

With the continued development of humanity, with continued technical achievements, and with further merging and mixing of nations, the patriotism of individual nations will transform on its own, and its chauvinistic aspects will disappear.

After all, it is rather obvious that a brother is closer to a brother, and that a brother understands a brother better than a stranger would. Similarly, people who have a common language, customs, and ideas will also understand and will be closer to each other than people who are entirely alien according to their traits. It would be insane and unnatural to try transforming these relationships with the help of brute force. Life itself should undertake this work; by calling for help on culture, technology, and common sense.

Your ears have heard my words. I hope that these will reach your common sense as well.   [[2030]]

Nakcia   01/13/45

Nakcia is speaking. The divine spirit Iligaya alighted past the Earth to the Deoss Temple. All the spirits are heading there in order to hear Iligaya's news about the creation of new worlds – worlds whose creation is based on entirely new bases. In twenty minutes, I will try to tell you the contents of Iligaya's news, if that will be permitted.

Iligaya stopped her legions of spirits for a moment at your door, and then proceeded on. Her lips did not open for a single word, but her eyes sought someone infinitely dear.

I alight away. [[1818]]

Nakcia   01/13/45 1918

Nakcia. Iligaya told The Almighty and the spirits about the task that she has accomplished, the creation and formation of a new group of stars – worlds – based on new principles. She requested the help of several high spirits, who are essential to her for continued successful accomplishment of the tasks. She asked The Almighty to assign to her, by releasing them from the accomplishment of their tasks on Earth, the following high spirits – who on Earth bear the human names of Alexander, Mary, Alexo, and Jenny.

Omega and God are raising objections of a categorical nature.

I hasten back. Wait for me!

Ilgya   01/13/45

Ilgya. Omega announced The Almighty's answer, "The divine Iligaya should go back to the new world. I will gradually release from their duties on Earth the spirits whom she requested. The Divine will have to wait!"

Stand up, the divine Iligaya is alighting away.

Your destinies have changed. New tasks arise before you. Devote all your efforts [to assure] that you will honorably accomplish Iligaya's distinguished selection and will justify The Almighty's thought.

The high Kolinto, Otranto, and Nakcia left along with Iligaya. They will await you in the world of Iligaya – the first spirit from among the living beings who has achieved the degree of divinity, but who has postponed accepting this degree until the moment when another spirit, still more worthy of it, will be able to accept this degree.

Nicholas's spirit will also alight to the new world.

I conclude.   [[1930]]

Domenito   01/16/45 1855

Servus, homo sapiens!

Ego Domenito. I am talking with you, the children of the old planet Earth – *terra*. Evil times have befallen on the chest of the Earth. The Earth breathes heavily. The horrible nightmares of her millions of years long sleep torment her. Dark clouds cover the sky, although rain does not fall from them. Unprecedentedly dreadful thunder rolls, even though stars shine in the sky. Terrible claws of steel scratch the chest of Earth. Unsightly heaps of rubble, instead of the beautiful cities, cover her face. The stately trees of the forests lie like piles of brushwood. There is no peace for old Earth. Her son, her pride – man – has raised his cruel hand against her – his mother – against his brothers, and against the guardian of culture, the gray time. The chest of Earth breathes heavily. The frightful nightmares oppress her.

"Oh, Almighty, when will Your morning come for once!" her parched lips whisper.

As if answering her, the eastern sky turns red. But, oh no! That is not the morning, that is not the rising of the sun! Instead, streams of fire flow from the east, streams of fire and blood. Meadows bend beneath millions of feet, and mountains disappear. It is not morning that comes, but death.

"Yet when will the morning come, when?"

"Then, when man will have overcome the night in his heart, and will have dissipated the fog of unreasonableness from his mind!" comes the answer from the starry distance.

That is what the Earth of this day is like. That is what she has always been like.

I lived on her once. That was recently, just a few moments ago. The strong Roman nation ruled the Earth then. The names of England, Germany, and Russia had not been born yet. No oracles yet predicted that there is also a part of the world that will be named after the name of the traveler Amerigo.

I ruled Rome back then. My legions had squeezed into the sandy land of the small, savage nation Afri. The land of the Hellenic gods lay beneath their heels. The nations of Asia looked at the unconquerable eagles of my legions with eyes full of fear. It seemed that I no longer had any worthy opponents in the world. Yet still there was no peace. After all, weapons could be heard here and there, and blood was being spilled. All that, however, was a trifle, an insignificant trifle, compared to what I see now.

My people, my Roman people, regardless of the endless hordes of slaves and endless riches that flowed to Rome, did not feel satisfied, did not feel happy. They grumbled about the difficult and boring life.

I gave them slaves so that they would have it easy. I gave them bread, fruit, and the fine clothing of the East. I gave them beautiful jewelry so that they would feel rich and satisfied. I had the most beautiful women and the handsomest young men from the entire world brought to Rome so that the Romans would not complain about a lack of lovers. I staged circus performances for them. I did just about everything so that the Romans would not be bored and would feel happy, so that they would praise me – the ruler of Rome!

All that was to no avail, though. They praised me in front of my eyes, but these cheers were unable to deceive me. While standing on the stairway of the palace on dark nights I could feel how heavily Rome breathed. I heard lamentations and laughter, but this laughter was more dreadful than the lamentations.

I was sitting in the palace garden one evening. Somewhere in the shadow of the streets the voice of *asinus*[3] could be heard. A gray, little *passer*[4] was hopping around at my feet. It was hoping to find something at the feet of the ruler of the Earth, but was bitterly disappointed. The last *alauda*[5] hung in the sky. *Feles domestica*[6] had noticed the small, gray *passer* and was sneaking through the bushes, but my old *canis familiaris*[7] ran along the road looking for its master and sniffing *terra*[8]. It scared the *passer* and the great house beast remained without its cherished dinner.

The sun was sinking into the distant sea. Night was approaching. Peace was coming, but only not over Rome. Only now aspirations lit up there for pleasure and for power over another. Desires awoke, which work during the day had deprived of the opportunity to impose themselves on man, with their demands.

Rome's great poet approached me with slow steps. I motioned to him and he came up to my seat.

"Tell me something about Rome. What are the Romans doing and what are they thinking about?" I asked.

"Oh, what can I tell you? My neighbor is ruined. His ship has sunk with all the merchandise. My wife is unhappy – I sold today her lover, my handsome slave. I am unhappy as well – my lover got caught, and my wife spanked her and sent her to our home in the provinces. Your great troop commander slipped in dishwater poured out in the street and broke his arm. On my way over here I heard the sound of fighting and curse words directed at...."

"You can skip at whom," I interrupted him, "but please continue."

"Two Jews in a side street were yanking at a beautiful slave girl until they tore the clothing from her and she fled naked down the street, pursued by sailors. A drunk was crawling in the middle of the street and your prison superintendent ran him over. Should I continue?"

"No, it suffices!" I said. "The same old Rome, the same old Romans! Nothing beautiful, nothing noble, nothing great. Oh, why do they call you the great Rome?

"Tell me rather about something else. Tell me something beautiful, uncommonly beautiful."

"Uncommonly beautiful," the poet said contemplatively. "Yet what then?"

"What? You are our greatest poet and if even you have nothing beautiful in your soul then it is no longer worth living."

We grew silent. The wings of darkness had spread over old Rome as well. The trees and bushes were immersed in the shadow of the evening. Silence reigned. We remained silent as well. Then a wonderful song came from a branch of a bush. The little bird *motacilla luscinia*[9] was singing.

The poet raised his head and said, "And you said that it is not worth living in the world, for there is nothing beautiful in it! What can be more beautiful than this song, though? Doesn't its beauty compensate for all the ugliness in the world? Raise your eyes toward the sky! Don't you see this dome of jewels above your head? Don't inexpressible beauty and divine tranquility breathe from this starry sky? Look at these heads of flowers that cling to your feet with their fragrance. Then look at your young slave girl who brings you your evening attire. Isn't she the beauty itself, and don't her eyes radiate a wonderful love? And you who are surrounded by so much that is beautiful ask me, a poor poet, for beauty!"

The cheers of the people were heard at this moment and the chief of the palace guard approached us with an announcement. "Ruler, your troop commander has brought back the conquered enemy king. He is lying in the dust in front of the palace. The people await you."

I rose and told the poet, "Yes, there is much that is beautiful in the world, but we do not have the time to notice this beauty and to comprehend it. We have to eat, drink, wage wars, judge, fight, be bored, make politics, envy, love, suffer, rejoice, and rule, but we have no time left over for beauty, because this beauty is not obtrusive and one does not have to pay money for it. One does not have to seek it, and therefore it cannot be found."

I walked off.

The gray ruler, my former enemy, lay in the dust, bound with chains. A beautiful young woman – his daughter – stood next to him. She was pale and tired, but her dark eyes burned like torches. It was not, however, the fire of love, but the fire of utter hatred that burned in these beautiful eyes.

I began feeling very sorry for this old ruler and his beautiful daughter. I walked up to her wanting to caress her and tell her some comforting and cordial words. She, however, misunderstood the intent of my movement, took a step back, and spat in my face.

The crowd froze for a moment, and then roared like an enraged beast, on seeing an insult like that to its ruler.

What could I do? In a few moments, two horribly torn bodies, rolled in the dust, lay at my feet.

I turned away, and told the poet, "You see what remains of beauty when the hand of the crowd touches it, and what comes of a desire to do good when it meets with an uncomprehending life!"

We parted.

My eyes did not close all night long. When the figure of the beautiful, young slave girl bent over me in the morning, I reached out with my arms in order to embrace her lovingly. In front of my eyes, though, appeared the face of the princess burning in hatred, and I lowered my arms – arms that while loving brought death.

I remember my life on Earth. I remember the thirst for beauty and happiness. I remember the unbearable fight against man's base nature. I still remember all that, but thousands of your years have passed, have passed but have not changed anything. How many millions of years will you, people, still need so that for once you will be able to tear to shreds these rusty chains of matter, and will be able to discern true love, beauty, and happiness?

I am glad that The Almighty has come to your aid. While alighting to my distant world, I stopped on my old Earth for a moment in order to see what she is like now, and to meet with you – The Almighty's envoys. My time has run out. The rays of the stars summon me. I take leave and tell you, "May we meet soon on the paths of the rays of the stars!" [[2100]]

Friedrich Schiller   01/19/45 1724

Friedrich is speaking. I do not come to you today on behalf of Heaven, but while remembering the old times on Earth. I come to you as a friend comes to friends, in order to remember in cordial conversations the good times that have passed. Specifically today, when people's minds are so alarmed while listening to the dreadful steps of fate – when the mind trembles, like a sparrow in the claws of a cat, awaiting the collapse of days and the bacchanalia of the night – I want to talk about something so unimportant and so commonly serene that it may seem strange that at a time when the destinies of nations, and yours as well, are being decided on the battlefields, one can talk about something this remote from everything that is important and acute. As you have already been told once, though, the worth of the spirits is expressed in the abilities of tranquility and withdrawal. Recall the story about the condemned Chinese and the book.

You have no basis for being alarmed, because you are the fortunate ones who know that life on Earth is merely a brief episode in your long, immeasurably long life of the spirits. This episode can be most beautiful, and it can also be very difficult and even horrible. Still, it is simply a brief episode, and it is not worth either rejoicing or grieving over such a brief episode, [and certainly not worth] becoming alarmed. So then, let us stuff the tobacco tighter in our pipes, push our chairs around the warm stove, and begin our friendly conversations. I feel that you want to give the advantage to me as the guest, and ask me to commence my story, for I have not yet carried out my promise to the full extent. Fine, I agree!

My story will be commonplace, and therefore unusual, for you will not hear anything regarding the affairs of Heaven in it. It will be an ordinary story of the Earth and is intended only for the pleasant passing of time. I can see Alexander frown, while probably thinking about his long and dark trip home. However, I hope that this time, and in the name of friendship, he will sacrifice himself without being surly. I wanted to pass my story on to you in German, but fearing that you would make too many mistakes, I will venture to pass it on in Latvian. Obviously, it will lose much in its expression, but that cannot be helped. So, let us close the door to the world, entwine ourselves in clouds of smoke, and submerge in the past.

There once lived a farmer. While dying, he left his home and land to his older son. The younger son had to head for the big city and seek his fortune there. Years passed. The sons died, and their sons as well. The same family continued to farm in the country, and lived in the same old home. The current owner of the home did not have any sons, but only a young, beautiful daughter. His kin in the city again had no daughters, but only a son – a nice, strapping young man. The two young people began corresponding; this became ever friendlier. The girl had never been to a city and the young man to the country.

Let us give them names, but quite common ones. Let us call the girl Joan and the young man John.

Joan wrote long letters to the city, singing praises to the beauty of the countryside. John also wrote equally long letters, singing praises to the magic of the city. Joan sent apples, pears, and other fruit to the city, but John sent Joan trinkets from the stores and books.

Having received Joan's latest package, John wrote, "Oh, these wonderfully delicious apples! How magnificent looking must be the tree on which these wonderful fruit grow!"

Joan replied, "Come visit, and see for yourself."

John wrote, "I'm on my way; meet me at the station. I will be with you and the apple trees for the entire fall."

Joan's hasty reply was, "I'm awaiting you impatiently, but while you're coming bring me the city's most beautiful book."

They met at the station. She smiled at him happily and held out her hand. Confused, he squeezed it hard, and then raised it to his lips and kissed it awkwardly.

"Why the hand, rather than the lips?" the girl said, obviously, not in words.

Then they headed homeward.

"After all, show me this famous apple tree right away!" John said impatiently.

"How simple – show me! No, my dear, you will have to find it yourself."

"And do you think that I will not find it? It will not be difficult to differentiate a tree like the apple tree from the other trees!"

They walked along the dry, fall-like road while chatting pleasantly.

"Look, there they are already!" John exclaimed in a happy voice, while pointing at some poplars.

"Are what?" the girl asked.

"What? Why, obviously, the apple trees! What could reach for the sky like that, except an apple tree? What could be so stately as it?"

They reached the poplars.

"You see, my friend, not a single apple, only branches and leaves! These trees don't even have decent seeds, let alone apples. We, country people, don't call these trees apple trees, but rather poplars."

The young man blushed and mumbled, "It's human to err."

They continued along the road.

"Yes, I confess, that could not have been an apple tree," John said.

"Why?"

"Because the apple tree is a mighty, thick, and tall tree. I see it now!"

"Come," said Joan.

They walked up to a huge tree which not even their four arms could encircle, and whose broad branches formed a complete roof above their heads and reached high into the sky. Joan bent down and picked up from the ground a few small, triangular nuts.

"Here are your apples!" she said. "We, however, generally call them beechnuts."

"A beech?" the young man drawled contemplatively. "Who could have imagined that such a gigantic tree would have such tiny fruit?"

"Tiny yes, as you can see that's actually how it is."

They proceeded once again.

"I'm not mistaken now!" John exclaimed. "That can only be an apple tree, and only an apple tree! How could I have erred like that? Obviously, only an apple tree can have such a mighty, majestic crown; huge, strong branches; and dark, beautiful leaves!"

"Then you'll also have to eat the apples of this majestic apple tree," the girl said.

She picked something hard and elongated from a branch and handed it to John. He took this strange apple hesitantly, and bit into it.

"How terrible and bitter!" John said while spitting [it out]. "After all, that's not an apple!"

"Sure is! Except until now we called it the acorn of an oak tree, but you, the smart city dwellers, know that better."

The young man blushed for the third time, and said, "Yes, I surrender."

They were getting close to the house.

"Look at these trees!" said Joan.

"What's there to look at? Short, ugly trees with twisted branches and pale leaves."

"Perhaps, though, it's worth after all! Let's walk up closer to them."

"As you wish," John drawled unwillingly, and approached the trees.

"But what's that?" he exclaimed in surprise. "After all, in the branches there, those are the very same sweet and beautiful apples that you had sent me! Could such beautiful fruit really grow on such an undistinguished tree?"

"As you can see – yes!"

"Who could have imagined that? How strange is this nature!" John said contemplatively.

"Now let's go home, though. Hot coffee and a pie await us on the table. I await your book as well."

"Oh yes!" said John. "Here it is now. It is the most beautiful book that is currently available."

He handed her a thin book, bound in golden covers.

"So thin!" Joan said sadly.

"Yes, but you will find in it the most beautiful poems of the greatest poet of our time. All people are enthused about this new book of poems, and memorize it. Nothing more beautiful than it has yet appeared in the world."

"I thank you," Joan said with a sigh. "I'll have to believe that, because there is so little of everything that is beautiful and expensive."

They went into the room.

The days passed quickly, happy days. One morning while passing by the lake, John noticed Joan on a bench with a book in her hands, the book that he had given her.

"I see that you can no longer part from this book at all. I see it in your hands in the mornings, day, and evenings. You probably keep it under your pillow at night."

"That's how it is," Joan replied. "This book has enchanted my soul. The songs that these meager gold covers hold between them are so beautiful. How handsome, noble, and young must be the poet who could have written them! All eyes probably follow him when he walks along the street; and all the wealthy, heroes, and kings seem inconsiderable and insignificant compared to him. Just listen to this poem which I am reading for the hundredth time already, even though it is still not the very best one! Listen!"

She read:

"Your hand slips into my hand
Just as the caress of a rose petal.
Your eyes in the arc of your dark eyelashes
Call me like the dreamlike story of the stars.
There's a sharp, sweet pain in your kisses,
We cannot find the word for it.
Like the brook that quenches the thirst of gods, resounds
Your voice, which brings me eternity.
Like a sea gull diving in the pearls of waves..."

The girl, though, became suddenly silent after these words, because the lips of the young man covered her lips.

"But John, how could you do that?" Joan whispered after a few minutes.

"How could I? After all, that was a challenge to fate. Such beautiful words from such beautiful lips! Not even a cliff could have resisted this challenge, let alone a human," said John.

"And a young, handsome, and infinitely dear human at that," Joan added dreamily. "You know something, my dear, I also am a poetess. I have poems as well. Obviously, not as good, but still poems. I want to meet this great poet, see him, and read him my poems in order to hear a verdict from his divine lips. You will take me along to the city and will take me to him, if only the servants will admit us into his dreamlike palace."

"All right, I'll take you along," John said, "except you will have to find his palace yourself and recognize the great genius, just as I had to find the apple tree."

They departed for the big city in a few days.

(Rest for twenty minutes.)

"Let us go now to seek the poet's palace," said Joan, after they had washed off the dust of the countryside in a white marble bathtub in the city.

"Let's go, but look carefully so that the same thing would not happen as happened to me," John added with a grin.

Carried by the stream of people, they wandered through the endless streets.

"Would that be the poet's palace? It does appear somber, but the windows are protected by bars and guards march around it," the girl said while pointing at a huge, somber building that occupied an entire block.

"Thank God," said John, "that the poet does not find himself yet inside this building of yours."

"Why thank God?" Joan asked.

"Well, simply because this palace of yours is the main jail. The most beautiful creations of humanity do not dwell in it, but the most hideous ones. You might as well blush for your first time!"

The stream of people carried them on.

"It seems to me that this will be the poet's palace!" Joan said while pointing at a huge building. A long stairway led to the entrance adorned with colonnades. Statues of gods stood along the edge of the stairway. In the windows, too, could be seen wonderful heads of heroes, carved in marble and stone.

"That is the real palace of the poet. Just look at this fabulous statue of a young woman! Isn't she the very one to whom he dedicated his beautiful poem?"

"Yes, it is a palace, but it is not the poet's palace. It is the palace of artists. They, themselves, however, don't live in it either, but only their immortal works – statues and paintings – for we, the city dwellers, call this palace – the art museum."

The waves of people lifted and carried them again, carried them to another fabulous palace, and streamed through its wide, fiery gate into a hall that sparkled in lights and glittered in gold.

"Stop, my dear!" the girl said in despair. "Look at these people who stream into the poet's palace. All of them are clad in such formal, expensive, and beautiful attire, and the ladies sparkle in jewels. How can we dare to insult the great poet in our ordinary, gray clothing!"

"Neither do we have to do that," the young man responded, "for the poet does not live in this palace. Only his works live in it, and this gray night watchman."

"I don't understand you," whispered the girl.

"You see, this splendidly attired crowd streams into this palace for only three hours. After that the suns of the lamps are again extinguished, the gold pales, and the voices fade. Only mice run along the silk seats and the dusty decorations, and the steps of the old, lonely night watchman sound hollowly in the empty, dark hall; for the show is over. The poet's divine words have grown silent, the curtain has been lowered, the show has ended, and the theater doors have been locked."

They entered a deserted side street now. The stream of people forgot them, and they walked all by themselves among small garden cottages.

"Where are we going?" Joan asked.

"There, where you wanted to. Tell me, how do you like this palace?"

"This palace?" the girl asked. "After all, that is not a palace but a plain garden cottage, even worse than some of our farm houses!"

"Yes, you are right, but perhaps we should go into it after all."

"But why? After all, no one is going into it! What could interest us there?"

"Merely [the fact] that in it lives the one whom we sought in the jail, museum, and theater. Your great poet lives here."

"You must be kidding! Surely that can't be!"

"Still, that's how it is. I will wait for you here, in order not to disturb the conversations of the two great poets. You go inside, though."

The girl opened timidly the small garden gate. An old man, with gray hair and sad eyes, in old, worn-out clothing, with old shoes on his feet, was pruning the roses.

"Mr. Gardener," the girl turned to him, "could you tell me where I might meet our great poet?"

"Why do you want to meet him?" the one who was pruning the roses asked her.

"Because…," stuttered the girl, "but you wouldn't understand that anyway. I have to talk with him personally. Perhaps he is busy, though, or else is sleeping, or else is sick?"

"No," came the response, "he is not sleeping and is not sick. Please go inside, he will see you."

The girl went into the small house. A maid met her and inquired.

"I want to talk with the poet," the girl replied.

"But, after all, he's in the garden!"

"He is not there. Only the old gardener is there."

"Oh, if only we could afford to pay a gardener!" the elderly maid sighed, "but go on ahead into his study, as long as he has already allowed you to do that."

She opened the door. The girl entered a room that was not large and whose walls were concealed behind bookcases. Books were lying on all the chairs as well, and even the floor of the room was not safe from them. Only the table, a simple wooden table was free of them, because entire mountains of paper lay on it. The girl walked up to the table. The sheets of paper were filled with rows of words – poems and again poems, completed and barely started, crossed out and corrected so that they couldn't even be read.

The door opened, and the one who had been pruning the roses came into the room. He had put on better shoes and a newer jacket. Having entered, he removed the books from a chair, pushed it toward Joan, and asked her to be seated.

He, himself, stopped next to the table and said, "I am the one whom you call the great poet. What has brought this beautiful girl to him?"

A few moments – extremely long moments – passed before the girl was able to come to her senses and regain her ability of speech. The poet remained silent, and his sad eyes looked kindly at Joan. Joan got up awkwardly and in silence handed the poet the small bundle of her poems. White, narrow, but weak hands, with slender, translucent fingers, took the small bundle and unrolled it.

He leafed through the papers for a few moments, and then handed them back to her, saying, "Read [them to me, my] dear child! My eyes are too weak for your dainty handwriting."

The girl began reading in a trembling, low voice. The poet remained silent. Only his eyes were alive – they became still sadder.

"My last poem now, the shortest one, in which I envision my old age and death.

> I am old. My hair is gray,
> My hands are weak, barely move my feet.
> The night is dark. Rumbles death's heavy cart.
> I lack the strength to close the door."

The girl grew silent, and leafed nervously through the sheets that she had read. The poet remained silent, and his sad eyes gazed somewhere out the window. Then he turned around and said slowly and thoughtfully, "Your last poem inspired in me an eerie scene, which I just clad in words. Listen to what they sound like.

> Beyond the dark window roll the steps of death,
> The hand of the storm rips open the shutters,

My feet bend beneath the burden of the years,
My weary hands permit me to open the door."

He grew silent. The girl's eyes lit up, and her heart beat fast, fast. Infinite love and adoration radiated in her eyes.

"Dear child, I can't tell you much of anything."

"Don't say anything! You have already told me so very much that it will suffice for me to work and to learn for many years."

Her beloved book of the poet fell from her handbag.

"Oh, this small, little book has found its way to you as well!" said the poet.

"I would give up my entire life, if I were able to write a book like that," the girl said dreamily.

The old poet responded sadly to these words of youth. "And I would give up this book in order to become young and handsome once again. Yes, my child, that is the irony of life, but it is not worth talking about. The wheel of time turns in only one direction – forward. It never turns backward, but only breaks if someone wants to stop it and turn it back."

"The immortal fame, though, which you have achieved, is it of that little value?"

"No, it is not worthless to humanity, but it comes too late for me. May The Almighty help you, and may the rays of fame fall on your gilded head, but not on the silver-clad," the poet said.

The girl bid farewell and left the poet's room.

John was waiting for her on the street. "You must have really liked the poet's beautiful palace, and the royally handsome, young poet himself!"

"Yes, very much!" the girl replied loudly. "Very much, and far more than you think, and than I thought! I entered an unreal, insecure fairy tale castle, but emerged from the wonderful palace of life, whose bright rays will accompany me on all my pathways of life and will protect me from the dead-end roads of delusions. My eyes acquired the ability to see in this palace, and they are capable of seeing now not only the somber stone palaces built by people's hands, but also the sunny and inexpressibly beautiful palaces of the human spirit!"

The young man felt the mightiness of the girl's words, and grew silent.

They headed homeward with silent steps, through the empty streets.

Their lips remained silent, but this silence was full of unexpressed yet fiery thoughts.

My story has ended. Your turn has come now. I, too, would gladly like to hear something, but, oh God, I have talked away the entire long evening all by myself, and your eyes are full of sleep and your mouths can't control the yawns. I take leave, but remember – it is you now, rather than I, who are the debtors.

Now then, until the next time. It seems to me that the hands of Janoss are holding a little bundle of paper. Too bad that it is so late, but let us hope that The Almighty will give us still another day.

While taking leave I ask Alexo to the table.

Ilgya   01/20/45 1720

Ilgya. All evening long yesterday, the spirit of the great German poet talked with you. There was no time left over for me, but I listened gladly to the great spirit's story of the Earth. Friedrich tends at times to express himself very briefly, to encompass broad ideas in a short phrase, which you, people, are not always able to fully understand. Thus perhaps to many of you his phrase regarding the girl having gained so very much during the time when she visited the poet will sound strange. After all, at least on the surface, nothing all that important happened there, and neither was it said. One has to know, however, how to form a majestic image from a few insignificant words.

I want to demonstrate to you how that occurs. The girl said that she had comprehended and learned extremely much, but from what? Can you tell me that? Janoss, please!

[[Janoss replies, "She gained the realization from the poems that there is much that she has to learn, and that she has to acquire instructions for her future."]]

Is that enough? The poem merely demonstrated that her, the girl's, poem was still only the work of someone who is learning. I ask Alexo.

[[Alexo declines to respond.]]

Mary then.

[[Mary responds, "From the poet's insight that fame always comes too late."]]

One can only suffer from this insight, rather than learn. I will answer in lieu of Alexander. Therefore, listen!

Little Nick will tell us what the girl saw on entering the poet's room.

[[Nick answers, "Chairs and shelves full of books."]]

Beautiful! Learn from your son. Yes, she saw books, endlessly many books. From that the girl understood that in order to become a great poet one also has to learn extremely much and has to know what other poets have said, so that the individual himself could say something new, something that has not been expressed by others.

[What was] the other thing which the girl noticed? Alexo will tell us that.

[[Alexo says, "The large pile of papers covered with writing, indicated how very much she'll have to work."]]

Now, the other thing that she noticed was the mountain of papers covered with writing. She saw how much work the writing of a good poem requires even from a genius. Every word has to be evaluated; steel has to be transformed into silver, silver has to be forged into gold, and the gold has to be illuminated with a diamond. That is what the work of the great poet is like. A poem that seems like the very perfection to everyone, seems like the tortured attempt of a child to him. He is never completely satisfied with his work, for he knows that there are yet more beautiful words, there is yet a more complete manner of expression.

The third thing that she learned was what should be expressed in a poem, and how. A poem should not be a photograph of life or of things, but the expression of the soul of life or of things – the revelation of their internal essence, and their unique perception from the poet's point of view.

The fourth thing that she learned was the understanding about how one has to develop the ability to create within oneself, in order to be able to readily and momentarily transform one's thoughts into a sonorous poem, rather than sweating for hours and even days in order to be able to achieve this transformation.

What else did the girl gain? She learned that a genius generally does not dwell within princes and handsome people, athletes and young men, but rather within people who can be ordinarily gray in their appearance, and even ugly and old. The beauty of the spirit currently has nothing to do with the beauty of the body, or as we say it, with that of matter. Later on, when matter will ascend to the level of the spirit, then the beauty of the body will reflect the beauty of the spirit as well.

She also attained the realization that spiritual work is recognized by people, but is not remunerated. The book, which the entire nation received with enthusiasm, and even with deification of the poet, brought him only illusory worth – fame and a little money; so little that the poet could not even afford to pay a gardener. The publisher of his book gained millions though; and built himself a mansion for whose upkeep he hired gardeners, yard keepers, maids, a chef, chauffeurs, and so on. The publisher also was a genius, obviously, a genius of business. The poet put the people and his work in first place, but the publisher put himself and his wallet in first place.

The main realization that the girl gained was that spiritual work is valuable, but that life itself is valuable as well, and that the greatest skill is the ability to combine the two of them harmoniously.

Those were the cognitions which the girl gained in the poet's house. Yet I did not enumerate all of them. There were others as well; still, those which I have expressed will suffice.

As you can see, my friends, these are the writer's ways of expressing his thoughts. You can see now that one also has to know how to read. Anyone who has read a book without striving to delve into the writer's thought, without attempting to comprehend the meaning of each of his words, has killed time for naught. It would have been better had he been chopping wood or drinking beer in a tavern.

You can also see now why the Tidings seem to be so unclear to you, and why it seems to you that the answer to all the questions regarding Heaven and life on Earth has not been given in them. It has been given, except it has not been found and comprehended, for you do not begrudge the time to discuss which bakery bakes better bread, but lack the time to consider the expressions in the Tidings.

I conclude. Ali will speak in twenty minutes. [[1820]]

[[This concludes Volume One. The Tidings of the spirits will continue in Volume Two.]]

EPILOGUE

On May 1, 1944, Santorino said, "I am capable of speaking only through Alexander and Mary. When one of you will depart, I, too, will grow silent. Omega speaks only through Alexander. Once he will depart, the gates of Heaven will close to humanity for ever and ever. All those who will speak in The Almighty's and our names will be nothing but false apostles. And, oh, woe! what awaits them and those who will believe them."

On June 28, 1944, Omega spoke on behalf of The Almighty, "I, The Almighty, will never again send any of My envoys to Earth. Whoever will speak in My name will be an impostor. What I have proclaimed, I will never supplement again. I will never, ever speak again, not with the tongue of a prophet, not through signs, not as I am talking today, nor in any other manner.

"So that you might receive answers to some remaining questions, which are still not clear to you, I permit My spirits to talk to the people on Earth only as long as I have not recalled My envoy Alexander to Me; and only through him, so that no false prophets could speak in My name and in yours."

On February 13, 1949, Mortifero passed on to humanity the words of The Almighty, "I repeat My previous words, that I come to man for the last time and will speak only through Alexander. This, My decision, is irrevocable. It places a huge responsibility on you, as well as a hard-to-endure test for Alexander's strength."

On March 20, 1959, Alvisego said, "These Tidings are the first and the last ones for the people on Earth. All communications with The Almighty will cease with Alexander's departure from Earth, and not one word expressed in the Tidings will be changed. Anyone who tries to represent himself as The Almighty's herald will be an impostor. Similarly, anyone who wants to alter even one sentence in *The Book of Tidings*, will be considered a fraud."

On February 28, 1969, Omega spoke, "The Almighty ordered me to announce to the heralds to Earth that, with respect to the Tidings, He talks to the people on Earth only through Alexander and His heralds, and only when they are together. He does not speak, and will never speak, through only one herald."

Alexander's immortal spirit departed from his mortal body on March 10, 1971.

Nick Mezins

ENDNOTES

1   "Messages to Mankind From The Almighty and His Spirits" (1976, Vantage Press); "Messages to Mankind, Vol. II" (1977, Valkyrie Press); and one of the fictional ones, "Ipsis" (1977, Valkyrie Press).

2   A regional food.

3   a donkey

4   sparrow

5   lark

6   A cat

7   dog

8   the earth

9   nightingale